Journal of Semitic Studies Supplement 4

STUDIA ARAMAICA

New Sources and New Approaches

Papers Delivered at the London Conference of
The Institute of Jewish Studies
University College London
26th-28th June 1991

Edited by M. J. Geller, J. C. Greenfield
and M. P. Weitzman

with the assistance of V. T. Mathias

Published by Oxford University Press
on behalf of the University of Manchester

1995

Oxford University Press, Walton Street, Oxford OX2 6DP
Oxford New York
Athens Auckland Bangkok Bombay
Calcutta Cape Town Dar es Salaam Delhi
Florence Hong Kong Istanbul Karachi
Kuala Lumpur Madras Madrid Melbourne
Mexico City Nairobi Paris Singapore
Taipei Toronto Tokyo

and associated companies in
Berlin Ibadan

Oxford is a trade mark of Oxford University Press

Published in the United States
by Oxford University Press Inc., New York

A catalogue for this book is available from the British Library

Library of Congress Cataloguing in Publication Data
(Data available)

ISSN 0022-4480
ISBN 0-19-922194-4

Subscription information for the *Journal of Semitic Studies* is available from

Journals Customer Services
Oxford University Press
Walton Street
Oxford OX2 6DP
UK

Journals Marketing Department
Oxford University Press
2001 Evans Road
Cary, NC 27513
USA

Printed by the Charlesworth Group, Huddersfield, UK, 01484 517077

CONTENTS

FOREWORD

The present volume is the written presentation of the international Conference held by the Institute of Jewish Studies, University College, London in 1991, on "Aramaic and Aramaeans: New Approaches and New Analyses". The Conference programme covered a wide range of subjects in Aramaic, with papers on a new Aramaic Elephantine papyrus, an Aramaic papyrus from Egypt in Demotic script, new Aramaic inscriptions from Egypt and Arabia, grammars of the Targum and Christian Palestinian Aramaic, Aramaic incantation bowls, Samaritan and Syriac versions of the Bible, and Palmyrene inscriptions. The Conference witnessed the last scholarly paper read by Goshen-Gottstein before his death.

All of the papers represent the latest progress in various aspects of the field of Aramaic, which served as a lingua franca in the Near East for many centuries. The contributions are relevant to Biblical studies, including exegesis. The full range of Aramaic is represented in this volume, from Persian period Aramaic of the fifth century BCE to Babylonian Aramaic of the fifth century CE. The dialects discussed were used by Jews, Christians, and Pagans, and the texts discussed in these papers offer new insights into the language and texts of the Hellenistic and Byzantine Near East.

The Institute of Jewish Studies was established by Alexander Altmann in Manchester in 1954 to promote the academic study of all branches of Jewish culture. Since his move to the USA in 1959 it has been located within the Department of Hebrew and Jewish Studies at University College London, while retaining its autonomous status. Funded by the private sector, it has its own governing body and Patrons. Its Director is Professor M. J. Geller.

During each academic term leading scholars from the UK and throughout Europe, Israel and the USA communicate the results of their research to scholars, students and the public, through a programme of public lectures and seminars.

In addition, the IJS hosts one or more international conferences each year, which focus on significant themes relating to Jewish civilisation. The conferences are intended to bring together eminent scholars working in the same or allied fields of research.

The Institute sponsors the publication of its conference proceedings in cooperation with various publishers, including Cambridge University Press, Oxford University Press and the Littman Library of Jewish Civilisation.

The volume has been edited by Jonas Greenfield of the Hebrew University, Jerusalem, and Michael Weitzman and Markham Geller of University College, London. The editors, who also organised and participated in the original conference, cover a wide range of expertise in Semitic languages. The cooperation of Dr J. F. Healey of the *Journal of Semitic Studies* is much appreciated, as is the detailed attention in the preparation of the manuscript by Miss Ginny Mathias of the Institute of Jewish Studies and Mrs Judith Willson, Editorial Assistant for the *Journal of Semitic Studies*.

The Institute of Jewish Studies acknowledges the valued contribution of the British Academy to this Conference. In its support the Academy has again shown its high regard for the work of the Institute which, with its active Board under the chairmanship of Dr Manfred Altman, fulfils an important role in the UK for Jewish scholarship worldwide.

It was with great regret that the other editors learned, as this volume was going to press, of the death of Jonas Greenfield on 13th March 1995.

ABBREVIATIONS

AAAS	Annales archéologiques arabes syriennes
AASOR	Annual of the American Schools of Oriental Research
ABL	R. F. Harper, Assyrian and Babylonian Letters (London-Chicago 1892-1914)
AC	A. Kohut (ed.), Aruch Completum (Vienna 1928^2)
Addit.	S. Krauss et al., Additamenta ad Aruch Completum (Vienna 1937)
AE	Ancient Egypt and the East (The British School of Archaeology in Egypt)
AHw	W. von Soden, Akkadisches Handwörterbuch (Wiesbaden 1965-81)
AIT	J. A. Montgomery, Aramaic Incantation Texts from Nippur (Philadelphia 1913)
AJA	American Journal of Archaeology
AKM	Abhandlungen für die Kunde des Morgenlandes
AnOr	Analecta Orientalia
AOAT	Alter Orient und Altes Testament
AoF	Altorientalische Forschungen
AOS	American Oriental Series
ARAB	D. D. Luckenbill, Ancient Records of Assyria and Babylonia (New York 1968 = Chicago 1926)
ArOr	Archiv Orientální
AS	Anatolian Studies
Assaf	S. Assaf, Gaonic Responsa from Geniza Mss. (Jerusalem 1929) [Hebrew]
b	Babylonian Talmud (followed by name of tractate)
BA	The Biblical Archeologist
BaM	Baghdader Mitteilungen
BASOR	Bulletin of the American Schools of Oriental Research
Ber	Berytus
Bibl Angelica	Biblioteca Angelica (Rome)
BIFAO	Bulletin de l'Institut Français d'Archéologie Orientale
BiOr	Bibliotheca Orientalis
BM	British Museum (bowls or tablets)
BN	Bibliothèque Nationale (Paris)
Bodl. Heb.	Bodleian MS Hebrew
BSAE	British School of Archaeology in Egypt
BSOAS	Bulletin of the School of Oriental and African Studies
BT	Babylonian Talmud
CAD	The Assyrian Dictionary of the Oriental Institute of the University of Chicago
CAL	Comprehensive Aramaic Lexicon
CAP	A. Cowley, Aramaic Papyri of the Fifth Century B.C. (Oxford 1923)
CBS	University Museum of the University of Pennsylvania, Philadelphia (tablets)
CCR	A. S. Lewis, M. D. Gibson, Codex Climaci Rescriptus (Cambridge 1909)
CdE	Chronique d'Égypte – Bulletin périodique de la Fondation égyptologique Reine Élisabeth (Bruxelles)
CIS	Corpus Inscriptionum Semiticarum
CNis	Des heiligen Ephraem der Syrers Carmina Nisibena, ed E. Beck, CSCO 240-241 (1963)
CPA	Christian Palestinian Aramaic

CPSH	M. Black, A Christian Palestinian Syriac Horologion (Cambridge 1954)
CRAI	Comptes rendus de l'Académie des inscriptions et belles-lettres
CSCO	Corpus Scriptorum Christianorum Orientalium (Louvain)
CTA	A. Herdner, Corpus des tablettes en cunéiformes alphabétiques découvertes à Ras Shamra-Ugarit de 1929 à 1939 (Paris 1963)
DISO	C.-F. Jean, J. Hoftijzer, Dictionnaire des inscriptions sémitiques de l'Ouest (Leiden 1965)
DJPA	M. Sokoloff, A Dictionary of Jewish Palestinian Aramaic of the Byzantine Period (Ramat Gan 1990)
DPD	G. J. Reinink, H. L. J. Vanstiphout (eds.), Dispute Poems and Dialogues in the Ancient and Mediaeval Near East (Leuven 1991)
Driver	G. R. Driver, Aramaic Documents of the Fifth Century B.C. (Osnabrück 1968 = Oxford 1954)
E.P.H.E.	École pratique des Hautes Études (Paris)
EA	J.A. Knudtzon, Die El-Amarna-Tafeln (Leipzig 1915)
ECR	Eastern Churches Review, amalgamated with Sobornost
EI	Eretz-Israel
Eps, Studies	J. N. Epstein, Studies in Talmudic Literature and Semitic Languages (Jerusalem 1983-88)
FMSD	A. S. Lewis, M. D. Gibson, The Forty Martyrs of the Sinai Desert and the Story of Eulogios (Cambridge 1912)
FuB	Forschungen und Berichte
GA	Genesis Apocryphon
GC	Gaonic Commentary: J. N. Epstein, The Gaonic Commentary on the Order Toharot Attributed to Rav Hai Gaon (Jerusalem 1982)
Harkavy	A. Harkavy, Responsen der Geonim (Studien und Mitteilungen aus der Kaiserlichen Öffentlichen Bibliothek 6, St. Petersburg 1887)
HArm	Hymnes de S. Éphrem conservées en version arménienne, ed. L. Mariès, C. Mercier, PO 30 (1961)
Heb.	Jewish National University Library (Jerusalem) (documents)
HEccl	Des heiligen Ephraem der Syrers Hymnen de Ecclesia, ed. E. Beck, CSCO 198-199 (1960)
HEO	Hautes Études Orientales (série de l'E.P.H.E., IVe section)
HFid	Des heiligen Ephraem des Syrers Hymnen de Fide, ed. E. Beck, CSCO 154-155 (1954)
HG	E. Hildesheimer (ed.), Sefer Halakhot Gedolot (Jerusalem 1971-1987)
HP	R. Yehudai Gaon, Sefer Halachot Pesuqot (Codex Sasoon 263), ed. S. Sasoon (Jerusalem 1948; facsimile edition, Jerusalem 1971)
HResur	Des heiligen Ephraem der Syrers Paschahymnen, ed. E. Beck, CSCO 248-249 (1964)
HS	Hilprecht Sammlung, University of Jena
HSM	Harvard Semitic Museum
HSS	Harvard Semitic Series
HVirg	Des heiligen Ephraem der Syrers Hymnen de Virginitate, ed. E. Beck, CSCO 223-224 (1962)
IEJ	Israel Exploration Journal
IFAO	Institut Français d'Archéologie Orientale
IGLS	Inscriptions grecques et latines de la Syrie (Paris)
IJ	E. S. Rosenthal, "Talmudica Iranica", in S. Shaked (ed.), Irano-Judaica, Studies Relating to Jewish Contacts with Persian Culture throughout the Ages (Jerusalem 1982)
IM	Iraq Museum (Baghdad) (bowls)
IOS	Israel Oriental Studies (Tel Aviv)

J	M. Jastrow, A Dictionary of the Targumim, the Talmud Babli and Yerushalmi and the Midrashic Literature (New York 1903)
JA	Journal asiatique
JANES	Journal of the Ancient Near Eastern Society of Columbia University
JAOS	Journal of the American Oriental Society
JARCE	Journal of the American Research Center in Egypt (Boston, Mass.)
JBA	Jewish Babylonian Aramaic
JBL	Journal of Biblical Literature
JEA	Journal of Egyptian Archaeology
JEOL	Jaarbericht van het Vooraziatisch-Egyptisch Genootschap "Ex Oriente Lux"
JHS	Journal of Hellenistic Studies
JIES	Journal of Indo-European Studies
JNES	Journal of Near Eastern Studies
JNSL	Journal of the Northwest Semitic Languages
JPA	Jüdisch-Palästinisch-Aramäisch
JQR	Jewish Quarterly Review
JRS	Journal of Roman Studies
JSS	Journal of Semitic Studies
JSSEA	Journal of the Society for the Study of Egyptian Antiquities (Ontario)
K	C. J. and B. Kasowski, Thesaurus Talmudis Concordantiae Verborum quae in Talmude Babylonico Reperiuntur (Jerusalem 1954-1982)
KAI	H. Donner, W. Röllig, Kanaanäische und aramäische Inschriften, Vols. I-III (Wiesbaden 1962-76)
Kraeling	E. G. Kraeling, The Brooklyn Museum Aramaic Papyri: New Documents of the Fifth Century B.C. from the Jewish Colony of Elephantine (New Haven 1953)
Kutscher, Studies	E. Y. Kutscher, Hebrew and Aramaic Studies (Jerusalem 1977)
KWIC	Key Word in Context Concordance
LÄ	Lexicon der Ägyptologie
LAPO	Littératures anciennes du Proche-Orient (Paris)
LCL	Loeb Classical Library
Le 00	A. S. Lewis, M. D. Gibson, Palestinian Syriac Texts from Palimpsest Fragments in the Taylor-Schechter Collection (London 1900)
Le 02	A. S. Lewis, M. D. Gibson, Apocrypha Syriaca (Cambridge 1902)
Lesh	Leshônênu – A Journal for the Study of the Hebrew Language and Cognate Subjects
LOT	Z. Ben-Hayyim, Literary and Oral Traditions of the Samaritans (Jerusalem 1957-1977)
LSp	Lexicon Syropalaestinum
LXX	Septuagint
m	Mishnah
MH	Mishnaic Hebrew
MMA	Metropolitan Museum (New York) (documents)
N	Targum Neofiti
NJPS	New Jewish Publication Society Bible translation
NPNF	Select Library of Nicene and Post-Nicene Fathers
OEL	Outline Etymological Lexicon
OGIS	W. Dittenberger (ed.), Orientis Graeci Inscriptiones Selectae (Leipzig 1903-5)
OH	Otzar ha-Geonim (Haifa-Jerusalem 1928-1943)
OIP	Oriental Institute Publications

OLP	Orientalia Lovaniensia Periodica
Or	Orientalia
OrChrA	Orientalia Christiana Analecta (Rome)
OrChrP	Orientalia Christiana Periodica
OrSyr	L'Orient syrien
P	Paris Fragment Targum
PO	Patrologia Orientalis
Ps-J	Pseudo-Jonathan
PT	Palestinian Talmud
R.A.I.	Rencontre Assyriologique Internationale
RB	Revue biblique
RdE	Revue d'égyptologie
REJ	Revue des études juives
RES	Revue des études sémitiques
RGTC	Répertoire Géographique des Textes Cunéiformes
Riv. Bibl. It.	Rivista Biblica Italiana
ROC	Revue de l'orient chrétien (Paris)
SA	Samaritan Aramaic
SAA	State Archives of Assyria (Neo-Assyrian Text Corpus Project, Academy of Finland, Helsinki University Press)
SbKAW	Sitzungsberichte der Königlichen Akademie zu Wien
SC	Sources chrétiennes (Paris)
SDB	Supplément au Dictionnaire de la Bible
Sef	Sefarad – Revista del Instituto "Arias Montano" de estudios hebráicos y del Oriente proximo C.S.I.C. (Madrid/Barcelona)
Segert	S. Segert, Altaramäische Grammatik mit Bibliographie, Chrestomathie und Glossar (Leipzig 1973, 1983[2])
SH	Samaritan Hebrew
SP	Samaritan Pentateuch
ST	Samaritan Targum
StOr	Studia Orientalia
T-S	Taylor-Schechter Collection
Targ	Targum
Tg. Ps.-Jonathan	Targum Pseudo-Jonathan
TM	Tibåt Marqe
TUAT	O. Kaiser (ed.), Texte aus der Umwelt des Alten Testaments (Gütersloh 1982-)
UET	Ur Excavations, Texts
VAB	Vorderasiatische Bibliothek, Berlin
VAT	Staatliche Museen, Berlin (texts)
VT	Vetus Testamentum
WVDOG	Wissenschaftliche Veröffentlichungen der Deutschen Orient-Gesellschaft
ZÄS	Zeitschrift für ägyptische Sprache und Altertumskunde
ZAW	Zeitschrift für die alttestamentliche Wissenschaft
ZDMG	Zeitschrift der Deutschen Morgenländischen Gesellschaft

Aramaic and the Jews

Jonas C. Greenfield — Hebrew University of Jerusalem

A cultural trait that has been noted by observers of the Jewish scene, past and present, is the ability of the Jews to adopt cultural elements that were initially foreign or even inimical and in the course of time to adapt them, and to make them their own. This is especially true in the sphere of language. In the Jewish experience there was often the desire on the part of a large segment of the people to hold on to the ancestral language which was not of necessity always Hebrew. The rival languages, however, when used by the Jews gradually became Jewish languages. A count of the major examples, in more or less historical order, would give us not only dialects of Palestinian and Babylonian Aramaic, but also Judaeo-Arabic, Judaeo-Persian, Judaeo-Spanish, that is Ladino, Judaeo-German, latter to become Yiddish, Judaeo-Romance, which would include Judaeo-French and the dialects of Judaeo-Italian, and, still others. I have not included a supposed Judaeo-Greek of the Hellenistic and Roman periods that some scholars have presumed for the Greek biblical translations and for other Greek writings of the Jews, but a case has been made for a Judaeo-Greek dialect in the Byzantine period and in modern times. This does not include the many vernaculars and modern languages for which Hebrew letters were used for writing. I treasure a letter in English written by my grandfather, who spoke a rather good, idiomatic English but was never sure enough of his spelling to write English in anything but his fine, cursive Hebrew hand.

Aramaic is foremost among the Jewish languages both by reason of its antiquity and its continuous use. By the mid-fifth century B.C.E., after the return from the Babylonian exile, it was widely, but far from exclusively, used among the Jews in their homeland and elsewhere. Hebrew remained in vernacular use in Palestine among the villagers of Judaea into the second century C.E. Aramaic is still in use among Jews, in a variety of important prayers, hymns and songs for synagogue and home use; for the reading of the Targum Onqelos, in the study of the Talmud and Midrash, and for writing in the worst of rabbinic jargons. It is also still in use as the vernacular among many Jews from Kurdistan.

If we follow the course of relationships between the Aramaeans on the one hand and the Israelites, and then the Judaeans, on the other, we find that from the earliest period these were not smooth. The pattern of mistrust that developed in historical times is projected back into the Patriarchal period. The Aramaeans were, according to the Biblical narrative, a kindred tribe — the family of Nahor, Bethuel, and Laban — from whom in patriarchal times one took one's wives and from whom one separated as soon as possible to return to the land of Canaan. It is in the narrative concerning the pact between Jacob and Laban that the earliest Aramaic words recorded in the Bible *yĕgar śahadūtā* are found. In the period of the Judges and the Monarchy, the Aramaeans — if we disregard those rare times when circumstances led to a shaky alliance — were usually seeking territorial aggrandizement at the expense of Israel or Judah. The relationship was nevertheless strong enough for the phrase *ʾărāmī ʾōved ʾāvī* "my father was a fugitive Aramaean" (Deut.26:5, with the NJPS) to be used by the Israelites to describe themselves.

Let us pick up the historical thread. With the spread of the Assyrian Empire in the eighth century, Aramaic achieved an important place as the *lingua franca* in the western part of this realm. There were two main factors for this: 1) the Aramaeans and Chaldeans were significant sectors of the population in Assyria and Babylonia and had assumed a leading role in all levels of society; and 2) the relative ease in writing alphabetic Aramaic in comparison with the more cumbersome cuneiform Akkadian. The use of two scribes, Assyrian and Aramaic, for recording tribute, counting spoils, etc., is attested to by reliefs from the time of Tiglath-pileser III on. We also know that Aramaic was also used for communications from the West to the Assyrian court. That Aramaic was understood and used outside the Aramaic-speaking area proper is shown by the well-known passage in 2 Kings 18:26 (and Isaiah 36:11). The Assyrian envoy, who spoke Hebrew (called *yehūdīt* "the language of Judah"), was requested by Hezekiah's officials to speak Aramaic, which they understood, rather than Hebrew. The public use of Hebrew by the Assyrian official would have enabled the populace to appreciate the Assyrian threat. Understandably, he continued in Hebrew. The so-called Assur ostracon (KAI 224), written in Babylonia — the earliest example of Eastern Aramaic — attests to the use of Aramaic for official communications in the seventh century within the Assyrian-Babylonian heartland. By the late sixth century Aramaic had spread to Egypt as the language of diplomacy. A letter found at Saqqara (KAI 266), whose exact date is a matter of dispute, sent by a ruler of one of the cities of the Philistine coast to the Pharaoh, is written neither in Egyptian nor in the language used in Philistia but in Aramaic. Jeremiah's message deprecating foreign gods is also quoted in Aramaic (Jer. 10:11).

After Assyria was conquered by the Medes and the Babylonians, most of the Assyrian territory in the West came under Babylonian control. The Aramaic used in Babylonia, an Eastern dialect, gradually replaced for official purposes the dialect used earlier — in all likelihood that used by the Aramaeans of Assyria which has been called Mesopotamian Aramaic. There can be no doubt that it was during this period that the many words of Akkadian origin that are found in various Jewish languages entered Hebrew via Aramaic. Some familiar examples from the the documentary and legal sphere are: *šěṭar*, *šěṭārā*, "document" from Akkadian *šaṭaru*; *geṭ*, *giṭṭā* "document" from Akkadian *giṭṭu* (in turn from Sumerian gid.da "[long] document"), used in later Jewish usage primarily for "divorce decree" and *ʾiggeret*, *ʾiggartā*, from Akkadian *egirtu* "letter". The word *šuttāf*, "partner" widespread in the Jewish dialects, also arrived via Aramaic from Akkadian *šutāpu*. Beside the usual Aramaic word for gate *tarʿā* one finds in the Eastern dialects *baba* from Akkadian *bābū*, its use in the name of several Talmudic tractates is well known, and in Arabic *bāb* is the ordinary word used for "gate".

The largest body of Aramaic documents from the Achaemenid period comes from the island of Yeb, Elephantine in Greek, situated across from the southern Egyptian city of Aswan. The Jews of Elephantine served as soldiers in the Persian army and as such were part of the Aramaean garrison of Syene. The texts are primarily legal documents, land sales and transfers, marriage and manumission documents and the like. There are also court decisions, letters, and lists. Literary texts are few, the Ahiqar story and proverbs are the best known. There is also the so-called Bar Punash text, and the fragmentary Aramaic version of Darius' Bisitun inscription. Beside the names of the participants in the various transactions the clear Jewish element in these texts is sparse — the fragmentary Passover letter, an inquiry on an ostracon as to when Passover might fall, and some not well understood references in the ostraca to the sixth day as *ʾarūbtā*, and the seventh day as *šabbah*. Were these literary texts actually read by the local Jews or were they in reality from Syene where some literate Aramaean treasured them, while the Jews used the other side of the papyrus for records and notes? What language did the Jews actually speak among themselves? The use of Aramaic for legal documents and other written forms of communication does not reveal a thing about *viva voce* communication at Elephantine. We know that there was a temple, a *BYT YHW*, at Elephantine, that there were *kohanim* there too, but we have no indication as to what sort of service there was beside the sacrifices and other offerings that are referred to in CAP 30/31 and 32, and in what language this service might have taken place.

In the Persian and Hellenistic periods the enmity between the Jews and Aramaeans, now a catch-all phrase for Aramaic speakers without reference to their origins, grew. In the course of time the phrase *ʾārāmī ʾōved ʾāvī* which in its original usage designated Jacob as an Aramaean took on the meaning, "an Aramaean sought to destroy my father" and as such it is used in the Passover *haggada*. In the Roman period, when any trace of Aramaean political power had long since ceased to exist, the term *ʾārāmī* had a derogatory tone. and was used to designate a pagan (see PT San. 3,6, 21b, where the contrast *yěhūdī/ʾārāmāʾi* is clear). It was also then used in a general way for the Romans (unless this is a form of internal censorship, but *ʾărāmīt* is Latin in PT Meg. 1, 11, 71c).

Nevertheless, Aramaic is the chief rival of Hebrew for the accolade "Jewish language". Aramaic was to become a serious rival of Hebrew first as a vernacular and then as a literary language, and at a later date would eclipse Hebrew in both spheres for some time. The literary works written in Aramaic, be they parts of the Bible — a line in Jeremiah, the chapters of Daniel and Ezra — be they the various Targums, the discursive parts of the Palestinian and the Babylonian Talmuds, the Aramaic *midrāshim*, various Geonic works, or such medieval compositions as the Zohar, are essential parts of the Jewish literary heritage. Jewish legal documents have been drawn up in Aramaic for over two thousand years utilizing ancient formulas. The two essential legal instruments for the polarities of family life, the *kĕtubbā* — the "marriage contract" — and the *geṭ* — the "divorce decree" — are still written in Aramaic. Even if by tradition the ministering angels do not understand any language other than Hebrew, the *qaddish* is still recited in Aramaic.

A characteristic of the later books of the Bible is the occurrence of Iranian terms and expressions. In the Aramaic documents of the Achaemenid period, such as the Elephantine documents and the Arsham letters, there are also quite a few administrative and commercial terms drawn from this source. Since Aramaic and various Iranian dialects were used in close proximity, it is a matter of linguistic discernment for the student of matters Aramaic and Iranian to sort out the lines of influence and development in this area. But there can be no doubt that words that are part and parcel of Aramaic, such as *ginzā* "treasure", *gizbārā (ganzabara)* "treasurer", *rāzā* "secret", and *pitgāmā (patigama)* "word, thing", were absorbed at an early stage of this contact with Iranian. I should add that these words were eventually also taken over by Hebrew and in their Hebrew form — *gĕnīzā*, *gizbār*, *rāz* and *pitgām* live on in modern Hebrew. The continued absorption of Iranian terms is also typical of later Aramaic dialects such as Jewish Babylonian Aramaic.

Although different Aramaic dialects were used in the various parts of the Achaemenian Empire, a remarkable uniformity prevailed as to the script in use. A single script type for Aramaic was dominant; it had developed at an early date from the Phoenician script, with monumental and cursive forms, and its development can be traced from the eighth century through the fourth. It served as a quasi-official script throughout the succeeding Assyrian, Babylonian, and Persian Empires and was widely used on papyrus, leather, and ostracon; it diverged from the Hebrew-Phoenician type and acquired a unique image of its own. With the breakup of the Achaemenian Empire, due to the conquests of Alexander the Great, local scripts began to emerge. In the West, the "Jewish script" is a descendant of the Aramaic script, and its development can now be traced in detail thanks to the Judaean Desert finds and other recent archaeological discoveries. It took the place of the ancient Hebrew script, and of the paleo-Hebrew script that emerged from it, and came to be used for both Aramaic and Hebrew. A cursive Jewish script also developed during this period and was widely used, but *seems* to have fallen into disuse after the Bar Kokhba rebellion. All the later Jewish scripts, square and cursive, we are told by the paleographers, descend from the Jewish script that developed in this period.

Alongside the Official Aramaic of the Achaemenian period, a literary dialect emerged which may be called "Standard Literary Aramaic". This development is comparable to the emergence of Late Babylonian as the standard language of most literary compositions and royal inscriptions of the Neo-Assyrian period, and to the emergence of the dialect of London as Standard English, or that of Paris as French. The framework story of the Proverbs of Ahiqar is the earliest example of Standard Literary Aramaic to reach us. The two large segments of Biblical Aramaic preserved in Ezra and Daniel contain elements of both Official Aramaic and Standard Literary Aramaic. The letters and documents in Ezra are in Official Aramaic while the narrative is in Standard Literary Aramaic. The variety and scope of this latter dialect can be best perceived in Daniel, for although this book was composed during the early part of the second century B.C.E., it contains material from earlier times in both prose and poetry. The language of these texts has been brought up-to-date and the themes made more topical by the pre-Hasmonean editor. During the late Achaemenian and the Hellenistic periods, Standard Literary Aramaic was in wide use in the West, to judge from contemporary and later sources in Aramaic. The various Aramaic literary works found at Qumran are, in my opinion in this dialect even though there are slight linguistic variations among them. These range from Tobit, in all likelihood originating in the late fourth century, to Enoch and the Genesis Apocryphon and other works from the third and second centuries, to the Job Targum, dating in all likelihood to the first century B.C.E.

Perhaps a word is in order concerning these texts. It was long thought by perceptive scholars, on the basis of the Greek text that has reached us in more than one version and the Old Latin text, that the original language of Tobit was Aramaic. Tobit was a work of piety and erudition, and the Ahiqar tale serves as a structural element in its composition. For a complete text of Enoch we have to fall back on the Ethiopic version but Aramaic fragments of all of Enoch, except for the Similitudes, have been found at Qumran. On the other hand fragments of the Book of Jubilees in Hebrew were also discovered there. These are not sectarian literature as such, but share with Qumran the peculiar solar calendar that is the basis of Qumran ritual, as well as other matters. There are a number of manuscripts of both these books at Qumran, and one may assume that they had quasi-canonical status there. The discovery of these works at Qumran may also help clarify the nature of those circles who constituted the immediate audience for these works. The Aramaic Levi Document (already known from the Cairo Geniza) and related literature in Aramaic have also been found there.

The Genesis Apochryphon, an expanded version of the Genesis story with midrashic and aggadic elements, may serve as an example of the retold and paraphrased Biblical text which was in all likelihood very popular among the Jews in this period. Literature of this sort, usually in Hebrew dress, is known to us from the Middle Ages. There are unexpected elements in the Genesis Apocryphon. Among these are a) the supposition of Lamech, Noah's father, that Noah was not his son, but rather the result of his wife's coupling with a heavenly being (col. 2:1); b) the detailed, poetic description of Sarah's beauty (col. 20:1-8), more befitting a Hellenistic, than a Jewish work, in which details of piety and ritual observance are important; and c) in relating the punishments visited on Pharaoh for taking Sarah from Abraham, we are afforded a glimpse into elements of folk magic such as the use of prayer in order to expel evil spirits and the laying on of hands for curing disease (col. 20:21-28). This sort of "treatment" was known from Hellenistic literature and also from the New Testament (see Luke 4: 40-41) but was hitherto unknown from contemporary and later Jewish sources. It is quite clear that none of the Aramaic texts found in the Qumran caves were written there, and although they were of prime interest to the sectarians they were not of necessity Essene (or Essenoid) in origin. An interesting point made by some scholars is that truly sectarian literature, such as the Rule of the Community, the Damascus Covenant, the Pesharim, the Hodayot and others, was usually written in Hebrew.

In the course of the last forty years a growing number of Aramaic epigraphic discoveries have been made for this period. Although some are of everyday items such as ostraca containing precise information about the delivery of goods and other types of lists, on the whole funerary inscriptions comprise the greater part of the discoveries. An unusual example is the inscription of the priest Abba, found in a burial cave on the Givᶜat ha-Mivtar in Jerusalem. The inscription related that Abba brought back the body of Mattathias, son of Judah, from Babylon and buried him in the cave which he had acquired by document. This remarkable inscription is written in the paleo-Hebrew script, a script of very limited use during this period. Some scholars have surmised that Mattathias was one of the last members of the Hasmonean dynasty. The ossuaries also contain short but significant inscriptions such as that of a person who is called a *bāneh hēkālā* "builder of the temple". Was he an architect, or simply a member of the Herodian building staff?

The Qumran discoveries led to other finds in the Judaean Desert. As with Qumran, the bedawin usually preceded the professional archaeologist. The documents from the Bar-Kokhba period present us with an extremely interesting variety of materials. There are documents in Aramaic, Hebrew, Nabataean, and Greek consisting of letters, judicial orders, legal and commercial contracts. This material may best be dealt with in accordance with the location of the finds. The first known discovery was at Wadi Murabbaᶜat in the Judaean Desert. It was from these documents that it was learned that Bar-Kokhba's real name was Shimeon Bar-Kosiba, a name which allowed two puns: the positive Bar-Kokhba "son of the star", and the negative Bar-Koziba "false son". There were among these texts a variety of contracts in Aramaic and Hebrew which testify to the actual use of the legal formulae recorded in the Mishna, the Tosefta, and later Talmudic literature. A prime example is the *geṭ* found there. The letters and documents in Hebrew attest both to the continued use of Hebrew as a vernacular and also to the influence of Aramaic upon it. For students of Jewish law, these documents have provided added information concerning the continuity and development of legal terminology and usage. Of special interest from this point of view are the two Greek documents. The first is a marriage contract P. Mur. 116 which is essentially a *kĕtubbā* written in Greek. It contains most of the clauses prescribed by the Mishna for this type of document (Ket. 4:7-12) and it is clearly based upon the Aramaic. The second is a remarriage contract P. Mur. 115; both the names of the participants and the legal formulae show that this is a Jewish document. Rather than the usual Greek formulae known from texts of this type discovered in Egypt, this contract contains many legal formulae which are also translated from Aramaic. It provides the only example of this type of document known from the pre-Geonic period.

The other Judaean Desert site was Naḥal Ḥever, not far from ᶜEin Gedi. The find made by the late Yigael Yadin in the "Cave of Letters" consists essentially of two archives, the first centered around Babatha, and enabled us to trace the fortune of that lady and her family from the year 120 to the year 132 in the area around Zoᶜar on the south-eastern shores of the Dead Sea. The Greek texts from this archive were published at the end of 1989 by the eminent papyrologist Naphtali Lewis and the Aramaic signatures and subscriptions were edited by me. The Nabataean and Aramaic texts include a long document in Aramaic in which Babatha's father gives his property as a gift to his wife after his death and also Babatha's *kĕtubbā*. This latter document follows Mishnaic prescriptions. The second archive consisted of letters and legal documents in Aramaic and Hebrew stemming from ᶜEin Gedi from the Bar Kokhba period, and reflected life during those dire times. I would note that from the Murabbaᶜat caves, we now have the earliest *geṭ* "divorce document" to reach us and from the Naḥal Ḥever archives we have Babatha's *kĕtubbā*, again the earliest example.

With the defeat of Bar Kokhba the focus of Jewish life moved from Judaea, where Hebrew was still spoken, to the Galilee, where Aramaic was the dominant language. A stress on the need to converse in Hebrew is found in the literature of the time. Rabbi Meir's remark that "he who speaks in the holy tongue is guaranteed a place in the world to come" (PT *Sheqalim* 3:4 87c) is symptomatic. Rabbi Judah the Prince took up the battle for Hebrew in the challenge to Aramaic quoted in his name: "In Palestine why Syriac? Either Hebrew or Greek!" (BT *Sota* 49b; *Baba Qamma* 82b). During this period the use of Hebrew declined, and when information about the meaning of a rare word was needed, one turned to one of the maids of the household of Rabbi Judah the Prince who came from the South (PT Shevi^cit 9:1 38c), or to a scholar from that area. Incidentally, scholars of this period were also the first to record Arabic usages in explaining Hebrew words and phrases. Hebrew did not give way entirely before Aramaic, it remained the major language of prayer and ritual; it was also used in the school house and study hall and important compilations of both *halakha* and *aggadah* continued to be composed in it. The varied origins of those buried in the great necropolis of Bet Shearim are often reflected in the languages used in the burial inscriptions. Greek and Aramaic are predominant, but the inscriptions belonging to the members of the patriarchal house are all in Hebrew. The inscription on the lintel of the study house whose remnants were found in Dabbura in the Golan Heights, reads: *zeh beit midrāšō šelĕrabbī ʾeliʿezer ha-qappār* "this is the study house of Rabbi Eliezer ha-Qappar". He lived in the second century C.E. and had his home in Lydda, a southern city, where Hebrew probably remained in use for some time after his death. It should be noted that the dialect of Aramaic known from a later period, that is called Christian Palestinian Aramaic, whose locale was primarily Judaea, has both morphological and lexical Hebraisms.

It was in Standard Literary Aramaic that the targum to the Pentateuch, usually known as *Targum Onqelos*, and that to the Prophets, known as *Targum Jonathan ben Uzziel*, were composed. Since they were not written in an identifiable Palestinian Aramaic scholars have disputed the geographic origin of these targumim; but it is quite clear that these targumim were composed in Palestine. It is because they were not intended solely for local consumption that they were written in a generally intelligible dialect. According to Talmudic tradition they had received the stamp of approval of leading authorities and were intended for use throughout the Aramaic speaking Jewish diaspora. In the course of time these targumim were transmitted and cultivated primarily in the Babylonian academies and therefore contain certain morphological features typical of Eastern Aramaic, and certain phrases and usages that may also point in that direction. It became the traditional mode of study in the academies, perhaps already by the second century C.E., to read the weekly portion of the Torah *šenayim miqraʾ we-ʾeḥad targum* "twice in Hebrew and once in Aramaic". This practice was adopted first by those under Babylonian influence and then by others. The significance of this custom was that there spread throughout the Jewish world an active, conscious use of this Aramaic text — the *Targum Onqelos* — and it was inevitable that its language set a standard for writing "correct Aramaic". The *Targum Onqelos* is still used in the Yemenite shabbat liturgy, a verse from the Torah is followed by its rendition in that targum. The *Megillat Taᶜanit* is another authoritative text in Standard Literary Aramaic. Some of the later targumim such as those to the Song of Songs, Ruth, Lamentations and Ecclesiastes were also composed in this dialect. At a much later date, the *Megillat Antiochus,* which was based on the Greek First Maccabees, was concocted in Standard Literary Aramaic to give the work an air of antiquity and veracity.

Which type of Aramaic was actually spoken in Palestine during this period? Some scholars have thought that the Qumran texts bring us closer to the vernacular in use, and not only to the literary language. They have assumed that this is the sort of Aramaic that stands behind the Greek of certain New Testament books. Others have claimed that Qumran notwithstanding, one must turn to later Palestinian Aramaic for evidence of the colloquial language. The latter position seems more plausible to me, since my view is that Qumran Aramaic is a variety of Standard Literary Aramaic. It would seem to me that the *ipsissima verba* of a Galilean ought best be recovered by using a later vernacular Galilean Aramaic than a literary language. However, if an Aramaic proto-Gospel, postulated by some scholars, was in literary Aramaic, then there is no reason why Qumran Aramaic may not be used to reconstruct it.

Clear distinctions among the dialects of Aramaic have been established and Palestinian Aramaic has emerged into its own in the last half century of research, so that it can now be said that we know what such a Galilean dialect was like. The three dialects of Palestinian Aramaic are Samaritan Aramaic, Christian Aramaic and Jewish Aramaic. Important texts in these dialects have been published, and valuable dictionaries and lexical and grammatical studies have aided scholars. The elements that are common to these Aramaic dialects are more numerous than those that distinguish them from each other. Three different scripts were used — Jewish, developed from the "Herodian book-hand" familiar from the Qumran scrolls, for Jewish texts; Samaritan, a continuation of the paleo-Hebrew, for Samaritan texts; and a modification of the Syriac script, for Christian Palestinian. The last mentioned is more conservative in orthography, since it follows its Syriac model. Jewish Aramaic was also bound by orthographic tradition — that of the Hebrew and Aramaic texts read and studied; but it is closer to the colloquial than is Christian Palestinian orthography, while Samaritan Aramaic has the laxest orthographic practices.

The area of Samaritan studies was fostered by Zeev Ben-Hayim and his leading disciple Abraham Tal, together with Rudolph Macuch, and his students, in a series of important works. The growth of interest in this field has been outstanding. The recently published collection of essays, *The Samaritans*, edited by Alan Crown, is a testimonial to this. In Christian Aramaic, there was the publication of important texts by M. Black and M. Goshen-Gottstein, of inscriptions from a variety of sites, and of some papyri from Khirbet Mird. The linguistic studies by Moshe Bar-Asher, and the *Grammatik des Christlich-Palästinisch-Aramäischen* by Christa Müller-Kessler are of great use to students and scholars alike. It has become clear in recent years that speakers of Christian Palestinian Aramaic were centered in Judaea; and there is reason to believe that many of these were ultimately of Jewish origin. It is therefore not surprising to find in this dialect traces of Mishnaic Hebrew influence. The great talmudist Saul Lieberman often used items from both Christian Palestinian Aramaic and Samaritan Aramaic to explain difficult lexical items in the Jewish texts.

Palestinian Jewish Aramaic of the Byzantine period — best known as the language of the Palestinian Talmud, called Talmud *Ereṣ Yiśraʾel* or the Yerushalmi, and the Midrashim and targumim noted below is the best known of the three dialects. The literature in it has been read and studied over the centuries and has achieved canonical status, as it were, among the Jews. The designation "Galilean Aramaic" used by E. Y. Kutscher for the Jewish Aramaic dialect may be defended since most of the material comes from the Galilee, but this may be too restrictive. The material in Jewish Aramaic consists of a growing number of dedicatory and memorial inscriptions found throughout the country; but it is best known from literary works, such as the Palestinian Talmud, the Aramaic parts of *Genesis Rabba* and *Leviticus Rabba* and other Midrashim (as found in the better manuscripts and Geniza fragments), and from the Palestinian Targums, as best represented by texts from the Cairo Geniza and the so-called *Neofiti Targum.* In recent years a steady flow of editions of both manuscripts and geniza fragments has given us fuller control of the rich resources of this dialect and a better appreciation of its literature. We now also have Michael Sokoloff's *Dictionary of Jewish Palestinian Aramaic of the Byzantine Period* as a useful resource and research tool. I would like to mention five areas in Jewish Palestinian Aramaic that have been opened to fuller research in recent years: 1) Targumic studies: We now have with the publication of the *Neofiti Targum* by Alejandro Diez Macho, despite the many problems that the text entails, a full Palestinian Targum of the Pentateuch, and with the edition of the Geniza material and of the *Fragment Targum* by Michael Klein the tools to examine closely the complexities entailed in these Targums; 2) Aramaic poetry: The corpus of Aramaic *piyyuṭim* from the Byzantine Period is being prepared for publication by M. Sokoloff and J. Yahalom. Some of these *piyyuṭim* such as *ʾezel moshe* and *ʾarkin shemayya* were well known since they had been preserved in the festival liturgy. Others were preserved as *tōsāfōt* "additions" to the Palestinian Targumim and as such some have been published by Klein in his edition of the *Geniza Manuscripts of the Palestinian Targum.* The forthcoming work of Sokoloff and Yahalom will present a full corpus of this invaluable material. One poem, *ʾtbḥr zhrh lqydwš yrḥyn* "the new moon was chosen for the sanctification of the months," is of particular interest. It consists of seventeen omens in poetical form belonging to a well known class of astronomical omens of Mesopotamian type. The poem deals with portents such as lunar eclipses, changes in the moon's color and other meteorological phenomena. In a recently published study by Sokoloff and myself the text has been edited and commented on. We have dealt with the close parallels in ancient Mesopotamian texts, and other Near Eastern traditions. This corpus will also contain a variety of poems for private occasions such as weddings and also eulogies and dirges. The poems are characterized by an accented verse with four stresses, typically Palestinian Aramaic vocabulary, and the use of a large number of Greek loan words. 3) Amulets and other magical texts: Joseph Naveh and Shaul Shaked have devoted a great deal of time and effort assembling a corpus of amulets, deciphering and interpreting the difficult texts. They have published the first volume containing such texts and are now preparing the second one. Whereas Babylonian Jewish magic was well known from material preserved in the Babylonian Talmud, and in the many "incantation bowls" discovered in Iraq and Iran, the Palestinian tradition was virtually unknown. The amulets and the chapbooks giving instructions on amulet writing from the Geniza have opened up an important field of study. I would add that these amulets are written for Jewish customers while the magic bowls in my opinion, although written by Jews, are usually for non-Jewish customers; 4) The *hekhalot* or *merkaba* literature: It was the late Gershom Shalom who revived interest in these texts and argued for their early date. A good number of Geniza texts have now been published, primarily by Peter Schaeffer, and the better preserved Aramaic texts among them are on the whole in good Palestinian Aramaic. Schaeffer and his students have given us a very useful Synopsis of the *hekhalot* texts. 5) Inscriptions: The growing number of inscriptions that have been found in recent years are relevant to the study of the Aramaic language. These are usually dedicatory inscriptions found in synagogues or other public places, or funeral inscriptions. Of unique importance is the sixth-century "halakhic" inscription found in a field near the village Rehov. It matches material known from the Palestinian Talmud and elsewhere and provides a useful witness for the text, the language, and the orthography of the period. The synagogue inscriptions from ʿEin Gedi, Hammath Tiberias, Beit Shean and elsewhere are both cultural and linguistic monuments. Joseph Naveh's *ʿAl psephas veʾven* has made them readily available.

A site like Dura Europos on the Euphrates may also testify to the importance of Aramaic among the Jews. It had a flourishing Jewish community and the remains of one of the oldest synagogues known to us was discovered there. The city, an important military post and emporium, was an outpost of Hellenistic civilization and most of the epigraphic material discovered there was in Greek. This consists of a great variety of inscriptions and a goodly number of documents. However, as far as we can tell, the Jews on the whole used Aramaic. The descriptive inscriptions accompanying the famed synagogue paintings are in Aramaic. The main ones being: a) Moses splitting the Red Sea: *mšh kd npq mn mṣrym wbzʿ yʾmʾ* and again *mšh kd b*[*z*]*ʿ yʾmʾ*; b) Samuel anointing David *šmw*[*ʿl*] *kd mšḥ* [*d*]*wyd*. Both phrases are the ones that are known from the Targumic tradition and would have been understood by the local Aramaic speaking Jews. There are other documents from Dura Europos in the Jewish Aramaic of the period. One of the commemorative inscriptions on the synagogue wall is close to a well-known prayer that is still found in the prayer-book. It is indeed a great pity that other sites in Mesopotamia which had large Jewish populations in late antiquity have not been excavated.

Our chief source for Babylonian Jewish Aramaic is the Babylonian Talmud. Although it contains a great number of texts in Hebrew, the language of discourse is Aramaic. As is well known the material in the Talmud is very varied. Beside the *halakhic* discussion of the pertinent Mishna text there is a great deal of what has been labeled by the tradition as *ʾaggadĕta*. This includes tales about personages, ancient and classical, stories concerning the rabbis, fables, legends, dream interpretations, astrological data, etc. Most of this is in Aramaic. Due to the fact that the Babylonian Talmud became the commentary par excellence on the Mishna, the source for law and lore, and the main textbook for ritual edification and religious education, it entered the conscience of the Jews and has remained so until our times. The Aramaic of the Babylonian Talmud therefore achieved a unique place in the traditional Jewish curriculum. It was never studied as such, but it was absorbed and it became common practice for scholars and scribes to rewrite the texts in other dialects to fit Babylonian Aramaic. This type of Aramaic is dominant in the legal documents and formulae in use among Jews to the present day.

A large number of "incantation" or "magic" bowls have been found in Iraq, in the Nippur region, and in Iran, in Khuzistan. These bowls, whose purpose was to ward off evil, are written not only in the Jewish script and Jewish Babylonian Aramaic, but also in the Syriac and Mandaic scripts and languages, as well as in a type of writing that some scholars have called the "pagan" Syriac script. Although some of the bowls are distinctly Mandaean or Christian (those in Syriac) in content, they represent an interesting cultural phenomenon since they share many common elements across religious boundaries. The dialect and script were determined by the community of the person for whose protection the bowl was written. Most of the Jewish bowls were surely intended for pagans as the names of the parties mentioned in the bowls demonstrate, and some of the Mandaic and "pagan" bowls are Jewish in content but were written for non-Jews. The divorce formula, known from the traditional *get*, is used in all the traditions to drive demons from human beings.

Long after the Islamic conquest Aramaic was spoken by Jews and others in Mesopotamia. The *Book of Commandments* of Anan, the early Karaite leader, was also written in this dialect. The Geonim composed many of their works in Babylonian Aramaic. These were responsa, commentaries on the Talmudic text and legal manuals. The *Letter* of Sherira Gaon, a prime source of historical and literary information, one of the last of these works, is a good example. Hai Gaon, his son and successor, who was the last of the Geonim, composed most of his works in Arabic, but referred to Aramaic as "our language" and reported that it lived on in the rural areas among Jews and Christians into the eleventh century.

Recourse must be had to good manuscripts, Geniza fragments, etc., for the proper study of Babylonian Aramaic. The differences between Eastern and Western Aramaic are found in the areas of vocabulary, phonology, morphology, and syntax.

1. Vocabulary. Lists of words typical of the Western dialect, in contrast to those of the East, are easily drawn up. A simple criterion from the earliest periods may be found in the word for "to see" — in standard Aramaic from the earliest periods and in the Eastern Aramaic dialects it is *ḥzy*; in the Western Aramaic dialects, *ḥmy*. There are naturally more Greek and Latin loanwords in the West, and more borrowings from Akkadian and Iranian in the East. A list of the words shared by all the Palestinian dialects can be made with ease.

2. Phonology. In all the Aramaic dialects, the gutturals — the laryngeals and pharyngeals — remain a subject for study, for there can be no doubt that they have been affected in all the dialects; but the degree to which this happened is not readily ascertainable everywhere. The Western dialect most conservative in its orthography is Christian Palestinian Aramaic, but even here there are indications that the gutturals have been confused. The same is true for Jewish Aramaic. The Palestinian Talmud (Ber. 2:2 4d) reports that residents of three cities — Haifa, Tibʿon, and Beit-Shean — were not allowed to lead the prayer service since they pronounced *ḥeṭ* like *he* and *ʿayin* like *ʾalef.* A recently discovered mosaic inscription on the floor of a synagogue at Beit-Shean proves that the Talmudic report was accurate, for in a blessing for the artisan "who made this work" the word for "made" *ʿbd* is spelled correctly with an *ʿayin,* but "work" *ʾavidta* is with an *alef* for the *ʿayin.* And *ḥada* "this" has a *ḥet for* the *he.* Other inscriptions from the Beit-Shean valley display the same orthographic idiosyncrasies. The dialect in which the loss of the gutturals is most pronounced is the Samaritan. In the traditional Samaritan pronunciation, all the gutturals are reduced to zero, and in writing real confusion reigns. In the East, it is Syriac which seems to be most conservative, for it has a set orthography established at an early period and maintained for the classical language despite phonological changes that must have taken place. Jewish Babylonian Aramaic and Mandaic have lost the gutturals; this is less apparent in the orthography of the Jewish texts, since scribal practice was influenced by the continuous recourse to Biblical and Targumic sources. But the Palestinians at times twitted their Babylonian colleagues in a way which makes clear that the Babylonians no longer distinguished the various gutturals.

There was a tendency in Eastern Aramaic to interchange *lamed* and *nun*. This may be seen in the development of the prefix of the third person imperfect in Syriac, and partially in Mandaic and Jewish Babylonian Aramaic, where the precative *lamed* replaces the usual indicative *yod* and then *l* > *n* (see below). In Jewish Aramaic this change is found in a variety of verbs and nouns; e.g., *lqṭ* "to take hold of" became *nqṭ*, *laḥmā* became *nahmā* etc. Note the ironic remark *hānē bablāʾē ṭipšāʾē dĕʾāklīn nahmā im nahma* "those foolish Babylonians who eat bread with bread" (B.T. Besa 16a). In the Babylonian dialects there was also a tendency for final *l m n r b* to be dropped, thus *lemāʾ* for "normal" *yeʾmar*.

3. Syntax and Morphology. (a) An important syntactic distinction between Eastern and Western dialects is the word order. In Early Aramaic and Western Aramaic the order is *usually* verb-subject-object, while in Eastern Aramaic — and this feature is already apparent in Official Aramaic — the order was much freer and the object often preceded the verb. These points become clear when the same tale is told in both the Palestinian and Babylonian Talmuds or when a Palestinian Aramaic text is quoted in its more or less original form in the Babylonian Talmud. (b) The Western dialects maintained the distinction between the absolute and the determined forms of the noun: *kĕsap/kaspā, gĕbar/gabrā*, etc. This distinction had been lost in the Eastern dialects, and the determined form was in general use.

Other features could be added. Certain tractates of the Babylonian Talmud use a type of Aramaic that appears at first glance to be closer to the language of Onqelos; the Talmud quotes a variety of legal formulae, magical formulae, folk sayings, etc. These diverge from the usual Babylonian Aramaic and are worthy of further study not only for their contents but also for the linguistic information they contain.

As noted above, the Babylonian Talmud was to become, for a variety of historical and cultural reasons, the main item in the curriculum of Jewish studies for about a thousand years. It is, therefore, not at all surprising that Jewish speech in the many languages that Jews made their own was spiced with words and phrases from Babylonian Aramaic. Such interrogative expressions as *mai ṭaʿmā* "why?", *lĕmai nāfqā minnāh* "what difference does it make?", *minnāh hānē millē* "how does one know?", *ʾippĕkā mistabbĕrā* "the opposite is correct" were widespread (the translations are functional rather than literal). A Hebrew speaker today, innocent of Aramaic, may be heard using the expression *bnīḥūtā* "calmly, quietly" or *bar-minān* "corpse, recently deceased" (an apotropaic expression meaning literally "outside, away from us"). A troublesome woman might be called a *klavta* "bitch" (the canine would always be Hebrew *kalbā)* or a *nafqa* "whore" (although the Hebrew equivalent *yaṣʾanīt is* more frequently used). A generation or so ago an accepted version of "Gesundheit" (after sneezing) was *ʾasūtā* "health" (in Yiddish pronunciation *asusa).* This word's history bespeaks the complexity of the material studied here, for *ʾasūtā is* borrowed from Akkadian *asûtu,* an abstract formed from *asû* "healer", which in turn is based on Sumerian a.zu "he who knows the water (urine)".

Hebrew was the usual language of prayer among the Jews but a variety of prayers in Aramaic were in use among the Jews of Babylon and the countries under the influence of the Babylonian academies during the Geonic period; these were to become in the course of time the common property of most of the rites. Among the better known examples of this are the *yĕqūm purqān* prayers recited in the Sabbath morning liturgy, the *hā laḥmā ʿanyā* recited at the beginning of the Passover Seder and a penitential prayer such as *maḥe u-mase*, known from the Selihot. Here too the Yemenite rite preserved the use of Aramaic to a greater extent than the other rites. During the early Middle Ages, it was quite popular for liturgists to compose in Aramaic alongside the more usual Hebrew. A good example would be the *ʾaqdāmūt millīn* recited on Shavuot in the Ashkenazic ritual. Aramaic was used by some of the poets of the Spanish Golden Age when they wanted to write complimentary poems to one another in as elusive language as possible to test the recipient's scholarship and erudition. Shmuel ha-Nagid wrote an Aramaic encomium to Elhanan ben Hushiel and received one in return; Yitzhaq ibn Ghiyat and Yehudah ha-Levi also tried their hand at this and the poem that Shlomo ibn Gabirol wrote in honor of Jonah ibn Janaḥ has attracted scholarly attention and acumen in recent years. It goes without saying that the language of these poems, both Ashkenazic and Sephardic, is artificial since the author made use of the great variety of texts of all periods and places available to him.

The most important medieval literary work in Aramaic is, of course, the Zohar. Written in Spain in the thirteenth century by Moses de Leon who created with great ingenuity an artificial Aramaic dialect which made use of both Palestinian and Babylonian linguistic traditions. It has been pointed out that alongside his own skillful inventions, he often used idiomatic expressions current in the Spanish spoken in his day. An example of this is *lĕbassōmē dīnā* "to mitigate the judgment", literally "to sweeten the judgment", based on Spanish *endulzar* "to sweeten, soften, mitigate"; this has in turn entered Hebrew as *lĕhamtīq ʾet ha-dīn.* De Leon manipulated dialogue and description in his work, invented words freely and managed to give the impression that he was using real Aramaic to describe a meeting of Rabbi Shimʿon bar Yohai and his disciples in the hills of Galilee, while in reality the landscape was that of his native Spain. From the Zohar, prayers such as the *brīk šmēh,* recited before the Torah reading on the Sabbath, entered the ritual.

In the sixteenth century, Rabbi Isaac Luria ("the Ari") of Safed composed hymns for the Sabbath meals in Aramaic; and the popular *yāh ribbōn,* which has become part of the Sabbath "table service," was written by Israel Najara. The "rabbinic style" popular among rabbis and scholars of a traditional cast contains a healthy dose of Aramaic phraseology. Among the Yemenites the great poet and mystic, Rabbi Shalem Shabazi (17th cent.) wrote hymns and poems in Hebrew, Aramaic and Arabic. A study of this sort of literary activity is much needed.

As is well known Aramaic is still spoken in various parts of the Near East. A descendant of Western Aramaic still lingers on, in ever diminished use, among Christian villagers in Maʿlula and Jubbʿadin near Damascus. The modern Eastern Aramaic dialects, usually called Modern Syriac, were spoken by both Christians and Jews in an area that extended from the Jezira in northern Syria through the Lake Van area of eastern Turkey, Soviet Azerbaijan, northern Iraq, and Iran. Some of the villages — Zakho and Dahok come to mind — that have been featured in the news reports about the fate of the Kurds had significant Christian and also Jewish population. Many of these Christians have emigrated to other countries, primarily the United States, and in recent years to Western Europe and especially Scandanavia. During the last century a literary revival developed under the aegis of the Protestant mission, and there was a similar revival fostered by native Catholic priests. The term "Assyrians" was used for the first group, while "Chaldeans" is usual for the second. Both use the Nestorian type of Syriac script. In recent years periodicals in this language, as well as books and pamphlets, were regularly published in Iran during the reign of the Shah. In various parts of the Assyrian diaspora magazines with names like the Assyrian Star, Gilgamesh and Nineveh appear.

The Jews who lived in the mountains of Kurdistan and adjacent areas spoke related dialects. They have an extensive oral literature consisting of liturgical poems, folktales, and a traditional oral translation of some Biblical texts. They had also developed in modern times a written literature in Hebrew script, but the influence of Hebrew and the classic Jewish Aramaic dialects has been noted in their language. Most of the Aramaic speaking Kurdish Jews, except for some still living in Iran, have migrated to Israel. It is worth noting that words that are in common usage in Modern Aramaic occur as variant readings preserved in some of the manuscripts of the Talmud, or in Syriac lexical lists. The spoken Aramaic of the Kurdish Jews resident in Israel has absorbed many Hebrew words and phrases, and one can hear such mixtures of the old and the new as *sappa sliqta* "a nice sofa". There can be no doubt that Hebrew will replace Aramaic totally among the Kurdish Jews in the course of the next generation or two. Here too there has been a quickening of scholarly interest. With scholars such as R. Macuch, K. Tsereteli, Olga Kapeliuk, E. Knudsen and F.

Pennacchietti dealing with the "Christian" dialects and G. Goldenberg, B. Hoberman, S. Hopkins and Y. Sabar with the Jewish dialects.

Aramaic has had a direct influence on the vocabulary of Hebrew throughout the long period of contact between the two languages. Scholars have pointed out loanwords and calques in Biblical Hebrew and Mishnaic Hebrew. This process continued through the medieval period, when neither Hebrew nor Aramaic was spoken by most Jews. Modern Hebrew has been greatly enriched by Aramaic — this was evident already at the beginning of its rebirth as a literary language; the process became more intense with the revival of Hebrew as a spoken language, since many of those who were involved in this revival brought with them traditional training in the classical Jewish sources. This is an ongoing process in the contemporary language. The close analysis of a page of a modern text in Israeli Hebrew will reveal the absorption and adoption of many Aramaic roots into current Hebrew — the natural result of an extended linguistic symbiosis. The verb root *nqṭ* may serve as an example. It entered the Hebrew of the Babylonian Amoraim from Aramaic, was widely used in the phrase *nāqaṭ kĕlāl* "to take as a rule" and in other expressions. In Modern Hebrew it is used in phrases such as *nāqaṭ ʾemṣāʿim neged* "he took measures against", or *nāqaṭ ʿemdā* "took a position" etc. The word for an "airplane taking off" is *nĕsīqā* based on a putative Aramaic root *nsq* and a "helicopter" is a *massōq*. In turn the word for a plane landing is *neḥita*, although the root *nḥt* exists in Biblical Hebrew, it is much more frequent in Aramaic. At times new phrases are formed by replacing part of an Aramaic expression with the equivalent Hebrew; thus, Talmudic *šilhē dĕqayṭā* "the end of summer" becomes *šilhē ha-qayiṣ;* the Aramaic *qayṭa* "summer" is retained in *qayṭānā* used for a "summer program for children" or a "day camp" or in *qayiṭ* "a summer camp". Still another way in which Hebrew has used Aramaic is in the formation of numerical and other prefixes: *ḥad* "one, single", familiar to Hebrew speakers from the expression *ḥad bĕdārā* "unique in the generation" or *ḥad min ḥabrāyā* "one of the company", not to speak of *ḥad gadyā* from the Passover *Haggada*, is used for "uni-" or "mono-" in compounds like *ḥad-gōni* "monotonous", *ḥad-siṭri* "one-way", *ḥad-miflagtī* "single-party" (political), etc. *tlat* "three" serves the same function for "tri-". A model for this use was found in such rare forms as Mishnaic Hebrew *dū-parṣūfīn* "Janus-faced", and *dū*, borrowed from Greek, functions for "two" or "bi-, di-", as in *dū-śiaḥ* "dialogue". So too *tat,* based on Babylonian Aramaic *tatta* "under, below", is "sub-" *tat-ʾenoš* "sub-human" (alongside *ʿal* "super-"); not to speak of *bar-* so well known from bar-mitzva and the like. In the following there are two lists of words taken from a recent scanning of a popular Israeli daily which illustrates this point. The first contains individual words, the second idiomatic expressions.

1) bram "but", *gimlā'ūt* "retirement", *hadādī* "mutual", *hitgander* "show off, boast", *pirzūl* "shoeing, fixing iron work", *shěkhiax* "usual", *shě'iltā* "question", *šūmā* "assessment, evaluation", *zuhmā* "filth", *zūṭār* "minor, cadet", *tērūṣ* "answer", *tinyānī* "secondary".

2) *'agav 'ūrxā* "by the way", *bar-minān* "corpse", *bědi^căvad* "post factum", *hā běhā tālyā* "mutually dependent", *měhēkā teyte* "how do you know?" *šaqlā vě-ṭaryā* "give and take, discussion", *vě-day lě-hakkīmā* "a word to the wise", *ze^cir 'anpīn* "miniature", *ze^cir poh ze^cir šām* "here a little, there a little".

By becoming the second Jewish language in Jewish history, Aramaic has in turn gained as much as it has given, and has become merged or better fused with Hebrew.

A Re-examination of the Berlin Aramaic Dockets[1]

Eleonora Cussini — The Johns Hopkins University

Twenty-two Achaemenian clay tablets with Aramaic epigraphs, found during the German excavations at Babylon, are today in the collection of the Vorderasiatisches Museum of Berlin. They all belong to a large archival unity of about three hundred tablets known as the *Kasr Archive*.[2]

The tablets record contracts written in cuneiform, in the Neo-Babylonian dialect. The Aramaic epigraphs are written on portions of the tablet left free after the completion of the cuneiform contract. They are either brief summaries — never exceeding three lines — of the object of the transaction contained in the operative section of the Akkadian document, or simply a record of the personal names of the parties involved, usually the debtor's name, which is sometimes followed by his patronym.

The first document in chronological order, a silver loan dated in the 15th year of King Darius I was published in 1890 by F. E. Peiser.[3]

The other twenty-one tablets did not appear until 1972 when they were rediscovered in the *Tontafelsammlung* in the Vorderasiatisches Museum, and published by the Assyriologists Liane Jakob-Rost and Helmut Freydank.[4] This group of tablets was found in Babylon between June and September, 1913. According to the

---

[1] This is a revised version of the paper presented at the Institute of Jewish Studies conference in London. I am grateful to the conference organizers and participants for their useful comments and remarks. In addition, I would like to thank D. R. Hillers and F. M. Fales for their criticisms and suggestions. I am indebted to L. Jakob-Rost, E. Klengel-Brandt and J. Marzahn for their help and courtesy during my stay in Berlin. Finally, I am extremely thankful to M. W. Stolper for reading the manuscript and offering numerous improvements and corrections.

[2] In addition to this group of tablets, other texts (some presenting as well still unpublished Aramaic endorsements) scattered in different Museums have been identified as part of the *Kasr Archive*. See M. W. Stolper, "Empire and Province: Abstract of Remarks on Two Late Achaemenid Babylonian Archives," *Paléorient* 11:2 (1985), p. 64, M. W. Stolper, "Belšunu the Satrap," in F. Rochberg-Halton, ed., *Language, Literature, and History: Philological and Historical Studies Presented to Erica Reiner* (American Oriental Series 67, New Haven 1987), p. 401. For the latest assessment of the *Kasr Archive* see M. W. Stolper, "The Kasr Archive," *AJA* 92 (1988), pp. 587-88, and especially M. W. Stolper, "The Kasr Archive," in H. Sancisi-Weerdenburg, A. Kuhrt edd., *Centre and Periphery. Proceedings of the Sixth Achaemenid History Workshop, Groningen 1986, Nederlands Instituut voor het Nabije Oosten* (Groningen 1990), pp. 195-205. Stolper considers the possibility that at least two — but likely more than two — archives were combined together in antiquity, resulting in the group of texts known as the *Kasr Archive*.

[3] F. E. Peiser, *Babylonische Verträge des Berliner Museums* (Berlin 1890), pp. 91-92 no. LXVII (VAT 356).

[4] L. Jakob-Rost and H. Freydank, "Spätbabylonische Rechtsurkunden aus Babylon mit Aramäischen Beischriften," *Forschungen und Berichte* 14 (1972), pp. 7-35 [hereafter texts appearing in this article are referred to as FuB]. The twenty-one tablets were found together with other similar tablets and tablet fragments for a total of about three hundred texts. On these texts, see also F. Vattioni's inventory of Aramaic epigraphs on clay tablets, *Orientalia* 48 (1979), nos. 168-188, pp. 140-42.

excavation journal the tablets were found in the ruins of Nebuchadnezzer's palace and citadel.[5]

I had the opportunity of collating the Aramaic dockets written on these documents in March 1991, and I am grateful to Dr. Liane Jakob-Rost for allowing me to study them. This paper is a summary of the results of my examination of this group of texts with Aramaic endorsements, which are part of the Kasr Archive, discussing their significance for the study of the Aramaic epigraphs on clay tablets of the Neo-Babylonian and Achaemenian periods.

I. State of the Archive

The tablets and the tablet fragments belonging to this archive are all extremely damaged as a consequence of a fire that destroyed or vitrified large portions of them. In seven cases the Obverse of the tablet — which contains the operative section of the contract and thus is crucial in order to understand the sketchy and unfortunately always damaged Aramaic epigraphs — is either completely burnt or broken off, and in nine cases it is damaged to the point that only bits and pieces of the original contract can be read. On the basis of internal evidence — such as recurrent names of witnesses and main parties — the editors have concluded that the twenty-one documents were part of one archive, and, since the tablets are burnt almost without exception on one side only, they have suggested that when the archive caught fire, they were lying in the same room on wooden shelves.[6] Due to the serious damage the tablets suffered, the dating formula is not always preserved or complete. The kings mentioned are Artaxerxes I (465-424 B.C.) and Darius II (424-404 B.C.). In three instances, only the name of the king is preserved, and in seven other cases the final portion of the tablet containing the dating formula is broken or unreadable. The oldest preserved date is 455 B.C. (10th year of Artaxerxes I) in document FuB 5, and the most recent one is 406 B.C. (18th year of Darius II) in FuB 11.

The place of issue is preserved in six documents only. In one case it is Babylon,[7] in another Borsippa,[8] in the remaining four cases smaller settlements are mentioned, which, according to Zadok, were located in the vicinity of Babylon and Borsippa.[9] The toponyms are: *URU ri?-bu-ú; Bīt-bārê*; *Bāb-surri*[10]; *Ālu-ša-Bēl*. The first two toponyms are attested for the first time in this archive.

---

[5]For a map of the excavation see R. Koldewey, *Die Königsburgen von Babylon.1. Teil: Die Südburg, WVDOG* 54 (Leipzig 1931), pl. I.
[6]L. Jakob-Rost and H. Freydank, *FuB* 14 (1972), pp. 7-8.
[7]In document FuB 6, E.KI.
[8]In document FuB 4.
[9]See R. Zadok, *Geographical Names According to New- and Late-Babylonian Texts, Répertoire Géographique des Textes Cunéiformes* Band 8 (Wiesbaden 1985), henceforth: R. Zadok, *RGTC*.
[10]According to Zadok, in the vicinity of Borsippa. For this reading, instead of the editors' EDIN.SUR.RU, see M. W. Stolper, "Bēlšunu the Satrap," *AOS* 67 (1987), p.391.

The names of the main parties in the transaction are not always preserved. The most active figure is *Bēlšunu* son of *Bēl-uṣuršu*, *pīḫat Bābili*, governor of Babylon, who is the creditor in four contracts, and possibly in two others.[11] The dated documents are issued during the reign of Darius II:

FuB	8:	417 B.C.	issued at *Bāb-surri*
FuB	21:	417 B.C.	-
FuB	1:	415 B.C.	issued at *Bīt-bārê*;
FuB	12:[12]	reign of Darius	-
FuB	15:	-	-
FuB	20:	-	-

Another individual appearing more than one time is *Uraš-nāṣir* (^{d}URAŠ-PAP) son of *Ibnâ* (DÙ-*a*).[13] He is the debtor in a contract featuring *Bēlšunu* as the creditor, FuB 1, 415 B.C., the creditor in another contract, FuB 13, 418 B.C.,[14] and the creditor in document FuB 16, dated in the reign of Darius.[15]

In the remaining cases, the names of the parties are attested once in each document, and in four instances are preserved in Aramaic only:

FuB	5:	455 B.C.[16]	^{m}*ḫaš*$^{?}$*-da-a-a*, creditor
			Bēl-apla$^{?}$*-iddin*, creditor
			Kāṣir$^{?}$, debtor?
FuB	7:	451 B.C.	*Dannat-Bēlet*
			Rammān-ʾayāli, lessees?[17]
			(Aramaic: *d⌜nt⌝rmnʾyly*)
FuB	9:	reign of Artaxerxes	*Nabû-naṣir* son of *Iddin-Bēl*, tenant
			Aplā, lessor
			(Aramaic: *ʾply*)
FuB	2:	417 B.C.	*Bēl-ittannu*, creditor

[11] Further attestations of this individual, as well as his role of *governor* of Babylon, are discussed by M. W. Stolper, "Bēlšunu the Satrap," *AOS* 67 (1987), pp. 389-402. In addition to the three occurrences cited by Stolper, FuB 1, 8, and 21, I would add three more instances where he appears as creditor: possibly FuB 12, reign of Darius, l. 2: ^{md}EN-x-x-x[ ]; FuB 15, date lost, l. 2: ^{md}EN-*šú-nu* A-*šú šá* ^{md}EN.URÙ-*šú*, and FuB 20, date lost, Lo.Ed. l. 2: [^{md}EN-*šú-nu*] A-*šú šá* ^{md}EN.URÙ-*šú*

[12] The Aramaic endorsement contains a personal name not preserved in the cuneiform part of the contract: *twkl*. See below, III. Onomastic Data.

[13] The name was previously read by the editors *Ilu-ibni* son of *Banija*. I am grateful to M. W. Stolper who suggested the correct reading, confirmed by syllabic spellings of the name. For an example, see below, note 14.

[14] The name is not preserved in l. 1, but appears in l. 6: *a-na* ^{md}URAŠ*-na-ṣir i-nam-din*. The debtor is *Niḫištum* son of *Bēlšunu*.

[15] See in l. 4: *ina* ^{GIŠ}*ma-ši-ḫu šá* ^{md}URAŠ-PAP, "in the measure of *Uraš-nāṣir*" (the creditor). The Aramaic epigraph contains part of a name not preserved in Akkadian, *nbw*[ ], most likely the debtor. See below, III. Onomastic Data.

[16] The date formula is restored on the basis of the Aramaic docket: l. 4: *šnt* 10, "year 10."

[17] The operative section of the contract is completely missing. The two individuals appearing in the docket and on the tablet's right edge in Akkadian are very likely to be the lessees.

		Bēl-eṭir [son of] *Nabû-ittannu*, debtor
		(Aramaic: *blʾṭr* son of *nbw*⌜ʾ*tn*⌝)
FuB 19:	417(?) B.C.	(Aramaic: *nbw*[ ] tenant?)
FuB 21:	417 B.C.	(Aramaic: *ppʾ*, proprietor)
FuB 4:	414 B.C.	(Aramaic: *nbwkṣr*, lessee?)
FuB 3:	410 B.C.	*Nabû-kuṣuršu*,[18] debtor?
		(Aramaic: *nbwkṣrš*)
FuB 11:	406 B.C.	[-]*tunē-su* son of *Surmunnaši* -x
		Šalam‹ma!›rē [19] (creditors?)
FuB 14:	-	(Aramaic: *blʾṣrš*, debtor)

The preserved names are mostly Babylonian, *Nabû-nāṣir*, *Uraš-nāṣir*, *Bēlšunu*, *Bēl-ittannu*, *Nabû-kuṣuršu* etc., with two West-Semitic names, *Rammān-ʾayāli*, *Šalammarē*, and one Persian name *Surmunnaši*-x.

The object of the transaction is preserved in fifteen documents. In most cases they are promissory notes for various commodities, mostly dates but also wheat, which are owed for the rent of leased land. In some cases the contracts are payment receipts.[20] In addition, three documents record amounts of silver, but the extant portion of the operative section does not allow us to determine the type of transaction involved.[21]

II. Data from the Aramaic epigraphs

The practice of writing Aramaic epigraphs on clay tablets is attested during the Neo-Assyrian, Neo-Babylonian and Achaemenian periods. In the relevant literature these epigraphs are commonly referred to as "endorsements," or "dockets."[22] The last term has been employed to define a particular type of document, that is "triangular corn loan dockets" recording Akkadian/Aramaic bilingual, or Aramaic monolingual

---

[18]The name is not preserved in the operative section of the contract, but appears on the left edge of the tablet: [mdN]À-*ku-ṣur-šú*.

[19]Contra Jakob-Rost's and Freydank's reading *Šalam‹ba›re*, I would suggest that the name in question is *Šalam‹ma!›re*, "**Mārē* is my peace." See R. Zadok, *On West Semites in Babylonia During the Chaldean and Achaemenian Periods* (Jerusalem 1977), p. 65: "**Marʾē* is (my) welfare, peace," where Zadok explains **Marʾē* as an Aramaic *pluralis maiestatis* of *Mār*. See K. Tallqvist, "Neubabylonisches Namenbuch," *Acta Societatis Scientiarum Fennicae* XXXII no. 2 (Helsingfors 1902), p. 187b. The Akkadian part of the contract is too fragmentary to allow us to understand the role of this individual. A *Šalammarē*, servant (LÚ.ARAD) of *Bēlšunu*, is mentioned in a document where *Bēlšunu* bears the title of "governor of Across-the-River," see M. W. Stolper, "Bēlšunu the Satrap," *AOS* 67 (1987), p. 390. Since the title refers to a posterior phase of *Bēlšunu*'s career, this *Šalammarē* may not be the same one of our document.

[20]FuB 7, 451 B.C. promissory note for dates; FuB 6, reign of Artaxerxes, possibly a promissory note for dates; FuB 9, reign of Artaxerxes, lease fragment; FuB 8, 417 B.C. promissory note for dates; FuB 21, 417 B.C., receipt for payment of silver; FuB 1, 415 B.C. promissory note for barley and wheat; FuB 4, 414 B.C. possibly a lease; FuB 3, 410 B.C. promissory note; FuB 16, 408 B.C. rent payment; FuB 11, 406 B.C., possibly a receipt for partial payment of rent; FuB 12, reign of Darius, contract dealing with commodity measured in *gur*; FuB 19, reign of Darius, promissory note for assessed rent.

[21]FuB 5, 455 B.C.; FuB 13, 418 B.C.; FuB 2, 417 B.C.

[22]See, in addition, "Aramaic Reference Notes," proposed by H. J. Stevenson, *Assyrian and Babylonian Contracts. With Aramaic Reference Notes*, (Vanderbilt Oriental Series, New York 1902) p. 10.

contracts.[23] Among the tablets with Aramaic epigraphs originating from Babylonia the "triangular-type tablets" are not represented, nonetheless the term "dockets" referring to the Aramaic epigraphs is frequently found also in recent studies.[24] As far as the Babylonian documentation is concerned, I believe that the term "dockets" can still be used in the sense of "abstract, summary" of a document, without clashing with Postgate's and Fales' specific documental classification, which, as we saw, pertains to the Northern (i.e. Assyrian) sphere only.

a) Physical appearance

The Berlin Aramaic dockets are incised on the tablets at different degrees of depth, and in some cases the letters are just very lightly scratched on the tablet's surface. It is known that usually the Aramaic dockets were written either by means of a stylus — in which case we have deeply incised letters — or painted with an ink-brush. In the last case, since the docket was written before the clay hardened up, in addition to more or less well preserved traces of ink, the scratches of the brush or stylus are visible on the tablet's surface as well.

None of the tablets here examined shows traces of ink, not even in the several cases in which the dockets are lightly scratched on the tablet's surface. This does not rule out the possibility that ink was used as, for instance, in many other contemporary Babylonian-Aramaic dockets.[25] The fire, in fact, could have very likely altered or effaced the black pigment traces.

b) Structure of the documents

The structure of the Aramaic dockets from Babylonia is not fixed or standardized. The information they convey can vary from the mere record of parties, to a summary of the Akkadian contract, including, in addition, the object of the transaction, silver, dates, barley, etc. In some cases a notation of the leased quantity, followed by the year of stipulation, can complete the epigraphs. Quite often, the epigraphs are introduced by the word *šṭr*, a loanword from Akkadian *šaṭāru* "document." The usage of this term is peculiar to the dockets from Babylonia.[26] Another Akkadian loanword frequently appears in documents from Assyria. The Aramaic epigraphs on Neo-Assyrian conveyance texts — that is, texts sanctioning the transfer of ownership of a slave or of a piece of property[27] — are in fact characterized

[23]J. N. Postgate, *Fifty Neo-Assyrian Legal Documents* (Warminster 1976), pp. 5-6; F.M. Fales, *Aramaic Epigraphs on Clay Tablets of the Neo-Assyrian Period* (Rome 1986), p. 18.
[24]See M. W. Stolper, *Entrepreneurs and Empire* (Leiden 1985) *passim*.
[25]Cf. several tablets belonging to the *Murašû* Archive: *CBS* 5308, *CBS* 5314, *CBS* 5377, *CBS* 5417, *CBS* 12859, *CBS* 12873, *CBS* 12989+13051, etc.
[26]I am grateful to Professor E. Lipiński for mentioning that the term *šṭr* is attested as well in the unpublished Aramaic texts from the Neo-Assyrian period held in the Koninklijke Musea voor Kunst en Geschiedenis of Brussels.
[27]J. N. Postgate, *Fifty Neo-Assyrian*, p. 3; F. M. Fales, *Aramaic Epigraphs*, pp. 4-8.

by the label *dnt* "deed", a loanword from Akkadian (*ṭuppu*) *dannatu*, attested in Neo-Assyrian documents in the form *dannutu*. The meaning of *dannutu* in the Assyrian juridical lexicon was "valid/legal document; deed."[28]

The word *šṭr* in the Babylonian dockets is not confined to one type of document only — unlike *dnt* which occurs only in documents of the "conveyance"-type — but it is found also in contract-texts, that is loans, leases, etc., and in receipts of payment. Out of about one hundred Babylonian dockets examined, forty follow the pattern *šṭr* + debtor's name, where *šṭr* is in construct state or followed by the relative particle *zy*.[29]

The Berlin dockets are structured as follows:

1) debtor's name only (and patronym), four cases:

VAT 356:	[*š*]*lb br ʾdnʾ*
FuB 21:	*ppʾ*
FuB 3:	*nbwkṣrš*
FuB 16:	*nbw*[ ]

2) *šṭr* or *šṭr zy* + debtor(s)'s name, four cases: "document of"

FuB 7:	*šṭr d⌜nt⌝bl wrmnʾyly gnnyʾ*[30]
FuB 9:	[*š*]*ṭr* [ ]*y*
FuB 19:	*šṭr zy nbw*[ ]
FuB 17:	[*š*]*ṭr* [ ]

3) *šṭr zy qdm* + debtor's name, one case: "document which is against"

FuB 12:	[*šṭ*]⌜*r*⌝ *zy qdm twkl*

4) *šṭr* + object of the transaction, two cases: "document concerning"

FuB 13:	*šṭr ksp m*⌜*n*⌝[*h* ?]
FuB 4:	*šṭr gnʾ z*[*y*] *nbwkṣr*

5) *šṭr* + object of the transaction *zy qdm* or *zy ʿl* debtor's name, four cases: "document (concerning ...) which is against"

FuB 8:	⌜*š*⌝[*ṭr t*]*mrn krn* 13 *zy qdm* [*Nergal-iddin*]...
FuB 2:	*šṭr ksp mn*⌜*y*⌝[*n*] *qdm blʾṭr br nbw*⌜*ʾtn*⌝
FuB 14:	*šṭr ʾgwrn zy* [ ] *blʾṣrš br bl*[ ]
FuB 1:	*šṭr* .... *zy ʿl nbwbls?ʾqb*[*y*] (co-debtor).

---

[28]See F. M. Fales, *Aramaic Epigraphs*, p. 8, and previous literature cited therein. As far as I am aware, the term *dnt* is not documented in Aramaic dockets from the Neo-Babylonian and Achaemenian periods.

[29]See E. Cussini, *Aramaic Epigraphs from Babylonia* (forthcoming).

[30]From the tablet's collation, on l. 1 the word following the second personal name, *rmnʾyly*, is *gnnyʾ*, "gardeners" a masculine plural in the emphatic state. Cf. FuB 7, p. 18: "*ḥ* o oy ʾ." The professional name refers to *Dannat-Bēlet* and *Rammān-ʾayāli*, very likely the lessees, despite the lack of information from the damaged Akkadian text. "Gardener," *gnn*, is attested elsewhere in Imperial Aramaic texts from Egypt, see B. Porten and A. Yardeni, *A Textbook of Aramaic Documents From Ancient Egypt*, 2, *Contracts* (Jerusalem 1986), B3.10:10, p. 86, and B3.11:6, p. 90.

c) Juridical value and juridical terminology

The Berlin dockets confirm the idea that Aramaic epigraphs of this type were essentially archival devices, devoid of binding legal value *per se*, and that the legal function of the document rested upon the cuneiform text only. When the operative section of the Akkadian document is preserved, the secondary character of the Aramaic epigraphs — which transcribe personal names, and translate short key-sections of the contract — is evident.

The yield of juridical terminology in Aramaic from the Berlin dockets is extremely meager. Worth noting is the usage of the prepositions *qdm* and *ʿl* in connection with the debtor's name. From a consultation of the cuneiform part of the contract — when preserved — it is evident that both prepositions correspond to Akkadian *ina muḫḫi*, with the meaning "(debt) against PN." The Berlin dockets show two attestations of *qdm* + debtor's name and one of *ʿl* + debtor's name:

1) FuB 8 *qdm* + [debtor's name] *ina muḫḫi* (Obv.3)
2) FuB 2 *qdm* + debtor's name *ina muḫḫi* (Obv.2)
3) FuB 1 *ʿl* + co-debtor's name *ina muḫḫi* (Obv.3)

In the other Babylonian dockets examined the situation can be represented as follows:

Prepositions		Party		Translation	Object
qdm	/ *ina muḫḫi*	(debtor)	=	"against"	(debt)
	\ *ina pāni*	(creditor)	=	"in front of"	(pledge)
ʿl	/ *ina muḫḫi*	(debtor)	=	"to, against"	(debt)
	\ *ina pāni*	(debtor)	=	"to, against"	(debt)

Both prepositions *qdm* and *ʿl* correspond to Akkadian *ina muḫḫi* or *ina pāni* and precede the debtor's name. In one case a pledged object is said to be *qdm* = *ina pāni* the creditor's name.[31]

[31]For a discussion of this text, BM 92722 dated to 407 B.C. (= L. Delaporte, *Epigraphes Araméens* (Paris, 1912) no. 101; F. Vattioni, "Epigrafia Aramaica," *Augustinianum* 10 (1970) no. 105), see E. Cussini, *Aramaic Epigraphs from Babylonia* (forthcoming).

III. Onomastic Data

The Aramaic dockets from the *Kasr Archive* have preserved fifteen personal names in Aramaic. These are alphabetic transcriptions of the debtors' names recorded in Akkadian in the cuneiform part of the contract. In one case the creditor's name is perhaps recorded as well. In six instances the names contained in the Aramaic docket are not preserved in the Akkadian contract.

ʾdnʾ	f. of [*š*]*lb*:	VAT 356	*Iddina*
ʾply		FuB 9	*Aplā*
blʾṭr	s. of *nbw*˹*ʾtn*˺	FuB 2	*Bēl-ēṭir*
blʾṣrš		FuB 14	[*Bēl-uṣuršu*]
d˹*nt*˺*bl*		FuB 7	*Dannat-Bēlet*
nbw[ ]		FuB 16	[*Nabû-*]
nbw[ ]		FuB 19	[*Nabû-*]
nbw˹*ʾtn*˺	f. of *blʾṭr*	FuB 2	*Nabû-ittannu*
nbwblsʾqb		FuB 1	*Nabû-balassu-iqbi*
nbwkṣr		FuB 4	[*Nabû-kāṣir*]
nbwkṣrš		FuB 3	*Nabû-kuṣuršu*
ppʾ		FuB 21	[*Pappā*?]
rmnʾyly		FuB 7	*Rammān-ʾayāli*
[*š*]*lb*	s. of *ʾdnʾ*	VAT 356	*Šellibi*
twkl		FuB 12	[*Tukkulu*?][32]

The theophoric elements contained in the names are *nbw-* (*Nabû*) in six cases, *bl-* (*Bēl*) in two cases, *-bl<*t>* (*Bēlet*) in one case, and *rmn-* (*Rammān*) in one case. In other words, three classical Babylonian gods and one West-Semitic deity.[33]

In the Aramaic transcriptions of the names, *aleph* is noted in initial position, corresponding to Akkadian *a-*/*i-*: *ʾdnʾ* for Akkadian *Iddina*; *ʾply* for Akkadian *Aplā*. In internal position, corresponding to Akkadian *-ē-*/*-i-*/*-u-*, in *blʾṭr*, for Akkadian *Bēl-eṭir*; *nbw*˹*ʾtn*˺, for *Nabû-ittannu*, *nbwblsʾqb*, for *Nabû-balassu-iqbi*; *blʾṣrš* (not preserved in Akkadian: [**Bēl-uṣuršu*]). In final position, corresponding to Akkadian *-a*, in the name *ʾdnʾ*, for *Iddina*. In final position *waw* is a marker of

---

32 The Aramaic docket is extremely lightly scratched. Instead of the editors' "Rs.unterer u.l.Rd.] o *z*?*y*? *q*?*n*?*h*? *q*? o o o [," I would tentatively suggest a new reading: Upper Edge [*šṭ*]˹*r*˺ *zy qdm* Left Edge *twkl*, "Document which is against PN," considering *twkl* the debtor's name, a transcription of Akkadian *Tukkulu*, attested at Nippur in the *Murašû* Archive, cf. M. W. Stolper, *Entrepreneurs and Empire*, p. 301. Unfortunately the name is not preserved in the Akkadian part of the contract, and this suggestion cannot be verified.

33 For other attestations of this divine name in Aramaic inscriptions, see R. Zadok, *On West Semites*, p. 49, J. C. Greenfield, "The Aramean God Rammān/Rimmōn," *IEJ* 26 (1976), pp. 195-98, and J. Teixidor, *Bulletin d'épigraphie sémitique (1964-1980)*, (Paris 1986) p. 428, no. 61, with references to this occurrence.

Akkadian -*û*, as in the transcription of the divine name *Nabû*: *nbw*. *Yod* appears in final position to mark the pronunciation of Akkadian -ā, for instance, *ʾply* for Akkadian Aplā.

The only Aramaic name recorded in the dockets is *rmnʾyly*. It appears in the Akkadian section of the document as *Rammān-a-a-li-ʾ* "the god *Rammān* is my help", with final -*y* for the first person singular pronoun.[34] In the same document, the name *dʿntʿbl*, a transcription of Akkadian *Dannat-Bēlet* "powerful is the goddess Belet" is an example of the influence of an Aramaic morphological rule according to which the feminine suffix -*t* is eliminated when the noun is not in the construct state.[35] In this case the scribe reduces the final / -*t*/ of Belet to Ø.

IV. Palaeographic analysis

The script of the Berlin dockets is not included in Naveh's study of Aramaic palaeography, because the tablets were not published until later.[36] According to Naveh, Aramaic dockets on clay tablets of the fifth century were mostly written in sub-styles he defines as "extreme cursive, sometimes tending towards the vulgar."[37] The names of the scribes of the Berlin tablets are preserved in eight documents, each scribe appearing only once. In the extant cases the name and patronym of the scribes are classical Babylonian.[38]

The script of the Berlin dockets shows mixed fifth-century cursive features, together with later developments mainly attested during the fourth and the third centuries. Here are some of the most distinctive shapes:[39]

Aleph — Three different types of aleph are attested: a conservative-upright type in which the right angle to the right of the oblique stroke becomes a vertical stroke. Secondly a later fourth-century form presenting the so called *crescent-shaped* left leg is attested. Finally, a third-century shape made of two crossed wavy oblique lines is found as well.

He — Presents a horizontal upper stroke which is a typical end-of-fifth beginning-of-fourth-century feature.

---

[34]The theophoric element in the name is written dKUR. On the basis of the Aramaic transcription *rmnʾyly*, L. Jakob-Rost and H. Freydank were able to establish the reading dKUR=*Rammān*. For a discussion of the root **ʾw/yl* with the meaning "to be strong, first", and the nouns "help", "strength", "deer", "ram", see F. M. Fales, "On Aramaic Onomastics in the Neo-Assyrian Period," *Oriens Antiquus* 16 (1977), p. 52. See also R. Zadok, *On West Semites*, pp. 49, 99, and J. C. Greenfield, *IEJ* 26 (1976), pp. 195-98.

[35]This rule has been amply documented by F. M. Fales for the Assyrian-Aramaic materials, see *Aramaic Epigraphs*, p. 67.

[36]J. Naveh, *The Development of the Aramaic Script*, Proceedings of the Israel Academy of Sciences and Humanities 5 (Jerusalem 1970).

[37]J. Naveh, *The Development*, p. 42.

[38]FuB 5 r. of Artaxerxes: - s. of *Bēl-iddin*; FuB 7 451/450: *Bēl-uballiṭ* s. of *Marduk-nāṣir*; FuB 6 r. of Artaxerxes: - s. of *Šum-uṣur*; FuB 8 417: *Nabû-balassu-iqbi* s. of *Rībat*; FuB 1 415: *Marduk-nāṣir* s. of *Bēl-ittannu*; FuB 4 414: *Nabû-bullissu* s. of *Nabû-iddin*; FuB 12 r. of Darius: *Bēl-ēriš* s. of - ; FuB 3 410: *Šum-uṣur* s. of *Šulum-Bābili*; FuB 14 date lost: *Bēl-erība* s. of - .

[39]See Table 1.

	ʾ	b	g	d	h	w	z	ḥ	ṭ	y	k	l	m	n	s	ʿ	p	ṣ	q	r	š	t
FuB 5																						
7																						
6																						
9																						
13																						
8																						
2																						
1																						
4																						
3																						
11																						
12																						
10																						
14																						
15																						

Table 1

Waw — Both the so-called *flag-form* with straight shoulder, and a later development with rounded shoulder are attested.
Zayn — Two forms are attested: the first one presenting the downstroke tending to the left — fifth-century feature — as well as later straight forms.
Yod — Has a typical fifth-century shape, consisting of an oblique stroke with a left descending or horizontal central small bar. Also one instance of a later *angular yod* is attested.
Lamed — Has a typical fifth-century shape. The later development with a descending tail to the right end of the bar is absent from the extant documentation.
Mem — On the basis of the extant material it is not possible to see if a distinction between medial and final forms is registered.
Nun — There is possibly one instance of medial form. It often appears without head.
ʿAyin — Shows a rounded head. There is one instance of a later shape with a tick at the bottom.
Pe — This letter has a typical fifth-century, quite long shape. No final/medial distinction.
Ṣade — The oldest type among the three varieties attested during the fifth century is here represented: the right arm is made of one stroke that bends at the right angle.
Šin — Fifth-century types made of three straight strokes, with the middle one ascending the left stroke not above its middle are documented. In addition, there is an example of a fourth-century development showing a raising of the middle stroke and the curving of the right stroke.
Taw — Has a typical fifth-century long shape. It sometimes shows a later feature, consisting of a bending of the long downstroke.

The Berlin dockets are an important addition to the corpus of the Aramaic dockets of Babylonia, which includes other texts from Babylon, Kiš, Sippar,[40] a large group of texts from Nippur (*Murašû* Archive), texts from Uruk, and from Tell Neirab.[41] Despite their poor state of preservation, the information they convey shows the similarity of this material — in typology and lexical data — to the other contemporary Aramaic endorsements on clay tablets. In line with the other material, the function of the epigraphs is that of filing devices, with no legal value by themselves.

[40]Mostly unpublished, see E. Leichty, A. K. Grayson, *Catalogue of the Babylonian Tablets in the British Museum. Volume VII: Tablets from Sippar 2* (London 1987), and E. Leichty, J. J. Finkelstein, C. B. F. Walker, *Catalogue of the Babylonian Tablets in the British Museum. Volume VIII: Tablets from Sippar 3* (London 1988).
[41]On this last group of texts found in Syria, but most likely originating from Babylonia, see the latest discussions by J. Oelsner, "Weitere Bemerkungen zu den Neirab-Urkunden," *AoF* 16 (1989), pp. 68-77, and L. Cagni, "Considérations sur les textes babyloniens de Neirab près d'Alep," *Transeuphratène* 2 (1990), pp. 169-85, with previous literature.

That all the documents belonging to the *Kasr Archive* were part of a single archive is open to objection, as was already pointed out by the editors, and has been recently amply discussed by Stolper.[42]

[42] M. W. Stolper, "The Kasr Archive," op. cit., pp. 195-205.

Greek and Aramaic in Palmyrene Inscriptions

Han J. W. Drijvers — Groningen

From the time of Alexander the Great (d. 323 B.C.E.) and the Seleucid dynasty Greek was the official language in Hellenistic Syria. It was used by the Seleucid administration for official, public, and legal documents and was undoubtedly spoken and understood, in particular, by the cultural and political élites in the cities.[1]

The local Aramaic dialects, however, remained in use in both spoken and written language, although only very few Aramaic inscriptions from the early Hellenistic period have come to light in Syria. This may be due not to the fact that Aramaic was less in use, but rather to the poor legacy of Seleucid Syria in general. We possess very few material remains from the Seleucid period in Syria, so that in comparison with other periods it is poorly known.[2] The region was, however, thoroughly bilingual, as the few preserved documents clearly demonstrate. Greek and Aramaic were both in use, although probably for different purposes. The language used for religious purposes in particular was mainly the native tongue and not Greek, although one of the earliest Greek inscriptions is a bilingual dedication from Tel Dan dating to the late third or early second century B.C.E.[3] When in the sixties of the first century B.C.E. the Romans appeared on the scene in Syria this linguistic situation did not fundamentally change. Greek remained the official language of the administration in the Roman Provincia Syria, and it was under the Roman empire that the distinctive mixed culture of Hellenistic Syria came to the fore.[4] The known Latin inscriptions from Syria are by contrast rather restricted in number and refer mainly to specific activities of the various legions, officers and Roman soldiers. Milestones along the Roman roads also usually bear Latin inscriptions. In Roman times the local varieties of Aramaic appeared again in written form in substantial quantities, due perhaps to strong nationalistic feelings in the divided province, where a range of local magnates exercised

---

[1]See e.g. the documents collected by C. B. Welles, *Royal Correspondence in the Hellenistic Period. A Study in Greek Epigraphy* (London 1934) and the inscriptions in W. Dittenberger (ed.) *OGIS* (Leipzig 1903-5) and in *IGLS*.

[2]See Fergus Millar, "The Problem of Hellenistic Syria", A. Kuhrt, S. Sherwin-White, (eds.) *Hellenism in the East* (Berkeley-Los Angeles 1987), pp. 110-133.

[3]J. Robert, L. Robert, *Bulletin Epigraphique* (1977), no. 542; cf. Fergus Millar, "The Problem of Hellenistic Syria", pp. 132f. for a discussion of this inscription.

[4]Cf. M. Sartre, *L'Orient romain. Provinces et sociétés provinciales en Méditerranée orientale d'Auguste aux Sévères* (Paris 1991), pp. 315s.; R. Schmitt, "Die Ostgrenze von Armenien über Mesopotamien, Syrien bis Arabien", *Die Sprachen in römischen Reich der Kaiserzeit*, Beiheft der *Bonner Jahrbücher* 40 (1980), pp. 198-205.

their power in the various cities and towns.[5] The independent kingdom of the Nabataeans produced almost exclusively Aramaic, i.e. Nabataean, inscriptions and only after 106 C.E., when the Romans converted it into the Provincia Arabia, did the number of Greek inscriptions increase substantially.[6] A similar situation prevailed at Edessa and in the little kingdom of Osrhoene in northern Mesopotamia. This area has preserved about seventy Old-Syriac inscriptions written in the local Aramaic dialect, but only when Edessa in 213 C.E. lost its independence and became a Roman colonia, do we find Greek inscriptions and papyri.[7] This does not mean that during the foregoing period Greek was not in use, but only that its cultural prestige was different in comparison with the local Syriac.

Palmyra, the caravan city in the midst of the Syrian desert, which came under Roman rule at the beginning of the first century C.E., is a good example of this general bilingual pattern.[8] The city has yielded a great many inscriptions, among them a substantial number of bilingual ones. Most of these are dedicatory inscriptions e.g. relating to a statue erected by the decision of the local council and people (*boule kai demos*) and in their formulae they are comparable with the countless official Greek dedicatory and honorific inscriptions from Asia Minor.[9] The Aramaic version is usually secondary, a translation from the Greek. In many cases the Aramaic is even no more than a summary of the Greek.[10] However, scholarly views of the relation of the Greek with the Palmyrene version differ. J. Cantineau drew attention to the fact that during the first century C.E. the majority of the bilingual inscriptions gave precedence to the Palmyrene and had only a summary in Greek, whereas in the third century it was the other way round.[11] J. Teixidor is of a different opinion. The Greek version of all bilingual inscriptions is always secondary: 'Occasionellement les textes palmyréniennes sont accompagnés d'une traduction grecque, mais en aucun cas le lexte grec ne l'emporte

---

[5]See J.-P. Rey-Coquais, "La Syrie romaine", *JRS* 68 (1978), pp. 44-73; for a useful survey of the available evidence, cf .M. Sartre, *L'Orient romain*, pp. 309-355.

[6]Cf.G. W. Bowersock, *Roman Arabia* (Cambridge-London 1983), pp. 76-89; R. Schmitt, *Die Sprachen im römischen Reich der Kaiserzeit*, pp. 205-209.

[7]For Syriac inscriptions see H. J. W. Drijvers, *Old Syriac (Edessean) Inscriptions* (Leiden 1972); idem, "Some New Syriac Inscriptions and Archaeological Finds from Edessa and Sumatar Harabesi", *BSOAS* 36 (1973), pp.1-14; for a recent find of Syriac and Greek papyri from this area see D. Feissel, J. Gascou, "Documents d'archives romains inédits du Moyen Euphrate", *CRAI* (1989), pp. 535-561; J. Teixidor, "Deux documents syriaques du IIIe siècle après J.-C., provenant du Moyen Euphrate", *CRAI* (1990), pp. 144-166; Sebastian Brock, "Some New Syriac Documents from the Third Century AD", *Aram* 3 (1991; appeared in 1993), pp. 259-267, gave an improved reading and translation of the two Syriac parchments published by J. Teixidor.

[8]See J. Starcky, M. Gawlikowski, *Palmyre* (Paris 1985), esp. pp. 27ff.; for the distribution of Greek and Palmyrene inscriptions see C. Dunant, *Le sanctuaire de Baalshamin, Palmyre III, Les inscriptions* (Rome 1971), pp. 11f.

[9]Cf. H. Seyrig, "Inscriptions grecques de l'agora de Palmyre", *Syria* 22 (1941), pp. 167-214 (= *Antiquités Syriens* III (Paris 1946), pp. 223-270).

[10]Cf. H. Ingholt, "Deux inscriptions bilingues de Palmyre", *Syria* 13 (1932), pp. 278-292, esp. p.279, 289; Ingholt published only the Greek inscriptions; for the Palmyrene version of the first inscription see J. T. Milik, *Dédicaces faites par des dieux* (Paris 1972), pp. 36-37.

[11]J. Cantineau, *Grammaire du palmyrénien épigraphique* (Cairo 1935), p.5.

sur la partie palmyrénienne.'[12] No systematic study of all known bilingual inscriptions from Palmyra and in particular of the translation techniques used exists so far.[13] It is my intention in this paper to demonstrate that the Aramaic of the bilingual Palmyrene inscriptions often shows certain characteristics and peculiarities in its choice of words, in its idiom and even in its syntax, that make clear that the Aramaic is translated from the Greek and only understandable in the light of the Greek version. In other words, the Aramaic of Palmyra is to a certain extent hellenized and displays expressions that are fundamentally alien to the Aramaic language. This is in particular the case when we are dealing with a *verbum e verbo* translation, where the linguistic differences between Greek and Aramaic cause some disadvantages and difficulties in rendering a Greek text into Aramaic. The lexicological peculiarities as well as the neglect of proper syntax consequent upon this translation method is deliberate and not due to incompetence on the part of the translator, since the receptor rather than the source language was his first language.[14]

The first example is a long, perhaps the longest known, dedicatory inscription commemorating the famous caravan-leader Soadu Bolyada dated 144 C.E. It is written on a bracket that once bore a bronze statue of the caravan-leader and was found in the excavations of Allat's sanctuary in the western quarter of Palmyra.[15] The inscription records the erection of four bronze statues of Soadu in the four sanctuaries of the four tribes that formed the body politic of Palmyra. As such the text is related to another honorary inscription about the same caravan leader discovered in the temple of Baalshamin dated 132 C.E. and published by C. Dunant.[16] It is noteworthy that in our inscription the sanctuary of Allat replaces Baalshamin's temple which is mentioned as one of the four sanctuaries in the text of 132 C.E. Both sanctuaries were religious centres of the Benê Mazin, one of the four tribes, and they were in many respects comparable with each other.[17] The reason for the lavish honour bestowed on Soadu by the other caravan leaders was his rescue of 'the caravan of all Palmyrenes' from an assault by a certain Abdallat and his gang of robbers, who had laid ambush over a long period to the Palmyrene merchants. Abdallat came from Aḥyt, an otherwise unknown

[12] J. Teixidor, "L'hellénisme et les 'barbares': l'exemple syrien", *Le temps de la réflexion* II (1981), pp. 258-274, esp. p.259.

[13] See for a useful survey of all techniques in use : S. P. Brock, "Aspects of Translation Technique in Antiquity", *Greek, Roman, and Byzantine Studies* 20 (1979), pp.69-87; idem, "Limitations of Syriac in representing Greek", in Bruce M. Metzger, *The Early Versions of the New Testament* (Oxford 1977), pp.83-98.

[14] S. P. Brock, "Aspects of Translation Technique in Antiquity", p.80.

[15] See H. J. W. Drijvers, "Das Heiligtum der arabischen Göttin Allât im westlichen Stadtteil von Palmyra", *Antike Welt* 7 (1976), pp. 28-38; M. Gawlikowski, "Le sanctuaire d'Allat, Palmyre. Aperçu préliminaire", *AAAS* 33 (1983), pp.179-198.

[16] C. Dunant, "Nouvelle inscription caravanière de Palmyre", *Museum Helveticum* 13 (1956), pp. 216-223; idem, *Le sanctuaire de Baalshamin, Palmyre III. Les inscriptions* (Rome 1971), pp.56-59; for some corrections of C. Dunant's reading of the inscription see: D. R. Hillers, E. Cussini, "Two readings in the Caravan Inscription Dunant, Baalshamin, No. 45", *BASOR* 286 (May 1992), pp. 35-37.

[17] M. Gawlikowski, "Allat et Baalshamîn", *Mélanges Paul Collart* (Lausanne 1976), pp.197-203.

place (or Arab tribe) in the desert east of Palmyra on the road to the Euphrates.[18] Although this bilingual inscription deserves an extensive commentary, I shall restrict myself now to drawing attention to the way in which the impeccable Greek text was translated into Aramaic.

The Greek Text

Front

1. [τὰς ἀνδριάντας τέσσαρας χαλκιάς, ἕνα] τοῦτον τὸν ἐν
2. [ἱερῷ 'Αθην]ᾶς, ἕνα τὸν ἐν ἱερῷ ἄλσει, ἕνα δὲ τὸν
3. [ἐν ἱερῷ 'Άρεο]ς καὶ ἕνα τὸν ἐν ἱερῷ 'Αταργάτειος
4. [τοὺς] ἐγηγερμένους παρὰ τοῖς πρώτοις
5. τέσσαρσι ἀνδριᾶσι τοῖς ἀνεγερθεῖσι
6. ὑπὸ τῆς πρώτης συνοδίας Σοάδῳ Βωλιάδους
7. τοῦ Σοάδου τοῦ Θαιμισάμσου εὐσεβεῖ καὶ φιλο-
8. πατρίδι τῷ διὰ τὴν αὐτοῦ εὔνοιαν καὶ μεγαλο-
9. φροσύνην τὴν πρὸς τοὺς πολείτας παντὶ
10. τρόπῳ κεκοσμημένῳ ἀρεταῖς καὶ μεγίσ-
11. ταις τειμαῖς ἀνέστησεν ἡ ἀπὸ 'Ολογασίας ἀνα-
12. βᾶσα συνοδία πάντων Παλμυρηνῶν ἐπεὶ
13. προώρμησεν ἐπισήμως παραλαβὼν μ[ε]-
14. θ' ἑαυτοῦ πολλὴν δύναμιν καὶ ἀντέστ[η]

Left Side

15. ['Αβ]δαλλάθῳ 'Εειθήνῳ καὶ τοῖς ὑπ'αὐτοῦ συναχθεῖσι ἀπὸ π̇[(7 letters)
16. [δ̇ (12 letters) ἱ]ριοῖς τοῖς ἐπὶ χρόνον ἐνεδρεύσασι ἀδικῆσαι τὴν σ[υνοδίαν]
17. [(10 letters)] προσδιέσωσεν αὐτοὺς. δια τοῦτο ἀνέγειραν αὐτῷ
18. [τοὺς ἀνδριάντας (?)] τειμῆς χάριν συνοδιαρχούντων Μαλη Συμωνου
19. [(12 letters) καὶ 'Ε]ννιβήλου Συμωνου τοῦ Βαζεκη
    ἔτους ενυ' μη[νὸς] Δαισίον (= 455 Seleucid era = 144 C.E.)

Hiatus in the preserved Greek text are supplemented as far as possible by comparison with the Greek version of the inscription from the Baalshamin temple and by retranslation of the Palmyrene version.

[18]M. Gawlikowski, "Palmyre et l'Euphrate", *Syria* 60 (1983), pp.53-68, esp. p.64.

Plate 1

Bracket of hard limestone. Front side dimensions: upper side: h. 44 cms.; w. 62 cms.; l. 70 cms.; lower side: h. 44 cms.; w. 40 cms.; l. 54 cms. Letters written in red: 2.5 cms. Palmyra Museum

Translation of the Greek:

(1) The four bronze statues), this one in (2) (the temple of Athen)a, one in the sacred garden, one (3) (in the temple of Are)s, and one in the temple of Atargatis,(4) (which) have been erected next to the first (5) four statues that were erected (6) by the first caravan for Soados (son) of Boliades (7) son of Soados (son) of Thaimisamsos, who is pious and patri(8)otic, through his benevolence and magn(9)animity towards the citizens in every (10) way adorned with distinctions and very grea(11)t honours (12) the caravan of all Palmyrenes which came back from Vologesias erected, because (13) he advanced in a distinguished manner taking with (14) him a large force and he protected (or: defended) (them) (15) against (Ab)dallathos, a man from Eeithe and the (robbers) that were brought together by him from............. (16) who for a long time were lying in wait in order to harm the (caravan) (17)...............he preserved them. Therefore they erected for him (18)..............(these statues) to honour him, when Malê (son) of Sumonos (19)..................(and) (E)nnibel (son) of Sumonos (son) of Bazekes were caravan-leaders in the year 455 in the month of June.

The Palmyrene Text

(1) *ṣlmyʾ ʾln dy nḥšʾ ʾrbʿtyhwn ʾḥd dnh bt ʾlt (wʾḥd bgntʾ ʾlym)*

(2) *wʾḥd bt ʾrṣw wʾḥd bt ʿtrʿth dy qymyn lwt ʾrbʿ(tʾ qdmyʾ dy)*

(3) *ʾqymw lh bny šyrtʾ qdmytʾ lšʿdw br blydʿ br š(ʿdw dy dḥl)*

(4) *ʾlhyʾ wrḥym mdynth dy mn ṭl ḥšh ṭbʾ wrʿynh rbʾ dy l(t.............)*

(5) *bkl gnsh wmṣbt bšbḥyn wbyqryn šgyʾyn dy ʾqymw l(h šyrtʾ dy)*

(6) *tdmr klh dy slqt mn ʾlgšyʾ bdyl dy npq bydyʿw(tʾ wʾyty ʿmh)*

(7) *ḥl šgy wqm bʾpy ʿbdlt ʾḥytyʾ wgyšyʾ dy knš (ʿm............)*

(8) *dy hww ytbyn zbn mḥṭʾ ʿl šyrtʾ whw šʿdw šw(zb ʾnwn bdyl kwt)*

(9) *ʾqymw lh ṣlmyʾ ʾln lyqrh brbnwt šyrtʾ ml(ʾ br šmʿwn...........)*

(10) *wḥnbl šmʿwn bzqʾ byrḥ sywn šnt 45(...)*

Translation of the Palmyrene:

(1) These four bronze statues, this one in the temple of Allat (and one in the sacred garden), (2) and one in the temple of Arṣu, and one in the temple of Atargatis, which are standing next to the (first) four ones, (which) (3) the members of the first caravan erected for Soadu son of Belyada son of S(oadu who fears) (4) the gods and loves his city, who because of his benevolence and magnanimity towards (................) (5) in every way and he was adorned with praises and many honours which erected for (him the caravan of) (6) whole Tadmor that came from Vologesias because he proceeded with knowledge (or: experience) (and took with him) (7) a large force and protected (them) against Abdallat the Aḥitaia and the robbers that he brought together (...........) (8) who were sitting a (long) time to harm the caravan. But this Soadu saved (them,

Plate 2

Bracket of hard limestone. Left side.

Therefore) (9) they erected for him these statues to honour him, when Malê (son of Sem'on (10) and Hanibêl son of Sem'on (son) of Bazeqa were caravan-leaders. In the month of Siwan of the year 455 (= June 144 C.E.)

Soadu was honoured by his fellow-citizens for his *eunoia*, "goodwill, favour", and his *megalophrosyne*, "greatness of mind, generosity" (ll. 8-9). These two stereotyped expressions are rendered in the Aramaic version (l. 4) as *ḥšʾ ṭbʾ* and *rʿynʾ rbʾ*, literally "good affection" and "great mind". The noun *ḥšʾ* (from the root *ḥš*, "to suffer") in contemporary Syriac had the meaning "pain, suffering" and also "ambition, desire, affection" and is used in later Syriac to denote the various passions of the mind. To the best of my knowledge the combinations *ḥšʾ ṭbʾ* and *rʿynʾ rbʾ* never occur in Aramaic or in later Syriac and can only be explained and understood as literal translations from the Greek text (*verbum e verbo*) for which bilinguism is a necessary condition.

The correct Greek phrase in l. 13 *proormesen episemôs*, "he advanced, moved forwards in a distinguished or notorious way", is rendered in the Aramaic version as *npq bydyʿwtʾ*, "he proceeded, went out, with knowledge, science or even cleverness". This is a rather odd expression in Aramaic and only due to the fact that the translator tried to render the Greek as literally as possible. The nearest rendering of the Greek adjective *episemos*, "notable, notorious, significant", is the *peʿil* form *ydyʿ*, which also has the meaning "notable, notorious". It consequently forms the base of the noun *ydywtʾ* which together with the preposition *b* renders the adverb *episemôs*. A noun with the preposition *b* is a very common way of forming an adverbial expression.[19]

In l. 15 of the Greek we are told that the robbers had lain in wait for the caravan for a certain time in order to harm (or assault) it: *tois epi chronon enedreusasi adikesai ten s(unodian)*. This correct Greek phrase is rather oddly translated as *hww ytbyn zbn mḥṭʾ ʿl šyrtʾ*. *Hww ytbyn* renders *enedreusasi*, *zbn* is meant as the equivalent of *epi chronon* and the infinitive *mḥṭʾ* (root: *ḥṭʾ*, "to sin") renders *adikesai*. The Aramaic is a literal translation of the Greek, but the result of the *verbum e verbo* rendering is a grammatically incorrect sentence. One would expect at least the preposition *l* before the infinitive *mḥṭʾ*, although another verb than *ḥṭʾ*, "to sin" would be more appropiate. The use of the absolute *zbn* is extremely odd and only understandable with the indefinite *chronon* in mind. If, however, the verb *ḥṭʾ* in Palmyrene Aramaic can render the whole range of meaning of the Greek *adikeo,* this would provide us with a better translation of the only other occurrence of this verb in Palmyrene epigraphy (Ber V 133, 10) *ʿl npšh ḥṭʾ*, "to wrong himself", instead of "to

[19]Cf. J. Payne Smith, *A Compendious Syriac Dictionary*, p.33: "*b* frequently helps to form adverbs"; G. Dalman, *Grammatik des jüdisch-palästinischen Aramäisch* (2te Aufl. Leipzig 1905, reprint Darmstadt 1960), p.211f.

sin against himself" (cf. DISO, 85: "pèchera contre soi-meme", which ought consequently be corrected; J. Hoftijzer and K. Jongeling, in *Dictionary of the North-West Semitic Inscriptions* I [Leiden 1995], p. 362, s.v. *ḥṭʾ*, translate the phrase: "...is sinning against his soul", which seems an odd interpretation.)

Finally I should like to draw attention to *mn ṭl* as two separate words, the equivalent of Greek *dia*, in l. 4 of the Aramaic version, instead of the common *mṭl*, which occurs in two other Palmyrene inscriptions (CIS 3913 I 6; 3932,6). The form attested here establishes the compound character of *mṭl* and excludes a derivation from the verb *nṭl* as suggested by Brockelmann, *Lexicon Syriacum* 2, 382. It can also provide us with a clue as to how to solve the enigmatic *mn ṭlʾ* in official Aramaic.[20]

A comparison of the Greek and Aramaic version of another honorary inscription of Soadu Bolyada dated 132 C.E., and found in the Baalshamin sanctuary can help to correct some mistakes in C. Dunant's edition of the text, in particular in the Aramaic part.[21] In l. 5 of the Aramaic version: *mṣbt bšm bwlʾ (wdm)s*, translated by C. Dunant as: "des statues au nom du sénat et du peuple", *mṣbt* evidently is the rendering of what C. Dunant in l. 12 of the Greek gives as *teteimemenon* — a restored reading —, but what certainly ought to be read as *kekosmemenon*; in the inscription of 144 C.E. *kekosmemenon* (L.10) is also rendered in the Aramaic version as *mṣbt* (L.5) "decorated". The translation "des statues" is therefore wrong.[22]

The next example is a bracket discovered in 1935 in front of Baalshamin's temple and first published by J. Cantineau.[23] The fragmentary bilingual honorific inscription was republished by C. Dunant. [24] The text is dated in 171 C.E. when Avidius Cassius was procurator of Syria.[25] The person to whom all the honours mentioned in the inscription was given is unknown. The Aramaic is a free rendering of the Greek part, although the Aramaic translates the technical terms as precisely as possible. The four tribes of Palmyra, together forming the *boule* and *demos* of the city, passed a decree in their separate assemblies to give good testimony for this unidentified but meritorious person and to inform the procurator of their decision. The Greek text refers to the four separate decrees with the words *dia psephismatôn*, "measures passed by a popular assembly" (Liddell & Scott, s.v. p.2022). The Greek *dia psephismatôn* is rendered in the Aramaic part as *bqblyn ʾrbʿʾ* and translated by C. Dunant following

---

[20]Cf. *DISO*, p. 100, s.v. *ṭlʾ*; E. G. Kraeling, *The Brooklyn Museum Aramaic Papyri* (New Haven 1953), Papyrus 5, l. 9 and Kraeling's commentary, pp. 185-186.

[21] C. Dunant, *Le sanctuaire de Baalshamin à Palmyre. III. Les inscriptions* (Rome 1971), nr. 45, pp. 56-59.

[22]For some other corrections of C. Dunant's reading and translation see D. R. Hillers, E. Cussini, "Two Readings in the Caravan Inscription Dunant, Baalshamin, No. 45", *BASOR* 286 (May 1992), pp. 35-37.

[23]J. Cantineau, "Tadmorea II", *Syria* 17 (1936), pp. 277-282.

[24]C. Dunant, *Le sanctuaire de Baalshamin a Palmyre.III. Les inscriptions* (Rome 1971), No. 48, pp.61-63.

[25]Cf. M. L. Astarita, *Avidio Cassio* (Rome, 1983); M. Sartre, *L'orient romain* (Paris 1991), pp. 49-51.

J. Cantineau as "en quatre ambassades(?)".[26] The noun *qbl'* in Palmyrene Aramaic apparently is the same as Syriac *qwbl'*, "acceptance, approval"; the *paʿel*: *qbl* "to receive, accept", also has the meaning of "to approve, to assent to".[27] The Palmyrene is a correct and precise translation of the Greek.

Thereupon the procurator had an equestrian statue, *ephippon andrianta*, erected in the local Caesareum. The Greek expression *ephippon andrianta* is rendered as *ṣlm mrkb swsy*, in which *mrkb swsy* is the equivalent of *ephippon*. According to J. Cantineau the Aramaic phrase means "riding a horse" ("chevauchant un cheval"). In my opinion *mrkb* is the participle *aphʿel* passive of *rkb*, "to mount, to ride", and the expression is a literal rendering of *ephippon andrianta*, "a statue mounted upon a horse". The termination *y* in *swsy* transforms the noun *sws*, "horse" into an adjective, so that *mrkb swsy* should be understood as a compound adjective corresponding to *ephippon*. It is a neologism in Aramaic due to the influence of Greek and an enrichment of the receptor language.

A possible, but unlikely misunderstanding of the Greek text can be found in CIS 3932, a honorific inscription for Julius Aurelius Zabdila dated 242 C.E., who was presented with a statue by the *boule* and *demos*. He was *agoranomos*, "clerk of the market", and spent lavish amounts of money, apparently for public purposes. The Greek text phrases it as follows: *agoranomesanta te kai ouk oligôn apheidesanta chrematôn*. The Aramaic, however, renders this as: *whw' rb šwq wḥsk rz'yn šgy'yn*, "and he was head of the marketplace and saved many *rz'yn*" (Aramaic version, l. 5). The meaning of *rz'yn* is disputed, but starting from *rz'* "secret, mystery" most scholars interpret *rz'yn* as "treasures"[28], and therefore conclude that the translator misunderstood the Greek, or overlooked the *alpha privans*. Although I cannot solve this riddle completely, a misunderstanding of the Greek seems unlikely in an inscription in honour of a high civilian official. The solution may lie in a meaning of *rz'*, which is other than "secret, mystery", in particular since the *aleph* is part of the root. A solution is offered by the Syriac *'trzy* "to be reduced, wasted away", which leads to the meaning "waste, expenditure, loss", for *rz'*. The meaning of the phrase, apparently, is that Julius Aurelius Zabdila, in his function of clerk of the market, spent lavish amounts of public money and in this way saved on private expenditure. The Aramaic version considered the negation *ouk* and the *alpha privans* as neutralizing each other and interpreted *chrematôn* correctly as "expenditures". It is an example of a characteristic mercantile interpretative translation of a common Greek expression in honorific inscriptions.

---

[26]Cf. *DISO*, p. 249, s.v. *qbl* iii.
[27]Cf. J. Payne Smith, *A Compendious Syriac Dictionary*, s.v. *qbl* and *qwbl'*.
[28]See *DISO*, p. 276, s.v. *rz'*; M.Lidzbarski, *Handbuch der nordsemitischen Epigraphik* (Weimar 1898), p. 368: "Geldminderungen, Ausgaben"; J. Cantineau, *Inventaire des inscriptions de Palmyre* III (Beirut 1930), p. 31: "détriment, perte matérielle"; cf. Syriac *'trzy* - "to be reduced, wasted away".

In CIS 3943, a bilingual inscription on one of the columns in the Great Colonnade belonging to a statue of the well-known Septimius Worod erected for him by Julius Aurelius Salma, Septimius Worod is called "friend" (*philos*) and "protector, patron" (*prostates*) of Julius Aurelius Salma. The Aramaic version translates *prostates* with *qywmʾ*, a literal rendering, "he who stands up" (for someone else). I conclude that the noun formation *qywmʾ* is a Aramaic neologism due to the frequent use of *prostates* in various social situations (also in CIS 3940). It is interesting to see that the Syriac *qywmʾ* has exactly the same range of meanings as Greek *prostates*: "manager, prefect", and "protector, patron".

An inscription in the agora accompanying a statue of Zabdila the scribe informs us that he performed his function with integrity (he evidently could not be bribed) *hagnôs grammateusanta*.[29] The Aramaic renders this phrase as *bgrmtyʾ dylh hlk špyr* "in his function of scribe he acted in an excellent (good) way". Since the Aramaic does not have a verb denoting the function of a scribe (the simple *ktb* would not do) the translator had to use a circumlocution and formed the apparently new expression *hlk špyr*, "to act in a good way". The combination of *hlk* (*paʿel*) and *špyr* does not occur elsewhere in the entire Aramaic literature and owes its existence to the translation technique used.[30]

A comparison of the wording of the Greek and Aramaic can sometimes help to correct evident mistakes in the reading of the Aramaic. An inscription in the agora mentioning the erection of a statue of Iarḥai son of Zabdila praises him for his benevolence and zeal shown towards the merchants of Palmyra: *eunoias kai spoudes heneken hes endedeiktai pros tous emporous*.[31] The Aramaic, as read by J. Starcky, renders this as follows: *lḥšbn ḥpywtʾ wḥšʾ ṭbʾ dy ʾšth lh lwt tgryʾ*. Here the Aramaic *ʾšth lh lwt tgryʾ* is odd; it corresponds with *endedeiktai pros tous emporous*. I suggest reading *ʾšthwh*, a reflexive of the *šaphʿel* of *ḥwy,* "to show", which corresponds in every detail with the Greek *endedeiktai*. The phrase *lḥšbn ḥpywtʾ* (Starcky: "pour la protection") is likewise odd, since it must correspond with *spoudes heneken*. I suggest reading *lḥšbn ḥpyṭwtʾ*, which is possible according to the published photograph of the inscription; *ḥpyṭwtʾ*, "diligence, earnest care" in Syriac is the exact equivalent of Greek *spoude*.[32] It is interesting that the Aramaic version renders Greek *heneken*, "on account of" with *lḥšbn*, which has exactly the same meaning; Syriac *nsb ḥwšbnʾ* means to "take account of, to reckon". The Aramaic version of this Greek honorific inscription is therefore as literal as possible.

---

[29]J. Starcky, *Inventaire des inscriptions de Palmyre* X (Damascus 1949), No. 39, pp. 26-28.

[30]Cf. *Inventaire* X, No. 53, L. 4: *bdyl dy hlk ʿmh špyr*; cf. Syriac *hlk* (*paʿel*): "to go, to walk; to act, to behave".

[31]*Inventaire* X, No. 127.

[32]Cf. J. Payne Smith, *A Compendious Syriac Dictionary* , p. 153, s.v. *ḥpyṭw*.

A first and surely not exhaustive study of some bilingual Palmyrene inscriptions has made clear that there were various translation techniques implied. Some texts display a literal rendering of the Greek, almost a *verbum e verbo* translation, which has produced various neologisms and unusual word combinations in Aramaic. But even more strikingly free renderings of the Greek, a *sensus e sensu* translation, have actually occasioned an enrichment of Aramaic, the receptor language. The Aramaic in use in Syria, since the period of the Seleucids more and more a bilingual area, thus underwent a substantial influence from both the Greek lexicon and idiom, not only in the use of Greek loan-words, but also in the formation of neologisms and new idiomatic expressions in Aramaic itself.[33] Not only urban architecture and art, but even the language itself, the most powerful cultural medium, was to a certain extent hellenized.[34] The native Aramaic speakers, however good their knowledge of Greek may have been (and in many cases it was impeccable), did the same in the linguistic arena as in other provinces of their cultural heritage: they adapted new forms and expressions to their own language and transformed them into real, although sometimes rather unusual, Aramaic. Hellenization was a real and longlasting enrichment of the local Semitic cultures and languages, as the Palmyrene bilingual inscriptions demonstrate.[35]

---

[33] See J. A. Fitzmyer, *A Wandering Aramean. Collected Aramaic Essays* (Missoula 1979), pp. 29-56, "The Languages of Palestine in the First Century A.D.", p. 41: a clear example of Greek affecting Aramaic in an official Aramaic papyrus of 120 C.E.; cf. p. 46: "Grecized Aramaic is still to be attested in the first century. It begins to be attested in the early second century and becomes abundant in the third and fourth centuries."

[34] See also M. T. Davis, L. T. Stuckenbruck, "Notes on Translation Phenomena in the Palmyrene Bilinguals", *Intertestamental Essays in Honour of J. T. Milik* (Kraków 1992), pp. 265-283, which basically deals with the semantic range of a single term.

[35] See now Fergus Millar, *The Roman Near East 31 BC - AD 337* (Cambridge-London 1993), pp. 319-336.

Lamedh-Yodh Verbs in Palestinian Targumic Aramaic

S. Fassberg — Hebrew University of Jerusalem

The modern study of Palestinian Targumic Aramaic began in 1930 with the publication of some 600 verses of Pentateuchal Targum from the Cairo Genizah by P. Kahle in *Masoreten des Westens* II.[1] The language of these fragments was quickly recognized as the best representative of the original Aramaic of the Palestinian Targum, far more reliable than the language found in the Fragment Targum and in Targum Pseudo-Jonathan. Despite the subsequent publication of a complete Pentateuchal Targum, Targum Neophyti, the linguistic value of the fragmentary Genizah material still far surpasses the value of all other non-Genizah material. The additional texts published by M. L. Klein in *Genizah Manuscripts of Palestinian Targum*[2] lend further proof to the importance of the Genizah fragments.

Now that almost all of the Genizah Targumic material has been published,[3] one is able to describe this variety of Aramaic in some detail. Such a description also serves as a basis for examining once again the non-Genizah Targumic material in an effort to recover the authentic Palestinian Aramaic embedded in those sources.

This paper will focus on one feature of Palestinian Targumic Aramaic that sets it apart from other Aramaic dialects, namely, the inflection of the perfect of *lamedh-yodh* verbs.[4] Although certain salient forms have been taken up in the literature, such as the 3 m.pl. and 3 f.pl., which have been treated in detail by A. Tal in his study of the appended *nun* in Palestinian Aramaic,[5] other forms still await discussion, or merit renewed discussion, e.g., the origin of הוינה "I was". The 1 s., 2 m.s., and 3 f.s. forms of the perfect of *lamedh-yodh* verbs will be examined first, followed by a discussion of the unique inflection of הוה. The data for this paper are drawn from the vocalized[6] and unvocalized fragments of straight[7] Palestinian Targum from the Cairo

---

[1]P. Kahle, *Masoreten des Westens* II (Stuttgart 1930), MSS A-F.
[2]M. L. Klein, *Genizah Manuscripts of Palestinian Targum*, 2 vols. (Cincinnati 1986).
[3]M. Sokoloff and J. Yahalom have collected unpublished Targumic poems that will appear in their forthcoming *Aramaic Poems from Eretz Israel of the Byzantine Period.*
[4]In this study I elaborate and expand on my discussion in Fassberg, *A Grammar of the Palestinian Targum Fragments from the Cairo Genizah* (HSS 38) (Atlanta 1990), paras. 143, 148, 151.
[5]A. Tal, "Layers in the Jewish Aramaic of Palestine: The Appended Nun as a Criterion," *Lesh* 43 (1979), pp. 165-184 (Hebrew).
[6]Some of the readings presented in this paper differ from those found in Klein, *Genizah Manuscripts*. In transcribing the Cairo Genizah forms, I use *e* to represent *ḥireq* (<*i), *ṣere*, and *seghol* since the fluctuation of these three signs *(seghol* is the most frequent) in the Genizah fragments points to one *e* phoneme. The free fluctuation of *pathaḥ* and *qameṣ (pathaḥ* is dominant) points to one *a* phoneme.
[7]Data from Targumic poetry and Targumic Tosephta are excluded.

Genizah fragments[8] that are free from the linguistic influences of Targum Onqelos. Although the data are at times limited, a coherent and consistent picture, nonetheless, emerges. Relevant forms will also be drawn from the non-Genizah Targumic material and from Galilean Aramaic.

A. Perfect: 1 s., 2 m.s., 2 f.s., 3 f.s.

1 s.: There are two pointed forms of the 1 s. Peal in the Cairo Genizah: חֲמֵית Gen 46:30 "I saw" (p. 145), חֲטֵית Exod 9:27 "I sinned" (p.185), as well as several unpointed forms with the same orthography: חמית Gen 7:1 (p.17); 31:10 (p.55); 40:16 (p.105); 41:19 (p.109); 41:22 (p.109); ברית Gen 7:4 "I created" (p.17). The Pael conjugation is represented by two pointed examples. The first is שׁוי֗ית Gen 40:11 "I placed" (p.103), where the positioning of the vowel sign under the *yodh* indicates a realization of *šawwĕyet̲* a second *yodh* added above the line confirms this pronunciation. The other pointed Pael example is סַכַּ[יֵי]ת *sakkăyet̲* Gen 48:11 "I awaited" (p.153).[9] Unpointed Pael forms include צלית Gen 30:8 "I prayed" (p.45) probably reflecting *ṣallet̲*, but possibly *ṣallĕyet̲*, and שוית Gen 40:12 "I placed" (p.103) realized as *šawwet̲* or *šawwĕyet̲*. The Aphel conjugation is represented by two pointed examples: אַיְיתִּיֵית *ʾayt̲iyet̲* Gen 31:39 "I brought" (p.61),[10] but also אַיְתֵי]ת] *ʾayt̲et̲* Gen 44:18 (p.141). In addition this verb occurs once unpointed with a double *yodh* suggesting *-yet̲*, אייתיית Gen 43:9 (p.121) and once with a single *yodh* reflecting either *-et̲* or *-yet̲*, אייתית Gen 42:37 (p.119). There is one more example of a 1 s. unpointed Aphel; however, the reading is difficult and one cannot tell whether the verb is written with a single or double *yodh*: ?אשרית/?אשריית Lev 23:43 "I caused to dwell" (p.319).[11] A 1 s. Ethpeel/Ethpaal is attested once with pointing: אִתְגַלֵית *ʾetg̲ălet̲*?/*ʾetg̲allet̲*? Exod 6:3 "I revealed myself" (p.175).[12] There is also one unpointed example of this verb: אתגליית Gen 31:13 (p.55); the double *yodh* indicates final *-yet̲*.

These examples suggest that the 1 s. Peal was realized as *bĕnet̲*, but in the derived conjugations there were biforms *bannet̲*/*bannĕyet̲*, *ʾab̲n et̲*/*ʾab̲nĕyet̲*, *ʾet̲bĕnet̲*/*ʾet̲banyet̲*, *ʾet̲bannet̲*/*ʾet̲bannĕyet̲*. Whereas the forms without the consonantal *yodh* are the rule elsewhere in Aramaic, the forms ending in *-yet̲* seem to be attested outside of Palestinian Targumic Aramaic only in Galilean Aramaic. The origin of the

[8] The page numbers cited in this study are from Klein, *Genizah Manuscripts*.

[9] The *pathaḥ* under the *kaph* reflects the pronunciation of *shewa* as an ultra-short *a*; this scribal practice is frequent in the fragments.

[10] The *shewa* has assimilated to the following *yodh* as is common in the fragments.

[11] Klein reads אשרית; Kahle reads אשריית. Cf. Targum Neophyti text אשרית, but marginal note אשריית.

[12] The Ethpeel was intended if the *pathaḥ* represents a *shewa* that was realized as an ultra-short *a*. The lack of *daghesh forte* in the *lamedh* does not, however, rule out Ethpaal, since *daghesh* is not always marked.

forms with -*yet̲* lies in the inflection of the strong verb of this dialect where one finds the 1 s. forms *qaṭlet̲, qaṭṭĕlet̲, ʾaqṭĕlet̲, ʾet̲qaṭlet̲, ʾet̲qaṭṭĕlet̲*.

Biforms of the 1 s. Peal with double *yodh* are attested, however, in non-Genizah Targumic material and in Galilean Aramaic, e.g., ברייית Gen 7:4 "I created" (Targum Neophyti), קרייית Exod 31:2 "I called" (Targum Neophyti, margin). The orthography with double *yodh* suggests the forms *baryet̲* and *qaryet̲* on the analogy of the strong verb *qaṭlet̲*.[13] In the light of these non-Genizah forms and the paucity of Genizah pointed forms, one could argue that Palestinian Targumic Aramaic may also have had a rare Peal biform *banyet̲*, similar to the form in the derived conjugations.

2 m.s.: There are no attested forms of the 2 m.s. Peal in the Cairo Genizah fragments. In Targum Neophyti, however, one usually finds forms like חמית Gen 20:10 "you saw" or מחית Num 22:28 "you struck", probably reflecting *ḥămet̲* and *măḥet̲*. The Pael conjugation of the Cairo Genizah fragments is represented by three unpointed forms: כסית Exod 15:7 "you covered" (p.245), רבית Gen 31:13 "you raised" (p.55), תנית Gen 31:27 "you told" (p.59); the orthography with single *yodh* would seem to reflect *kasset̲, rabbet̲, tannet̲,* though one cannot rule out a realization of *kassĕyet̲, rabbĕyet̲, tannĕyet̲*. The only other attested forms of the 2 m.s. are four occurrences of the verb אתגלי: אֶתְגְלֵית Gen 35:9 (p.73),[14] אֶתְגַלֵית Gen 35:9 (p.73), אֶתְגְלִית Gen 35:9 (p.73), אתְגְלִית Gen 35:9 (p.75). Two of the four forms are pointed with *ṣere* and two are pointed with *ḥireq*. In the light of the frequent fluctuation of *ṣere/ḥireq/seghol* (< **i*, **ay*) in these fragments representing one underlying phoneme *e*, it may be that the two pointings with *ḥireq* are in imitation of the Tiberian Biblical Aramaic pointing of the 2 m.s. in derived forms, e.g., מַנִּיתָ *mannit̲ā*, whereas the pointings with *ṣere* reflect the vulgar pronunciation.

The limited evidence would appear to indicate that there are no biforms of the 2 m.s. with consonantal *yodh* of the type *bannĕyet̲, ʾab̲nĕyet̲, ʾet̲banyet̲, ʾet̲bannĕyet̲*. Like the 1 s. ending, which is formed on the pattern of the strong verb ending, the 2 m.s. forms of the derived conjugations *bannet̲, ʾab̲net̲, ʾet̲bĕnet̲, ʾet̲bannet̲* seem to follow the pattern of the 2 m.s. strong verb, *qaṭṭelt, ʾaqṭelt, ʾet̲qĕṭelt*. The assumed vowel *e* of *lamedh-yodh* verbs in the Pael and Aphel conjugations[15] agrees with the vowel of the strong verb. Compare the *i* vowel found in Biblical Aramaic, Targum Onqelos, and Syriac. It should be noted, however, that a 2 m.s. ending -*yet̲* is found in

---

[13]For additional examples, see G. Dalman, *Grammatik des jüdisch-palästinischen Aramäisch* (Leipzig 1905²), p. 343; C. Levias, *A Grammar of Galilean Aramaic* (New York 1986), p. 133 (Hebrew).

[14]Klein reads אֶתְגְּלֵית with *daghesh*. The dot in the published plate seems to be beneath the *taw*, suggesting that it is an ink spot.

[15]This assumption is based on the pointings of אתגלֵית (see above). If אתגלית is an Ethpeel verb, then its ending follows that of the strong verb *ʾet̲qĕṭelt*. If it is Ethpaal, it too follows the strong verb: **ʾet̲gallayt* > *ʾetgallet̲* (contraction of the diphthong).

Galilean Aramaic and infrequently in non-Genizah Palestinian Targum sources.[16] These rare forms raise the possibility that the language of the original Palestinian Targum, in addition to the regular 2 m.s. ending *-eṯ*, also had infrequent biforms with *-yeṯ*.

2 f.s.: There are no examples in the Cairo Genizah material. In Targum Neophyti one finds ס טית Num 5:20 "you turned aside," perhaps reflecting *sĕṭeṯ*.[17]

3 f.s.: The form of the 3 f.s. Perfect Peal is בנת *bĕnaṯ*, and 13 of the 14 pointed forms (including the verb הוה) have *pathaḥ*, e.g. הֲוַת Gen 4:16 "she was" (p.9), הֲווַּת Exod 9:24 (p.183), בְעַת Gen 38:25 "she sought" (p.89), קְהַת Gen 32:26 "it was benumbed? dislocated"[18] (p.67), חֲמַת Gen 38;25 "she saw" (p.89), תְלַת Gen 38:25 "she lifted up" (p.89). Only one example is pointed with *qameṣ* in accordance with the rules of Tiberian Biblical Aramaic: הֲוָות Gen 38:21 (p.87).[19] There are 13 unpointed examples whose orthography also reflects *-aṯ*, as well as 12 unpointed examples of קראת "she called", which, despite the historical orthography, also must have been realized as *-aṯ* (*qĕraṯ*), e.g., Gn 29:32-35 (p.43). In the derived conjugations one finds *-yaṯ*. The Pael conjugation is represented by one pointed example: זְנִית Gen 38:24 "she whored" (p.89). There are three unpointed forms whose orthography agrees with the pointed form: זניית Gen 38:24 (p.95), שווית Gen 31:34 "she placed" (p.59), תניית Gen 29:12 "she told" (p.39). There are five pointed examples of the Ethpeel/Ethpaal: אֶתְּלְיַית Gen 7:17 "it was suspended" (p.21), אֶתְבְּרְיַת Gen 2:23 "she was created" (p.3), אֶתְבְּרְיַת Gen 2:23 (p.3), אתגלְיַת Num 20:6 "it was revealed" (p.325), אֶתְרְעִית Gen 49:6 "she was pleased" (p.167).[20] In addition there are three more 3 f.s. Ethpeel/Ethpaal verbs attested unpointed, and their orthography suggests final *-yaṯ*: אתמליית Gen 9:19 (p.27), אתגליית Exod 19:20 (p.263), 20:17 (p.271).

As is the case with the 1 s. and the 2 m.s., the 3 f.s. of the derived conjugations has been remodelled on the forms of the strong verb in this dialect: *qaṭṭĕlaṯ, ʾaqṭĕlaṯ, ʾeṯqaṭlaṯ, ʾeṯqaṭṭĕlaṯ*. The *i* vowel of Biblical Aramaic *-iyyaṯ* (e.g., אִתְכְּרִיַּת *ʾiṯkĕriyyaṯ*) and Targum Onqelos *-iyyaṯ* > *-iʾaṯ* (e.g., אִתְבְּנִיאַת *ʾiṯbĕniʾaṯ*) has been reduced to *shewa* in the Cairo Genizah fragments as in the strong verb. A reduction is also attested in Syriac (e.g., Pael *rammĕyaṯ*). In Galilean Aramaic there is

---

[16] See below n. 47.

[17] For the 2 f.s. הוויית, see below.

[18] J. A. Lund, "On the Interpretation of the Palestinian Targumic Reading WQHT in GEN 32:25," *JBL* 105 (1986), pp. 99-103.

[19] *Pathaḥ*, however, can also be found in Tiberian Biblical Aramaic. See H. Bauer, P. Leander, *Grammatik des Biblisch-Aramäischen* (Halle 1927), p. 174.

[20] The *shewa* under the *reš* occurs in place of *pathaḥ; shewa* in place of *pathaḥ* is attested elsewhere in the fragments.

a biform of the Peal 3 f.s. with consonantal *yodh*: בעיית/בעית *baᶜyaṯ*.[21] Similarly, there are infrequent 3 f.s. Peal biforms attested in Christian Palestinian Aramaic of the type חמית.[22]

B. Perfect of הוה: 1 s., 2 m.s., 3 f.s.

1 s.: As J. Lund has shown, the form הוינא functions as the 1 s. Perfect of הוה in Palestinian Targumic Aramaic and in Galilean Aramaic, as opposed to הוית in older Aramaic and in the Western Aramaic dialects of Christian Palestinian Aramaic and Samaritan Aramaic.[23] Examples of הוית or הויתי in Targum Pseudo-Jonathan, the Fragment Targum, and Targum Neophyti are the result of external influence. There are four examples of this form in the Cairo Genizah fragments: הֲוֵינָא מְשַׁלֵּם Gen 31:39 "I used to repay" (p. 61)[24]; הֲוֵינָא מְשַׁלֵּם Gen 31:39 (p.61) הֲוֵינָא Gen 31:40 "I was" (p. 61), לא הווינה רחימה Gen 29:33 "I was not loved" (p.43).

The origin of this form is disputed. G. Dalman,[25] followed by W. Stevenson,[26] listed הוינא as a participle with the 1 s. independent pronoun אנא suffixed, but did not elaborate. E. Y. Kutscher cautiously suggested that הוינא was formed from the passive participle הֲוֵי (<*$qaṭīl$) and the 1 s. independent pronoun אֲנָא;[27] he thought that this passive participial form was part of the phenomenon attested in Galilean Aramaic, and to a greater extent in Maᶜlula, of passive participles functioning as the perfect, e.g., Galilean Aramaic אנה שמיע "I have heard", or Maᶜlula *nišqel* "I have taken" where the independent pronoun is proclitic.[28] Tal has also taken הוינא as a participial form.[29] Lund, on the other hand, prefers to explain הוינא as a backformation from the 1 pl. Perfect הוינן.

---

[21]Dalman, *Grammatik*, p. 338.

[22]F. Schulthess, *Grammatik des christlich-palästinischen Aramäisch* (Tübingen 1924), p. 72. M. Bar-Asher points out in his *Palestinian Syriac Studies* (Jerusalem 1977), p. 185 n. 54 [Hebrew] that these forms are found in late manuscripts.

[23]J.A. Lund, "The First Person Singular Past Tense of the Verb הוה in Jewish Palestinian Aramaic", *Maarav* 4/2 (1987), pp. 191-199.

[24]So according to Kahle. Klein, however, reads הֲוֵינָא. One cannot identify the vowel sign from the published photograph.

[25]Dalman, *Grammatik*, p. 352.

[26]W.B. Stevenson, *Grammar of Palestinian Jewish Aramai c* (Oxford 1962[2]), p. 58.

[27]E.Y. Kutscher, "Two 'Passive' Constructions in Aramaic in the Light of Persian," in *Proceedings of the International Conference on Semitic Studies held in Jerusalem, 19-23 July 1965* (Jerusalem 1969), pp. 137-138 n.29: "Apparently also הוינא — I was, in Galilaean Aramaic, equals הוי (קְטִיל) + נא (= אנא)."

[28]A. Spitaler, *Grammatik des neuaramäischen Dialekts von Maᶜlula (Antilibanon)* (AKM 32.1) (Leipzig 1938), p. 211.

[29]A. Tal, "Ms. Neophyti 1: The Palestinian Targum to the Pentateuch. Observations on the Artistry of a Scribe," *IOS* 4 (1974), p. 40 n. 37.

2 m.s.: There are four attestations of the 2 m.s. Perfect: הְוִיתְּ תָּבַע Gen 31:39 (p.61) "you used to demand", הֲוִיתְּ משׁ]יזב Gen 49:9 (p.167) "you used to save", הֲוִית־אָמַר Gen 44:18 (p.133) "you used to say", הֲוִית משקי Gen 40:13 (p.103) "you used to give drink". It seems significant that in the four examples, all from different manuscripts, the final vowel is *i*.[30] Also significant is the fact that in two of the four examples, one finds a *daghesh* in the final *taw*. While it is possible that the *daghesh* in in the *taw* of הוית תבע could reflect the sandhi assimilation of *ṯ* to *t*, as noted by Muraoka,[31] the *daghesh* in the second example is more difficult to explain away. On occasion one finds that the use of *daghesh* in the Cairo Genizah material parallels that in the "Palestinian-Tiberian" system (also known as the "Fuller Palestinian" system), in which *daghesh* can mark the beginning of a new syllable, e.g., the *qoph* in אֶתְקַבַּל Gen 4:8 (p.7) "it was accepted". This, however, is not the case in these examples since the *taw* closes a syllable. It must be stressed that with regard to the two examples of הֲוִית without *daghesh*, the *daghesh* is not consistently marked in the manuscripts, even in those manuscripts that tend to be fully pointed.

2 f.s.: As is the case with other *lamedh-yodh* verbs, there are no examples of the 2 f.s. in the Cairo Genizah fragments. In Targum Neophyti Gen 24:60 (also in Galilean Aramaic - Palestinian Talmud Shab. 7d), however, one finds the 2 f.s. written הוויית reflecting possibly *hăwayt*, *hăwayṯ*, or *hawyet*, *hawyeṯ*.

Muraoka has suggested that both the vowel *i* and the plosive pronunciation of *t* in the 2 m.s. form reflect an attempt to distinguish the 1 s. הוית from the 2 m.s. of הוית as well as the 1 s. of all *lamedh-yodh* verbs from the 2 m.s.[32] He compares Biblical Aramaic 1 s. *bĕneṯ* and 2 m.s. *bĕnayṯā*, Syriac l s. *bĕneṯ* and 2 m.s. *bĕnayt*. A difference between the two forms also exists in *lamedh-yodh* verbs in Maʿlula 1 s. *eḥmiṯ* < *ḥmīṯ* and 2 m.s. *eḥmič* < *ḥmīt*,[33] and occasionally in Targum Onqelos 1 s. *bĕneṯ(i)* and 2 m.s. *bĕneṯ(a)*.[34] Note the 2 f.s. forms Syriac *bĕnayt* (kethibh *bĕnayti*), Targum Onqelos *bĕneṯ*, Maʿlula *eḥmiš*. Muraoka rejects the idea that the pointing of 2 m.s. הוית is a reflex of an original intransitive verb of the type **qaṭila*, since it is not attested in this form anywhere in Aramaic and the other inflected forms of הוה in the Cairo Genizah all reflect original **qaṭala*. It should be added that there are no examples of **qaṭila* verbs in *lamedh-yodh* in the Cairo Genizah material; they have all gone over to **qaṭala*. Cf. סגון Gen 7:17 "they increased" (p. 21), שתון Gen 43:34

---

[30]Klein reads הֲוֵית Gen 44:18 (p.133).

[31]T. Muraoka, "A Study in Palestinian Jewish Aramaic," *Sef* 45 (1985), pp. 7-9.

[32]Ibid.

[33]Spitaler, *Grammatik*, pp. 164-165. This difference also exists in the strong verbs.

[34]Dalman, *Grammatik*, pp. 337-359; A. Dodi, "The Grammar of Targum Onqelos According to Geniza Fragments," Ph.D. thesis, Bar Ilan University (Ramat Gan 1981), pp. 347-386 (Hebrew).

"they drank" (p.125) רבון (= רוון) Gen 43:34, "they became drunk" (p.125), which in other dialects have **qaṭila* reflexes.

It is possible to explain the creation of הוינא (Lund) and/or הוית with plosive *t* and *i* (Muraoka) as arising from an effort to distinguish the 1 s. from the 2 m.s. Nevertheless, one cannot ignore the fact that the Perfect 1 s. and 2 m.s. forms of the verb הוה behave differently from the 1 s. and 2 m.s. of other *lamedh-yodh* verbs in the Cairo Genizah fragments. This would seem to be true too for the 2 f.s. form of הוה if the unattested Cairo Genizah forms are the same as Targum Neophyti הויית and סטית. In other verbs the 1 s. ends in *-eṯ* (e.g., חְמֵית) as does the 2 m.s.[35] When an innovation takes place distinguishing persons in *lamedh-yodh* verbs in other dialects, it is levelled through all *lamedh-yodh* verbs and is not lexicalized, e.g., in Samaritan Aramaic the new endings of the 2 m.s. perfect ־יך (*-ək*) and 2 m.pl. ־יכון (*-īkon)*.[36] The fact that the endings of הוינה and הוית differ from those of other *lamedh-yodh* verbs in the Cairo Genizah fragments suggests that the attempt to distinguish the different persons is not at play in the creation of these two unique forms.

For this reason, Kutscher's proposal to view הוינא as a passive participle with an enclitic pronoun merits serious consideration. Moreover, the pointing of the forms of הוית with *daghesh* could conceivably reflect the suffixing of the independent 2 m.s. pronoun *ʾat(t)* to the passive participle of הוה.[37] Also there is clear evidence in later Aramaic that the passive participle (< **qaṭīl*) of intransitive verbs (הוה is the intransitive verb *par excellence*) with suffixed independent pronouns can function as the preterite, as has been shown by S. Hopkins[38] in his description of the Jewish Neo-Aramaic dialect of Kerend.

In Kerend, which is representative of all the Jewish dialects of Iranian Kurdistan, the old passive participle with suffixed *l-* pronouns serves as the preterite of transitive verbs (e.g., *qṭilli* "I killed"), but the passive participle with suffixed independent pronouns serves as the preterite of intransitive verbs (e.g., *qīmna* "I stood"). The suffixing of the independent pronouns is attested with 1 s. and pl. and 2 s. and pl. pronouns:[39] 1 m. *qīmna*, 1 f. *qīman(a)*, 2 m.s. *qīmet*, 2 f.s. *qīmat*, 1 pl. *qīmex(īn)*, 2 pl. *qīmetu*. Although the use of the passive participle followed by the

[35]This is based on the pointings of אתנלֵית.

[36]Z. Ben-Ḥayyim, *The Literary and Oral Tradition of Hebrew and Aramaic amongst the Samaritans*, Vol.III, Part II, p. 110 (Hebrew); R. Macuch, *Grammatik des samaritanischen Aramäisch* (Berlin-New York 1982), p. 204.

[37]It is difficult to explain why *hăwe* + *ʾăna* > *hăwena* but *hăwe* + *ʾat(t)* > *hăwit*, unless the pointings with *ḥireq* should be seen in the context of the fluctuation of *ṣere* and *ḥireq* and thus reflect *e*. The existence of *ḥireq* in four different manuscripts, however, strongly suggests a realization of *hăwit*.

[38] S. Hopkins, "Neo-Aramaic Dialects and the Formation of the Preterite," *JSS* 34 (1989), pp. 413-432.

[39]The 3 person forms are 3 m.s. *qīm*, 3 f.s. *qīma*, 3 pl. *qīmi*.

preposition *l-* with pronouns functioning as a perfect (e.g., קים לי "I have stood") can be found on occasion in Late Eastern Aramaic dialects (Syriac, Mandaic, Babylonian Talmudic) and the passive participle with suffixed *l-* pronouns is a salient feature of the verbal system in Eastern Neo-Aramaic, the variety of Neo-Aramaic reported by Hopkins is the first in which the passive participle of intransitive verbs with enclitic independent pronouns expresses the preterite.[40]

Similarly, it is conceivable that the 1 pl. הֲוֵינַן נְחָתִין Gen 44:18 "we came down" (p.133) is a reflex of *hăwe* + *ʾanan* and that הוויתון Exod 22:20 "you were" (p.293) reflects *hăwe* + *ʾatton*. The 3rd person forms of the perfect, however, all reflect **qaṭala* הֲוָוה *hăwa* Gen 31:42 (p.61), הֲוָות *hăwaṯ* Exod 9:24 (p.124), הֲוֹון *hăwon* Gen 4:8 (p.7), הווין *hăwen* Gn 41:21 (p.109).

Even though the parallel of the passive participle with enclitic independent pronoun comes from an Eastern variety of Neo-Aramaic, and the language of the Cairo Genizah fragments is of the Western Aramaic variety, it certainly is relevant that the verb הוה in Western Neo-Aramaic develops differently from other *lamedh-yodh* verbs. It is not inflected by itself, but rather the verb can fuse with either 1) the enclitic passive participle *yhīb* > *yīb* (*hwā* + *yīb* > *wōb* "he was"), which is then fully inflected, or 2) the predicator of existence *īt* (*hwā* + *īṯ* > *wōṯ* "he was"; *hāwē* + *īṯ* > *ōṯ* "there is/was").[41]

Could הוינא and הוית reflect the suffixing of independent pronouns to the active participle *hāwe*? One reason Lund cites for taking הוינא as a backformation from the 1 pl. perfect הוינן is the pointing with a reduced vowel, for in his opinion, were this the active participle *hāwe*, one would expect הָוֵינָא. Here too there is evidence in Aramaic for the inflection of an active participle with enclitic pronouns like a perfect. S. Morag has shown that the active participle with enclitic pronouns in the Yemenite reading tradition of the Babylonian Talmud becomes identical in form to the perfect[42], and this is related to the increasing use of the participle in narrating past events replacing the perfect form.[43] Evidence of this process can also be found in Yemenite Talmud manuscripts[44] and manuscripts of Targum Onqelos.[45]

---

[40]In Jewish Azerbaijani the passive participle of intransitive verbs with enclitic independent pronouns expresses the perfect. See Hopkins, n. 35.

[41]Spitaler, *Grammatik*, pp. 206-209. It should be added that the classical Aramaic perfect conjugation has survived in Central and Eastern Neo-Aramaic only in the fossilized past-converter *-wa* (<*hwā*).

[42]The initial vowel of the participle reduces to *shewa*.

[43]S. Morag, *The Yemenite Tradition. Historical Aspects and Transmission, Phonology, The Verbal System* (Jerusalem 1988), pp. 134-135 (Hebrew). For *lamedh-yodh* verbs, see, pp. 260-261.

[44]Y. Kara, *Babylonian Aramaic in the Yemenite Manuscripts of the Talmud: Orthography, Phonology and Morphology of the Verb, Eda weLashon* X (Jerusalem 1983), pp. 175-178 (Hebrew).

[45]Dalman, *Grammatik*, pp. 289, 340, 352.

C. Conclusion

In conclusion, the inflection of the perfect of *lamedh-yodh* verbs as reflected in the Cairo Genizah fragments differs from the inflection of *lamedh-yodh* verbs in other dialects, with the exception of Galilean Aramaic. The influence of the strong verb on *lamedh-yodh* verbs is striking.[46] The patterning of *lamedh-yodh* on the strong verb manifests itself in the creation of biforms in the derived conjugations. One finds the 1 s. *bĕnet̲* in Peal, but in the derived conjugations the biforms *-et̲/-yet̲*: *bannet̲/bannĕyet̲, ʾab̲net̲/ʾab̲neyet̲, ʾet̲bĕnet̲/ʾet̲banyet̲, ʾet̲bannet̲/ʾet̲bannĕyet̲*. In the 2 m.s., the vowel *e* of the ending *-et̲* has its origin in the derived conjugations of the strong verb. The influence of the strong verb is also apparent in the inflection of the 3 f.s. in the derived conjugations: *bannĕyat̲, ʾab̲nĕyat̲, ʾet̲banyat̲, ʾet̲bannĕyat̲*.

These biforms are also reflected in forms found in the non-Genizah sources of Palestinian Targum and in texts of Galilean Aramaic,[47] including reliable manuscripts. It must be added that in other texts of Palestinian Targum and of Galilean Aramaic, biforms of the 1 s., 2 m.s., and 3 f.s. can be found in all conjugations, including Peal. The vocalization of forms like 1 s. בעית as *bĕʿayit̲*, 2 m.s. חטיית as *ḥăṭayit̲*, or 3 f.s. חמית as *ḥămayit̲* as suggested by Dalman[48] and Odeberg[49] is not supported by the pointed evidence of the Cairo Genizah fragments. Both Dalman and Odeberg explain the forms with double *yodh* as having been created on the pattern of the strong verb of Targum Onqelos 1 s. *qĕṭalit̲*, 3 f.s. *qĕṭalat̲*. While they are certainly correct in seeing the influence of the strong verb, the forms with double *yodh* are to be explained on the analogy of the Palestinian Targum strong verb forms *qaṭlet̲, qaṭlat̲*.

The inflection of the perfect of the verb הוה is unique to the Palestinian Targum and to Galilean Aramaic and it differs from other *lamedh-yodh* verbs in these dialects. While הוינא may be a backformation from the 1 pl. הוינן, it, together with the pointed forms of the 2 m.s. הַיִּת with *daghesh*, could point to an original participial form with enclitic pronouns (perhaps too the 2 f.s. הוייה of Targum

---

[46]It should be added that strong verb influence on the weak verb is discernible too in other verbal classes in the Cairo Genizah fragments, for example, verbs *lamedh-* guttural (e.g., אתבוע Gen 9:5 "I shall demand" [p.25]) for expected אתבע), and *ayin-waw/yodh* verbs (Ethpeel/Ettaphal אֶתְנַיַּיח Gen 35:9 "he rested" [p.75], אִתְנְיַיח Exod 20:11 [p.267] for expected אֶתְנִיח or אֶתְנָח; or the ultimate stress on מִיתַתְ Gen 35:9 "she died" [p.75], קָמַתְ Gen 38:19 "she arose" [p.87] for expected קָמַת, מִיתַת).

[47]B. Levy, "The Language of Neophyti 1: A Description and Comparative Grammar of the Palestinian Targum," Ph.D. thesis, New York University 1974, p. 161; D.M. Golomb, *A Grammar of Targum Neofiti* (HSM 34) (Chico 1985), p. 156. The pointings of Galilean Aramaic forms given by Dalman (*Grammatik*, pp. 341-343), Odeberg (H. Odeberg, *The Aramaic Portions of Bereshit Rabba with Grammar of Galilaean Aramaic* (Lund-Leipzig 1939), II, pp. 32-39) and Levias (*Grammar*, 1986, pp. 132-133) are not based on reliable manuscripts.

[48]Dalman, *Grammatik*, p. 338.

[49]Odeberg, *Grammar*, II, p. 33. He also suggests the realizations of 1 s. *binyēt̲(i)*, 3 f. *binyat̲*. Levias (*Grammar*, pp. 130-135) is the only grammarian to vocalize the 1 s. as *banyēt̲*.

Neophyti, and the 1 pl. הוינן, 2 m.pl. הוויתון from the Cairo Genizah). Kutscher's suggestion to take הוינא as a passive participle with past meaning is supported not only by Aramaic dialects where the passive participle functions as a perfect (e.g., Galilean Aramaic אנה שמיע "I have heard"), but particularly in those varieties of Aramaic in which the passive participle with enclitic pronouns functions as the preterite, as in the Jewish Eastern Neo-Aramaic dialects of Iranian Kurdistan. There is also evidence, however, for taking הוינא not as an originally passive participle with enclitic pronoun, but rather as an originally active participle that has been remodelled on the pattern of the perfect, as in the Yemenite reading tradition of the Babylonian Talmud. This merging follows from the growing use of the participle in past tense narration.

Pagan Incantations in Aramaic Magic Bowls

Tapani Harviainen — University of Helsinki

In the ancient Near East there was a close connection between religion and the alphabetical script system. A similar phenomenon is observable at later periods, e.g. in Eastern Europe. Today, we find this kind of marked boundary in Yugoslavia, in particular. The great majority of the citizens of the dissident republics of Slovenia and Croatia profess the Roman Catholic faith and, as a consequence, they have written Slovenian and Serbo-Croat in the Latin (Roman) alphabet. By contrast, the Serbs have been Eastern Orthodox Christians and, consequently, they spell the same Serbo-Croatian language in the traditional alphabet of Orthodox culture, i.e. an adapted form of the Cyrillic characters.

How is one to define the connection between religions and magic bowls after such an introduction? The reply seems to be the classic one: the bowls written in Hebrew characters were written by Jews, those in Mandaic letters are Mandaean in regard to religion, and the Syriac characters were those used by Christians, even in Palestine, outside the East Aramaic area.

However, we know that the content of bowl incantations is not in harmony with this response. The main obstacle consists in the enormous number of syncretistic features which appear in the texts themselves. It is a well-known fact that the bowl incantations deviate radically from the main lines of Judaism or Christianity. In this paper I shall designate incantation texts Mandaean, Jewish or Syriac solely *on the basis of the script.*[1]

With regard to the syncretistic nature of bowl incantations we may resort to at least one adequate explanation. *Horror vacui*, the avoidance of empty space, is a leading principle of popular magic. To be on the safe side, it is also worthwhile to pay attention to foreign cults, demons, and deities. The avoidance of dangerous gaps is demonstrated by the alphabet which appears at the end of several bowl incantations. Since all words, both beneficent and evil, are included in the alphabet, the last circle with a complete alphabet may be considered to render the incantation complete.[2]

---

[1]Occasionally the term "Aramaic incantation" has been used with reference to the "Jewish" bowls. However, this designation makes the terminology even more unsatisfactory, since all three dialects represent different branches of the Aramaic language; in addition, the Jewish script used in bowls derives its origin from Jewish-Hebrew characters developed by the Jews in Palestine.

[2]When employed in magic bowls, it is more likely that the alphabet has a magical reason than a scholastic or educational one, cf. Alan R. Millard, "*ʾbgd* ... — Magic spell or educational exercise?", *Eretz-Israel* 18 (Nahman Avigad Volume 1985), pp. 39*-42*.

In our view, texts displaying a pronounced syncretistic nature could be called pagan. At all times and in all places there has been a discrepancy between the high-level ideology of a religion and its manifestations among the masses. However, alongside syncretistic phenomena in the bowls, we must pay attention to expressions which, in my opinion, are distinctive marks of religious identification. First, I should like to deal with the question of the opening formulae of bowl texts.

Mandaean texts. In the thirty-one Mandaic texts published by Edwin Yamauchi[3] the opening phrase appears in three main forms: (1) *asuta* (etc.) *thui-lẖ l-X bar Y* "may there be salvation[4] to (with the name of the client)", this wish occurring seven times; (2) *ʿpika krika ʿsir* "repulsed, averted, bound (are all the curses etc.)", this occurring ten times, while (3) the third phrase: "in the name of Life" *b-šuma ḏ-hiia*, introduces an incantation eleven times. These three formulae cover 28 cases out of the total of 31. The Mandaic incantations published since Yamauchi's book do not alter the general picture.[5]

Jewish bowls. In one hundred and four Jewish bowls which I have examined — obviously I have not been able to find all of the most recent publications[6] — the most common initial phrases constitute five groups with slighter variation: (1) "This is the amulet of" — and then a personal name (*haden qemiʿa / ṣilma d-NN*) — eight occurrences;[7] (2) "This bowl is designated for the salvation of NN" (*mezamman hana kasa / qemiʿa le-ʾasuta de-NN*) — this phrase occurs seven times,[8] (3) "Salvation from the heavens for" plus personal names (*ʾasuta men šemayya le-NN*), eleven or thirteen instances;[9] (4) "Sealed and doubly-sealed and bound are the house etc. of X bar Y" (*ḥatim wa-mḥattam beteh* etc. *d-X bar Y*) — ten bowls;[10] and (5) "In your name, Lord of salvation, great Saviour of love" (*bi-šmak mare ʾasuta ʾasya rabba de-raḥme*),[11] which in this form occurs six times[12] and as shorter variants eleven times

---

[3]*Mandaic Incantation Texts* (American Oriental Series 49, New Haven 1967).

[4]Or "healing", "health", "cure"; German "Heil" would be an apposite rendering of *ʾasuta.*

[5]For the exceptional text, McCullough Bowl D, see below note 22.

[6]In agreement with the method adopted by Isbell (Charles D. Isbell, *Corpus of the Aramaic Incantation Bowls.* Society of Biblical Literature, Dissertation Series, Number 17 [Missoula 1975], p. 2), only those bowls which have been published with legible photographs or facsimiles have been included in this examination. I quote the bowls included in the Corpus of Isbell according to the text numbers given by him; for the original publications and other details, see ibid. Several hundred unpublished bowls are kept in various museums and collections; thus all general conclusions concerning magic bowls must be considered preliminary.

[7]Isbell, Text nos. 1, 16, 18, 54, 55, 61, 69; M.J. Geller, "Eight incantation bowls", *OLP* 17 (1986), pp. 101-117), Aaron Bowl A.

[8]Isbell nos. 14, 42, 47, 53, 59, 60; Joseph Naveh, Shaul Shaked, *Amulets and Magic Bowls. Aramaic Incantations of Late Antiquity* (Jerusalem-Leiden 1985), Bowl 7.

[9]Isbell nos. 17, 23, 24, 32, 34, 64, 66, 72, (20), (68); Naveh–Shaked, Bowl 3; M.J. Geller, "Two incantation bowls inscribed in Syriac and Aramaic" *BSOAS* 39 (1976), pp. 422-427, Bowl B; Tapani Harviainen, "An Aramaic incantation bowl from Borsippa – another specimen of Eastern Aramaic "koiné". Appendix: A cryptographic bowl text or an original fake?" *Studia Orientalia* 51 (1981), p. 14

[10]Isbell nos. 28, 29, 30, 31, 38, 50, 51; A.J. Borisov, "Epigraficheskie zametki", *Epigrafika Vostoka* 19 (1969), pp. 1-13, ii; K.A.D. Smelik, "An Aramaic incantation bowl in the Allard Pierson Museum", *Bibliotheca Orientalis*, 35, cols. 174-177); Geller 1986, Aaron Bowl F.

[11]We may ask, who is *mare ʾasuta ʾasya rabba de-raḥme*, "Lord of salvation, great Saviour of love"? An answer seems to be implied by a number of wordings in other Jewish bowls: "in your name I am

(*bi-šmak mare šemayya, bi- / li-šmakh ʾani ʿośe* etc.).[13] These five groups include 57 cases out of the total of 104 texts. Individual openings as well as combinations of the aforementioned phrases are rather numerous — 37 instances — and in ten bowls the beginning has disappeared.

Alongside the concrete evidence, it is important to notice which types of opening phrase *do not* appear in Jewish bowls. No Jewish Aramaic bowl text begins with the Mandaean formula "in the name of Life". Other Mandaean phrases also have very few parallels in Jewish bowls. We shall soon encounter the expression: "This bowl is designated for the salvation of NN", in connection with Syriac bowls.[14]

Syriac bowls. With regard to the opening phrase, the Syriac bowls are the most stereotyped. Of twenty-six Syriac bowl texts, the beginning is visible in sixteen. Twelve of these sixteen begin with the words "This bowl / amulet is designated for the salvation / for the sealing of the house etc. of NN" (*mezamman hana kasa / qemiʿa l-asyuta / la-ḥtamta de-bayteh* etc. *de-* + personal name). The phrase *ḥatim bayteh de-NN* ("sealed is the house of NN") twice opens a Syriac bowl text. As mentioned above, the first type of incipit (*mezamman hana kasa le-ʾasuta de-NN*) occurs in seven Jewish bowls.

We may further ask, what is lacking in Syriac bowls? There is no invocation of a god or deity at the beginning. Syriac is considered to be the language of eastern Aramaic Christians. This being the case, it is quite probable that Christian formulae would occur in Syriac incantations. In fact, only one bowl *ends* "in the name of the Father and of the Son and of the Holy Spirit".[15] None begins with these words.

In this respect the Syriac amulets published by Philippe Gignoux[16] differ from the bowl texts; Gignoux dates the amulets to the sixth or seventh century, i.e. to the period of Syriac bowls. Two of his three very syncretistic amulet incantations commence *be-šum ʾaba wa-bra we-ruḥa qaddišta*, "in the name of the Father and of the Son and of the Holy Spirit". It is also the normal introductory formula of the near-

acting, Yahwe the Great God" (Isbell no. 9), "in the name of God, the God of Gods" (Borisov, iii, p. 11, end), and "in the name of Yahwe Sebaoth, the God of Israel" (Smelik, c. 176, line 2). Thus it is most probable that the Lord of salvation refers to the God of Israel, Yahwe, the Saviour and Healer of his people.

[12]Isbell nos. 3, 4, 6, 8, 21, 44.

[13]Isbell nos. 9, 12, 19, 20, 26, 36, 39, 70; Naveh–Shaked, Bowl 5; Geller 1986, Aaron Bowl B; J. Oelsner, "Naveh, Joseph, and Shaul Shaked: Amulets and Magic Bowls" (review article, *Orientalistische Literaturzeitung* 84 [1989], cols. 39-41).

[14]In the Jewish bowls known to me, the only distinctly "heretical" or "pagan" initial phrase reads: "By the power of the Great One (*rabba*), and by the command of the angels, and by the name of the lord Bagdana ʾAziza, the great one of the gods (*rabba de-ʾelahe*), and the king, head of sixty kingdoms, etc.". However, this text, Naveh–Shaked Bowl 13 (pp. 198-214), is also unique in many other respects.

[15]Victor Hamilton, *Syriac Incantation Bowls* (Dissertation, Brandeis University 1971, University Microfilms International, Ann Arbor, 71-30,130), Text 2 (= J.A. Montgomery, "A Syriac incantation with Christian formula", *American Journal of Semitic Languages and Literatures* 34 [1917-18], pp. 137-139). In this article the Syriac bowls have been referred to according to the text numbers given by Hamilton.

[16]*Incantations magiques syriaques*. Collection de la Revue des Études Juives dirigée par Gérard Nahon et Charles Touati (Louvain-Paris 1987).

modern Syriac amulets published by Hermann Gollancz.[17] The contents of the Syriac amulets and the bowl texts do not differ much from each other; in the Syriac bowl texts, however, all Christian connotations are very rare.

The bowls vary in respect of the script and language or dialect, as well as in respect of the initial sentences. It is not only the alphabet and script, but also the opening phrases which separate the different groups of Eastern Aramaeans. The Mandaeans do not borrow opening formulae from Jewish texts, and despite the considerable number of different opening phrases in the Jewish bowls, the introductory formulae of other bowls have not been introduced into them. "This bowl / amulet is designated to the salvation of NN" (*mezamman hana kasa / qemiᶜa l-asyuta*) is the sole phrase which passes over from one script and from one group to another. It occurs in Jewish and Syriac bowls, but not in the Mandaean ones.

This observation becomes increasingly significant when we bear in mind that other phrases, demons, gods, angels, *nomina barbarica*, and even complete incantations were used by the Mesopotamian bowl magicians as common material. Also magic signs, crosses, drawings, and pictures on bowls are similar.[18]

A conclusive example of the working methods adopted by the bowl magicians is presented by a Jewish bowl which I published in 1981.[19] A kind of Mandaean *Vorlage* of this text was discovered by Jonas Greenfield and Joseph Naveh on a Mandaean lead amulet,[20] and a close parallel to this Mandaean lead roll text was published by Rudolph Macuch in 1967-1968.[21] In Macuch's text, however, the beginning of the incantation is broken and has disappeared.[22]

The main differences between the Mandaean *Vorlage* and its Jewish adaptation consist in the opening formulae as well as in the list of helpers. In the opening phrase of the lead roll, salvation is invoked for the Mandaean gentleman *Aban bar Sisin-anahid* in the name of Life: *b-šumẖ/a ḏ hiia asuta (u-zrzta u-htmta) thui lẖ l-aban br*

17 *The Book of Protection, Being a Collection of Syriac Charms* (London 1912, repr. APA-Philo Press, Amsterdam 1976).

18 Hamilton, pp. 8-9, 96.

19 *Studia Orientalia*, 51 (1981), p. 14 see above, note 9.

20 Jonas Greenfield, Josef Naveh, "Qamiᶜ mandaᶜi baᶜal arbaᶜ hašbaᶜot", *Eretz-Israel*, 18 (Nahman Avigad Volume 1985), pp. 97-107, and Plates xxi-xxii); Text *beth*, lines 3-29, and Text *gimel*, lines 2-20, include the counterparts of the Jewish bowl published by me. On the basis of Mandaic words and expressions in the Jewish bowl text, Greenfield and Naveh conclude that a Jewish magician or writer copied the Mandaean text without understanding it completely (p. 97).

21 "Altmandäische Bleirollen", I d, lines 65-84, in Fr. Altheim, R. Stiehl, *Die Araber in der Alten Welt*, IV (Berlin 1967), pp. 91-203 and V/1 (Berlin 1968), pp. 34-72.

22 On the other hand, a couple of Syriac (Hamilton, Texts 1 and 4) and Mandaean (McCullough, Bowl D, see below) bowl texts obviously go back to Jewish incantations, see J. N. Epstein, "Glosses babylo-araméennes", *Revue des études juives* 73 (1921), pp. 27-58, and 74 (1922), pp. 40-72); Naveh–Shaked, pp. 18-19. The Mandaic Bowl D published by W.S. McCullough (*Jewish and Mandaean Incantation Bowls in the Royal Ontario Museum* [Toronto 1967], pp. 28-47) is almost completely devoid of Mandaean features but includes numerous parallels to Jewish expressions, see Jonas C. Greenfield, "Notes on some Aramaic and Mandaic magic bowls" *JANES* 5 (The Gaster Festschrift 1973), pp. 149-156), pp. 154-155. It is important to note that the opening phrase (*asara u‹a›suta uhtamta uzr‹z›ta ... l-baita ...*) of this exceptional bowl does not occur in the same form in other bowls known to me.

sisinanahid (*ʾalef* 1, *bet* 1, *dalet* 1). And a mighty angel (*mlaka taqipa*) will be a wall and boundary for him between good and evil (*gimel* 2-3). The opening phrases: "in the name of Life" and "may there be salvation to-X", are each typical of Mandaean bowl incantations, as mentioned above.

However, the Jewish adaptation written for *Keyaniḥaye bar Ḥatai* does not refer to the name of Life. Instead, it commences with an exceptional request written horizontally in the centre of the bowl: *šemaʿu we-qabbelu h de-zahar yy*. The letters *he* and *yod-yod* refer to the Lord of the Jews, and the request reads "accept the Lord who has warned, Yahwe!" This invocation is followed by a common opening formula: *ʾasuta men šemayya li-Kyaniḥaye*, a phrase which is typical of Jewish bowl texts. The helpers of Keyaniḥaye include the mercies of heaven (*raḥme di-šmayya*, line 3) and three angels called Sariel, Mazdat (?) and ʾEkhrum (8); at the end of the text, Keyaniḥaye bar Ḥatai is bound and sealed "with the signet-ring of Great Selitos" (12).

The dangers and adversaries are almost identical in both incantations. However, the Jewish version differs from the Mandaean source in respect of the openings and the helpers.

This is exactly what is to be expected. The outside world, dangers external to ourselves, are equal irrespective of each in-group. Consequently, the description of the dangerous external world may be outlined with general expressions used in common. By contrast, dependence on one's own group demands the employment of internal characteristics, one's own catchwords. And it is safer to rely on one's own helpers.

Obviously, it is not too far-fetched to draw a parallel between the initial phrases of the incantations and the different types of *basmala*, i.e. the headings which in many cultures indicate the religious affinity of a writer.

Next we may examine the contents of the Jewish bowls in respect of the opening formulae as well as of Jewish features, viz. biblical names and epithets of God, quotations from the Bible and references to it.

In 57 bowl texts beginning with one of the five initial formulae mentioned above, only ten do not reveal these types of Jewish features.[23] On the other hand, 23 bowls[24] could be placed under the heading "texts without a special opening phrase but with Jewish features". However, an equal number of bowls (24) are without a special opening phrase and without Jewish features.[25]

---

[23] Isbell nos. 21, 28, 29, 30, 31, 32, 36, 38; Geller 1986, Aaron Bowl F; Oelsner. The classification of bowl texts cannot be totally unambiguous with respect to these features.

[24] Isbell nos. 13, 16, 17, 20, 22, 25, 33, 43, 44, 48, 52, 55, 65, 67, 69; Naveh–Shaked, bowls 9, 13; Charles D. Isbell, "Two new Aramaic incantation bowls", *BASOR* 223 (1976), pp. 15-23, A and B; Borisov (1969), iv; Harviainen (1981); Cyrus H. Gordon, "Two Aramaic incantations", *Biblical and Near Eastern Studies: Essays in Honor of William Sanford LaSor*, ed. Gary A. Tuttle (Grand Rapids 1978), pp. 231-244, i; McCullough, Bowl A (for the reading of the text, see Harviainen 1981, p. 10, n. 1).

[25] Isbell nos. 1, 2, 5, 7, 11, 15, 18, 27, (40), 41, 46, 54, 57, 58, 61, 62, 71; Naveh–Shaked, Bowls 4, 6, 8, 12a, 12b; Geller 1986, Pearson Bowl and Aaron Bowl D. It is worthy of note that among the three parallel texts, Naveh–Shaked Bowls 12 a, 12 b, and Oelsner, which do not include Jewish

Without going into details, such an examination leads to the conclusion that in the majority of Jewish bowls there is an evident connection between (1) the Jewish script, (2) the distinctive initial phrases typical of these texts, and (3) the Jewish features of the contents.

Similarly, the opening phrases distinguish the Mandaean incantations from their Jewish and Syriac counterparts; so especially the typically Mandaean *basmala*: *bu-šmi ad-heyyi*, "in the name of Life". Also the specifically Mandaean supernatural beings lend a distinctive character to these texts.

In the light of these observations, a reconsideration of the Syriac bowls yields interesting results: by contrast to the Jewish and Mandaean incantations these texts do not offer distinctive opening phrases — almost the sole opening is the neutral statement: *mezamman hana qemiʿa / kasa l-asyuta de-bayteh (etc.) de-NN.* This opening is the only one which has crossed the boundaries between the main groups of Mesopotamian bowl texts. In addition to this lack of a typical basmala, the Syriac bowl texts also lack references to Christianity, Judaism or Zoroastrian religion. This *dual* evidence provides significant concrete support for the hypothesis of a pagan origin for the Syriac bowl texts; previously it has been proposed on the basis of general impressions.[26]

Finally, a few words about the script used in Syriac bowls. There are bowls written in Syriac Estrangela.[27] However, in the majority of the bowls[28] the Syriac script resembles Palmyrene cursive, on the one hand, and Manichaean writing, on the other. Joseph Naveh calls this script proto-Manichaean and — hypothetically — explains it as an offshoot of the cursive style of the eastern Aramaic script which was probably used in the Seleucid empire. This eastern cursive was adopted by both the Syrians and the Palmyrenes. In Mesopotamia it was preserved "presumably in some religious circles" and, later, in the Manichaean texts and in Syriac incantation bowls. Elsewhere the Syriac script underwent a rapid development into Estrangela and other Syriac forms.[29]

According to Javier Teixidor and Joseph Naveh, the Syriac bowls date back to the period c. 600 A.D.[30] The lack of discoveries intermediate between these Syriac

---

features, 12a is without an opening phrase, 12b has an opening without an exact counterpart in other bowls while the bowl published by Oelsner begins with the common phrase: "In your name I make this amulet".

[26]E.g. by Naveh–Shaked, p. 18.

[27]Hamilton, Texts 11-16; Tapani Harviainen, "A Syriac incantation bowl in the Finnish National Museum, Helsinki. A specimen of Eastern Aramaic 'koiné'", *Studia Orientalia* 51, (1978-81),1.. Instead of I.M. 7863, the correct Iraqi Museum number of the bowl is I.M. 78630 (I am grateful to Dr. Erica Hunter for the clarification); Naveh–Shaked, Bowl 10. For various types of Estrangela, see Moller 1988 (below, note 35).

[28]Hamilton, Texts 1-9 and 16-21; Naveh–Shaked, Bowl 1.

[29]Joseph Naveh, *Early History of the Alphabet* (Jerusalem-Leiden 1982), pp. 149-153; Naveh–Shaked, p. 126.

[30]"The Syriac incantation bowls in the Iraq Museum", *Sumer* 18 (1962), pp. 51-62, pp. 61-62; Naveh, p. 151.

bowls and the supposed ancestors of their type of script leaves a number of questions open.

I have proposed new arguments for the pagan nature of the Syriac bowls and I have referred to the close connection between religion and script in the Near East. In my opinion, the employment of the proto-Manichaean script in Syriac bowls could be connected with the paganism of these Syriac texts. The question is: in which script did pagans write Aramaic in Mesopotamia? Although we have to bear in mind that Gentiles too may learn Hebrew, Jewish Aramaic and Mandaic, the Hebrew and Mandaic scripts bear characteristics of closed religious groups. Nevertheless, the 24 Jewish bowls without Jewish phraseology and without a *basmala* typical of Jewish bowls should be noted carefully in any discussion of paganism in bowl incantations.

Syriac script derives its origins from the pre-Christian period and, consequently, it was used originally by pagans. After the Christianization of the area, which was only partial, pagans continued to read and write books. One proof of this is included in the prophecy of Baba, who lived in Harran before the 8th century and "whose books the pagans continuously read, (and) who is renowned as a prophet amongst them".[31] Similarly, it is quite improbable that the Syriac Bar-Theon Amulet[32] would represent a Christian or Jewish text.

In the third century, Estrangela was used in early Syriac documents which do not reveal any Christian features — I refer to the Deed of Sale from Dura Europos as well as to the two documents described recently by Javier Teixidor.[33] However, in the fifth century the Syriac Estrangela script (and later also Serto and the Nestorian script) was employed for writing a rich Christian literature, in particular. As a consequence, *this* script came to be considered the script of Christians.

As far as I know, we do not possess specimens of pagan Syriac autographs or inscriptions from the fourth, fifth or sixth centuries. Thus the following analogies may be worthy of consideration.

In Russia, the Church Slavonic characters have continued to be employed, especially in religious texts, icons and cultic utensils, and also in the Russian language, despite the introduction of the new Russian alphabet by Peter the Great at the beginning of the 18th century; of late, the old characters have been invested with a nostalgic flavour of "Holy Russia". On the Jewish side, Hebrew square script, Rashi script and

[31]See Sebastian Brock, "A Syriac collection of prophecies of the pagan philosophers", *OLP* 14 (1983), pp. 203-246, § 27, p. 233 (in Syriac, p. 224; *terminus ante quem* the 8th century, pp. 207-212). For the use of Syriac by pagans (in Harran) see also J.B. Segal, *Edessa and Harran* (Inaugural lecture, London 1963), p. 21, and Sebastian P. Brock, "Three Thousand Years of Aramaic Literature", *Aram* 1 (1989), pp. 11-23, p. 13: "It is very possible (and indeed quite likely) that there also existed a pagan Aramaic literature ... but which has all been lost. ... A few relics of such a pagan literature do, however, survive in Syriac: amongst these is a letter of advice from a certain philosopher Mara to his son Serapion, and some utterances which are attributed to the prophet Baba of Harran."

[32]Naveh–Shaked, Amulet 6, pp. 63-69; the dating of the amulet is insecure.

[33]"Deux documents syriaques du IIIe siècle après J.-C., provenant du Moyen Euphrate", *Comptes rendus de l'Académie des inscriptions et belles-lettres*, (Paris, January-March 1990), pp. 144-166.

various types of cursive could be mentioned as an example of the ideology of sacred and less sacred forms of the characters. And if we return to the beginning of this paper, Croatia offers us an instructive case of a special connection between script and religion: the originally eastern Greek-Orthodox (Church Slavonic) Glagolitic script has been retained as the script of liturgical books by the Roman Catholic Church in Croatia until this century, while in Orthodox countries Glagolica was replaced by Cyrillic characters not later than the 12th century; by contrast to the "Orthodox" Cyrillic letters, the Glagolitic alphabet was considered to be the Roman Catholic Slavonic script, which in the Middle Ages was also occasionally used in other Slavonic countries of Roman Catholic faith.[34]

As a parallel phenomenon, Syriac pagan bowl texts could be explained as representing the last vestiges of non-Christian Syriac writings in which the employment of the proto-Manichaean, non-Christian script was an important distinguishing mark. The preservation of a sacred, pagan proto-Manichaean script in magic objects, in particular, is in agreement with what we may expect; the bowls in Estrangela reflect the disappearance of this distinction.[35] The exceptional features in the Syriac language of the bowls accord well with this suggestion. The hypothesis implies that a pagan tradition of writing in a type of Syriac was in existence to a greater extent than we have previously thought. If we take into account the longevity and variety of pagan cults in Mesopotamia, the absence of pagan literary traditions during the first half of the first millennium is very improbable. Much more probable is the almost complete disappearance of their achievements at the hands of active religions with a new message.

[34]For the interesting history of Glagolitic script, see Josip Hamm, "Glagoljica", *Enciklopedija Jugoslavije* 4 (Zagreb 1986), pp. 391-398; I am grateful to Father R. Murray for reminding me of the rôle of Glagolica in Croatia. As a case of a religious alphabet boundary in Lutheran countries, one could mention the long-lived employment of Gothic type as true Lutheran characters in Northern European pietistic devotional literature until the middle of this century; Roman type was considered to be characteristic of secular texts.

[35]In fact, the development and ramification of Estrangela have a considerably more complicated history than has been thought, see Garth I. Moller, "Towards a new typology of the Syriac manuscript alphabet", *Journal of Northwest Semitic Languages* 14 (1988), pp. 153-197. Nevertheless, the proto-Manichaean script deviates from various variants of Estrangela to such an extent that a significant opposition can be seen to prevail between these two types of script.

Combat and Conflict In Incantation Bowls : Studies On Two Aramaic Specimens From Nippur

Erica C.D. Hunter — Faculty of Oriental Studies, Cambridge

In 1989 the Oriental Institute of the University of Chicago conducted its 18th season at Nippur, marking a centenary of archaeological work at this site. A century earlier, in 1889 the campaign of the University of Pennsylvania led by John Peters excavated part of the West mound, discovering in the process a Parthian "villa with a Court of Columns".[1] In the stratum above, more than a hundred incantation bowls were found, in a residential quarter that was termed a Jewish settlement. Forty specimens were published by James Montgomery in his celebrated work, *Aramaic Incantation Texts from Nippur* (Philadelphia 1913). Whilst numerous incantation bowls have been found in both disturbed and undisturbed contexts at Nippur over the last hundred years, the group of six specimens which were excavated in 1989 are distinguished by their location; Area WG adjoins the Jewish settlement.[2]

The incantation bowls came to light in Level III of the WG area which spans the transition from the late Sassanid era to the Islamic period. This level is found directly below Level II that has been designated as Early Abbasid, with its *terminus post quem* being fixed by the discovery of a coin minted in Basra in 782 A.D. At what stage within Level III (extending from the late sixth century A.D.–mid eighth century A.D.) the incantation bowls were buried is difficult to say. However, this chronology would accommodate Montgomery's conclusion that the Nippur texts should be placed "in a period not earlier than the sixth or the beginning of the seventh century."[3] A later date in the eighth century A.D. for the incantation bowls could also be proposed, on the basis of a recent find from the Abbasid stratum of Bidjan, near Ana in west Iraq which Michel Gawlikowski assigned to the eighth century A.D.[4]

The placement of the incantation bowls in the WG area re-affirms the information recorded by Hilprecht in his monograph, *Exploration in Bible Lands during the 19th Century* (Philadelphia 1903), that includes an *in situ* photograph of the 1888 finds.[5] As with the earlier discoveries, those from 1989 are from a domestic

[1]See J. P. Peters, *Nippur*, 2 vols., (New York 1897), II, pp. 172 ff.
[2]See Erica C. D. Hunter, "Aramaic and Mandaic Incantation Bowls from Nippur", in McGuire Gibson (ed.) *The Sasanian-Islamic Transition at Nippur, Excavations at Area WG* (Oriental Institute Publications) (in press), for a comprehensive report on the incantation bowls from the 18th season.
[3]Montgomery, op.cit., p. 105.
[4]M. Gawlikowski, "Une coupe magique araméene", *Semitica* 38 (1990), p. 137 where the recent find at Bidjan, near Ana (Iraq) was, according to the excavator, "enfouie sous un sol attribué avec certitude au VIIIe sie, grâce a d'autres poteries".
[5]Hilprecht, op. cit., p. 447.

context; five specimens being buried in a courtyard in which an oven also was found and the sixth being located in a room with a storage bin.[6] Following a widespread and common practice, four incantation bowls, 18N18, 18N19, 18N97 and 18N98 were found down-turned and appear to have been placed randomly.[7] Yet, on closer observation, the four specimens divide into two pairs: 18N18 and 18N19 in Locus 30, floor 4 and secondly 18N97 and 18N98 in Locus 14, floor 2. The fragmentary incantation bowl, 18N20, was buried just above this floor level and thus appears to be slightly later.

The pairs of incantation bowls in the WG area immediately attract attention since they present a mixed bag in terms of their scripts, with two of the texts being written in Aramaic and two in Mandaic.[8] The Mandaic specimens 18N19 and 18N97 were written for the sons of MḤLPTʾ, a commonly encountered matronym which also occurs in several of Montgomery's Aramaic texts.[9] 18N19 merely lists DʾNYŠ, whilst 18N97 also cites his two brothers, RWʾY and DWMʾ. The two Aramaic incantation bowls, 18N18 and 18N98 are concerned with a sister-brother combination, ḤWRMYZDWK and NYPRʾ, the children of MʾRWY, a couple who are also cited by another Aramaic incantation bowl from Nippur, HS 3003 of the Frau Prof. Hilprecht collection. Yet, the physical arrangement of the four incantation bowls cuts across the two language groups, for each of the pairs consists of an Aramaic and a Mandaic specimen.

This paper concentrates on the two complete Aramaic incantation bowls, 18N18 and 18N98, which were excavated from the courtyard of Area WG. They are especially important since each of the incantation bowls is paralleled by a number of duplicates, thus allowing insight into the transmission histories of the texts. The supplementary information afforded by the known chronology and provenance of 18N18 and 18N98 augments these studies. Since both specimens were written by the same hand, their palaeography casts valuable light onto the praxis of writing incantation bowls. Here the spontaneity of the practitioner, the person who penned the texts on the pottery vessels, is clearly attested. A *Vorlage* was used, but rather than being rigidly adhered to, it was interpreted flexibly, thus suggesting the oral transmission of incantation texts.

18N98 is duplicated by five incantation bowls and one amulet. HS 3003, found during Hilprecht's campaign in 1900, has been recently published by Joachim Oelsner following its partial translation by Cyrus Gordon in *Orientalia* X (1941) 346-8.[10] Two

---

[6]See p. 63: Nippur. Area WG. Sasanian-Early Islamic Level.
[7]F. Franco, "Five Aramaic incantation bowls from Tell Baruda (Choche)", *Mesopotamia* 13-14 (1978/9), p. 233 and H. Pognon, *Inscriptions Mandaïtes des Coupes de Khouabir*, (Paris 1898), p. 3.
[8]See Erica C.D. Hunter, "Two Mandaic Incantation Bowls from Nippur" *Baghdader Mitteilungen* 25 (1994), pp. 605-618 for the two Mandaic texts.
[9]Montgomery, op. cit., Texts 17, 19 and 24.
[10]J. Oelsner, Review of J. Naveh and S. Shaked, "Amulets and Magic Bowls. Aramaic Incantations of Late Antiquity", *Orientalistische Literaturzeitung* 84 (1989) 1, cols. 38-40.

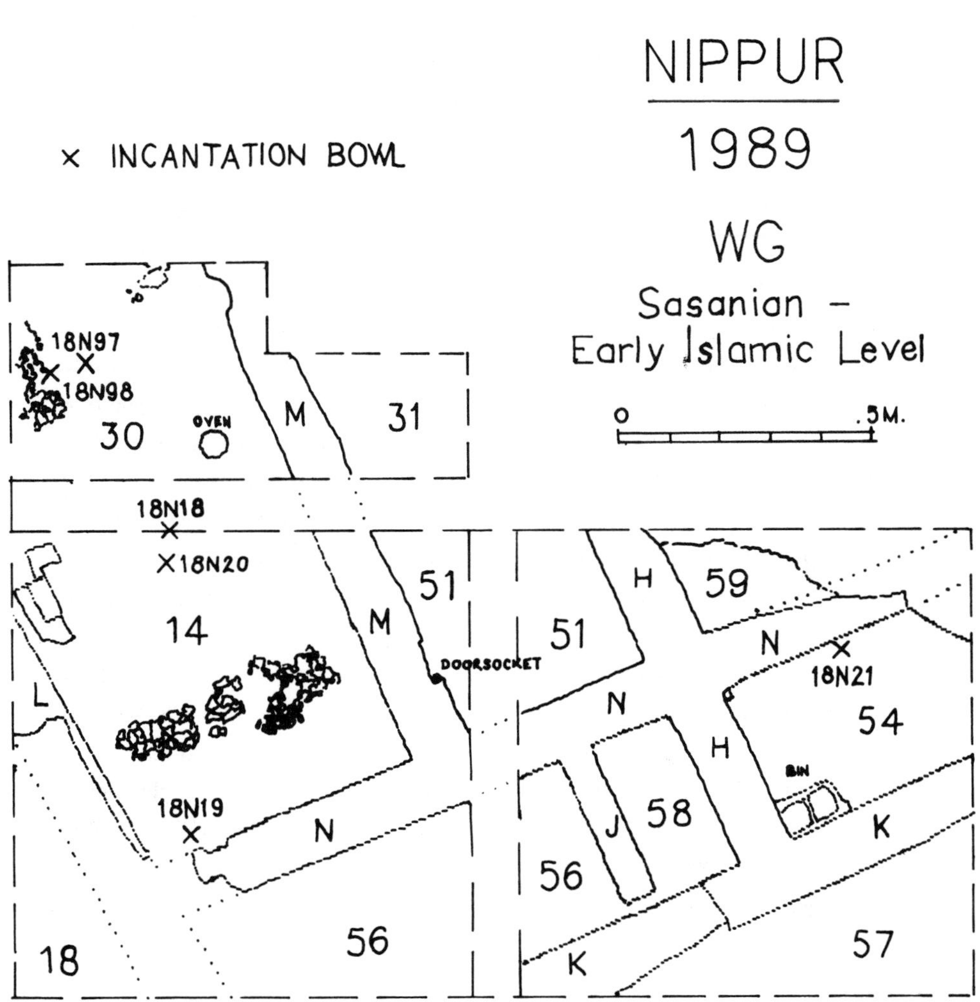
NIPPUR
1989
WG
Sasanian -
Early Islamic Level
0
5M.
× INCANTATION BOWL
18N97
18N98
30
OVEN
M
31
18N18
18N20
14
M
51
51
H
59
N
18N21
DOORSOCKET
L
N
54
H
BIN
58
J
18N19
N
K
56
56
18
56
K
57

more incantation bowls, Heb. 4 6079 of the Jewish National University Library, (Jerusalem) and Metropolitan Museum, (New York), MMA 86.11.259 have been simultaneously published by Joseph Naveh and Shaul Shaked in their monograph, along with a metal (silver) amulet: Israel Museum, (Jerusalem): 69.3.146.[11] A specimen housed in the Museum für Vor- und Frühgeschichte, (Berlin) (XI c 5178) and an incantation bowl from a private collection in Berlin provide the fifth and sixth duplicates.[12]

One of the duplicate texts to 18N98, HS 3003 comes from Nippur, having been excavated during the 1900 campaign of Hilprecht.[13] Apart from citing the same clients, ḤWRMYZDWK and NYPR', the children of M'RWY,[14] 18N98 and HS 3003 are linked by several other features which intimate their common source of production. The palaeography of both specimens is identical, intimating that they were written by the same hand. It is likely that the scribe also produced the drawings of the figure which occur in the interior centre of both HS 3003 and 18N98. Indeed, the iconography is differentiated only in its detail, such as the number of scallops on the head-dress which the figure sports.[15] Furthermore, HS 3003 and 18N98 are hemispherical in form and of approximately similar dimensions.[16] Although incantation bowls of the simple rim-rounded base type are very common, it is possible that the practitioner may have preferred a particular shape.

Using the above criteria, it may also be proposed that Heb 4 6079 and the Berlin specimens came from Nippur, being written by the same scribe as 18N98 and HS 3003. The palaeography of the Berlin specimens appears to be identical with 18N98, as Müller-Kessler has reported.[17] This inference may also be extended to Heb 4 6079, since Müller-Kessler comments in reference to its relationship with the Berlin incantation bowls; "[s]o ist schon vom Photo her erkennbar, dass derselbe Schreiber am Werk war. Der Schriftduktus ist eindeutig der gleiche".[18] Furthermore, Heb 4 6079 and the Berlin specimens feature, like 18N98 and HS 3003, the same distinctive drawing in which only minor stylistic differences may be detected. Finally, the Berlin

---

[11]J. Naveh and S. Shaked, *Amulets and Magic Bowls: Aramaic Incantations of Late Antiquity*, (Leiden 1985), Amulet 15, Bowls 12a and b. The three texts are compared on pp. 188-93 .

[12]C. Müller-Kessler, "Eine aramäische Zauberschale im Museum zu Berlin", *Orientalia* 63 (1994), pp. 5-9.

[13]The author wishes to thank Dr. J. Oelsner for his information about the Hilprecht campaign and collection of incantation bowls.

[14]Oelsner, op. cit., p. 40, has spelt the name M'RWJ and in n.6 refers to Naveh–Shaked, op. cit., Bowl 7 line 6 to support his reading over the reading M'DWY of Gordon, op. cit. (1941), p. 346. Later in n.8 he considers the possibility of the name being read as M'D/RN, and states that this would mean that ḤWRMYZDWK and NYPR' were not brother and sister. Whilst the palaeographic difficulties of distinguishing Resh and Dalath cannot be overlooked, the script of 18N98 and 18N18 suggests the former letter and the spelling M'RWY.

[15]These vary from seven in 18N98 to five in HS 3003.

[16]Oelsner, op. cit., p. 40 records the dimensions of HS 3003 as 18.8 x 7.2 cm, whilst those of 18N98 are 17.3 x 6.7 cm.

[17]Müller-Kessler, op. cit.

[18]Ibid.

bowls and Heb 4 6079 have the same typology as 18N98 and HS 3003, possibly suggesting that the scribe selected his hemispherical vessels from the same source.[19]

The core texts of 18N98, HS 3003, Heb 4 6079 and the Berlin bowls are distinguished only by minor variants. The most significant difference between the five incantation bowls concerns the quotation of Isaiah 40:12 מי מדד בשעלו מים "who was it measured the water of the sea in the hollow of his hand?", referring to God's majesty. 18N98 together with HS 3003 and the Berlin specimens uniformly present a variant on the quotation: *bmy šmdd bšʿlw mym* that occurs in the Sefer ha-Razim I : 226, viz: *bm‹y› šmdd* {*mdd*} *bšʿwlw mym*. In all cases, the *Yodh* following the *Mem* has been omitted and the second combination of *mdd* may be interpreted as a dittography.[20] Since the quotation appears in Heb 4 6079: *bmy šmdd bšʿwlw mym* the scribe may have corrected the errors which he had perpetrated. Alternatively, 18N98, HS 3003 and the Berlin specimens may have been written after this incantation bowl.

The practitioner's improvisation is demonstrated by HS 3003 which begins with an introductory formula: *byšmk ʾny ʿwšh hwdyn qmyʿh lḥtmt*[*h*] *wlnṭrth lbytyh dnwpryʾ br mʾrwy* "In deinem Namen mache ich dieses Amulett, um zu siegeln und zu bewachen das Haus des Nufija(?), des Sohnes des Maroj".[21] By contrast, 18N98, Heb 4 6079 and the Berlin bowls have no introductory formula but commence immediately with the core text. In her discussion of Heb 4 6079, the Berlin bowls and HS 3003, Müller-Kessler claims that the basic form of these duplicate texts was varied for different clients, so that in effect each received an 'individual' incantation.[22] Her premise is, however, contradicted by the evidence supplied by HS 3003 and 18N98. Unlike the former, the latter has no introductory formula, even though it was written by the same practitioner for the same brother-sister clientele.

The situation is further highlighted by the fact that HS 3003 does not have a concluding formula, unlike 18N98 and Heb 4 6079 which end with lists of evil beings, each of which is accompanied by the participle *ʿsyrʾ* "bound". Both specimens commence with the combination; *lylytʾ* ... *mbkltʾ* ... "Lilith ... tormentors ... ",[23] but then diverge. Heb 4 6079 names; סתא [ ] [ ] (זכ)נא פתכרא כל מזיקין בישין the

[19]Naveh and Shaked, op. cit., p. 188 do not supply the dimensions of Heb 4 6079, whilst Müller-Kessler, op. cit., appears to give only approximate dimensions of the two Berlin bowls, these being 17 cm (diameter) and 7 cm (height). For the dimensions of HS 3003 and 18N98, see fn. 14.

[20]Correspondence between Oelsner and Hunter [23.3.91].

[21]Oelsner, op. cit., p.40. The badly damaged text of HS 3003 caused difficulties in the decipherment of NYPRʾ. Gordon, could only read the first two letters as *Nu* ... and given the palaeographic similarity between the characters *Yodh* and *Waw*, it is not surprising that he made this interpretation. Gordon's ellipsis did, however, indicate that three letters were required to complete this name. Oelsner proposed initially the reading NWPJʾ, but has now amended it to NYPRʾ. Oral communication between Oelsner and Hunter [London, 26. 6 91].

[22]Müller-Kessler, op. cit. "Jeder Klient erhielt eine andere Variante, so begegnet der Text einmal mit einer Einleitungsformel (Jena), dann lediglich mit Schlußformel (Jerusalem), mit beiden gleichzeitig (New York anderer Schreiber) oder wie im Falle der beiden hier vorgelegten Dubletten (Berlin und Privatbesitz) gleich ganz ohne diese Elemente."

[23]Naveh and Shaked, op. cit., p. 193 transliterate the word as Mevakkalta.

idol ... evil harmers", whilst 18N98 continues; *šdʾ* ... *dywʾ* ... *dnḥyš* ... *dyny* ...*zkyʾ* ... *ptkrʾ* ... "the demon ... the devil ... Danahiš ... the judges ... the acquitted one ... the image-spirit".[24] The final word of 18N98 is *ptkrʾ* "image-spirit", indicating that the practitioner simply stopped in mid-sentence when he reached the edge of the interior rim.[25] The practitioner could, of course, have continued on the exterior of the bowl writing Canticles 3:7-8 which finishes Heb 4 6079 or at least the customary concluding formulae, but chose not to do so.

The Metropolitan Museum incantation bowl, MMA 86.11.259 can be distinguished from 18N98, HS 3003, Heb 4 6079 and the Berlin specimens on several grounds. Firstly its palaeography differs from these specimens. Secondly and noticeably, it does not feature the drawing of the torso in the centre of its interior, its only decoration being a circle drawn with a single line; a feature that is common in incantation bowls. Thirdly, MMA 86.11.259 differs in its form and size. Smaller than the other duplicates, its dimensions being 13.3 x 5.4 cm, the Metropolitan Museum specimen is not a bowl, but its flat-base and everted upper sides suggest that it is a stopper. That it is clearly the product of another hand from the group comprising 18N89, HS 3003, Heb 4 6079, and the Berlin specimens is, however, most graphically attested by the detailed analysis of its language which has been published by Joseph Naveh and Shaul Shaked.[26]

Like the duplicates: 18N98, HS 3003, Heb 4 6079 and the two Berlin specimens, the Metropolitan Museum incantation bowl has ultimately derived from the same *Vorlage,* that may originally hark back to a Palestinian source.[27] But, there are significant variants between the texts as is shown by the collation compiled by Naveh and Shaked of the Metropolitan Museum bowl with Heb 4 6079.[28] Some suggest the Metropolitan Museum bowl's adaptation to the cultural milieu in which it circulated. In this category falls the preference of MMA 86.11.259 for *srgys* over *sdrws*, which appears in the duplicates, especially since the proper name Sergius would have been more familiar to Semitic speakers than the Greek Sideros. Similarly, the quotation of Isaiah 40:12 by MMA 86.11.259 contrasts with the clause מים במי שמדד בשעולו of the duplicates that is taken from the Sefer ha-Razim. Other differences, such as the Metropolitan Museum's opening and closing formulae, simply result from the practitioner's improvisation.

---

[24]Idem.

[25]Montgomery, op. cit., pp. 72-3 for the *ptkry* that were "properly 'images, idols', but used at large of gods and goddesses". He notes their reduced status from the position of this term in lists of evil beings. See S. Shaked, "Bagdana, king of the demons, and other Iranian terms in Babylonian Aramaic magic", *Acta Iranica* 25 (1985), p. 512 for the derivation of this term from the Persian *pat(i)kar.*

[26]Naveh and Shaked, op. cit., p. 196-7.

[27]Ibid., p. 194.

[28]Ibid., pp. 187-93, and accompanying commentary pp. 194-7.

No less than six duplicates to 18N18 are extant. Two, coming from the 1889 excavations at Nippur, were published by Montgomery as Texts 11 and 18.[29] He compared these texts together with a Mandaic version which was published by Mark Lidzbarski in *Ephemeris für Semitische Epigraphik*,[30] as well as BM 91710, translated by Thomas Ellis in A.H. Layard, *Discoveries in the Ruins of Nineveh and Babylon* (London: 1853) [Text 1] p.510. Further editions of this incantation bowl, reputedly from Babylon, have been made by Charles Isbell and more recently by Ben Segal.[31] In 1934 Cyrus Gordon presented two more Aramaic texts, both from the collection of the nascent Iraq Museum : IM 9377 in the *Annual of the American Schools of Oriental Research* 14 and IM 5497 in *Archiv Orientální* 6.[32] The latter publication expanded the original collation made by Montgomery to include this new specimen, a "wide-bellied, narrow-mouthed storage jar" where the text was written on the exterior.[33]

The introduction of 18N18 immediately distinguishes it from the duplicates, all of which cite Bagdana and Lilith Haldas as the two principal evils against whom the incantation texts were written.[34] 18N18 commences: *byšmk ʾny ʿwšh hwdyn qmyʿh lḥtmh wlnṭrtʾ lḥwrmy‹z›dwk bt mʾrwy* "by your name I made this amulet for the sealing and guarding of ḤWRMYʾZʿDWK daughter of MʾRWY", this formula also beginning HS 3003 which was written for the same client. Then follows a statement, *t[y]tḥtm wtytnṭr bʿzyqtʾ dḥtymyn bh ʾrʿʾ wšmyh* "may she be sealed and protected by the signet-ring by which earth and heaven are sealed" which leads into an inventory of fiends that concludes: *kl mydyʿm byš ... [lylytʾ] byštʾ ... mlwytʾ ḥṣyptʾ* "all evil things ... the wicked Lilith ... the impudent companion". At the string of verbs *dmḥyḥ wšrpʾ wṭrp* "who strikes, smites and claws" qualifying the pair *lylytʾ byštʾ* and *mlwytʾ ḥṣyptʾ* the parallel between 18N18 and the duplicate texts begins.

The following collation demonstrates that the core of 18N18, i.e. ll. 5-9 has derived from the same *Vorlage* as Montgomery Texts 11, 18, Gordon (*AASOR*) and (*ArOr*), Lidzbarski V and BM 91710. The accompanying comments highlight their textual affinities with 18N18 and simultaneously acknowledge the intricacy of the duplicates' transmission history.

---

29 Montgomery, op. cit., [Texts 11 and 18].

30 Lidzbarski, op. cit., pp. 103-5 [Text V].

31 See C. Isbell, *Corpus of the Aramaic Incantation Bowls*, (Missoula 1975), Text 18 which incorporates the edition by Jeruzalmi which the author was unable to consult. The author wishes to thank Prof. J. B. Segal for his generous assistance in allowing his reading of British Museum 91710, which is at present in preparation for publication, to be quoted.

32 C. H. Gordon, "An Aramaic exorcism", *Archiv Orientální* 6 (1934), pp. 466-74. C. H. Gordon, "An Aramaic incantation bowl", *Annual of the American School of Oriental Research* 14 (1934), pp. 141-4. These two specimens are differentiated in the subsequent discussion by the abbreviations of the journals in which they were published.

33 Gordon, *ArOr* 6, p. 466.

34 A collation of the duplicates is given in Gordon, ibid., p. 467 .

Section I (18N18 l.5)

dmḥyḥ wšqpʾ wṭrpʾ drdqy wdrdqt ʾ wmrmyṣy wmrmyṣytʾ

who strikes, smites and claws male and female children and male and female infants.

Montgomery 11:6	*[wš]qpʾ drdqy [wd]rdqtʾ*
Montgomery 18:6	*dmḥy[ʾ] wṭrpʾ wḥnqʾ wʾklʾ dyrqy w[dyrqtʾ] myṣh mymyʿṣ*
Gordon (*AASOR*)**:6**	*[w]mḥyʾ wšrpʾ drtqy wdrtqtʾ mr myṣy wmr mṣytʾ*
Gordon (*ArOr*)**:4**	*mḥyʾ šqpʾ wrmyʾ wḥnqʾ wqṭlʾ wrmyʾ drtqʾ wdrtqtʾ wmr mṣy wmlr myṣytʾ*
Lidzbarski V:4	*wmʾ[h]ʾ wgʾtlʾ wšʾqpʾ whʾnqʾ dʾrdqyʾ wdrdqʾtʾ*

The string of verbs is absent in BM 91710, but none of the duplicates' combinations reproduce that of 18N18. The opening pair introduces Gordon (*ArOr*) and the first and third combination *ṭrpʾ* occurs in Montgomery Text 18 as do the nouns, *mr myṣy wmr myṣytʾ*. They are conspicuously absent from Montgomery Text 11 and Lidzbarski V; however this enigmatic pair may not have been used in Mandaic, for even in Aramaic their occurrence is restricted.[35]

Section II (18N18 ll. 5 - 6) :

ʾšbʿyt {ʿyl} ʿlyky dtymhw bṭrps lybyky bmwrnytyh dsqrwṭ gybwrʾ

"I adjure you to be struck in the membrane of your heart by the lance of the mighty SQWRT".

---

[35] J. N. Epstein, "Glosses babylo-araméenes", *Revue des Études Juives* 73 (1921), p. 49 corrected Montgomery 18 : 6 to *mrmyṣy wmrmyṣytʾ*, but supplied no translation. In both of his 1934 articles, Gordon has only transliterated the characters, however in, "Two magic bowls in Teheran", *Orientalia* 20 (1951), p. 308 he rendered *drdqy wdrdqʾtʾ mrmyṣy wmrmyṣytʾ* "boys and girls, lads and lassies". In his accompanying comments, Gordon states that, "the relative clarity of the present text at last provides a basis for understanding the construction and attempting a translation [i.e. of the earlier texts]. The second word is here written plene with a (i.e. the eighth letter) showing that the form is feminine plural". Gordon's classification of the noun's morphology was sound, but his tentative interpretation "lads and lassies" lacked specificity. C. Isbell, *Corpus of the Aramaic Incantation Bowls* (Missoula 1975), Texts 19 : 4, 20 : 6 and 22 : 5 [respectively editions of Gordon (1934), Montgomery 18 and Gordon (1934 *AASOR*)], prefers "male and female foetuses (?)", and in 57 : 4 "lads and lassies" for *mrmyṣy wmrmyṣytʾ*. In the light of Lilith's reputation as the slayer of infants, "Male and female foetuses" may be derived from √RṢM "press, flatten". See M. Jastrow, *Dictionary of the Targumim, the Talmud Babli and Yerushalmi and the Midrashic Literature* (London 1903), p.1494. Rather, a new interpretation may be attached to *mrmyṣy wmrmyṣytʾ* as "male and female infants" since Jastrow, op. cit., p.826 records √MṢY II "wring", Pael "to give suck". This idea is further developed in Syriac where R. Payne Smith, *Thesaurus Syriacus* (Oxford 1890-1901), II, col. 2188 lists √MṢ as "suxit, lactavit". The first two letters of both *mrmyṣy* and *mrmyṣtʾ* may indicate a group or category of persons, as occurs in Akkadian. Or, the combination may reproduce the morphology of the previous pair of nouns, *drdqʾ wdrdqtʾ* which are classified as being Parpel. See Jastrow, op. cit., p. 319 *dqqʾ* "tender child" √DQQ "crush, pound".

Montgomery 11:6-7	*mšbʿnʾ ʿlyky dtytmhyn bṭrwps lybbky wbmwrnytyh dqyl..s*
Montgomery 18:6-7	*ʾšbʿyt ʿlyky dtymhwn bṭrps lylbyky wbmwrnytʾ dsq .. [gbr]*
Gordon (*AASOR*)**:5**	*ʾšbʿyt lky dtmhn bṭprs l{l}bky wbmrʾnyt‹y›h dqtrws gwbrʾ*
Gordon (*ArOr*) **4**	*ʾšbʿt ʿlky dtmhyn bṭwpry lybky {wbmrnytyh} wbmrnyth dqtrys gwbr*
Lidzbarski V:5	*ʾšbyt ʿlyk wmwwmynʾlyk hʾldʾs lylytʾ wtʾklʾt lylytʾ pt brʾth dzʾrnyʾ lylytʾ dtytmhʾy bṭʾrpws lybyk wbmrwnytẖ dqʾṭryʾwys mlʾkʾ*
BM 91710	*mšbʿnʾ ʿlyky dtymyḥn bṭyprs lylbkwn wbmwrnyth dtyqs gybrʾ*

1st person Perfect Aphel √ŠBʿ "adjure" is used by 18N18, and also Montgomery Text 18, Gordon (*AASOR*) and (*ArOr*) and Lidzbarski V, whilst Montgomery Text 11 and BM 91710 prefer the participial form + 1st singular pronominal suffix. Lidzbarski's Mandaic text cites the grand-daughters of Lilith Zarni which are notably absent in the Aramaic incantation texts where the proper name Qaṭros has been garbled.[36]

Section III : (18N18 l.6)

[dhw]ʾ š[ly]ṭ ʿl šydy wʿl dywy wʿl lylytʾ byštʾ

who has authority over demons, devils and the wicked Lilith.

Montgomery 11:7	*dhw šlyṭ ʿl šydy wʾl dywy wʾl ptkry wl wʾl lylytʾ*
Montgomery 18:7	*dhw šlyṭ ʿl šydy wʾl dywy wʾl ptkry wl wʾl lylytʾ*
Lidzbarski V :7	*dmšʾlʾṭ ʿl shryʾ wdywyʾ wšydyʾ wrwhyʾ whwmryʾ wlylyʾtʾ*
BM 91710	*dhwʾ šlyṭ ʿl šydy wʿl l{y}lylytʾ*

Variation in lists of evil spirits cited by incantation texts is common and to be expected. These are absent in Gordon's texts, but the opening combinations of Montgomery Texts 11 and 18 parallel that of 18N18; viz : *š [ly]ṭ... šydy ... dywy,* but then insert *ptkry* "image-spirits", before Lilith. Since *shryʾ* was the preferred Mandaic noun for

[36]Qaṭros might be a derivative of √QṬR "tie". See Jastrow, op. cit., p. 1353; Payne Smith, op. cit., II, col. 3587 ff. The special connotations of this verb may be intimated by the quotation, *qitria qatria uharsia harsia*, "tie (magic) knots and make spells" in E. Drower, R. Macuch, *A Mandaic Dictionary*, (Oxford 1963), p. 410. See M. Lidzbarski, "Uthra und Malakha" in C. Bezold, (ed.) *Orientalische Studien Theodor Nöldeke zum Siebztigsten Geburtstag*, 2 vols. (Giessen 1906), I, p. 543 for the development of the apotropaic character of angels' names.

"demons", the use of *šydy* in Lidzbarski V is noteworthy, and was presumably overlooked when the text was translated from Aramaic.[37]

Section IV : (18N18 l. 7)

hʾ ktbyt lyky gyṭʾ wpṭryt ytyky mn (+ name)

Behold, I have written you a divorce-writ and I have banished you from (name)

Montgomery 11:7	*hʾ ktbyt lyky whʾ pṭryt* [*ytyky mn* (+ name)]
Montgomery 18:8	*hʾ ktbyt lkyn gyṭʾ whpṭryt yt*[*kyn*]
Gordon (*AASOR*)**:6**	*hʾ ktbyt lyky w.ʾ whʾ trykt ytyky*
Gordon (*ArOr*)**:5**	*hʾ ktbyt lyky hʾ pṭryt ytyky whʾ šbyqt ytyky whʾ trykt ytyky bgṭ pyṭwryn wʾmn mydlbpwʾy t .ṭ ʿwʾyryql*
Lidzbarski V:9	*hʾzyn ktʾbylyk hldʾs lylytʾ whʾzyn pṭʾrtyk mn ʾyth̲ wpgrh̲* (+ name) *wmn bnh̲ wbnʾth̲*
BM 91710	*hʾ ktbyt bkwn hʾ hʾ bṭlyt ytkwn mnh wmn byth* (+name)

Only Montgomery Text 18 and 18N18 specifically state that a *gyṭʾ* i.e. a divorce-writ has been written.[38] On the other hand, Montgomery Text 11, Lidzbarski V and BM 91710, like 18N18, have appended the name of the client to the actions, although only the Mandaic version names the respondent, Lilith Haldas.

Section V : (18N18 ll. 7 - 8)

kmʾ dk‹t›byn š[*yd*]*ʾ* [*gy*]*ṭʾ lynšyhwn bqwšṭʾ wtwb lʾ hdryn ʿlyhwn*

as the demons write divorces for their wives in truth and they do not return to them again

---

[37]See W. von Soden, *Akkadisches Handwörterbuch* (Wiesbaden 1976), III, 1, 1208 and Montgomery, op. cit., pp. 73-4, for the term *šydy,* cognate to Akkadian *šēdu*. Also, R. Campbell Thompson, *Devils and Evil Spirits of Babylonia*, 2 vols. (London 1903), I, p. 11 for the *šydy*. How the *shryʾ* differed from the *šydy* is not clear. Lidzbarski derives *shryʾ* from the Akkadian *sāḫiru* "sorcerer", and in *Das Johannesbuch der Mandäer*, (Giessen 1905), p. 194n, states "doch für den Plural *sʾhryʾ* wenigstens die Bedeutung 'Dämonen' gesichert ist". Presumably *shryʾ* was some type of "sorcery-spirit" possibly one which span or turned around. See von Soden op. cit., II, 1009. Edwin Yamauchi, *Mandaic Incantation Texts* (New Haven 1967) preference for "crescent spirits" would appear to be derived from *shrʾ* "moon" and possibly from the moon shaped ornaments of gold recorded by Targ. Jud. VIII 21, 26 which Jastrow, op. cit., p. 960 lists under *shrnʾ*. Payne Smith, op. cit., II, col. 2359 which records *shrnʾ* as crescent-shaped ornaments which hung on camels' necks, presumably acting as amulets. On the other hand, the interpretation may be based on the Old Aramaic *shr* "moongod" and Tapani Harviainen, "An Aramaic Incantation Bowl from Borsippa", *Studia Orientalia* 51 (1981), p. 12 suggests that the vocalism of this noun with an i sound may indicate its relation to Jewish Aramaic *syhrs* and Mandaic *sira* "moon".

[38]See B. Levine, "The Language of the Magic Bowls". Appendix in J. Neusner, *A History of the Jews of Babylonia*, (Leiden 1970), V, pp. 348 - 9 for incantation texts which include *gyṭʾ*, this term already having been noted in Layard, op. cit., p. 512.

Montgomery 11:7-8	[*km*ʾ *šydy*] *dktbyn gyṭy lynšyhwn wl*ʾ *h*[*dry*]*n* ʿ*lyhyn*
Montgomery 18:8	[*km*ʾ *ktb*]*yn šydy gyṭ*ʾ *lynšyhwn wtwb l*ʾ *hdryn* ʿ*lyhyn*
Gordon (*AASOR*)**:6**	*km*ʾ *dktbyn šydy gyṭ*ʾ *lnš‹y›hwn wtwb l*ʾ *hdry*
Gordon (*ArOr*)**:6**	*ky*(*m*)ʾ *dktbyn wyhbyn šydy wdyw*ʾ *gyṭy lynš*(*y*)*hyn wtwbw l*ʾ *hdryn* ʿ*lyhynbmwtym ydk*[39] ʿ*p lylyt*ʾ *byšt*ʾ *lyly* {*b*}*dykr*ʾ *lyly*ʾ*t*ʾʿ *nqbt*ʾ *wḥnqt*ʾ *wbrt*ʾ *wšlnyt*ʾ *w*ʿ*t.t*ʾ *whllt*ʾ
Lidzbarski V:10	*kd dk*ʾ*tby*ʾ *šydy gyṭ*ʾ *l*ʿ*nš*ʾ*ywn bkwšt*ʾ *wtwm l*ʾ *h*ʾ*dry*
BM 91710	*km*ʾ *dktbyn šydyn gyṭyn wyhbyn lynšyhwn wtwb l*ʾ *hdryn* ʿ*lyhwn*

Lidzbarski's text is noteworthy for the second occurrence of *šydy* where *shry*ʾ might be expected and also for its inclusion, like 18N18 of *bkwst*ʾ after *l*ʾ*nš*ʾ*ywn*. Like 18N18, Montgomery Text 18 inserts *wtwb* before *l*ʾ but otherwise there is little to distinguish between it and Montgomery Text 11.

Section VI : (18N18 l. 8)

*k*ʿ*n šqwly gyṭyky wqbyly mwmtky* ʿ*qyry mdwrtyky wšnw mlkwtky*

now, take your divorce-writ, receive your exorcism, uproot your dwelling and depart your kingdom

Montgomery 11:8	*šqwly gyṭyky*
Montgomery 18:9	*šqwl gyṭykyn wqbyl mwmtkyn*
Gordon (*AASOR*)**:6-7**	*wšqwly gṭky wqbly mwmtky*
Gordon (*ArOr*)**:7**	*šyqly gyṭ‹yky› wsprt yr‹n›b‹y›ky w*ʾ*grt šybwqyky*
Lidzbarski V :11	*šqwl gyṭyk wq*ʾ*byl mwm*ʾ*tyk*
BM 91710	*šqwl gyṭykwn wqbylw mwmtkyn*

18N18 has expanded the basic combination of √ŠQL + *gyṭ*ʾ and √QBL + *mwmt*ʾ that occurs in Montgomery Text 18, Gordon (*AASOR*), Lidzbarski V and BM 91710. Montgomery Text 11 presents only the first half of the formula.

[39]Gordon's collation of the duplicates ceases at this point.

Section VII : (18N18 l. 9)

qrḥy tbʾry pwqy wʾytrḥqy mn bytyh wmn dwrtyh wmn ḥyklyh wmn ʿyṣqwptyh (+name)

razed, shattered, go and be far away from the house, dwelling, homestead and threshold of (name)

Montgomery 18 :9	*wqrḥw wy[ʿryqw mn by]tʾ* (+ name)
Gordon (*AASOR*)**:7**	*wqdḥy wʿqyry wpwqy mn byth wmn gwph* (+ name)
Gordon (*ArOr*)**:7**	*wʿqry wʿqdḥ wpqy wtʿqry* (+ name)
Lidzbarski V :12	*wqdʾ wpwq wʿrwq wʿtrʾhʾq mn bʾytẖ dʾwrẖ hyklẖ wbynyʾnẖ wmn ʻrsẖ wbysʾdyẖ* (+ name)
BM 91710	*wpwqw wqdḥw wʿyrwqw wʾyzlw mn byth* (+name)

The duplicates, with the exception of Montgomery 11, present variant strings of imperatives to 18N18, but include √QDḤ/√QRḤ and √PWQ.[40] The usage of *tbʾry* in 18N18 is unique, but the Ethpeal/Ethpael √RḤQ does occur in Lidzbarski V.

18N18 diverges from the duplicates at this point to present a dramatically abbreviated version. The closing formula, *ʿšbʿyt ʿlyky bʿbd ʻbrhm bṣwr yṣḥq bšdy yʿ[qb] dlʾ tyḥṭwn bḥwrmyzdwk bt mʾ‹r›wy* "I adjure you by the servant of Abraham, by the rock of Isaac, by the Shaddai of Jacob, that you should not injure ḤWRMYZDWK daughter of Mʾ‹R›WY", is unattested in the duplicates which have multiple references to the signet-ring. The scribe of 18N18 may have chosen not to repeat a common motif, since the signet-ring was already mentioned in the introduction, selecting instead a formula favoured by the clients. Or, his production of a shorter incantation text may have been dictated by space factors. "Amen", "Selah" and "Halellujah" which are customary concluding formulae are noticeably absent in 18N18,

[40] *qrḥw* has been variously read, probably due to the palaeographic difficulty of distinguishing the characters Resh and Dalath. In commenting on the preference of Montgomery Text 18 for *wqrḥw*, Epstein, op. cit., p. 41 claims that it should be read as a conjugation from √QDḤ "bore, perforate" and also "[break through], grow forth, sprout". See Jastrow, op. cit., p. 1314 and Payne Smith, op. cit., II, col. 3486. Gordon followed Epstein but Montgomery's reading appears to be accurate. Jastrow, *op. cit.*, p. 1415 records under the masculine substantive QRḤ "bald, bald head", Gitt. viii, 9 *gṭ qʾ* being a letter of divorce that lacks signatures. Furthermore, Jastrow lists the feminine *qrḥt* B. Bath. 1320 *qʾ mkʾn wmkʾn* meaning that she is bald on both sides i.e. has forfeited both claims on her husband's estates. The legal connections of QRḤ which have been cited would be compatible with the tenor of the text, for as Montgomery, op. cit., p. 159 has noted, "the magical writ affects the same forms and formalism as that of the divorce-courts in that the demon loses rights over the client". Alternatively, an extract from an incantation cited in Pes 110a bot. *qʾ qrḥyyky* "bald be your baldness" (may the hair with which you practise your witchcraft fall out) may suggest another application of √QRḤ. See Jastrow, op. cit., p. 1415 √QRḤ Hiphel "make bare, raze", and Payne Smith, op. cit., II, col. 3738 √QRḤ Peal "calvus evasit". Demons often sported long, flowing tresses as many of the drawings on incantation bowls indicate. Since Montgomery, op. cit., p. 153 notes that "[a]ny portion of a person's body, especially hairs, nails, etc. as detachable could be used in magic directed against him", presumably this principle may also be applied to demons. Such practices are recalled by the episode of Samson and Delilah in Judges 16:17 *sqq*. The concept of stripping or razing a demon, be its application physical or legal, would seem to be particularly appropriate.

giving the impression that it is unfinished. This may have been a scribal idiosyncracy, for 18N98 and the duplicates which the same practitioner wrote also conclude almost in mid-sentence.

Montgomery Texts 11 and 18 indicate that, in addition to 18N18, two more versions circulated in the quarter of the Jewish settlement at Nippur. However, the textual affinity between 18N18 and Montgomery Text 18, over and above that of Montgomery Text 11, is attested by the following summary of Sections I -VII of the collation :

(I) the use of the pair of nouns, *mr myṣy* and *mr myṣtʾ*.

(II) 1st person Perfect Aphel √ŠBʿ, and the orthography of Qaṭros.

(III) the sequence of demons following *dhw šlyṭ*.

(IV) the use of *gyṭʾ*.

(V) the word-order of *kmʾ k‹t›byn šydy gyṭʾ* and the use of *wtwb*.

(VI) the use of *wqbyly mwmtkyn* after *šqwly gyṭyky*.

(VII) absent in Montgomery Text 11.

The excavation of the two Aramaic specimens, 18N18 and 18N98, from Area WG at Nippur has allowed the transmission history of incantation texts to be charted, for the first time, in the framework of chronological, provenance and palaeographic factors. Two very different patterns have emerged. 18N98 and its duplicates, with the exception of the Metropolitan Museum bowl, were the product of one scribe and emanate from Nippur. These duplicates represent a localised and contemporary circulation, although the Greek words of this text, that has been termed an "historiola", point to its foreign origins.[41] The unique genre of the text may have enhanced its transmission in its entirety and consequently may account for the lack of textual corruption. On the other hand, this may result from the fact that the duplicate texts and 18N98 were the product of the same practitioner; compared to the Metropolitan Museum bowl whose text Naveh and Shaked have termed as "inferior".[42]

By contrast, 18N18 and its duplicates have a broad distribution, both in terms of provenance and script. In spite of their many differences, the duplicates have derived from a common *Vorlage*. The dissemination of these texts, not only in different cities of Mesopotamia, but also their writing in Aramaic and Mandaic, might be expected to be accompanied by increasing changes. Certainly the textual tradition is intricate indicating a long and varied transmission history yet, surprisingly, Lidzbarski V reveals little of the specific phraseology that is usually associated with Mandaic incantation bowls, so much so that it has been commented: "[s]ie verrät mehr als die übrigen jüdischen Einfluss".[43] Indeed, Lidzbarski V appears simply to be a translation from Aramaic.

---

[41]Naveh and Shaked, op. cit., p. 192.
[42]Ibid., p. 195.
[43]Lidzbarski, op. cit., p. 90.

Furthermore, comparison between 18N18 and the duplicate texts, from Nippur and Babylon, does not indicate any substantial differences that intimate the development of regional or "urban" traditions.

18N18 and 18N98 are incantation texts with diametrically different transmission histories. Yet they are linked by their recitation of a common inventory of evils. 18N98 concludes with the repeated binding, *ʿsyrʾ* of multiple fiends : *lylytʾ* ... *mbkltʾ* ... *šydʾ* ... *dywʾ* ... *dnḥyš* ... *dyny* ... *zkyʾ* ... *ptkrʾ* "the Lilith ... the tormentors ... the demon ... the devil ... Danahiš ... the judges ... the acquitted one ... the image-spirit". Similarly 18N18 ll. 3 -4 lists : *šydy* ... [*dywy*]... *lylytʾ* ... *dnḥyš* ... *dyny* ... *zkyʾ* ... *ptkrʾ* "demons ... [devils] ... Lilith ... Danahiš ... judges ... the acquitted one ... the image-spirit." In 18N18 *šydy* and *dywy* precede rather than follow *lylytʾ*; otherwise the order of *dnḥyš* ... *dyny* ... *zkyʾ* ... *ptkrʾ* is identical with 18N98.

The citation in 18N18 and 18N98 of these evil spirits exemplifies scribal innovation and spontaneity in incantation texts. The selection by the practitioner of this unusual concatenation, which also partially occurs in Heb 4 6079, is enigmatic. That he did not compose it himself, is indicated by the occurrence of a similar string of evils in another incantation bowl, also concerned with Lilith's defeat.[44] For this reason, the practitioner may have considered it appropriate for 18N18 and 18N98, where Lilith is a central figure. Yet the Berlin bowls, duplicating 18N98, also written by the same practitioner, do not include this inventory. It is possible that the concatenation was requested by ḤWRMYZDWK and her brother MʾRWY, the clients for whom both 18N18 and 18N98 were written. But, paradoxically, it is not present in HS 3003 which was also produced for the same couple.

The variations which occur between 18N98, 18N18 and their duplicate texts casts light onto the praxis of writing incantation bowls. The practitioner improvised the opening and closing formulae, probably writing them as they came to mind. His failure to conclude both 18N18 and 18N98 with the usual expressions, such as "Amen", "Selah" and "Hallelujah", together with the mis-spelling of the clients' names, suggests a careless production of the two incantation bowls.[45] It simultaneously indicates that the practitioner did not consider these formulae crucial for the efficacy of the incantation texts. Whilst the core of an incantation text was essentially retained, improvisation did take place, being particularly noticeable in 18N18, which is a much abbreviated version compared to its duplicates. However, the spontaneity of the practitioner is exemplified in both 18N18 and 18N98, by the inventories of fiends whose presence invoked the combat and conflict inherent in incantation bowls.

---

[44]Naveh and Shaked, op. cit., p. 199 [Bowl 13 : 7].
[45] ḤWRMYZDWK occurs on 18N18 l.2 as ḤWRMY‹Z›DWK, while MʾRWY is variously spelt as MʾRW‹Y› on 18N18 l.2; Mʾ‹R›WY on 18N18 l.10 and MʾRW‹Y› in 18N98.

The practitioners who wrote the incantation texts may have been peripatetic, travelling from city to city within a certain area, or even between different regions, plying their profession. The known locations of 18N18 and its duplicates, Montgomery Texts 11 and 18 at Nippur and BM 91710 at Babylon, suggests this possibility. Alternatively, the writing of incantation texts may have been a local industry, performed by men or women living in a particular village, with whom this activity was associated. It may even have been an hereditary occupation of a particular family. The paradigm offered by 18N98 and its duplicates, which emanate from Nippur, lends support to such a proposal, although the practitioner could have produced multiple copies of the incantation text during a visit to the city. Whichever method was adopted, the tailoring process that went to the very heart of incantation texts supports their oral transmission over and above the rigid adherence to a prototype incantation.

Les inscriptions araméennes de Cheikh-Fadl (Égypte)

André Lemaire — E. P. H. E., Paris-Sorbonne

I - Histoire de la recherche

Les inscriptions araméennes de Cheikh-Fadl en Moyenne Égypte ont été découvertes par Flinders Petrie au cours d'une excursion sur la rive droite du Nil, lors de sa campagne de fouilles 1921-22 à Bahnésa. Flinders Petrie identifia immédiatement les inscriptions comme araméennes et fit appel à Noël (Aimé-)Giron pour leur déchiffrement et leur publication. Ce dernier examina et copia sommairement les inscriptions pendant deux jours, en mars 1922. A nouveau, pendant trois jours, en décembre 1922, il étudia et copia sur place ces inscriptions, accompagné alors de M. Lacau, Directeur Général du Service des Antiquités, et de M. Busutil, photographe du Musée du Caire. Ce dernier prit de bonnes photographies de la plupart des textes; cependant, par suite du manque de plaques, il ne put photographier les panneaux I, VI, VII, X, XIV, XV et XVII.

Dès 1923, N. Giron publiait, dans une note de 6 pages d'*Ancient Egypt*,[1] une présentation préliminaire du contenu de ces inscriptions avec un aperçu que lui-même qualifiait de "malheureusement bien incomplet". Cette "note" rapportait la découverte de la tombe, présentait la situation des inscriptions avec un croquis (reproduit *infra*) et proposait une lecture préliminaire des passages les mieux conservés accompagnée d'une seule photographie de trois lignes fragmentaires. Giron concluait provisoirement à une inscription funéraire présentant le *curriculum* d'un ancien fonctionnaire assyrien, à dater "entre le milieu du VIIème et la fin du VIème siècle avant J.-C.", en remarquant que l'édition définitive demanderait "encore beaucoup de temps et plusieurs visites nouvelles à Cheikh-Fadl pour contrôler la vraisemblance des nombreuses hypothèses qui viennent à l'esprit".[2]

Ce pronostic pessimiste sur le délai de publication s'est réalisé, puisque c'est seulement aujourd'hui, environ 70 ans après leur découverte, que nous essayons de présenter cette *editio princeps*. Que s'est-il passé? Il est difficile de le savoir dans le détail puisque N. Giron n'a rien publié ensuite sur Cheikh-Fadl. En fait, il semble avoir été très vite dérouté et découragé par ces inscriptions si fragmentaires mentionnant Taharqâ, Nékô et Psammétique, et d'un genre littéraire si énigmatique (funéraire?

[1]N. Giron, "Note sur une tombe découverte près de Cheikh-Fadl par Monsieur Flinders Petrie et contenant des inscriptions araméennes", *AE* 8 (1923), pp. 38-43, spéc. p. 38.
[2]Ibid., p. 43.

historique?...). Il a donc cherché à les confier à un autre grand spécialiste des inscriptions araméennes d'Égypte qu'il estimait peut-être, modestement, plus compétent pour traiter ces inscriptions originales. Une note dans une publication de Flinders Petrie parue en 1925 nous apprend, en effet, que le dossier a été confié à A. Cowley[3] qui venait de publier, en 1923, son livre classique sur les papyri d'Éléphantine, *Aramaic Papyri of the Fifth Century B.C.* Cependant Cowley lui-même ne semble avoir jamais rien publié sur ces inscriptions. Bien plus, des recherches pour retrouver le dossier des inscriptions de Cheikh-Fadl constitué par N. Giron (photographies, copies détaillées et transcriptions préliminaires), aussi bien en Égypte[4] que dans sa famille,[5] n'ont rien donné, pas plus que des recherches du côté d'un dossier laissé par A. Cowley à Oxford, à l'Ashmolean Museum[6] ou dans la Bodleian Library.[7]

Cependant, depuis 1923, l'existence des inscriptions araméennes de Cheikh-Fadl n'a pas été totalement oubliée des spécialistes, aramaïsants ou égyptologues, qui les ont mentionnées en ne pouvant se référer qu'à la présentation préliminaire de N. Giron: ainsi R. A. Bowman[8] en 1948, H. de Meulenaere[9] en 1951, S. Sauneron et J. Yoyotte[10] en 1952, E. Y. Kutscher[11] en 1954, J. Yoyotte[12] en 1960, J. J. Koopmans[13] en 1962, J. Naveh[14] en 1966, S. Segert[15] en 1973 et E. Bresciani[16] en 1985. En l'absence d'*editio princeps* ou, au moins, de photographies, ces spécialistes n'ont pu porter de jugement critique ni sur les lectures préliminaires proposées par N. Giron, ni sur son interprétation générale provisoire. Seul J. Naveh, dans son livre classique sur la paléographie araméenne, a-t-il pu apporter un élément nouveau:

---

[3]W. M. F. Petrie, *Tombs of the Courtiers and Oxyrhyncos*, British School of Archaeology in Egypt and Egyptian Research Account XXVIIIth Year 1922, BSAE 37 (London 1925), p. 1: "...Here are references to Taharqa, Nekau and Psemtek I showing an early settlement of Syrians, probably Jews. The inscriptions were copied by M. Noël Giron, and photographed by the Museum staff. M. Giron's account appeared in Ancient Egypt 1923, pp. 38-43, and he then preferred to place the materials in the hands of Dr. Cowley."

[4]Nous remercions Mme. P. Posener-Krieger et M. M. Dijkstra pour leurs indications.

[5]Nous remercions M. M. Dewaechter pour ses conseils.

[6]Nous remercions M. P. R. S. Moorey pour ses indications.

[7]Nous remercions M. R. A. May pour ses indications.

[8]R. A. Bowman, "Aramaeans, Aramaic and the Bible", *JNES* 7 (1948), pp. 65-90, spéc. p. 76.

[9]H. de Meulenaere, *Herodotos over de 26ste Dynastie (II, 147 - III, 15)*, Bibliothèque du Muséon 27 (Leuven 1951), p. 54, n. 50.

[10]S. Sauneron, J. Yoyotte, "Sur la politique palestinienne des rois saïtes", *VT* 2 (1952), pp. 131-136, spéc. p. 134.

[11]E. Y. Kutscher, "New Aramaic Texts", *JAOS* 74 (1954), pp. 233-248, spéc. p. 246.

[12]J. Yoyotte, "Néchao ou Néko", *Dictionnaire de la Bible, Supplément (SDB)* VI (1960), col. 363-393, spéc. col.365.

[13]J. J. Koopmans, *Aramäische Chrestomathie*, 2 tomes (Leiden 1962), n° 15.

[14]J. Naveh, "The Scripts of Two Ostraca from Elath", *BASOR* 183 (1966), pp. 27-30, spéc. p.28, n. 9.

[15]S. Segert, *Altaramäische Grammatik mit Bibliographie, Chrestomathie und Glossar* (Leipzig 1973 = ^{2}1983) (*infra* : *Segert*), p.462.

[16]E. Bresciani, "The Persian Occupation of Egypt", dans I. Gershevitch (ed.), *The Cambridge History of Iran II, The Median and Achaemenian Periods* (Cambridge 1985), pp. 502-528, spéc. p. 517.

"Fortunately, all the photographs taken by Aimé-Giron on his visit to Sheikh-Faḍl were brought to Jerusalem by the late Mr Joseph Leibovitch formerly Director of Publications of the Egyptian Department of Antiquities. Mr. Leibovitch kindly placed these photographs at my disposal. They are of excellent quality, though the condition of the inscriptions is too poor for exact decipherment. The photographs enable us, however, to conclude, palaeographically, that the inscriptions are from approximately the second quarter of the fifth century B.C.E.....Let us hope that a basic re-examination of the inscriptions will make a more complete understanding of this material from Sheikh Faḍl possible."[17]

En décembre 1983, J. Naveh a eu l'amabilité de nous transmettre une copie de ce jeu de photographies et, du 9 au 15 avril 1984, une mission en Égypte nous a permis de nous rendre sur place avec l'autorisation du Service des Antiquités.[18] Malgré l'approximation de la localisation indiquée par N. Giron et le peu de temps disponible sur place (environ 2 h.), nous avons pu repérer à nouveau la tombe et photographier ses inscriptions en noir et blanc et en couleur. Malheureusement cette visite a révélé que, depuis 1922, la tombe avait subi de nouveaux outrages du temps et des hommes (en particulier, par de nombreux graffiti) et que les inscriptions y étaient encore en plus mauvais état que lors des premières photographies prises par M. Busutil. Finalement, M. J. Naveh nous a généreusement transmis aussi sa transcription préliminaire du panneau II,[19] en nous laissant toute latitude de préparer la publication de ces textes si originaux et si fragmentaires[20] que nous présentons ici malgré toutes les incertitudes qui entourent leur lecture et leur interprétation.

II - Localisation des inscriptions

Le village de Cheikh-Fadl est situé sur la rive droite du Nil, à environ 186 km au sud du Caire et 48 km au nord de Minieh. On y parvient en traversant le Nil au bac de Beni-Mazar, petite ville située sur la rive gauche du Nil. N. Giron avait situé la tombe "à 8 kilomètres environ à l'E.N.E. de Cheikh-Fadl";[21] celle-ci semble plutôt se

---

[17] J. Naveh, *The Development of the Aramaic Script* (Jerusalem 1970), p. 41.

[18] Cette mission a bénéficié de l'aide de l'IFAO, dirigée alors par Mme. P. Posener-Krieger, du Service des Antiquités, et surtout de M. P. Vernus, directeur d'études à l'E.P.H.E., ainsi que de Mlle. Pantalucci, stagiaire à l'IFAO, qui a mis sa voiture à notre disposition. Qu'ils en soient tous cordialement remerciés ici.

[19] Nous tenons à l'en remercier très cordialement.

[20] Nous avons présenté ces inscriptions, de façon préliminaire mais avec les diapositives en couleur, à Paris, à la Société Asiatique, lors de sa séance du 9 décembre 1988, sous le titre "Les inscriptions de Cheikh-Fadl et la littérature égypto-araméenne au Ve siècle av. J.-C." (cf. *JA* 277 [1989] pp. 413-414; nous remercions particulièrement M. J. Leclant pour sa remarque à propos du martelage du nom de Taharqâ: cf. *infra*) et à Londres, lors de la conférence "Aramaic and the Aramaeans" (26 juin 1991), sous le titre "Nouvel aspect de la littérature araméenne d'époque perse: les inscriptions de Cheikh Fadl (Égypte)".

[21] *AE* 8 (1923), p. 38.

situer à 4-5 km de Cheikh-Fadl à vol d'oiseau et à environ 2 km au nord de Kynopolis, la nécropole des chiens. Elle est creusée dans le sommet d'une colline du début de la montagne arabique et, de son entrée, tournée approximativement vers l'Ouest-Sud-Ouest, on a une vue générale sur la vallée du Nil à cet endroit.

Suivant le plan déjà publié par N. Giron (fig. 1), cette tombe se compose d'une sorte de parvis, actuellement encombré de matériaux rapportés mais peut-être primitivement recouvert d'un toît (?). "A la suite venait le tombeau proprement dit, une pièce rectangulaire d'environ 4 m de large sur 5 m de long et 2 m de hauteur creusée dans le calcaire dont le plafond est constitué par la plateforme même du sommet de la montagne. Au fond, en retrait, une niche béante qu'on retrouve dans les tombeaux congénères. Dans l'angle sud-est de la tombe, s'ouvre un puits carré qui donne accès à trois (?) chambres que nous n'avons pu visiter".[22] En 1984, la pièce principale était, en partie, encombrée de débris et son toît percé d'un trou triangulaire d'environ 20-30 cm de côté dans l'angle Nord-Nord-Est; de plus, son sol avait été percé, à peu près en son milieu, par une grosse fosse de pillage. La tombe n'a pas pu être nettoyée, pas plus qu'une autre tombe, apparemment du même type mais encore plus encombrée de débris, située quelques mètres plus au sud.

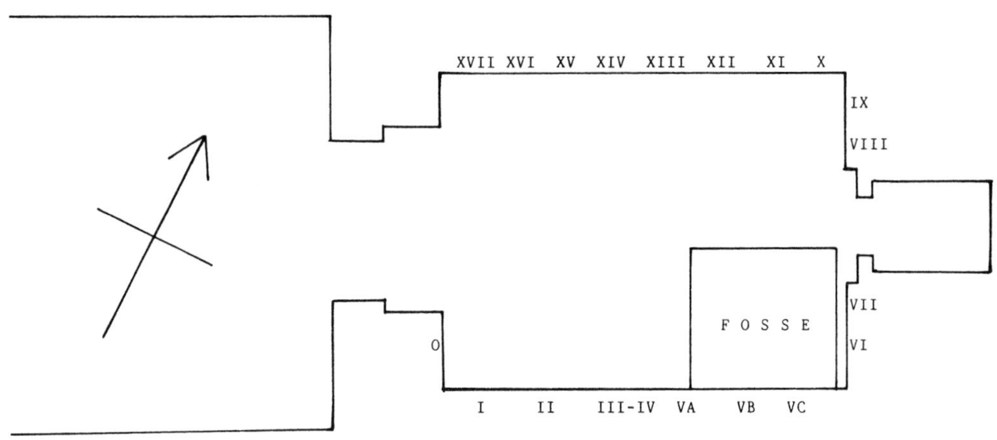

Fig. 1. Plan de la tombe avec numérotation des panneaux.

[22]Ibid. pp. 38-39.

La décoration primitive de la pièce principale de la tombe comportait plusieurs panneaux de fresques à dominante rouge, formant un bandeau se déroulant tout autour de la tombe, sur les quatre parois, et occupant "un registre d'une hauteur de 0 m 74 à compter du plafond",[23] sauf pour les panneaux du fond (paroi Est) comportant, sous les panneaux supérieurs descendant déjà un peu plus bas, des panneaux inférieurs dont la limite basse se situe à peu près à 1,40 m du plafond. "Toute la partie supérieure du registre comportant les figures était peinte sur un banc de calcaire plus friable que le reste; elle a presque complètement disparu".[24] Malgré son état lamentable aujourd'hui, ce registre semble avoir été délimité par un gros trait rouge horizontal proche du plafond et un ou deux gros traits rouges horizontaux parallèles marquant la limite inférieure, tandis que les panneaux étaient délimités, à intervalles assez irréguliers, par un ou deux traits rouges verticaux, plus ou moins épais, attestés aussi près des angles. Pour la numérotation de ces panneaux, nous suivrons celle proposée par N. Giron, quitte parfois à la compléter, et même si cette numérotation n'est pas toujours logique (un même panneau reçoit deux numéros consécutifs tandis que le panneau suivant correspond, en fait, à trois panneaux différents que nous avons appelés A, B et C).

Vu l'état de conservation de ce registre, il est souvent très difficile, voire impossible, d'identifier les représentations peintes primitivement. On devine cependant:
— en entrant, à droite (panneau O), un animal assis peint en rouge, tourné vers l'entrée, peut-être pour la garder; un animal similaire pourrait avoir été peint à gauche de l'entrée (panneau XVIII), mais ce qui reste de ce panneau rend toute identification conjecturale;
— au début de la paroi Sud (panneau I), "un bateau rouge à 21(?) rameurs";[25]
— plus loin peut-être "des personnages debouts, face à gauche, c'est à dire marchant vers la niche, dont les pieds seuls subsistent";[26] en fait, même cette interprétation de N. Giron reste conjecturale et, peut-être, illusoire, car on discerne seulement plusieurs traits verticaux, plus ou moins épais, probablement des séparateurs de panneaux;
— sur la paroi du fond, à droite de la niche, "restes d'une barque... au-dessus personnages marchant vers la niche dont un a disparu";[27] en fait, on reconnaît bien les restes d'une barque dans le panneau inférieur, ainsi qu'un homme debout dans le panneau supérieur proche de la niche (VII), mais on n'aperçoit aucun reste de représentation identifiable dans le panneau supérieur de droite (VI).
— A gauche de la niche, le panneau supérieur gauche (IX) comporte un personnage peint en bleu-vert marchant vers la droite et semblant conduire devant lui un veau(?)

[23]Ibid. p. 39.
[24]Ibid.
[25]Ibid.
[26]Ibid.
[27]Ibid.

peint en rouge. Le contenu primitif du panneau supérieur droit (VIII) et du panneau inférieur reste indistinct.

— La paroi Nord a été très abîmée, en particulier par des graffiti dont certains sont récents. N. Giron proposait de reconnaître (à partir de la gauche?): "deux quadrupèdes(?) momifiés, disque et cornes en tête, encadrés de raies rouges, plus loin un épervier, plus loin encore des personnages face à droite tenant un sceptre vertical".[28] Ces représentations sont parfois difficiles à reconnaitre aujourd'hui.

Les inscriptions araméennes n'apparaissent que sur les panneaux des parois Sud, Est et Nord; on ne voit aucune trace d'inscription de part et d'autre de l'entrée. Ces inscriptions sont au moins en aussi mauvais état que les fresques. Comme la partie supérieure du registre est très abîmée, "il est impossible de savoir à quelle hauteur se trouvait la première ligne des textes de chaque panneau et, dans plusieurs cas, on ne peut également déterminer avec certitude où commençaient et finissaient les lignes".[29] Pour N. Giron, il était "impossible également de préciser si les textes araméens, peints à l'encre rouge et très mal conservés qui coupent les figures, présentent un rapport quelconque avec elles. C'est cependant improbable".[30] En fait, il apparaît que les inscriptions sont postérieures aux fresques, comme le montre clairement le panneau XII avec ses lettres rouges écrites sur le vêtement vert, et sans rapport avec elles, puisque les inscriptions coupent les figures. Il semble donc que les scribes n'ont utilisé le registre peint de fresques que comme un support pratique pour une inscription à l'encre parce que bien aplani et parfois déjà recouvert d'un certain enduit (peinture).

Même si l'écriture à l'encre rouge est généralement régulière, le scribe ayant marqué la séparation des mots par un espace blanc, il apparaît que l'on peut discerner plusieurs changements de mains et donc plusieurs scribes. Comme la partie supérieure du registre est très abîmée, la numérotation des lignes présentée ici ne prétend pas représenter la numérotation primitive.[31] D'après les panneaux les mieux conservés, surtout dans leur partie inférieure, chaque panneau pouvait comporter au moins 15 lignes.

III - Texte, traduction, commentaire

Panneau I

En 1923, N. Giron avait proposé de voir "sous le grand bateau à rames deux lignes comprenant quelques caractères seulement",[32] mais, en 1984, il était devenu

---

[28]Ibid.
[29]Ibid.
[30]Ibid.
[31]On notera que la numérotation des lignes de N. Giron (ibid., p. 40, n. 1) était inversée et commençait par le bas. Bien qu'une telle numérotation puisse s'appuyer sur le fait que les lignes inférieures sont les plus claires, nous n'avons pas cru devoir garder cette numérotation mal commode.
[32]Ibid., p. 40.

impossible d'identifier des lettres à cet endroit: les traces sont trop indistinctes pour qu'on propose une quelconque lecture. Il est même douteux qu'il y ait eu primitivement deux lignes inscrites à cet endroit.

Panneau II

Selon N. Giron, "ce texte comprenait au moins 12 lignes (10 mots à la ligne). 9 d'entre elles sont encore susceptibles d'être déchiffrées dans les parties conservées". Selon lui, "il est certain que la fin manque" sans qu'on puisse savoir si nous possédons le commencement des lignes.[33] En fait, il paraît assez vraisemblable que nous ayons le début des lignes puisque ce que nous voyons de lisible au début des 8 dernières lignes semble aligné verticalement; la fin des lignes semble plus difficile à préciser: on pourrait proposer de la situer au trait vertical assez fin visible dans la partie gauche de la deuxième photographie de M. Busutil.

N. Giron avait proposé la lecture de plusieurs expressions de 4 lignes de ce panneau et J. Naveh nous a communiqué une lecture préliminaire des 8 dernières lignes avec quelques propositions de restitution. S'il semble évident que nous ayons les 12 dernières lignes de ce panneau, il est impossible de préciser où se situait primitivement la première ligne; on peut seulement noter que, au-dessus des 11 dernières lignes, on reconnaît un tout petit reste d'une 12e ligne, puis un espace ayant pu contenir deux autres lignes, enfin les restes de plusieurs lettres non identifiables d'une ligne antérieure.

4'. ?ḣ.....l̇..
5'. ... ṁṭ̈ʾ ẅʾl̇ḣn ....
6'. ... żẏ ḥ/l̇... ṁ. ḃẗ....ṫ .ṫṅḣṁ ḃʾn ̈ʿlt ẇl̈ʾ ...ṫ[........]
7'. l̈ʾ .. l̈ʾ ẏḣẇẏ l̇k̇ṅ ̈ʿl [š]ṁš ẏ/ʾ.l̇ šṁš ḣṅ/k̇ tṁṭ̈ʾ ʿmh ṡṗẇṙ .. q̇[.?]
8'. lʾ ʾk̈l̇ ʾšḃq̇ṅḣ ʾšk̇ḃ ʿmh ṙḥm ʾṅḣ l̇ḣy šgÿʾ ẇ/ḧʿ[..........]
9'. ʿl ʾṫṫʾ wʾškḥẏḣtbh bbẏṫḣ ẅʾ[m]ṙ ḣn tškbṅ ʿm ḥ̇rʾ l̇ʾ[..........]
10'. ʾ/ẏntn lk?k̇ṡṗ k̈ṙš] [w]ʿnṫ ẅʾṁṙṫ ḋn̈ʾ ḥrʾ lʾškb ʿm gbṙ zy [...........]
11'. ḥ̇rʾ ḣ. l̇k̇ ẅʿn̈ṫ?ṫ.q̇[b]l ʾtmnḃn ʾlhʾ zy lḣ hn tntn lẏ[..........]
12'. [.]ṅ [..]k̇m ʿmẏ wʾzl wʾmr lḥrʾ ʾnh lm ʾmrt l.. hn tm[..........]
13'. ... ʾškb ʿmh rḥm ʾnh lhy šgyʾ wʿlymʾ ʾz̈l̇ ̇ʿl ʾṡrẏ[......]
14'. l̈ʾ ÿṫṅtn lkẏ k̇ṡ[p] k̈ṙš] ḣ... ʿm ... ̈ʿlẏṁ̈ʾ żṅḣ q̇ḃ[l ʾ]ṫmnḃn [?]
15'. l̇ʾ ʾškb ʿmh wlʾ thẇtbnḣ ḃẏṫẏ wʾmr l̇ʾ ṫṁ[..]ṅ ẇṅṫṅṫṁ ̇ʿ[......]

[33]Ibid.

5'. .... *il est arrivé et les dieux* ....

6'. *qui* .... *leur*......... *dans Héliopolis je suis entré et ne* .... *pas* ....

7'. *ne* ...... *pas* ..... *que ne soit pas pour vous(?) vers(?) le soleil* ..... *soleil. Et si tu arrives auprès de lui/elle, raconte(?)* ....

8'. "Je ne pourrai pas l'abandonner, *je coucherai* avec *lui/elle*; moi je l'aime beaucoup ...." ...?

9'. vers *la* femme et *il la trouva demeurant* dans *sa* maison *et il d(i)t: "Si tu* couches avec Ḥorâ ....

10'. *je/il te donnera(i) 1 karsh d'argent". (Et) elle prit la parole et dit ceci(?)*: "Ḥorâ, je ne coucherai pas avec un homme qui ....

11'. *Ḥorâ* ...... *et elle prit la parole* .... *de(va)nt* Atoumnebôn son dieu; si tu *me* donnes ....

12'. .... avec *moi*. Et il alla et dit à Ḥorâ: "En vérité, moi, j'ai dit *à* ....: *'Si tu* ....

13'. ...... *je* coucherai avec *lui/elle*; moi, je l'aime beaucoup". Et le jeune homme *alla vers Osiris(?)* ....

14'. *et il ne te sera pas donné 1 karsh d'argent* .... *avec* ..... *ce jeune homme deva(nt A)toumnebôn* ...?...

15'. Je ne coucherai pas avec *lui/elle et tu ne le/la feras pas habiter dans ma* maison. Et il dit: *"Tu/vous ne* .... *pas et vous avez donné* ..?...

5'. *mṭ' w'lhn* est une lecture très incertaine.

6'. *b'n ʿlt* est une formule qui peut être rapproché de Cowley 7, 8:[34] *bbytk* [*l'*] *ʿlt*; *'on/'ôn*, "Heliopolis", est déjà attesté dans la Bible (Gn 41,45. 50; 46,20; cf. Ez 30,17). On retrouve *'n mṣrym* et peut-être *'n*[*y*] dans un graffito phénicien d'Abydos à l'époque perse (*KAI* 49, 34).[35]

7'. La lecture du début de la ligne reste très incertaine, de même que *lkn̊* (on pourrait aussi proposer *lkẘ*). A la fin, la lecture *spwr*, "histoire" ou "raconte"(?), est, elle aussi, très incertaine. Ensuite, on pourrait proposer la lecture conjecturale *q*[*r'*], *"pro(clame)/l(is)"*. On notera que, auparavant, le suffixe personnel de *ʿmh* peut être masculin (*-ēh*) ou féminin (*-āh*). Par ailleurs, il est difficile de préciser si *šmš* est ici un nom commun, "soleil", une divinité, "Shamash",[36] ou un titre désignant un pharaon.[37]

8'. N. Giron avait déjà proposé la lecture *l'*... jusqu'à *šgy'*, cependant il lisait l'avant-dernier mot *lḥy* en proposant d'y voir éventuellement un nom propre "Lehi(?)", alors

---

[34]*Cowley* = A. Cowley, *Aramaic Papyri of the Fifth Century B.C.* (Oxford 1923 = Osnabrück, 1967).

[35]Cf. de façon générale: L. Kàkosy, "Heliopolis", *LÄ* II, 7 (1977), col. 1111-1113.

[36]Cf. déjà N. Giron, *AE* 8 (1923), p. 40.

[37]Cf., par ex., *EA* 49,1; 53,1; 55,1; 60,1... : W. L. Moran, *Les lettres d'El Amarna*, LAPO 13 (Paris, 1987), pp. 219, 224, 226, 233....

que paléographiquement, avec J. Naveh, on lit clairement *lhy*. En araméen ancien, le verbe *ykl/khl* peut être suivi soit d'un verbe à la même forme personnelle comme ici, soit d'un infinitif précédé du *l*, cette deuxième construction devenant de plus en plus fréquente à partir de l'araméen d'empire.[38] On notera aussi le *n energicum* dans la forme *ʾšbqnh*[39] ainsi que, à nouveau, l'ambiguïté du suffixe personnel -*h*, masculin ou féminin, dans *ʿmh*; cependant le contexte, avec la mention de "*la* femme" (début de 9'), semble plutôt indiquer ici le féminin. Le problème devient encore plus compliqué avec la forme *lhy*: l'emploi de la particule *l*- devant un complément d'objet direct est tout à fait normal[40] mais le suffixe -*hy* est surprenant; on attendrait la forme masculine *lēh* ou, plutôt, d'après le contexte, la forme féminine *lāh*.[41] La graphie *lhy* suppose probablement une vocalisation *lāhī*. On pourrait songer éventuellement à une faute, à une métathèse pour *lyh*, écriture pleine de *lēh*,[42] mais comme la même forme se retrouve à la ligne 13, cette interprétation semble exclue. On pourrait alors songer à une influence du suffixe masculin -*hy*[43] après une voyelle finale[44] mais le contexte semble indiquer qu'il s'agit d'un suffixe personnel féminin; en effet, *rḥm ʾnh lhy* (lignes 8' et 13') a un sujet masculin, puisque la forme *rḥm* est masculine, et le contexte, avec "*la* femme" au début de la ligne 9', semble indiquer qu'il s'agit d'un amour hétérosexuel. Dès lors, un tel suffixe féminin anormal -*hy* pourrait s'expliquer:
— soit par une tendance à confondre les suffixes des deux genres,[45]
— soit parce que la finale -*y* a pu être sentie chez certains locuteurs comme caractéristique habituelle des suffixes verbaux et pronominaux personnels féminins,
— soit enfin, mais moins vraisemblement à cause du contexte, parce que ce suffixe personnel aurait été assimilé à un pronom personnel indépendant à fonction démonstrative;[46] dans ce cas, on pourrait rapprocher *rḥm ʾnh lhy* de *hy mlbš ʾnh* dans *Hermopolis* IV, 6-7.[47]

A la fin de la ligne 8', J. Naveh (inédit) a proposé de restituer *wʿ*[*lymʾ ʾzl*] d'après la ligne 13'; cette restitution semble raisonnable; cependant la lecture du *w* reste très incertaine; on pourrait aussi proposer de lire *ḣʿ*[... ou même *żẇʿ* [...

---

[38]*Segert* § 6.6.8.1.5.
[39]Cf. *Segert* § 5.6.5.3.1.; 5.7.9.4.5-8.
[40]Cf. *Segert* § 6.5.2.3.6.; 7.2.3.6; cf aussi, déjà, Tell Fekheriyeh 3: *mšqy lmt kln*.
[41]Cf. *Segert* § 5.5.2.9.
[42]Cf. *Segert* § 5.5.2.8.2.
[43]Pour une discussion récente de ce suffixe, cf. E. M. Cook, "The Orthography of Final Unstressed Long Vowels in Old and Imperial Aramaic", dans *Sopher Mahir: Northwest Semitic Studies Presented to S. Segert, Maarav* 5-6 (1990) p.52-67, spéc. p. 56-60.
[44]Cf. *Segert* § 5.1.3.3.5.6.
[45]Cf. *Segert* § 5.5.2.8.2;.6.3.1.3.2.
[46]Cf. *Segert* § 5.1.2.3.5.
[47]Cf. E. Y. Kutscher, *Hebrew and Aramaic Studies* (Jerusalem 1977) pp. 54, 106; B. Porten, A. Yardeni, *Textbook of Aramaic Documents from Ancient Egypt I, Letters* (Jerusalem 1986), p. 10: A 2.1, 6-7.

9'. N. Giron n'avait rien lu pour cette ligne dont J. Naveh a présenté une lecture préliminaire que nous avons légèrement modifiée. Ainsi J. Naveh avait-il proposé de lire *wʾškḥh ytbh* mais, paléographiquement, on lit assez clairement *wʾškḥyhtbh*, probablement une faute de scribe par métathèse pour *wʾškḥh ytbh*. Puisque *ytbh* est au féminin, le suffixe personnel *-h* de *ʾškḥh* doit, lui aussi, être féminin. Dès lors, *tškbn* est plutôt la 2e pers. fém. sing. (*tiškᵉbīn*)[48] que la 2e pers. masc. ou fém. pluriel (*tiškᵉbūn* ou *tiškᵉbān*). Le nom propre *ḥrʾ* semble nouveau dans les textes araméens d'Égypte mais on peut le rapprocher de *ḥry*, *ḥwr* et *ḥwry*;[49] il s'agit probablement d'un hypocoristique comportant le théonyme "Horus". A la fin de la ligne, après le *l*, la trace de lettre pourrait être celle d'un *ʾ (lʾ)*, d'un *y (ly)*, d'un *h (lh)* ou d'un *z*.

10'. Au début de la ligne, N. Giron avait proposé de lire [ʾ]*ntn lkmrn*[50] et J. Naveh (inédit): [*yt*]*ntn lky ksp krš*|. D'après l'alignement probable des débuts de ligne, il ne semble y avoir qu'une lettre avant *ntn*; d'après les traces, il s'agit probablement d'un *y* ou d'un *ʾ*. Après *lk*, la présence d'un *y* reste très incertaine: certaines traces pourraient correspondre à cette lettre mais celle-ci ne laisserait aucun espace de séparation avant *ksp*. Le *karsh* est une unité de poids perse bien attestée dans les documents araméens d'Égypte et valant environ 83,35 g.[51] Vers le milieu de la ligne la lecture *wʾmrt* reste très incertaine, de même que le début du mot suivant que J. Naveh proposait de lire *ḥrʾ*; *dnʾ* pourrait se rattacher à ce qui précède: ... "et elle dit ceci ..." (cependant on attendrait alors plutôt *kdnʾ* [52]), ou à ce qui suit: "celui-ci (est) Horâ" ou "ce Ḥorâ". L'association des deux verbes *ʿnh* et *ʾmr* est bien connue en araméen littéraire[53] tandis que *lʾškb* semble un emploi de la particule négative *l-* attestée à l'époque ancienne jusqu'au milieu du VIIe s.,[54] à moins qu'il ne s'agisse d'une graphie fautive par haplographie pour *lʾ ʾškb*. A la fin de la ligne, la lecture *ʿm gbr zy*, un peu abîmé, paraît pratiquement certaine.

11'. Le début de la ligne reste très incertain. N. Giron avait proposé de lire ensuite *ʾtmnd/rn ʾlhʾ zy lh hn ʾntn lh* ..., suivi en grande partie par J. Naveh (inédit) qui ajoutait, au début, *q*[*b*]*l* et corrigeait *ʾntn lh* en *tntn ly* à la fin. Cette dernière correction est tout à fait justifiée même si le *y* final reste quelque peu incertain. La *crux* de cette ligne est le mot qui précède *ʾlhʾ*; il peut se lire *ʾtmndn*, *ʾtmnrn* ou *ʾtmnbn*. Avec N.

---

48 Cf. *Segert* § 5.6.4.6.3.

49 Cf. W. Kornfeld, "Onomastica aramaica und das Alte Testament", *ZAW* 88 (1976), pp. 105-112, spéc. pp. 107-109; *id.*, *Onomastica aramaica aus Ägypten* (Wien 1978), pp. 80, 81.

50 *AE* 8 (1923), p. 40.

51 Cf., par ex. P. Grelot, *Documents araméens d'Egypte*, LAPO 5 (Paris 1972), p. 81, n. f; p. 175, n. c.; p. 510.

52 Cf. Jr 10, 11; *Kraeling* 5, 3.

53 Cf. en araméen biblique: Dn 2,5.7.8...; cf. aussi Ahiqar 14-15, 19-20(?), 45, 54(?), 58(?), 59(?), 67(?), 110, 118, 121, 166(?); Ḥor fils de Pawenesh recto 2(?) cf. B. Porten, *Select Aramaic Papyri from Ancient Egypt* (Jerusalem, 1986), p.16 (= *Cowley* 71,32); B. Porten, A. Yardeni, *Textbook ... III, Literature, Accounts, Lists* (Jerusalem 1993), p. 54.

54 Cf. *Segert* § 5.5.6.1.4.

Giron, on peut y reconnaître "un nom divin composé avec le nom du dieu égyptien Atoum".[55] Ce grand dieu égyptien est bien connu comme le grand dieu d'Héliopolis,[56] ville déjà mentionée à la ligne 6'. En fait, le titre *nb Iwnw*, "maître d'Héliopolis", est le titre le plus souvent donné à Atoum, spécialement à l'époque tardive,[57] tandis qu'Atoum peut être considéré comme le dieu principal de Saïs à l'époque de la XXVIe dynastie.[58] On notera, en particulier, que "Atoum maître d'Héliopolis (*ʾtm nb ʾnw*)" est attesté dans plusieurs textes littéraires tardifs,[59] ainsi que dans l'inscription égyptienne de la fameuse statue de Darius Ier découverte à Suse, très probablement la copie d'une statue déposée dans le temple d'Atoum à Héliopolis.[60] Dès lors, il semble évident qu'il faut préférer la lecture *ʾtmnb̊n*, contraction de *ʾtm nb ‹ʾ›n*, "Atoum maître d'Héliopolis", où l'association du théonyme originel et de son titre habituel est devenu un nouveau théonyme: "Atoumnebôn".

12'. N. Giron était resté silencieux sur cette ligne que J. Naveh (inédit) proposait de lire [*lʾ ʾškb*] *ʿmḣ wʾzl wʾmr lḥrʾ ʾnh lm ʾmrt l*[ ]*n tm*[*h...lʾ ʾkl ʾšb*]. Sur la photographie de M. Busutil, il semble qu'on puisse lire au début [*h*]*ṅ* [..]*k̊m ʿmẏ*. Ensuite *wʾzl wʾmr* peuvent être à la 3e pers. du masc. sing. de l'accompli, soit à la 2e pers. du masc. sing. de l'impératif. Les paroles adressées à Ḥorâ restent fragmentaires et difficiles à saisir: *lm* est la particule assérative souvent employée au début d'un discours direct[61] tandis que *ʾmrt* ne peut être ici que la 1ère pers. du sing. de l'accompli renforcée par *ʾnh* qui précède. Après *ʾmrt*, on reconnaît un *l* suivi, peut-être, de *mz*, *my*, *mr* ou *kʾ*, puis, peut-être, d'un espace de séparation, de *ḣn* et de *tm.*[, qui pourrait être le début d'un verbe à la 2e. pers.

13'. N. Giron avait déjà lu la partie centrale de cette ligne: *ʾškb ʿmh rḥm ʾnh lḥ̇y šgyʾ ẇʿl̇ẏmʾ*; outre la correction justifiée de *lḥy* en *lhy*, J. Naveh (inédit) a proposé de lire au début *q̇nh* pour retrouver la même formule qu'à la ligne 8'; cependant ce serait le seul cas, dans ce panneau, de coupure d'un mot en fin de ligne; de plus, paléographiquement, on lirait plutôt *ẇl̇ʾ/ẇl̇ẏ/ẇlṁ* ou, à la rigueur, *żṅḣ*. Après le milieu de la ligne, la lecture *ʿlymʾ* semble pratiquement certaine; *ʿlym* peut désigner aussi bien le "jeune homme" que le "serviteur".[62] A la fin de la ligne, J. Naveh (inédit) proposait de lire *ʾt*[*tʾ*;

---

[55]*AE* 8 (1923), p. 40.

[56]Cf. J. Yoyotte, "Prêtres et sanctuaires du nome Héliopolite à la basse époque", *BIFAO* 54 (1954), pp. 83-115, spéc. p. 85, n. 4; L. Kàkosy, "Atum", *LÄ* I, 3 (1973), col. 550-552; K. Myśliwiec, *Studien zum Gott Atum, II, Name, Epitheta, Iconographie* (Hildesheim, 1979), pp. 85ff; B. Watterson, *The Gods of Ancient Egypt* (London, 1984), pp. 45-50.

[57]K. Myśliwiec, *Studien... II*, pp. 112-114.

[58]Ibid., p. 118.

[59]Cf., par example, W. Spiegelberg, *Demotische Texte auf Krügen*, Demotische Studien 5 (Leipzig 1912), pp. 22-23.

[60]Cf. J. Yoyotte, "Les inscriptions hiéroglyphiques: Darius et l'Egypte", *JA* 260 (1972), pp. 253-266; cf. aussi B. Ockinga, "Inschrift Darius I. aus Susa", *TUAT* II, 4 (1988), pp. 552-554.

[61]*Segert* § 5.5.6.2.1.

[62]Cf., par exemple, *Driver* 8,2; H. Z. Szubin - B. Porten, "Royal Grants in Egypt: A New Interpretation of Driver 2", *JNES* 46 (1987), pp. 39-48, spéc. p. 42-43.

cependant les traces qui restent correspondraient plutôt à *ʾsry*[qui pourrait être soit le théonyme “Osiris”,[63] soit un anthroponyme comportant ce théonyme.
14’. N. Giron n’avait rien proposé pour cette ligne dont la lecture suit, en partie, les propositions de J. Naveh et reste généralement très incertaine.
15’. La lecture de cette ligne suit aussi, en partie, les propositions de J. Naveh qui, vers le milieu de la ligne lisait *wlʾth tbn ʿl byth*. Paléographiquement, il semble préférable de lire *wlʾ thẇtbnḣ ḃẏṫẏ*, en comprenant *thwtbnh* comme l’inaccompli haphel de *ytb*, suivi du *n energicum* et du suffixe personnel *-h*. A la fin de la ligne, la lecture probable *wntntm* semble comporter le suffixe *-tm* surtout attesté en araméen ancien tandis qu’en araméen d’empire on a habituellement le suffixe *-tn*.[64] Cependant l’interprétation de la plus grande partie de cette ligne, visiblement la dernière de ce panneau, reste très incertaine.

Panneau III-IV

Les restes des inscriptions de ce panneau ont été accidentellement séparés en deux groupes, d’où la double numérotation que lui a donné N. Giron. Selon ce dernier, “on peut déchiffrer quelques lettres de 8 lignes; il semble que nous possédions la fin des lignes; tout le commencement manque”[65]. En fait, il semble possible d’identifier une lettre d’une 9e ligne inférieure et de reconnaître des traces non identifiables de deux lignes supérieures.

3’.		l̇ṁ.ṅ/ṫ ḥ̇....
4’.		]....ʾ̇lḣʾ̇
5’.		]ṁ..ʾ̇ ...ṙ/ṁ..ṅ
6’.		]yq̇ṁ ẇk̇..ż.. żẏ
7’.		]ṅ k̇l̇ḣ l̇.ẏ... bʿḋn
8’.	ṁ. ẇ lhm wl̇ʾ . [	]ṗ/k̇slhm ṅṫṅ lʾḥrnn
9’.	ʿ̇l̇.... ṁṅ ...lnʾ .ṫ. ʿ̇ḋ[	]kl ʾn[š] ẏhwy tmh
10’.	ḣṁẇ ... ṁ..ṅẏl̇ ʾ̇p l̇k̇l ʾ̇[	]hmẇ ṅṫṅ
11’.		]l̇

4’.		]...... *le dieu*
5’.		]................
6’.		]*il se dressera* .... *qui*
7’.		].. *tout entier* .... *au moment*
8’.	.... *à eux* et *ne* ... *pas*[	]*leur pierre taillée il donna* à d’autres

---

[63]Cf. *ʾwsry ʾlhʾ* : *KAI* 267, 2; 269, 1; 272; cf. aussi 268, 1-2.3-4; 269, 3.
[64]*Segert* § 5.6.4.4.3.
[65]*AE* 8 (1923), p. 40.

9'...... *depuis* ... à nous...*jusqu'à*[ ]tout *hom(me) (qui?) sera* là
10'. *eux* .... aussi *à tout* ...[ ]*eux, il a donné*

A la ligne 9', N. Giron avait déjà lu ..*kl ʾn*[*š*] *yhwy tmh*..[66]

Dans ce texte très fragmentaire, il semble difficile de saisir une quelconque allusion ou référence au texte du panneau précédent, sauf, peut-être, *ʾlhʾ* (ligne 4').

Panneau V

Selon N. Giron, ce panneau est "le plus important de la série malheureusement dans un état lamentable". On discerne les "restes d'au moins 11 lignes (12 mots à la ligne)... Les lignes de ce texte paraissent bien commencer immédiatement à gauche de la robe d'un personnage encore visible. Un large trait rouge vertical marque la fin des lignes de la première tranche du texte, la suite également incomplète par le haut est comprise entre ce trait et un second trait de la même couleur qui lui est parallèle. De ce deuxième texte, 5 lignes (7 mots à la ligne) seulement peuvent être utilement étudiées... Entre la fin du N° 5 et l'angle peut-être y avait-il encore place pour un texte où rien ne subsiste".[67] Tel qu'il est compris par N. Giron, ce triple panneau fait quelque 2m de long. Il est divisé en trois parties (A, B, C) par deux gros traits rouges verticaux. Il est difficile de préciser si ce sont les mêmes lignes qui continuent en A, B (et C?), chevauchant les deux traits verticaux, ou s'il faut distinguer trois panneaux différents: VA, VB et VC, aucune ligne de ce dernier n'étant conservée. En effet:

— apparemment les lignes de VA et de VB semblent suivre la même orientation; elles sont presque horizontales, descendant légèrement vers la gauche;

— apparemment aussi la graphie est la même et il semble s'agir du même scribe;

— cependant, si certaines lignes de VA (5', 6', 7') semblent se continuer en VB, d'autres (4', 8', 9', 10') ne le semblent pas;

— de plus, le panneau est déjà un grand panneau; si on lui adjoignait VB et VC, ce panneau aurait des lignes d'environ 2 m de longeur, sans commune mesure avec la longueur des lignes des autre panneaux;

— enfin, le peu que l'on peut suivre du texte ne permet pas de préciser si les mêmes lignes se continuaient de VA en VB.

Nous présenterons donc séparément les panneaux VA et VB mais avec une numérotation approximativement harmonisée des lignes permettant facilement un éventuel raccordement des lignes de VB à celles de VA. Les deux gros traits rouges verticaux sont marqués par deux traits verticaux parallèles.

---

[66]Ibid., p. 41.
[67]Ibid., p. 41.

VA

1’. ....
2’. ....
3’. ṗṡl̇ żẏ [ʾ]ṅh th......................
4’. ṁl̇k̇ ....ṗ ṁl̇ẏ l̇.............ẏk̇...ṁ..... żṅḣ ...||
5’. ... l̇pṡṁšk̇ ṗṙʿḣ ḥ̇.ṫ l̇..............k̇š ...k̇.. ẇḃẏṫḣ ẏḣẇ[h?]||
6’. lpṡṁšk ṗṙʿḣ ḥḋ/ṙ żẏ ʾżl̇ l̇ḣẏ ʿm ... ... ẇḃẏṫ[...]ẏḃ lpṡṁšk̇ ṗṙʿḣ||
7’. ?ḥḋ/ṙ ṣḋ/ṙy ż.. mlṅ ʿ.t wnḥ̇t bʾlṗ. .ṅ/q̇.... wmṅ/ṫ..ṅš̈ʾ ʿṁḣ ẇšṗḋ/ṙ||
8’. hq̇m ṗ̈r[ʿh?] ʿl thrqʾ ṁl̇k̇ k̇šẏʾ żẏ ṁl̇k̇ tmh q̇ṁ [q?]ḋṁ thrq̇ʾ ẇ/ḥ̇||
9’. ʾṅ/l̇hʾ.. żṅḣ mrʾẏ ṫh[r]q̈ʾ ṙ/ḋḣ.? ṁẇẗḃ ..?ṁṙʾẏ ẇ... ṁl̇ṅ/k̇ zy [ʾ?]ṅḣ||
10’. ʾmr q[d]ṁ mrʾy mlkʾ ʾyṫ ṁl̇ṅ żẏ ...?ḣ l?ʾ̈t/ṅḣ ....?ḣṁ k̇š||
11’. ṁṗ?ḥ̇ṅḣ .l̇ḥ̇ ʿl prʿh nk̇[w?]..... l̇ḥ̇ẏṅ l̈ʾ .... nḥṙ?ṗ̈r...
12’. .... ẇ/k̇ḣṅ l̈t........................
13’. lnšyhṁ wṗryhm ..ʾ̇ ʾzrʿ mlḥ ẇk/ṗ.....? ṙḥ̇l ṗṙḣ .?ṙ.. ẏṅḥ?ẇṗṙ?

3’. *pierre taillée/statue que moi ......*
4’. *roi .... paroles .... ceci ....* ||
5’. *..... au pharaon Psammétique .... et sa maison ser[a]* ||
6’. *au pharaon Psammétique, quelqu’un qui est allé à lui avec ... et la maison .... au pharaon Psammétique* ||
7’. *mon ennemi(?) .... des paroles ...... et il est descendu en bateau ... et depuis(?) ..... il a pris lui/elle et il a bien fait(?)* ||
8’. *Il a dressé pha[raon] contre* Taharqâ, *roi des Nubiens qui règne* là-bas; il *s’est levé [fa]ce à/devant* Taharqâ *et(?)* ||
9’. *moi je .... ceci*; *mon* maître *Taharqâ .... siège/résidence ... mon maître et ...... des paroles(?) que [m]oi(?)* ||
10’. *disant de[v]ant* mon maître le roi *des paroles que .... Nubie(?)* ||
11’. *Memphis(?)* .... au pharaon *Nék[ô?] .... mauvais(?), ne ... pas ....*
12’. .... *et si(?)* ....
13’. à leur femmes et leurs *agneaux* ..... je sèmerai du sel et .... *brebis, agnelle ....*

3’. La lecture du début de cette ligne reste conjecturale; pour *psl*, cf. III-IV, 8’; pour *zy* [ʾ]*nh*, *infra*, 9’(?).

4’. Lecture conjecturale.

5’. Sauf *psmšk*, qui est probable, la lecture de cette ligne reste conjecturale. *Psmšk*, nom égyptien d’origine libyque ou éthiopienne (*p3-ś-n-mṯk*), est déjà attesté en transcription araméenne dans les documents araméens d'Égypte.[68] Ce nom revient deux fois à la ligne 6' de ce panneau, chaque fois suivi, semble-t-il, de *prʿh*, "pharaon". Dans ce panneau, il est mentionné aux côtés de Taharqâ (8', 9') et de Nékô (11');[69] il s'agit donc très probablement du "pharaon Psammétique" Ier (664-610), fondateur de la XXVIe dynastie.[70]

6'. Dans cette ligne, *ʾzl* reste conjectural, de même que le *prʿh* final. *Ḥd* semble employé ici comme un pronom indéfini[71] mais on pourraît aussi bien proposer de lire ici un nom propre *ḥr*, "Ḥor"[72].

7'. Malgré plusieurs lettres certaines ou probables, l'interprétation de cette ligne reste très incertaine. Vers le milieu de la ligne, on pourrait proposer de compléter *ʿ[š]t*, "il a pensé, comploté". A la fin de la ligne, *špr* pourrait être un verbe, un nom commun, "bien", ou même un nom propre.[73]

8'. N. Giron avait déjà proposé de lire ... *thrqʾ mlk k? w? ṡyʾ*(?) *zy mlk tmh* ... en notant que la lecture *kwšyʾ* était "très douteuse".[74] Il semble préférable de lire *k̇ṡyʾ*; on en rapprochera l'hébreu *kušîm/kušiyyîm* (Am 9,7; Dn 11,43) qui désigne les "Ethiopiens" ou, plus précisément, les "Nubiens". La graphie *thrqʾ* pour "Taharqâ" est conforme à l'égyptien alors que la Bible a transcrit ce nom avec une métathèse: *tirhāqāh* (2 R 19,9; Is 37,9). Avec N. Giron, on note que le titre de Taharqâ n'est pas "pharaon" ou "roi d'Égypte", ou encore "roi des Égyptiens", mais "roi des Nubiens/Éthiopiens", ce qui correspond à son appartenance à la dynastie "éthiopienne" (XXVe dynastie).[75] On le comparera au titre biblique *melek-kūš* (2 R 19,9; Is 37,9) et au titre assyrien habituel *šar Kūsi*.[76] Apparemment les Assyriens se sont présentés comme les libérateurs de l'Égypte contre le conquérant nubien/éthiopien et l'alliance/vassalité de Nékô Ier et de Psammétique Ier pouvait être interprétée comme un appui assyrien à la libération de l'Égypte.[77] La terminologie de notre texte pourrait donc refléter la terminologie de la dynastie saïte et de ses alliés/suzerains assyriens.

9'. N. Giron avait déjà noté le titre *mr.ʾy* appliqué à Taharqâ dans cette ligne. Malheureusement la lecture des autres mots reste très incertaine. Vers le milieu de la

---

[68]Kornfeld, *Onomastica*, pp. 91-92.
[69]Cf. déjà N. Giron, *AE* 8 (1923), p. 41.
[70]Cf., par exemple, K. A. Kitchen, *The Third Intermediate Period in Egypt (1100-650 B.C.)* (Warminster 1986²), pp. 399-408.
[71]Cf. *Segert* § 5.1.7.2.
[72]Cf. Kornfeld, *Onomastica*, p. 122.
[73]Ibid., p. 75.
[74]*AE* 8 (1923), p. 41.
[75]Cf., par exemple, Kitchen, *Third Intermediate Period*, pp. 387-393; J. Leclant "Taharqa", *LÄ* VI, 3 (1985), col. 157-184.
[76]Sur la distinction entre *Muṣur* et *Kusu* dans les textes assyriens d'Assarhaddon et d'Assurbanipal cf. A. Spalinger, "Esarhaddon and Egypt: An Analysis of the First Invasion of Egypt", *Orientalia* 43 (1974), pp. 295-326, spéc. pp. 320-324.
[77]Cf. Id., "Assurbanipal and Egypt: A Source Study", *JAOS* 94 (1974), pp. 316-328; id., "Psammetichus King of Egypt, I", *JARCE* 13 (1976), pp. 133-147.

ligne, on pourraît songer à restituer, de façon hypothétique, quelque chose comme: *mrʾy thrqʾ rḥ[q] mwtb*, "mon maître Taharqâ a éloigné (sa) demeure".

10'. La deuxième partie de cette ligne est très incertaine. Vers le milieu de la ligne, la lecture incertaine *ʾyṫ ṁl̇ṅ* pourrait fournir un indice chronologique puisque la *nota accusativi* araméenne *ʾyt* est essentiellement attesteé en araméen ancien jusque vers 650 av. J.-C.[78]

11'. Cette ligne commence à la base du "pilier" rouge à droite, descend légèrement sous la ligne horizontale reliant la base des traits rouges verticaux et semble se terminer sous et un peu à gauche du premier trait rouge vertical. N. Giron avait déjà proposé de lire *prʿh n[kw]*. Dans cette ligne, seul *ʿl prʿh* est sûr tandis que la mention de Nékô y est probable et tout le reste très incertain. Le syntagme se retrouve probablement dans les panneaux VIII et IX. Aux côtés de Taharqâ et de Psammétique, il s'agit très probablement de Nékô Ier (c. 672-664), prince de Saïs et père de Psammétique.[79] On notera que notre texte lui donne très probablement le titre de "pharaon" (*prʿh*) tandis que la transcription *nkw/nᵉkô* (*infra*: VIII) était déjà attestée dans la Bible (Jr 46,2; 2 Ch 35,20.22; 36,4), à côté de *nᵉkōh* (2 R 23,29.33.34.35), pour le pharaon Nékô II.

12'. Cette ligne, écrite sur un gros trait rouge horizontal marquant la limite inférieure du registre des fresques, est presque totalement illisible.

13'. La lecture de la deuxième partie de cette ligne, écrite aussi sur les restes d'un gros trait rouge horizontal, reste très incertaine. Le sens exact de *pryhm* reste quelque peu incertain car, en hébreu, *par* désigne un "taureau" ou un "taurillon",[80] tandis qu'en syriaque et mandéen, il s'agit d'un "agneau", comme en accadien (*parru*); *pr* semble attesté ici pour la première fois en araméen ancien. L'expression *ʾzrʿ mlḥ*, "je sèmerai du sel", pourrait faire référence à un rite de malédiction (cf. Sfiré I A 36). Dès lors, cette dernière ligne, ainsi que VB 7' (*infra*) pourrait faire allusion à la prise et au pillage d'une ville (Memphis ou Thèbes ?).[81]

VB

4'. ....ṅ ... ẇl̇k̇l̇ ....ṫ ..?||
5'. ?ẇṁṅ .... żṅḣ .. ẇṁṅ ..?ḣẏ l̇ʾṫḣ||
6'. l̇ḣṁ ʾṅḣ ...? l̇ṁṣṙẏṅ ẇṁṣṙẏṅ ..q̇ żẏ ṁ/ʿl̇ ||
7'. ż/ṙḥl̇ .... ẇṅšẏḣṁ ṫṙẏḣṁ ʾḥḋẇ ẇḃżẇ||
8'. ʾṧ...? šl̇ṁ šl̇ṁ

---

[78]Cf. R. Degen, *Altaramäische Grammatik* (Wiesbaden 1969), pp. 95-96; *Segert* § 5.5.3.1.2.

[79]Cf., par exemple, J. Yoyotte, "Néchao ou Néko", *SDB* VI (1960), col. 363-367; Kitchen, *Third Intermediate Period*, pp. 145-147, 391-395.

[80]Cf. R. Péter, "*Pr* et *šr*, note de lexicographie hébraïque", *VT* 25 (1975), pp. 486-496.

[81]Comparer la description de la prise de Memphis par Assarhaddon dans la stèle de Zencirli (*ARAB* II, § 580).

10'. ? |̇|̇| ?

12'. ? żṅḣ ḣ. ʿ̇l̇ ḣṗ/ṡq̇ẇ ?

4'. .... *et à tout* ....

5'. *et depuis(?) .... ceci ..... et depuis .... il n'est pas venu(?)* ||

6'. *pour eux; moi je ...... pour l'Égypte et l'Égypte .... que .....* ||

7'. *brebis(?) .... et leur femmes, leurs bovins, ils ont saisis et pillés* ||

8'. *............... paix(?), paix.*

10'. ? *3* ?

12'. ? *ceci .... ils ont fait sortir/monter(?)* ?

6'. La double mention de *mṣryn* semble très probable mais *zy* reste très incertain: il pourrait aussi s'agir du chiffre 2.

7'. Le sens exact de *tr* est difficile à préciser: "taureau", "boeuf", ou, plutôt, "bovidé" en général.[82]

8'. Le premier *šlm* est très incertain, le second probable. Après ce dernier, on ne reconnaît plus aucune trace d'inscription sur cette ligne qui pourraît donc s'arrêter au milieu.

9'ss. Il ne semble pas y avoir de ligne correspondant à VA 9'; à la ligne suivante, la présence du chiffre 3 reste incertaine. Ensuite, il ne reste que quelques traces de la deuxième partie d'une seule ligne qui, d'après sa situation, correspond mieux à VA 12' qu'à 11' ou 13'; cependant cette correspondance reste approximative. La lecture proposée pour cette moitié de ligne reste très incertaine.

VC

Il ne reste aucune trace d'inscription à cet emplacement.[83]

Panneaux VI et VII

Ces deux panneaux sont situés sur la paroi orientale, à droite de la niche. N. Giron, qui ne disposait pas de photographie de ces panneaux, avait simplement noté: "N° 6. Traces de quelques mots dont je n'ai qu'une copie et où je distingue seulement ... *ʾlhʾ ʾmr ... le dieu dit.* N° 7, un seul mot ... *šmš* ...".[84]

En fait, le panneau supérieur VII, où on reconnaît les jambes d'un homme marchant à gauche, ne comporte apparemment (au moins, en 1984) aucune trace d'inscription à l'encre et le mot *šmš* se trouve, de fait, à droite du trait vertical rouge

[82]On remarquera que, dans Tell Fekheriyeh 20, la forme masculine correspondante, *swr*, désigne clairement des "vaches". Pour le champ sémantique du correspondant hébreu, cf. R. Péter, op. cit.

[83]Cf. déjà N. Giron *AE* 8 (1923), p. 41.

[84]Ibid.

marquant la séparation entre les panneaux VI et VII. Il ne reste apparemment rien de la fresque du panneau VI et très peu de lettres de son inscription primitive.

VI

1'. ......
2'. ..?ḣ..... ? ...šmš ṙ̈ʿ||
3'. ....
4'. ....
5'. k̈lhm ʿṁ...
6'. ʾḥ̇rnn ḣṅ p̈r...
7'. .ḃ. ʾlhʾ ʾmr ?
8'. ẗr........
9'. ....
10'. ....ṅ...

2'. .... ? .... *le soleil Raʿ(?)*||
5'. eux *tous avec ....*
6'. *d'autres, si ......*
7'. ......*le dieu a dit* ?

A la fin de la ligne 2, la lecture incertaine *rʿ*, suivant *šmš*, indiquerait-elle le dieu soleil Raʿ ?
Au début de la ligne 7', il semble y avoir trois lettres avant *ʾlhʾ*, la deuxième paraissant un *b* incertain tandis que les traces des deux autres ne permettent pas de proposer d'identification sérieuse.

Panneau VIII

Les panneaux VIII et IX sont situés à gauche de la niche et bien encadrés par deux gros traits rouges parallèles dont il ne reste plus qu'une partie près du plafond. Les deux panneaux sont séparés l'un de l'autre par des restes d'une sorte de gros pilier rouge. Comme l'avait déjà remarqué N. Giron, le panneau VIII "devait contenir pour le moins 13 lignes (10 mots à la ligne)".[85] Il ne reste qu'une ou deux lettres à la fin des premières lignes, puis des restes plus étendus des 5 ou 6 dernières lignes très abîmées.

1'. ? m||
2'. ? ṙ ||

[85]Ibid.

3'. ? l̇ḣ||
4'. ? ḥ̇ż||
5'. ? ṅ/ṁ||
6'. ?
7'. ?
8'. ....ḋ/ṙ....ṫ/ṅ..ʿ̇............
9'. l̇k̇ ṁl̇ṅ šṗṙṅ ẇʿṅḣ wʾmṙ l.ʾ̇... ʿ̇l̇ ....||
10'. ṁl̇k̇ tḣṙq̇ʾ ṫṁḣ ʾḥṙ/ḋ ...... šl̇ṁ ẇṭ̇ḃ ....ṗṁ ẇ||
11'. ?bʿ̇ḋn ʾnh ?ṅṫṅ ʾ̇l̇ṅ .....ṡ l̇......ṅ ẇl̇...?ṗm ẇʿ||
12'. .... lpṙʿh nk̇w ẇʿṅḣ .....ṅ ẇ/ḣṗq̇ l̇ḣṁ ṁ?||
13'. ... lḣṁ ......

9'. *à toi de belles paroles; et il prit la parole* et dit .... *contre/vers(?)* ....||
10'. *Taharqâ est roi là-bas, ensuite* ...... *paix et bonheur* .... *bouche(?) et(?)* ||
11'. *au moment, moi je donnerai(?) ceux-ci* .... *bouche(?) et(?).*||
12'. ....au pharaon Néḱô *et il prit la parole* ..... *il a fait sortir(?) pour* eux ..||
13'. .... *pour eux* ......

Il ne reste que quelques traces très indistinctes dans la partie droite des lignes 6' et 7', tandis que la lecture du début de la ligne 9' reste conjecturale. A cette ligne N. Giron avait déjà lu *ʿnh wʾmr*, de même que *thṙq̇ʾ tmh* à la ligne 10'.[86] Le début de cette dernière ligne, avec *mlk* qui reste très incertain, évoque VA 8' (*supra*). A la ligne 12', *lprʿh nkẇ* avait déjà été lu par N. Giron.[87] Le reste est très incertain.

Panneau IX

Ce panneau comportait primitivement la représentation d'un personnage avec vêtement bleu-vert marchant à droite et conduisant devant lui un veau(?). Apparemment l'inscription, presque totalement disparue dans sa partie droite, ne descendait pas jusqu'au bas du panneau mais s'arrêtait juste au-dessus du veau.

1'. ? ....
2'. ? ẇ...... ẇ.....................
3'. ? .q̇..? ḃ... ẇẏ....................
4'. ? ...ẏṅ ʿ̇ṅ.?ṅ. ?ẇ..ṅ ʿ̇...n..........
5'. ? ....ṅ. lm.?ḋ/ṙ l̇ẏ ..ḣ.? k̇ʿṅ ʿ̇l̇ żṅḣ||
6'. ? ... ṗṙʿ̇ḣ ʿ̇l̇ ḥbl ṁṩṙẏṅ ẇ...ẏṅ ..||

[86] Ibid.
[87] Ibid., p. 42.

7'. ? ʾl̇....ṁṅ? šlḥ̇ ʿl̇ẏḣṁ .....ẏṅḥ̇tẇ ṗṙ||
8'. ṗṙ ? ....ẇ/ṗ........ ʾl̇ḣ[y?] ṁṩṙẏṅ ḣṅ||
9'. l̇̈ʾ ? ...ḣ?l̇..... wʿnh wʾmr l̇ṁṙʾ l̇k̇ẇ/ṅš||
10'. . ? ...prʿh [n]k̇[w] ẇʾmr ....ẇ l̇..ṁ||
11'. ...

5'. ? .... *à moi* ..... *maintenant concernant cela* ||
6'. ? ... *le pharaon sur* le malheur *de l'Égypte et* ....||
7'. ? .....*il envoya vers eux* .... *ils feront descendre un agneau* ||
8'. *agneau(?)* ? .... *les dieu[x] d'Égypte si* ||
9'. *ne .. pas(?)* ? .... et il prit la parole et dit *au maître* .... ||
10'. .. ? .... le pharaon *[Né]k[ô] et* il dit .... ||

Les lectures de ce panneau sont généralement très fragmentaires et très incertaines.
A la ligne 6', *ḥbl mṩryn* avait déjà été lu par N. Giron[88]; on serait tenté de restituer ensuite *w[mṣr]yn*.
A la ligne 7', *šlḥ ʿlyḣṁ* avait été lu par N. Giron; la finale reste très incertaine.A la ligne 8', la restitution *ʾlh*[*y*] est conjecturale. Le syntagme *ʾlhy mṣryn* est déjà attesté au moins deux fois dans l'histoire de Ḥor fils de Pawenesh.[89]
A la fin de la ligne 9', la lecture est très incertaine; on pourrait songer à *kwš*, "Nubie" ou à *knš*, "rassemblement".
A la ligne 10', *prʿh* avait déjà été lu par N. Giron; la restitution [*n*]*k̇*[*w*] est très conjecturale.

Panneau X

N. Giron signalait "au moins 4 lignes dont on ne distingue presque plus rien, j'y ai cependant noté la présence du verbe *škb* ".[90] En 1984, on ne voyait plus rien de ce panneau, probablement en partie à cause de graffiti récents. Comme M. Busutil ne semble pas avoir photographié ce panneau, son inscription doit être considérée comme perdue.

Panneau XI

La plus grande partie de ce panneau est aussi perdue: nous n'en avons plus que des fins de ligne limitées à gauche par un gros pilier rouge. La partie supérieure, aujourd'hui disparue, nous a été en partie conservée sur la photographie de M. Busutil.

---

[88]Ibid.
[89]*Cowley* 71,8.26 = Porten, *Select Aramaic Papyri* (1986), p.16; verso II,2.8; B. Porten, A. Yardeni, *Textbook ...III*, p. 56.
[90]*AE* 8 (1923), p. 42-43.

1'. ? ....||
2'. ? ....żẏ l̇ẏ ytḃthm ||
3'. ? ...ṅ ẇk̈‘ṅ ḥ̇żẏ zy ẏšm̈ṙ ||
4'. ? ʾ̇/ẏ ṙḥṁ ṁ.. żẏ q̇[b]l̇ ḋṅḣ ||
5'. ? ṅ q̇b̈l ..... šm. ʾ̈l̇ṗ ||
6'. ? ṙḥṁ lḣ .... ..ṫẏ šgyʾ ||
7'. ? ṅ ʾ̇ṁṙ żṅḣ ......? k̇ḥ̇ḋḣ ||
8'. ? ḃ mt‘štn ʾnḥn l̇/‘̇m thrqʾ ||
9'. mṅ/ẇ kmrn ‘bdn hm qrb[?]||

2'. ? .... *qui est à moi, je les ai installés* ||
3'. ? ..... *et maintenant vois ce(lui) qui gardera* ||
4'. ? . *aime* .... *qui (est) de[v]ant ceci/celui-ci* ||
5'. ? . *devant* .... *il a placé(?) .. bateau* ||
6'. ? *l'aime* .... beaucoup ||
7'. ? . *a dit ceci* .... *ensemble* ||

8'. ? . nous pensons*: en vérité*, Taharqâ ||
9'. ? ... les prêtres, eux, ils font *une offrande/un combat* ||

La lecture des 5 premières lignes est très incertaine.
A la ligne 8', N. Giron avait déjà lu *mt‘štn ʾnḥn ..m thrqʾ*. Avant *m thrqʾ*, la trace de lettre pourrait être celle d'un *l* ou d'un *‘*.
A la ligne 9', N. Giron avait lu *...mṅ kṁrn ‘bdn hm qrbʾ*... Cependant on ne discerne aucune trace de lettre après *qrb* qui peut désigner une "offrande" ou "un combat/une bataille".[91]
On remarquera, dans ce panneau, des mots tels que *rḥm* et *šgyʾ* qui évoquent le contenu du panneau II, tandis que la mention sûre de Taharqâ rappelle le panneau VA.

Panneau XII

Ce panneau comportait primitivement la représentation d'un homme marchant à droite, les pieds peints en rouge et le pagne en vert. L'inscription est très inégalement conservée: toute la partie supérieure et la fin des premières lignes identifiables ont disparu, tandis que l'inscription sur le pagne est relativement bien conservée; une photographie avec lecture préliminaire en avait d'ailleurs été déjà publiée par N. Giron.

---

[91]Pour un emploi assez fréquent de *‘bd qrb*, cf. J. C. Greenfield, B. Porten, *The Bisitun Inscription of Darius the Great, Aramaic Version* (London 1982), p. 29.

D'après ce que nous pouvons voir des lignes 10'-14' sur la photographie de M. Busutil, la fin primitive des lignes de ce panneau pourrait ne pas avoir été liée à un gros trait rouge vertical.

1'. ? hm ẇṁṅ ?
2'. ..ḣṁ ?
3'. żẏ l̇ḣṁ ? ʾth hwʾ blʿdyhm ?
4'. ...... ? l̇ḣm kʿn wymṭʾṅ ḃḋ/ṙẏ ?
5'. ḥk̇mẏḣm ẏṅṫṅ? lhm ẇygḋ/ṙ? ....? ʾbhyhṁ ?
6'. ?ṅ k̇l̇ żẏ ṁ......... ẇš ?
7'. l̇ṗṙʿḣ ṗs̈/k̇...? ṁṣṙyn ...? l̇ʾ ?
8'. ..?ṁ[ṣr]ẏṅ ḥ...... l̇ḣ ?
9'. ḃṙ ḣ..? ṫhṙq̇ʾ ?żṙ....... l̇m ..... ẏẇṁṅ ||| l̇ żẏ ʾṁwn
10'. ṗʾṅḣ ..st ṁḣ ẏṅ.?ṗ.....ṫ.ẏṅ ẇṁṅ .....ẇ ʾḃ ..?ṫḣ
11'. tmḣ ? q̣ ẇl̇.....?l̇ẇ ḃẏwm? zy ʾmwn
12'. .ẇʾtṅ ...k̇ .. mṗ w...... s̈ʾl̇ẇ ʿṁ ...ṁ šyṁ s̈ʾlṫʾ
13'. ʾṁṙ .... ṫšṫḣ ...

1'. ? *leur .... et depuis ...* ?
2'. ... *leur/(à) eux ...* ?
3'. *qui est à eux ....* ? *il est venu*, lui, sans eux ?
4'. ..... ? *à eux* maintenant et ils arriveront .... ?
5'. *leurs sages* leur *donner(ont?) et ....* leurs pères ?
6'. ... *tout(?) ce qui ....et ...* ?
7'. *au pharaon .... l'Égypte ..... ne ... pas* ?
8'. .... *l'É[gy]pte ....*
9'. *fils de(?) ...... Taharqâ .... en vérité ...... 4 jours d'Amon*
10'. *et moi ..... ce que ....et depuis ....*
11'. là-bas ....*et*.................. *au(x?)* jour(*s*?) d'Amon
12'. *et je donnerai(?) ...... Memphis(?)* et ..... *ils ont demandé auprès de ...... il a posé la question*
13'. *il a dit .... tu boiras*

La ligne 2' ne semble pas avoir continué sous toute la ligne 1'; il y avait peut-être ici une sorte de fin de paragraphe.

A la ligne 3', ...*th hwʾ blʿdyhm* ... avait déjà été lu par N. Giron.[92]

A la ligne 4', ...*hm kʿn wymṭʾṅ ḃḋẏ*.. avait déjà été lu par N. Giron.

[92] *AE* 8 (1923), pp. 42-43.

A la ligne 5', N. Giron avait lu ...*wygr* .....*y ʾbhyhm* ... La lecture et l'interprétation de cette fin de ligne restent difficiles à préciser. On peut hésiter entre *wygr*[et *wygd*[, peut-être suivi de la terminaison du pluriel -*n* dans la lacune. Il semble y avoir ensuite traces de trois ou quatre lettres dont les trois dernières pourraient être *ḥzy*. S'agirait-il du pluriel de *ḥz*, "vision", attesté, semble-t-il, en *CIS II*, 137 A 5? A la fin de la ligne *ʾbhyhm* est presque certain; cette forme avait été lue par Cowley dans le papyrus de Ḥor fils de Pawenesh (*Cowley* 71,2) mais B. Porten et A. Yardeni ont, à juste titre, corrigé cette lecture en *ʾlhyhm*.[93]

7'. Après *ps*, il serait tentant de restituer *ps*[*mšk*], cependant les traces ne sont pas claires et cette lecture serait purement conjecturale; ensuite *mṣryn* est une lecture paléographiquement très probable.

9'. *Thrqʾ* est une lecture probable. Après *ywmn*, lecture elle aussi probable, on reconnaît clairement un groupe de trois barres verticales suivi d'un trait vertical légèrement incliné et un peu abîmé; la présence d'un cinquième trait vertical entre le groupe de trois et le dernier n'est pas tout à fait exclue mais paraît peu vraisemblable. La lecture probable *ʾmwn* semble renvoyer au grand dieu de Thèbes, "Amon"; la même orthographe est attestée en Jr 36,25. Ces "4 jours d'Amon" pourraient correspondre à quatre jours de fête[94] en l'honneur d'Amon, plus précisément à la nouvelle lune de Paḥons (IXe mois).[95]

10'. L'emploi de la conjunction *p*- pourrait être une indication sur la date relative de la rédaction de ce texte puisque *p* ne semble attesté en araméen ancien que jusqu'au tout début de l'araméen d'empire (VIe s.).[96]

11'. A la fin de la ligne, il est difficile de préciser s'il faut restituer une lettre (un *y* ?) après *bywm*, cependant la mention des "4 jours" à la ligne 9' invite à restituer ici le pluriel *bywm*[y]. La finale *zy ʾmwn* est pratiquement sûre.

12'. La lecture *mp*, "Memphis", reste quelque peu incertaine.

13'. On notera que *tšth*, "tu boiras", apparaît aussi dans le papyrus de Ḥor fils de Pawenesh.[97]

Panneau XIII

Comme le notait déjà N. Giron, l'inscription de ce panneau semble avoir été brève et ne comporter que 4 lignes assez courtes, chevauchant une sorte de sceptre

[93]Porten, *Select Aramaic Papyri* (1986), pp.14 et 16; B. Porten, A. Yardeni, *Textbook ... III*, p. 56.
[94]Cf. déjà N. Giron *AE* 8 (1923), p. 42: "certaines fêtes (?)".
[95]Cf. S. Schott, *Altägyptische Festdaten* (Wiesbaden 1950), p.104; H. Altenmüller "Feste", *LÄ* II (1977), col. 171-191, spéc. col.181.
[96]*Segert* § 6.5.3.2.2.
[97]*Cowley* 71,22; Porten, *Select Aramaic Papyri*, p.16, recto, ligne 6; B. Porten, A. Yardeni, *Textbook ... III*, p. 54.

renversé verticalement. En 1984, elle était encore plus abîmée qu'en 1922. Il est possible que les deux dernières lignes aient été écrites par une autre main que les deux premières.

1'. .....?ẏ l̇.q̇ṙʾ ḣk̇tḃ zn
2'. ..l̇ ṅḋṙ/ḃʾ/ẏ kllh bšnt ||| ||? ktḃ
3'. ṁṅṫ q̇/ṫl̇ḃṫ? wtl̇ḣ ʿṙkẏ
4'. bżẇh k̇lmt hyʾ ʾḥḋ/ẏẏ

1'. .... *il a fait écrire* ceci
2'. .... l'a terminé, en l'an *5, il a écrit,*
3'. ....?..............
4'. .... elle ....

A la ligne 1, on pourrait proposer, d'après la trace de lettre qui reste, soit *lmqrʾ*, soit *lbqrʾ*; *lmqrʾ* pourrait signifier "pour la lecture", ce qui irait bien avec le mot suivant *hktb*, "il a fait écrire", "il a dicté"; *lbqrʾ* pourrait se rattacher à la racine *bqr*, "chercher, examiner", et on pourrait proposer de traduire "examen".
La lecture du deuxième mot de la ligne 2 reste très incertaine, ainsi que son interprétation (nom commun ou nom propre?). La suite, *kllh bšnt* ||| || avait été lue par N. Giron qui avait noté: "Malheureusement de ce qui suit impossible de tirer un nom de roi. Le souverain n'était probablement pas indiqué". Il y a clairement cinq traits verticaux, cependant il ne serait pas impossible qu'un sixième trait ait disparu dans la grande rayure verticale qui suit. La lecture et l'interprétation de la ligne 3 restent très incertaines: *mnt* serait-il la 1ère pers. du sing. du verbe "compter"? *tlbt* doit-il être rapproché du syriaque *talbūtōʾ*, "le langage, les mots"? *tlh* se rattache-t-il au verbe *tlh/y*, "élever"? *ʿrky* correspondrait-il à l'hébreu *ʿrk*, "montant", "estimation"? Y aurait-il une référence au compte des mots pour estimer le montant dû au scribe?
Le sens exact de la ligne 4 semble aussi nous échapper: *bzwh* se rattacherait-il au verbe *bzz*, "piller", ou au verbe *bzy*, "mépriser"? *klmt* se rattache-t-il à *klm*, "être honteux", ou au mot judéo-araméen *kalm*^{e}*tāʾ*, "la vermine"? *ʾḥḋ/ẏẏ*, incertain, se rattache-t-il au verbe *ʾḥd*, "saisir" ou au verbe *ḥyy*, "vivre"?[98]

Malgré toutes ces incertitudes, ces quatres lignes semblent former un ensemble particulier se référant à l'écriture et à un achèvement en l'an 5 d'un roi non nommé. S'agirait-il d'une sorte de colophon?

98On pourrait en rapprocher *ʾḥyy*, bien attesté pour le roi nabatéen: cf. *DISO*, 87.

Panneau XIV

Selon N. Giron, on ne discernait que "quelques signes tracés au travers d'un reste de peinture", mais, probablement à la suite de graffiti récents, on ne voit plus rien aujourd'hui.

Panneau XV

Selon N. Giron, il n'y avait "qu'un mot isolé entre un personnage et un objet indéterminé". On ne voit plus rien aujourd'hui.

Panneau XVI

Selon N. Giron, on discerne les "restes d'une dizaine de lignes, 4 en haut et 6 en bas du panneau; tout ce qui existait dans l'intervalle a disparu. Les deux textes paraissent avoir été tracés par deux mains différentes… Entre les deux textes un graffito araméen". Ce panneau contient donc trois inscriptions différentes se situant l'une en dessous de l'autre et que, pour plus de clarté, nous appellerons A, B, et C. Il n'est pas sûr que le panneau ait été primitivement écrit à l'encre de haut en bas, comme le pensait N. Giron. En effet, B a très bien pu être écrit après A, et C après B. On ne discerne aucune trace de lettre dans la partie droite du panneau qui pourrait ne pas avoir été inscrite; la fin des restes visibles de lignes est proche du gros trait rouge vertical et épais qui marquait la limite gauche du panneau.

A — 1'. ṧ.....ẇ......? ʿmhm
2'. ......ẏḣ..? żṅ nbwṧn
3'. ....ḣ...ẏ ʿ̇ḋṅ.?ẇṁl̇ṅ
4'. .....ṧḣ ......ẏẗʾ

B — ṗṁn dgl nqmn

C — 1'. ..ṅ....ẗʿ̇ṅ......
2'. ...? żṅḣ ....
3'. ʿ̇ṁḣṁ ṅ.....?l̇ẏ ...
4'. kṅ ʾ̇ṁṙ ẅʾ ....?ṁ.
5'. .kẇ ʾ̇mrẇ ʾ̈l̇ḣ. ṭḃʾ š̈l[m?]
6'. lsprʾ ży ktb ktbʾ ḋṅḣ[?

A — 1'. ....avec eux
2'. .... *ceci Nabu....*
3'. .... *et des paroles*
4'. ....

B — *Pamin* du régiment de Naqmân

C — 1'. ....
2'. .... *ceci* ....
3'. *avec eux* .... *à moi* ...
4'. *Ainsi a dit* ....
5'. ...... *ont dit le(s?) dieu(x?): bon(heur?), pai[x]*
6'. au scribe qui a écrit *cette* inscription [?

A. — 2'. Il est difficile de préciser s'il faut lire *nbw šn* ou *nbwšn* en un seul mot. Dans ce dernier cas, il pourrait s'agir d'un hypocoristique d'un nom d'origine babylonienne comportant le théonyme "Nabou".[99]

B. — Ce graffito est assez clair, sauf au tout début où on pourrait hésiter quelque peu entre *pmn* et *mn*. *Pmn*, "Pamin", est probablement un nom égyptien: "celui qui appartient à Min", déjà attesté en *CIS II*, 122.4; 148,3 (= *Cowley* 74,3),[100] ainsi que sur un sceau d'époque perse.[101] *Dgl*, primitivement "drapeau, étendard", désigne une unité militaire de plusieurs centaines d'hommes: une compagnie ou, mieux, un régiment. Cette unité pouvait aussi avoir une fonction administrative et économique au sein de l'empire perse.[102] *Nqmn*, probablement *naqmān*, "vengeur", "vindicatif", semble nouveau dans l'onomastique araméenne ancienne; cependant on peut le rapprocher de noms comportant l'élément *nqm* en ougaritique,[103] en phénicien d'Égypte[104] et en épigraphie paléo-hébraïque.[105] On notera qu'à Eléphantine les éponymes des régiments

[99]On pourrait penser à un nom tel que *Nabū*[-*šallim*-]*šunu*, avec chute de l'élément central (cf. K. L. Tallqvist, *Assyrian Personal Names* [Helsingfors 1914 = Hildesheim 1966], pp.158-160), ou à *Nabū-š*[*ēzib*]*anni*, attesté en particulier comme le nom assyrien de Psammétique Ier (*ARAB II*, 774.805), en en rapprochant certains noms araméens d'Égypte tels que *nbšlı/nbwšlı/nbwšzb* (Kornfeld, *Onomastica*, pp. 61-62).

[100]Ibid., p. 90.

[101]Cf. N. Avigad, "Three Ornamented Hebrew Seals", *IEJ* 4 (1954), pp. 236-238, spéc. pp. 237-238.

[102]Cf. A. Temerev, "Social Organisations in the Egyptian Military Settlements of the Sixth-Fourth Centuries B.C.E. *dgl* and *m'ʾt*", dans C. L. Meyers - M. O'Connor (éds.), *The Word of the Lord Shall Go Forth, Essays in Honour of D. N. Freedman* (Winona Lake 1983), pp. 523-525.

[103]Cf. F. Gröndahl, *Die Personennamen der Texte aus Ugarit* (Rome 1967), p. 168.

[104]Cf. *nqmʾl* : M. Lidzbarski, *Ephemeris für semitische Epigraphik III* (Giessen 1909), p. 126; F. L. Benz, *Personal Names in the Phoenician and Punic Inscriptions* (Rome 1972), pp. 147, 363.

[105]Cf. les trois incisions sur des anses de jarres trouvées à Tell en-Nasbeh, Ramat-Rahel et Jérusalem: J. Prignaud, "Notes d'épigraphie hébraïque I. Un grand vengeur", *RB* 77 (1970), pp. 50-59, spéc. pp. 57-59, n. 31.

(*dgl*) semblent d'abord iraniens et ne deviennent sémitiques qu'après 459 av. J.-C.,[106] ce qui pourrait constituer un indice pour une datation de ce graffito au plus tôt vers 460 av. J.-C. La place de ce graffito, entre XVA et XVC semble indiquer qu'il est à peu près contemporain de ces deux inscriptions à l'encre, leur étant structurellement lié. On devra tenir compte de ce fait dans l'interprétation générale (*infra*).

C — Les trois premières lignes de cette inscription sont presque illisibles. Aux lignes 4' et 5', il semble possible de reconnaître deux formes du verbe *ʾmr*, "dire". Vers le milieu de la ligne 5', il semble qu'il y a des traces d'une lettre après *ʾlh*; on peut hésiter à restituer soit *ʾlh*[*n*], "les dieux", peut-être le sujet de *ʾmrw*, soit plutôt, d'après les traces qui restent, *ʾlh*[ʾ], "le dieu" auquel pourrait se rattacher *ṭbʾ*, *ʾlhʾ ṭbʾ*, "le dieu bon", étant un syntagme bien attesté en palmyrénien et peut-être déjà dans le papyrus Amherst 63 comme qualificatif du dieu *mr*.[107] Ici *ʾlhʾ ṭbʾ* pourrait correspondre à l'égyptien *nṯr nfr*, qui peut qualifier un pharaon vivant ou mort.[108] A la fin de la ligne, le *l* reste incertain et la restitution *šl*[*m*], "pai[x]", conjecturale. Ce terme, ainsi que le précédent, pourrait être lié à la ligne 6'.

A la ligne 6', la lecture *lsprʾ zy ktb ktbʾ* avait déjà été proposée par N. Giron. Elle paraît pratiquement sûre, tandis que *dnh* reste assez incertain.

Panneau XVII

N. Giron avait déjà noté que ce panneau, le dernier avant l'angle, comportait les "restes de trois mots qui terminaient un texte". Ces trois mots semblent constituer la fin d'une seule ligne inférieure, continuée à partir de la dernière ligne du panneau précédent.

?]y.? q̇dm ʾṫṁ[n]ḃn ʾlhnʾ

?]..? *devant/de la part d'Atoum[ne]bôn* notre dieu.

La lecture de cette ligne reste paléographiquement assez incertaine; *ʾlhnʾ* est assez clair; il est précédé par un mot commençant par ʾ et se terminant par *n*. Nous avions d'abord pensé à *ʾ*[*mw*]*n*, "Amon", mais cette restitution semble un peu courte et un examen plus attentif nous conduit à proposer la lecture *ʾṫṁ*[*n*]*ḃn*, les lettres *t*, *m* et

[106]Cf. C. Tuplin, "Xenophon and the Garrisons of the Achaemenid Empire", *Archaeologische Mitteilungen aus Iran* 20 (1987), pp. 167-245, spéc. pp. 219-220.
[107]Cf. R. C. Steiner, C. F. Nims, "You can't offer your Sacrifice and eat it too. A Polemical Poem from the Aramaic Text in Demotic Script", *JNES* 43 (1984), pp. 89-114, spéc. pp. 95-96: 6,2. Ici, une lecture *l̇mṙẇ ʾlh* [ʾ] *ṭbʾ* ne serait pas totalement à exclure car, pour la première lettre, on peut hésiter quelque peu entre ʾ et *l*.
[108]Ce titre est attesté pour Taharqâ (cf. R. A. Caminos, "The Nicrotis Adoption Stela", *JEA* 50 [1964], pp. 71-101, spéc. pp. 74, 77) et pour Nékô (cf. H. de Meulenaere, "Une statuette égyptienne à Naples", *BIFAO* 60 [1960], pp. 117-129, spéc. p. 121).

b restant très incertaines; *ʾtmnbn ʾlhnʾ* peut être rapproché de *ʾtmnbn ʾlhʾ zy lh* du panneau II, 11'. Auparavant, on lit assez clairement *q̇ḋm*, précédé, à quelque distance, d'un *y*. On pourrait proposer de restituer [*br*]*y*[*k*] précédé éventuellement d'un verbe tel que *yhwy*, pour obtenir la formule "qu'il soit béni...". En effet, plusieurs textes araméens d'Égypte[109] attestent une formule similaire avec Osiris. Ainsi l'unique ligne du panneau XVII, complétant la dernière ligne du panneau XVI, semble signifier: "... au scribe qui a écrit *cette* inscription, *[qu'il soit bé]n[i] devant Atoum[ne]bôn* notre dieu!".

Cette formule finale évoque celle des colophons attirant la bénédiction sur le copiste. Puisqu'il semble y avoir déjà une sorte de colophon en XIII, on pourrait éventuellement penser que le premier colophon visait le scribe rédacteur du texte tandis que celui-ci viserait le ou les copistes.

IV - Essai d'interprétation générale

N. Giron avait assez naturellement proposé d'interpréter cette inscription trouvée dans une tombe comme une inscription funéraire:

"Le tombeau aurait donc été réutilisé pour quelque fonctionnaire civil, militaire, voire religieux, de langue araméenne, dont l'inscription retracerait à grands traits le *curriculum.* Si réellement ce fonctionnaire, comme il semble, dépendait de Taharqa on pourrait songer à un ancien fonctionnaire assyrien qui aurait trahi son roi, Asarhaddon ou Assurbanipal, pour passer au service des maîtres provisoires de l'Égypte. Cela fixerait approximativement la date des inscriptions entre le milieu du VIIème et la fin du VIème siècle avant J.-C."[110]. Cependant cette interprétation se heurte à la fois à la datation paléographique et au contenu de ces inscriptions.

N. Giron avait déjà, lui-même, remarqué que "Paléographiquement ces textes ne paraissaient pas s'écarter de l'époque des papyrus araméens d'Égypte".[111] Or ceux-ci datent essentiellement du Ve s. av. J.-C. et non de l'époque néo-assyrienne. Après un examen des photographies de M. Busutil, J. Naveh a confirmé et précisé cette datation au Ve. s.: "the photographs enable us, however, to conclude palaeographically, that the inscriptions are from approximately the second quarter of the fifth century B.C.E. It may be assumed that these inscriptions on the walls of the tomb were written within a short period. If this is so, it would allow us to follow various hands within a given time, since developmental differences are actually more stylistic than chronological. The

[109]*CIS II*, 122 (= *KAI* 267); 141, 1.3 (= *KAI* 269); *RES* 1367,1; 1368,1; 1370; 1372B; 1375; 1376; 1377.
[110]*AE* 8 (1923), p. 43.
[111]Ibid., p.42.

script of Nos. 2-4 is more developed than that of the others, such as No. 5, but even so, it is not later than the middle of the fifth century B.C.E."[112]

Même si elle reste toujours approximative, particulièrement lorsqu'il s'agit d'inscriptions aussi fragmentaires et mal conservées, l'analyse paléographique (cf. tableau, fig. 2) fait d'abord ressortir la présence probable de plusieurs mains. Utilisant en particulier les différentes manières d'écrire le ʾ, on peut proposer de reconnaître au moins six mains différentes, sans compter le graffito:

1 - Panneaux II, III-IV.
2 - Panneaux VA.B, VI(?), VIII(?), IX(?), XI(?), XII(?).
3 - Panneau XIII (lignes 1-2) [=XIII.A].
4 - Panneau XIII (lignes 3-4) [=XIII.B].
5 - Panneau XVIA.
6 - Panneau XVIC - XVII.

Cette diversité de mains révèle la difficulté d'une datation purement paléographique qui risque d'interpréter des styles différents comme indiquant une différence chronologique, alors qu'ils sont contemporains. Ici, la comparaison avec les manuscrits datés d'Éléphantine semble montrer que les différentes formes de lettres des inscriptions de Cheikh Fadl ont très bien pu coexister dans la première moitié ou vers le milieu du Ve. s. av. J.-C., confirmant approximativement la datation proposée par J. Naveh.

Cette datation contredit l'interprétation funéraire proposée par N. Giron. En effet, les inscriptions datent d'environ deux siècles après l'époque des personnages historiques mentionnés: Taharqâ, Nékô Ier et Psammétique Ier! Un tel hiatus chronologique entre la datation du texte et les événements évoqués ne surprendrait pas dans le cas d'une tradition littéraire, c'est à dire en comprenant les inscriptions comme la copie d'un manuscrit.

La disposition concrète des inscriptions s'expliquerait beaucoup mieux suivant cette dernière hypothèse. En effet, il n'y a apparemment aucun lien entre les inscriptions et les fresques primitives de la tombe puisque le texte a été écrit sur des parties peintes, à une époque où on se souciait visiblement assez peu du respect de ces peintures. Cette disposition, qui paraît exclure une interprétation funéraire, pourrait convenir à la copie d'un manuscrit littéraire généralement présenté écrit en colonnes éventuellement séparées par de gros traits rouges verticaux.[113]

---

[112]Naveh, *Development of the Aramaic Script*, p. 41.
[113]Sur cette interprétation et le parallèle des inscriptions de Deir ʿAlla cf. A. Lemaire, "Manuscrit, mur et rocher en épigraphie nord-ouest sémitique", dans R. Laufer (éd.), *Le texte et son inscription* (Paris 1989), pp. 35-42.

D'après les traces que nous avons relevées, les inscriptions à l'encre comportaient au moins 116 lignes et on peut raisonnablement penser que le texte primitif pouvait comporter autour de 200 lignes réparties en une quinzaine de colonnes. Ces données chiffrées approximatives sont comparables à celles des manuscrits littéraires araméens de cette époque: ainsi, la copie de la version araméenne de l'inscription de Behistun doit avoir comporté "eleven columns of 17-18 lines each, yielding a total length of ca. 190 lines",[114] tandis que le manuscrit des proverbes d'Ahiqar comportait au moins 9 colonnes avec des restes d'environ 144 lignes.[115]

Enfin, on rappellera la présence d'un (XVIC-XVII) ou même de deux (cf. aussi XIII) colophons, ce qui semble confirmer que ces inscriptions représentent essentiellement la copie d'un manuscrit littéraire, au moins jusqu'au panneau XII inclus.

Il resterait à expliquer pourquoi un tel texte littéraire a été recopié à Cheikh Fadl: le graffito (XVIB) mentionnant un "régiment" (*dgl*) de Naqmân pourrait laisser entendre qu'il y avait une garnison militaire et, peut-être, une place forte (*birtāʾ*) de l'armée perse dans les environs pour surveiller la vallée du Nil. Mais alors, pourquoi cette copie sur la paroi de la pièce principale d'une tombe? On pourrait se rappeler que cette pièce semble avoir été ouverte au public et proposer qu'un tel lieu couvert, avec des murs pouvant facilement servir de support à une inscription à l'encre, a pu servir occasionnellement de lieu d'enseignement à un petit groupe (d'apprentis scribes?) dont chacun des membres a pu recopier une partie du manuscrit étudié sur la paroi de la tombe. Il va sans dire que, à défaut d'une fouille archéologique de cette tombe et d'une exploration de surface de ses environs, il ne s'agit là que d'une conjecture, dans l'attente éventuellement d'une explication plus satisfaisante.

V - Essai d'identification de la tradition littéraire

Etant donné le caractère très fragmentaire de ces inscriptions dont aucune ligne ne semble pouvoir être lue complètement et avec certitude, il nous faut reconnaître que leur contenu nous échappe en grande partie. Cependant plusieurs thèmes littéraires semblent affleurer dans ces fragments lus avec plus ou moins de probabilité:

1 — Une histoire d'amour semble le thème dominant du panneau II avec deux fois la formule *rḥm ʾnh lhy šgyʾ*, "moi, je l'aime beacoup", et plusieurs fois l'expression "coucher avec" (*škb ʿm*). Ce thème pourrait réapparaître en XI, 3'.5',. et, éventuellement, en X d'après la lecture *škb* de N. Giron. Le héros de cette histoire semble un certain Ḥorâ (*ḥrʾ*); il est plus difficile de préciser si c'est lui qui est désigné sous le terme *ʿlymʾ*, "le jeune homme" ou "le serviteur".

---

[114]Cf. J. C. Greenfield, B. Porten, *The Bisitun Inscription of Darius the Great, Aramaic Version* (London 1982), p. 2.

[115]Cf. J. M. Lindenberger, *The Aramaic Proverbs of Ahiqar* (Baltimore-London 1983), p. 13.

2 — Une histoire royale, ou plutôt "pharaonique" semble évidente avec les mentions de Taharqâ, "roi des Nubiens", et des "pharaons" Nékô et Psammétique (panneaux VA, VIII, IX, XI, XII).

3 — Cette histoire ou ces histoires baignent dans une atmosphère religieuse avec la mention explicite des dieux (II, III-IV, VII, IX, XVI), spécialement d'Atoumnebôn (II, XVII), Amôn (XII), et, peut-être, le soleil Raᶜ (VII?) et Osiris (II?), ainsi que des "prêtres" (XI, 9').

4 — L'atmosphère semble typiquement égyptienne comme le montrent les pharaons (*supra*), les divinités (*supra*) et les toponymes (Héliopolis, Memphis) mentionnés. D'ailleurs le nom de "l'Égypte" semble revenir assez souvent (VB, IX, XII).

Ces différents thèmes se rattachaient-ils à différentes histoires ou à une seule histoire? Il est difficile de le dire, cependant l'évocation de l'amour, de Taharqâ et des prêtres dans le panneau XI semble indiquer qu'il s'agit vraisemblablement d'une seule et même histoire ou tradition littéraire. D'ailleurs, la tradition littéraire araméenne d'Ahiqar, connue, elle aussi, en Égypte au Ve. s., révèle qu'il n'est pas étonnant de retrouver plusieurs thèmes dans une oeuvre littéraire de cette époque.

Pour mieux cerner le genre exact de cette tradition littéraire, essayons de la replacer dans son contexte historique, vrai ou supposé (l'Égypte sous Taharqâ, Nékô et Psammétique), littéraire (histoires parallèles) et culturel (l'araméen et la tradition littéraire égyptienne).

A) L'histoire égyptienne de Taharqâ à Psammétique Ier nous est assez bien connue, en particulier par les études d'A. Spalinger[116] et de K. A. Kitchen.[117] Le règne de Taharqâ (ca. 690-664 av. J.-C.) se divise approximativement en 13 années de paix et 13 années de conflit avec l'Assyrie. Dès 677, Assarhaddon vainquit et déposa, puis exécuta Abdimilkutti, roi de Sidon; en 674, il essaie d'envahir l'Égypte mais est défait par Taharqâ. En 671, il réussit à pénétrer en Égypte, défait Taharqâ et le chasse de Memphis; il meurt en 669, à nouveau en route vers l'Égypte, qui s'était révoltée. En 667-666, son successeur, Assurbanipal, envahit l'Égypte, défait Taharqâ qui s'enfuit

[116] A. Spalinger, "Esarhaddon and Egypt: An Analysis of the First Invasion of Egypt", *Orientalia* 43 (1974), pp. 295-326; *id.*, "Assurbanipal and Egypt: A Source Study", *JAOS* 94 (1974), pp. 316-328; *id.*, "Psammetichus, King of Egypt", *JARCE* 13 (1976), pp. 133-147 et 15 (1978), pp. 49-57; id., "The Foreign Policy of Egypt Preceding the Assyrian Conquest", *CdE* 53 (1978), pp. 22-47; *id.*, "Notes on the Military in Egypt during the XXVth Dynasty", *JSSEA* 11/1 (1981), pp. 37-58.

[117] Cf. Kitchen, *Third Intermediate Period* (1986²), pp. 387-408, 455-461. Cf. aussi S. Sauneron, J. Yoyotte, "Sur la politique palestinienne des rois saïtes", *VT* 2 (1952), pp. 131-136; J. M. A. Janssen, "Que sait-on actuellement du pharaon Taharqa?", *Biblica* 34 (1953), pp. 23-43; W. Wessetzky, "Die Familiengeschichte des Peteêse als historische Quelle für die Innenpolitik Psammetiks I", *ZÄS* 88 (1962), pp. 69-73; F. Gomaa, *Die libyschen Fürstentümer des Deltas vom Tod Osorkons II bis zur Wiedervereinigung Ägyptens durch Psametik I* (Wiesbaden 1974); A. K. Grayson, "Assyria's Foreign Policy in Relation to Egypt in the Eighth and Seventh Centuries B.C.", *JSSEA* 11 (1980), pp. 85-88; D. B. Redford, "Necho I", *LÄ* IV/3 (1980), col. 368-369; S. M. Burnstein, "Psammetik I and the End of Nubian Domination in Egypt", *JSSEA* 14/2 (1984), pp. 31-34; J. Leclant, "Taharqa", *LÄ* VI/2 (1985), col. 156-184; id., "Tanutamun", ibid., col. 211-215.

vers Thèbes puis vers Napata. Assurbanipal reçoit la soumission des dynastes du Delta et de la Haute Égypte menés par Nékô Ier, prince de Saïs. Vers 665, après le retour d'Assurbanipal et une révolte des dynastes égyptiens, ceux-ci sont arrêtés et envoyés à Ninive; ils y sont exécutés sauf Nékô et son fils, Psammétique. Nékô, gracié, est renvoyé comme roi de Saïs et de Memphis, tandis que son fils reçoit le nom assyrien de Nabū-sêzibanni et le gouvernorat d'Athribis. En 664, Tantamani, neveu et successeur de Taharqâ, remonte vers le Nord, enlève Memphis et envahit le Delta. Nékô qui essaie de lui résister est exécuté. En 664/3, les Assyriens reconquièrent Memphis et pillent Thèbes (663). Psammétique Ier succède à son père comme roi de Saïs, Memphis et Athribis; il établit ensuite une sorte de protectorat sur les autres dynastes du Delta, puis, de 656 à 654 étend sa domination au reste de l'Égypte, y compris Thèbes. Son règne dure 54 ans (664-610). Ainsi Nékô et Psammétique, fondateurs de la dynastie "saïte", ont-ils été les vassaux/alliés des Assyriens qui les ont appuyés militairement dans leur guerre de libération de l'Égypte de la domination des rois "nubiens/éthiopiens": Taharqâ et Tantamani; on notera, en particulier, que le dieu principal de Saïs durant cette XXVIe dynastie semble avoir été Atoum,[118] mentionné dans les inscriptions. Il est clair que d'autres expressions des inscriptions, en particulier les titres donnés à Taharqâ ("roi des Nubiens"), à Nékô et Psammétique ("pharaon"), prennent un relief particulier dans ce contexte historique et semblent refléter l'idéologie de la dynastie saïte. Cependant ces expressions et cet arrière-plan historique ne suffisent pas à faire de ces inscriptions un texte historique au sens limité du terme; le thème littéraire d'une histoire d'amour (cf. surtout panneau II) semble indiquer qu'il s'agit plutôt d'une histoire romancée ou d'un roman historique, genre assez bien attesté en Égypte vers cette époque.

B) En effet, l'Égypte de basse époque semble avoir connu plusieurs traditions littéraires que l'on peut, plus ou moins, rapprocher de nos inscriptions:

1 — L'histoire de *Ḥor fils de Pawenesh* nous est connue par deux fragments de papyri araméens trouvés à Eléphantine (*Cowley* 71) réédités récemment.[119] Il semble qu'elle soit aussi attestée en démotique, bien qu'on n'ait pas encore, semble-t-il, découvert de véritables passages communs en démotique et en araméen.[120]

Les quelques fragments araméens de "Hor fils de Pawenesh" comportent plusieurs mots ou syntagmes que nous avons lus dans les inscriptions de Cheikh Fadl: *mlkʾ*, *znh*, *ʿnh wʾmr*, *kn*, *mln/mlyʾ zy*, *ywmn*, *tšth*, *šnn/šntʾ/šnt*, *ʾlhn*, *ʾlp/ʾlpy*, *yntn/ntn lh*, *ʾbwhy/ʾbhyhm*, *mṣryn*, *ʾlhy mṣryn*, *ʾḥrnn*, *ksp/ksph*, *mrʾy/mrʾh/mrʾyhm*, *yḥtwn/nḥt/ynḥtw*(?), *wyhnpq/hpqw*(?), mais il est difficile de

---

[118]Cf. Myśliwiec, *Studien zum Gott Atum II* (Hildesheim 1979), p. 118.
[119]Porten, *Select Aramaic Papyri*, pp.14-16; R. Porten, A. Yardeni, *Textbook ... III*, pp. 54-57.
[120]Cf. K. Th. Zauzich, "Neue literarische Texte in demotischer Schrift", *Enchoria* 8 (1978), p. 36.

préciser s'il s'agit là d'une simple coïncidence ou si cette convergence est significative. Même s'il s'agit, dans les deux cas, d'une tradition littéraire typiquement égyptienne attestée en araméen au Ve. s. av. J.-C., rien n'indique vraiment, au moins jusqu'à maintenant, qu'il s'agit de la même tradition littéraire. En effet, dans un cas, le héros s'appelle "Ḥor fils de Pawenesh", dans l'autre apparemment "Ḥorâ"; dans cette dernière, il est fait mention de Taharqâ, Nékô et Psammétique, absents des deux fragments que nous possédons de l'autre tradition. Ainsi, même si, étant donné l'état très fragmentaire de notre documentation, une identification des deux traditions littéraires ne peut être totalement exclue, il nous semble préférable, actuellement, de rester sur la réserve et de les distinguer.

2 — L'arrière-plan historique du *cycle de Pédubaste* se situe, comme les inscriptions de Cheikh Fadl, au début de l'époque saïte car le héros de ce cycle, le roi Pédubaste de Tanis, semble avoir été Sehetepibenre Pédubaste II de Tanis vers 665 av. J.-C.[121] Cependant ce cycle n'est attesté que par des manuscrits démotiques d'époque gréco-romaine et certaines histoires semblent intégrer des données de l'époque perse. Elles semblent donc relativement tardives et il n'est pas étonnant qu'aucun des textes publiés ne corresponde aux inscriptions fragmentaires de Cheikh Fadl. On y note d'ailleurs l'absence de Taharqâ, Nékô et Psammétique.[122]

3 — La tradition littéraire démotique a aussi conservé au moins deux histoires se rapportant à un personnage appelé *Setné* : la première est une histoire de séduction qui, par certains aspects, pourrait être rapprochée de l'histoire d'amour apparaissant en particulier dans le panneau II de Cheikh Fadl. Cependant la thématique semble légèrement différente et il n'y a apparemment aucune correspondance exacte des fragments araméens avec cette histoire démotique. La deuxième histoire de Setné se présente comme une histoire de magie; elle mentionne plusieurs personnages "Ḥor" ou "Ḥorus", ainsi que "Atoum, maître d'Héliopolis" et les "dieux d'Égypte";[123] cependant aucun passage ne semble correspondre exactement aux fragments de Cheikh Fadl.

4 — L'histoire d'*Ahiqar* l'Assyrien était certainement bien connue en Égypte à la basse époque, comme le montrent le papyrus d'époque perse trouvé à Éléphantine[124] et deux fragments de papyri démotiques.[125] Si cette histoire est bien censée se dérouler au début du VIIe s., sous Sennachérib et Assarhaddon pratiquement contemporains de

---

[121] Kitchen, *Third Intermediate Period*, pp. 445-461, spéc. p. 458.

[122] Cf. W. Spiegelberg, *Der Sagenkreis des Königs Petubastis* (Leipzig 1910); E. Bresciani, *Letteratura e poesia dell'antico Egitto* (Torino 1969), pp.642-676; M. Lichtheim, *Ancient Egyptian Literature III* (Berkeley 1980), pp. 151-156; W. Helck, "Petubastis-Erzählung", *LÄ* IV/7 (1982), col. 998-999.

[123] Bresciani, *Letteratura*, p. 638; Lichtheim, *Ancient Egyptian Literature III*, p. 149.

[124] Cf., par exemple, Grelot, *Documents*, pp. 425-452, B. Porten, A. Yardeni, *Textbook ... III*, pp. 24-35.

[125] Cf. K. Th. Zauzich, "Demotische Fragmente zum Aḥikar-Roman", dans H. Franke, W. Heissig, W. Treue (éds.), *Folia rara W. Voigt LXV* (Wiesbaden 1976), pp. 180-185; id., "Neue literarische Texte in demotischer Schrift", *Enchoria* 8 (1978), pp. 33-34.

Taharqâ, ni son thème, ni sa formulation ne correspondent au texte fragmentaire des inscriptions de Cheikh Fadl.

5 — L'*histoire des deux frères*, conservée en langue araméenne mais en transcription démotique dans le papyrus Amherst 63, est une histoire romancée de la révolte de Shamash-shum-ukin à Babylone vers 650.[126] Le fait qu'elle a été transcrite en démotique nous montre qu'elle était bien connue en Égypte, cependant il s'agit là d'une histoire assez typiquement assyrienne, différente de celle des fragments de Cheikh Fadl.

Dans l'état actuel de nos connaissances, tous ces textes araméens et/ou démotiques ne permettent pas encore d'identifier la tradition littéraire des inscriptions de Cheikh Fadl et donc de proposer éventuellement des restitutions plausibles pour les fragments conservés. Cependant ils révèlent qu'une intense activité littéraire s'est développée au Proche Orient au VIIe s. av. J.-C., spécialement lors de la renaissance égyptienne sous la dynastie saïte.

Peut-on essayer de dater plus précisément la rédaction de la tradition littéraire attestée à Cheikh Fadl? Il est clair que cette date doit être distinguée de la copie des inscriptions dans la tombe de Cheikh Fadl et ne peut lui être qu'antérieure. Puisqu'elle mentionne Taharqâ, Nékô et Psammétique, elle ne peut être que contemporaine ou postérieure au règne de Psammétique Ier (664-610).

La langue de ces inscriptions pourrait indiquer plutôt le début de cette "fourchette". En effet, l'emploi du verbe *ykl/khl* avec un verbe à la même forme personnelle,[127] de la particule négative *l-*,[128] du suffixe *-tm*,[129] de la particule *ʾyt*[130] et de la conjonction *p-*[131] semblent indiquer que la langue de ces inscriptions est plutôt celle du VIIe s. que celle de ca 500 av. J.-C.

Le contenu de ces inscriptions semble confirmer cette datation: l'idéologie nationale, royale et religieuse semble celle de la dynastie saïte et donc antérieure à la fin de cette dynastie en 525 av. J.-C. (invasion de Cambyse). Les diverses mentions de Taharqâ paraissent tout à fait confirmer cette datation. En effet, les noms royaux de la dynastie "éthiopienne" ont été l'objet d'une *damnatio memoriae* systématique à l'occasion d'une guerre menée par Psammétique II vers les contrées situées au sud de son royaume en l'an 3 de son règne (591 av. J.-C.).[132] Cette *damnatio memoriae*, bien attestée par le martelage des cartouches dans les inscriptions monumentales, a dû aussi

[126]Cf. surtout R.C. Steiner, C.F. Nims, "Ashurbanipal and Shamash-shum-ukin. A Tale of Two Brothers from the Aramaic Text in Demotic Script", *RB* 92 (1985), pp. 60-81.
[127]*Supra* II, 4'; cf. *Segert*, § 6.6.8.1.5.
[128]*Supra* II, 7'; cf. *Segert*, § 5.5.6.1.4
[129]*Supra* II, 15'; cf. *Segert*, § 5.6.4.4.3.
[130]*Supra* VA, 9'; cf. *Segert*, § 5.5.3.1.2.
[131]*Supra* XII, 10'; cf. *Segert*, § 6.5.3.2.2.
[132]Cf. J. Yoyotte, "Le martelage des noms royaux éthiopiens (591 av. J.-C.)", *RdE* 8 (1951), pp. 215-239, spéc. p. 239; J. Leclant, "Kuschitenherrschaft", *LÄ* III,6 (1979), col. 893-901, spéc. col.894, 896-897; *id.*, "Taharqa", *LÄ* VI,3 (1985), col. 156-184, spéc. col.167.

avoir un effet dans la tradition littéraire et il paraît très improbable qu'une histoire égyptienne mentionnant plusieurs fois Taharqâ ait pu être rédigée après 591.

A titre de conjecture, on peut encore remarquer que Thèbes ne semble pas mentionné dans les fragments de Cheikh Fadl, à la différence de Memphis et d'Héliopolis, c'est dire que l'arrière-plan historique de ces histoires pourrait s'être arrêté au tout début du règne de Psammétique, alors qu'il dominait seulement le Delta. Dès lors, il n'est pas impossible que l'histoire racontée ait été censée se terminer en l' "an 5" (Panneau XIII) de Psammétique Ier, c'est à dire en 660. Il ne s'agit là que d'une conjecture qui voudrait souligner que la rédaction d'une telle tradition littéraire paraîtrait particulièrement à sa place durant le règne long et glorieux de Psammétique Ier.

Cette tradition littéraire a-t-elle été primitivement écrite en araméen ou le texte araméen est-il une traduction d'un texte démotique? Etant donné l'état fragmentaire et incertain du texte, il nous semble pratiquement impossible de répondre à cette question liée, en partie, au problème du début de l'emploi de l'araméen en Égypte. Il semble que la première attestation épigraphique araméenne en Égypte soit l'inscription *blsrʾṣr*[133] de l'époque néo-assyrienne. Cependant il est probable que le jeune Psammétique a reçu une certaine éducation à Ninive puisqu'il a porté le nom assyrien "Nabū-sêzibanni".[134] Or, à cette époque, l'araméen était la langue officielle de l'ouest de l'empire assyrien, presque à égalité avec l'accadien.[135] Les campagnes militaires assyriennes et l'alliance/vassalité des princes saïtes vis à vis de l'Assyrie se sont probablement traduites par un certain rayonnement de l'araméen à la cour égyptienne dès le début de la dynastie saïte, ce qui explique que le papyrus de Saqqarah envoyé de Palestine au pharaon vers 603 av. J.-C. ait été rédigé en araméen.[136] Dans ce contexte, on notera que, en égyptien, l'écriture araméenne est appelée *sh ʾisr*, c'est à dire "l'écriture assyrienne",[137] ce qui constitue un nouvel indice en faveur de l'introduction de l'araméen en Égypte à l'époque néo-assyrienne. On notera, enfin, qu'il n'est pas impossible que la garnison/colonie araméenne et juive d'Eléphantine remonte au VIIe s. av. J.-C.[138] Tous ces indices révèlent un contexte culturel où la rédaction directe en araméen de la tradition littéraire

---

[133]Cf. M. Lidzbarski, "Aus dem Museum in Cairo", *Ephemeris für semitische Epigraphik III* (Giessen 1909), pp. 117-118; Naveh, *Development of the Aramaic Script*, p. 18.
[134]*ARAB II*, § 774.
[135]L'aramaïcisation de l'empire assyrien est déjà bien attestée au VIIIe s. av. J.-C.; cf. P. Garelli, "Importance et rôle des Araméens dans l'administration de l'empire assyrien", dans *Mesopotamien und seine Nachbarn, XXV. R.A.I.* (Berlin 1978), pp. 437-447; H. Tadmor, "The Aramaicization of Assyria: Aspects of Western Impacts", ibid., pp. 449-470; A. Lemaire, J. M. Durand, *Les inscriptions araméennes de Sfiré et l'Assyrie de Shamshi-ilu*, HEO 20 (Genève-Paris 1984), pp. 47, 89-90, 105.
[136]Cf. *KAI* 266; B. Porten, "The Identity of King Adon". *BA* 44 (1981), pp. 36-52. Ce papyrus comporte une suscription en démotique.
[137]Cf. la chronique démotique à propos de la codification de Darius en 519 av. J.-C.; cf. E. Bresciani, "Egypt, Persian Satrapy", dans *The Cambridge History of Judaism I, Introduction, The Persian Period* (Cambridge 1984), pp. 358-372, spéc. p.360.
[138]Cf. avec diverses nuances: Sauneron–Yoyotte, *VT* 2 (1952), pp. 131-136, spéc. pp. 131-135; B. Porten, *Archives from Elephantine* (Berkeley 1986), pp. 8-12; R. Contini, "I documenti aramaici dell'Egitto persiano e tolemaico", *Riv. Bib. It.* 34 (1986), pp. 73-109, spéc. pp. 84-87; F. M. Fales, "La tradizione assiria ad Elefantina d'Egitto", *Dialoghi di Archeologia* 5 (1987), pp. 63-70, spéc. p.70.

des inscriptions de Cheikh Fadl ne paraît pas impossible, même si elle est loin d'être prouvée.

Quelle que soit la date et la langue de la rédaction primitive de la tradition littéraire des panneaux II à XII de Cheikh Fadl, comment se fait-il que cette histoire, typiquement égyptienne et apparemment liée à la dynastie saïte, ait été recopiée dans la première moitié ou vers le milieu du Ve s., en pleine époque perse? Ce phénomène s'éclaire quelque peu à la lumière du fait que les rois perses, spécialement Cambyse, se sont présentés comme les descendants légitimes de la dynastie saïte, les nouveaux "pharaons" de ce qui sera appelé plus tard la XXVIIe dynastie.[139] Darius lui-même (522-486) suivit cette politique en faisant rédiger un code de lois égyptiennes en démotique et en araméen[140] et cette politique semble avoir, au moins en partie, réussi si l'on en juge par l'inscription et le rôle joué par Udjahorresnet qui, sur l'ordre de Darius, restaura des "maisons de vie" et un temple de Neith à Saïs, berceau de la dynastie saïte.[141] On notera tout spécialement que la version égyptienne de la statue de Darius découverte à Suse montre que Darius lui-même semble avoir voué un certain culte à "Atoum maître d'Héliopolis".[142] Dans ces conditions, la copie, probablement par des membres d'un régiment (*dgl*) de l'armée perse en Égypte, d'un texte littéraire égyptien avec appel de la bénédiction d'"Atoumnebôn, notre dieu", n'a pas de quoi surprendre. C'est vraisemblablement du début de la période perse, peut-être du règne de Darius, que l'on peut proposer de dater l'ajout incertain: "*1 karsh* " (I, 10'.14').

---

[139]Cf. K. Atkinsons, "The Legitimacy of Cambyses and Darius as Kings of Egypt", *JAOS* 76 (1956), pp. 167-177; Bresciani, "Egypt..." (1984), p. 359.
[140]Cf. *supra*, n. 137.
[141]Cf. Bresciani, "Egypt..." (1984) (*supra*, n.137), p. 361; A. B. Lloyd, "The Inscription of Udjaḥorresnet", *JEA* 68 (1982), pp. 166-180, spéc. pp. 173-174; J. Blenkinsopp, "The Mission of Udjahorresnet and those of Ezra and Nehemiah", *JBL* 106 (1987), pp. 409-421.
[142]Cf. Yoyotte, "Les inscriptions..." (1972), pp. 253-266.

Cheikh Fadl — A. Lemaire : Illustrations

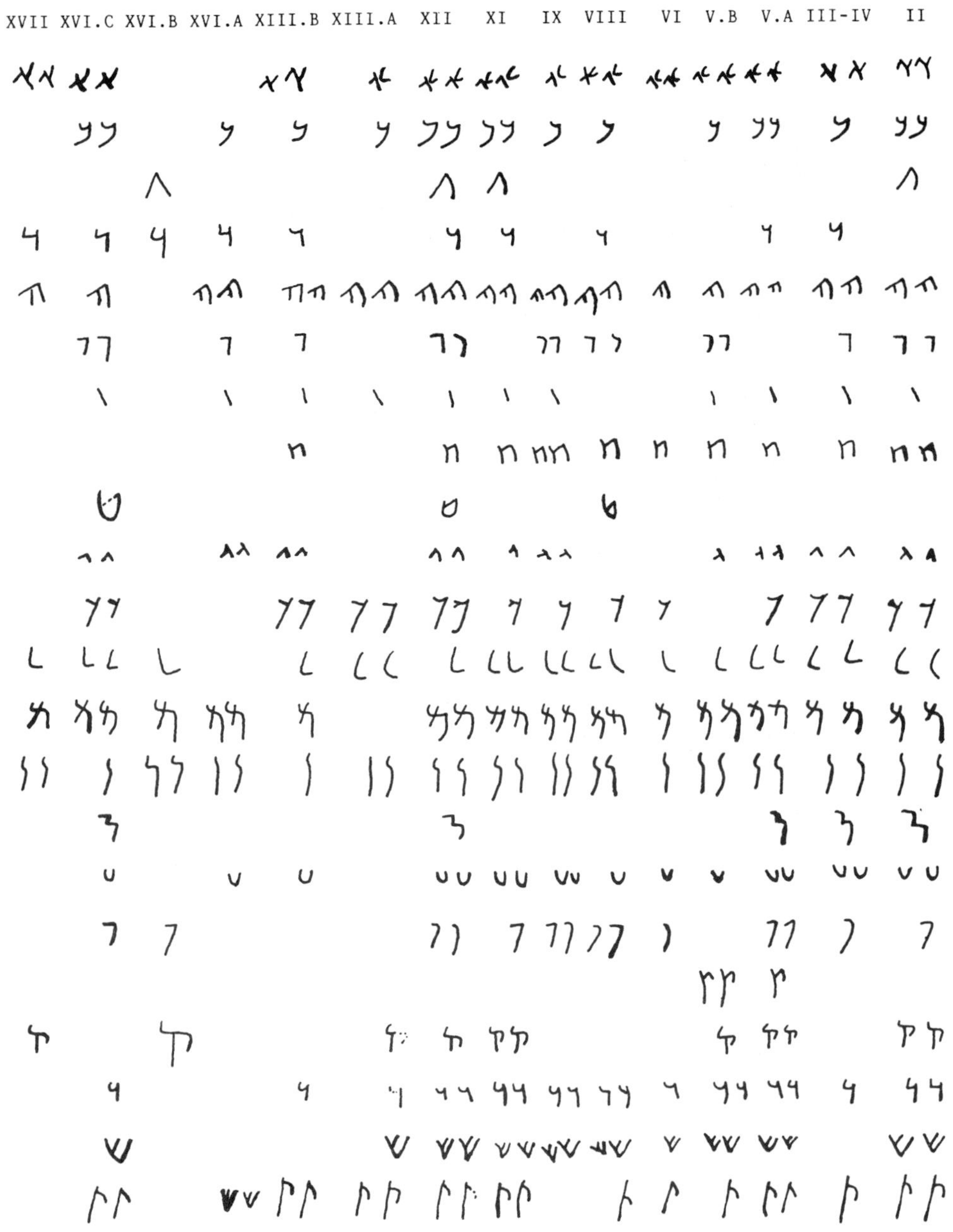

XVII XVI.C XVI.B XVI.A XIII.B XIII.A XII XI IX VIII VI V.B V.A III-IV II

Fig. 2. Tableau paléographique.

Fig. 3. Panneau I (1984).

Fig. 4. Panneau II : hauteur (1984).

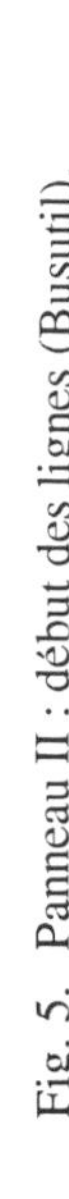

Fig. 5. Panneau II : début des lignes (Busutil).

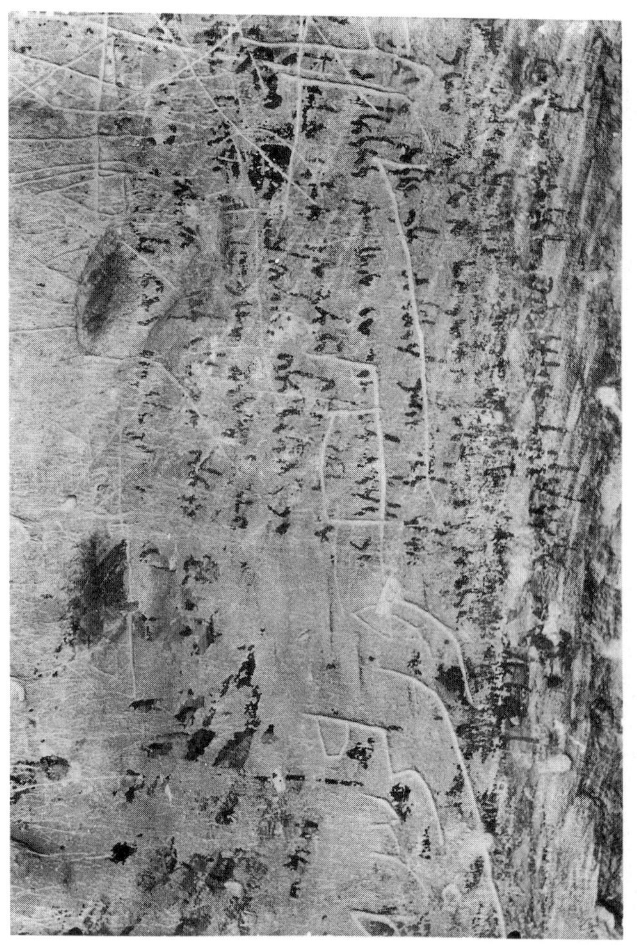

Fig. 6. Panneau II : fin des lignes (Busutil).

Fig. 7. Panneau III-IV (Busutil).

Fig. 8. Panneau VA : début des lignes (Busutil).

Fig. 9. Panneau VA : fin des lignes (Busutil).

Fig. 10. Panneau VB (Busutil).

Fig. 11. Panneaux VI et VII (1984).

Fig. 12. Panneau VI (1984).

Fig. 13. Panneau VIII (Busutil).

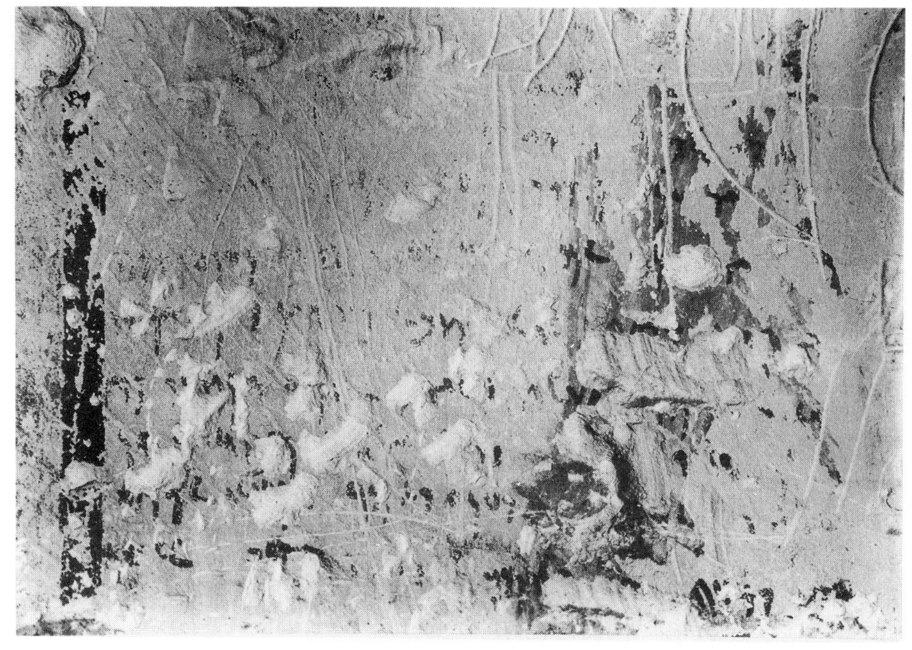

Fig. 14. Panneau IX (Busutil).

Fig. 15. Panneau XI (Busutil).

Fig. 16. Panneau XII (Busutil).

Fig. 17. Panneau XII : partie supérieure (Busutil).

Fig. 18. Panneau XIII (Busutil).

Fig. 19. Panneau XVI (Busutil).

Fig. 20. Panneau XVI B-C (1984).

Fig. 21. Panneaux XVI et XVII (1984).

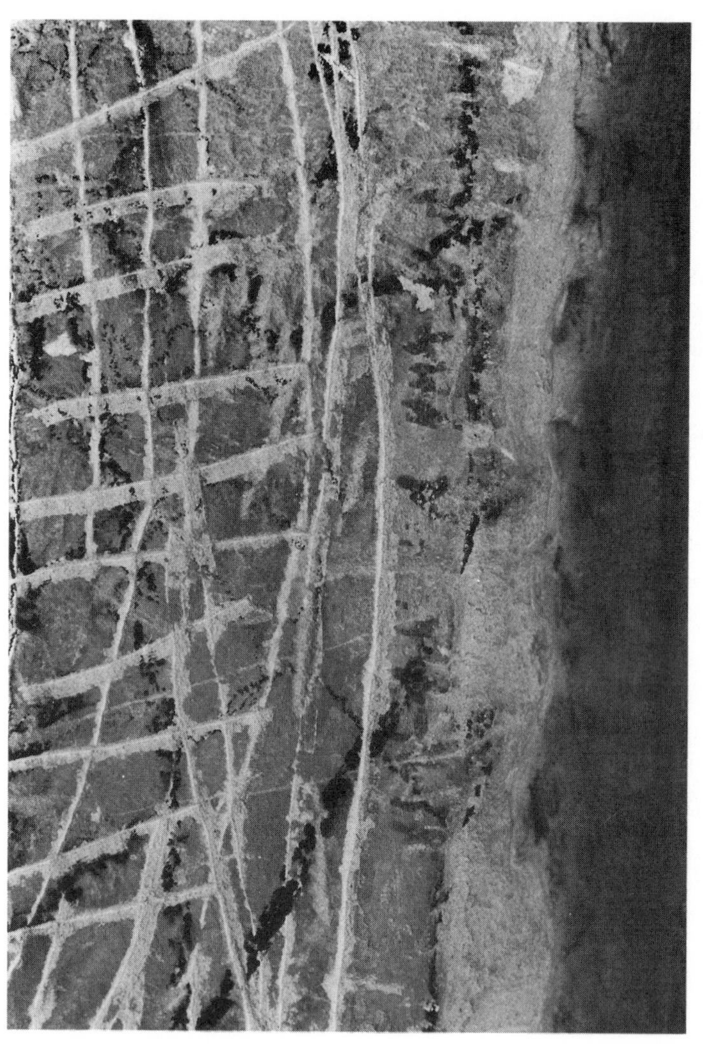

Fig. 22. Panneau XVII (1984).

New light on the ancient town of Taimā'

Alasdair Livingstone — Birmingham

While knowledge of the ancient history and archaeology of Palestine, Syria, Anatolia and Iraq advanced for almost two centuries by leaps and bounds, knowledge of ancient Arabia is still in its infancy. To take the single site of Taimā' as a case in point, it is easy to see from recent publications that significant new finds are no rarity.[1] Aramaic and the Aramaeans have of course been closely associated with Taimā' in modern historical research since the discovery in 1880 of the Taimā' stele now in the Louvre[2] and recent archaeological reconnaissance at the site resulted immediately in comparable finds. At the same time, the ever increasing corpus of cuneiform and related sources offers occasional items to bridge the gap over periods of obscurity in ancient Arabian history or further illuminate other periods where merely local information is available. The purpose of the present contribution is the following. Firstly, two new and complementary though disparate pieces of evidence will be adduced. Secondly, the implications of this will be considered in relation to some problems which have been brought up in respect to Taimā' by two authors who have recently made contributions offering overviews of the subject, namely W. G. Lambert on Nabonidus' activities in North Arabia and Taimā'[3] and P. J. Parr on the archaeological context of the town.[4] Finally, some information provided by the onomastica of the newly found Aramaic inscriptions will be summarised.

The first new and previously unsuspected piece of evidence comes from the royal inscriptions of Yariris of Carchemish in hieroglyphic Luwian, the second from the recently published Suḫu texts. It seems impossible on the basis of this evidence to avoid positing the existence of Taimā' as a place of some importance already in the 8th century B.C., whereas the earliest known inscriptions from the town itself date from some three or four centuries later.[5]

---

[1]See the successive reports in *Aṭlāl: The Journal of Saudi Arabian Archaeology* on Taimā' by various survey and excavation teams under the aegis of the Saudi Arabian Dept. of Antiquities.

[2]See H. Donner and W. Röllig, *Kanaanäische und aramäische Inschriften*, vol. I: Text (1962) Text Nr. 228, vol. II: Commentary (1964); J. C. L. Gibson, *Textbook of Syrian Semitic Inscriptions, Vol. 2 : Aramaic Inscriptions including inscriptions in the dialect of Zenjirli* Nr. 30 (1975).

[3]W. G. Lambert, "Nabonidus in Arabia", *Proceedings of the fifth Seminar for Arabian Studies* (1972), pp. 53-64.

[4]P. J. Parr, "Archaeology of North-west Arabia", in *L'Arabie préislamique et son environnement historique et culturel* (1989), ed. T. Fahd, pp. 39-66.

[5]K. Beyer and A. Livingstone, "Die neuesten aramäischen Inschriften aus Taimā'", *ZDMG* 137 (1987), pp. 285-296.

Taking the Yariris inscriptions as a starting point, the relevant evidence is best presented in the chronological order of modern research. The most important passage was rendered by Meriggi in 1967 as follows:

... 4URU-*sa-ā*-ti k	DUB-*li-ā-ti*	"..... in lingua cittadina,
Šu-r-wa-na-ti URU k	DUB-*li-ā-ti-a*	in lingua siria,
Á-šú-r KUR-*wa-n*o-*ti* URU k	DUB-*li-r-ti-a*	in lingua assira,
Ta-a-ma-na-ti-ha URU	DUB-*li-ti*	e in lingua tamanese".[6]

Though translating "language", Meriggi indicated in an accompanying note that "script" could also be possible. Since the appearance of Meriggi's *Manuale* considerable progress has been made in Hieroglyphic Luwian studies, substantially due to the work of J. D. Hawkins. In 1974 Hawkins made the observation that no native term for the writers of the hieroglyphic inscriptions or their language is known from these inscriptions themselves, the term Luwians being derived by equation with the second millennium Luwian of the Boğazköy texts.[7] To this comment he added the following footnote (p.68, n.6), which is of relevance here:

> The nearest approach to it is in CARCHEMISH A15 b 4, where we find - "[...] in the script of the City and in the script of Sura and in the script of Assur and in the script of Taiman, twelve languages I -ed." The script of the City is surely hieroglyphic as used in Carchemish, the script of Assur Assyrian cuneiform. Sura could refer to "Syrian", i.e. Aramaic, or possibly to Urartian, since the kings called themselves "King of the land *Šura*". It is not clear what language or script can be associated with Taiman, which is usually associated with Teman in Hanigalbat."

Before returning to these suggestions and observations, later developments must be summarised. In a further article published a year later, Hawkins had occasion to present his transliteration and translation of the text, and the passage is given in full here:[8]

> CARCHEMISH A 15 b, 4:
> (i)[...] URBS-si-ia-ti / SCRIBA-li-ia-ti sù+ra/i-wa/i-ni-ti (URBS) / SCRIBA-li-ia-ti-i à-sú+ra/i-(REGIO)-wa/i-na-ti (URBS) / SCRIBA-li-ia-ti-i ta-i-ma-ni-ti-ha (URBS) SCRIBA-li-ti

6 P. Meriggi, *Manule di Eteo Geroglifico,* pt. II, p. 34 (1967).
7 J. D. Hawkins, 'Assyrians and Hittites', *Iraq* 36 (1974), pp. 67-83.
8 J. D. Hawkins, 'The Negatives in Hieroglyphic Luwian', *AS* 25 (1975), pp. 119-156.

(ii) 12-ha-wa/i-ᵓ / "LINGUA"-la-ti-i-na / u+LITUUS-ni-ha

(iii) wa/i-mu-u ta-ni-ma-si-na REGIO-ni-si-na-ᵓ / INFANS-ni-na / ("VIA") ha+ra/i-wa/i-hi-ta$_5$-ti-i CUM-NA ARHA-sa-ta DOMINUS(-)na-ni-i-sa á-mi-i-sa / "LINGUA"-la-ti SUPER+RA-ᵓ

(iv) ta-ni-mi-ha-wa/i-mu (273) wa/i +ra/i-pi-n u+LITUUS-na-nu-ta

[...] in the script of the City, the script of Sura, the script of Assyria and the script of Taiman(?).
I knew twelve languages,
and to me my lord gathered the son of every country by (means of) travelling for (the sake of) language,
and he caused me to know every wisdom."

Three years later the same author, this time with A. Mopurgo-Davies as co-author once more had occasion to refer to the text, rendering it in agreement with Hawkins' previous translation "... nella scrittura della Città, nella scrittura di Sura, nella scrittura di Assiria e nella scrittura di Taiman. Ho conosciuto (?) 12 lingue...".[9]

Mentioning in his 1975 publication the well-known example of Assurbanipal, Hawkins pointed out that what is here at hand is a reflex of the motif of the wise ruler.[10] There is however also an interesting contrast. Assurbanipal, as ruler in the context of a high civilisation in its advanced phase, had an education which was almost exclusively assyro- and babylonocentric in character. Yariris, on the other hand, from his position on the cultural and trade crossroad of North Syria was a man of cosmopolitan accomplishments. The geographical allusions in the lines quoted above did not escape attention from Hittitologists or Semitists. In two articles E. Lipiński put forward the idea that *surawaniti* should best be understood as Tyrian.[11] The same idea was adopted by F. Starke in his Habilitationsschrift, published in 1990.[12] There are various considerations which make the suggestion that *sura* is *ṣūr*, "Tyros" attractive.

---

[9]A. Mopurgo-Davies and J. D. Hawkins, "Il sistema del luvio geroglifico", *Annali della Scuola Normale Superiore di Pisa* 8, 3 (1978), pp. 755-6.
[10]The earliest (3rd millennium) substantial example is the Ur III king Šulgi, see G. R. Castellino, *Two Šulgi Hymns (BC), Studi Semitici* 42(1972). For Assurbanipal see especially the inscription classified as L^4 , M. Streck, *Assurbanipal und die letzten assyrischen Könige bis zum Untergange Niniveh's*, pt. II: Text (1916), pp. 252-272.
[11]E. Lipińksi, "De fenicische inscripties uit Karatepe", in K. R. Veenhof (ed.), Schrijvend Verleden, Leiden-Zutphen 1983, pp. 46-54 (see p. 54) and in "Phoenicians in Anatolia and Assyria", in *OLP* 16 (1985), pp. 81-90, (see p. 82).
[12]F. Starke, *Untersuchungen zur Stammbildung des keilschriftluwischen Nomens, Studien zu den Bogazköy-Texten* 31, p. 231.

The idea that it is Syrian seems doubtful since it is questionable whether Syria was seen as a cultural or political entity in the 8th century B.C. The suggestion that it is Urartian (*Šūra*) could be doubted since the Urartian hieroglyphic did not attain a significant development or wide currency and more seriously since the Urartian inscriptions of this period are written in Assyrian cuneiform, even closely following the neo-Assyrian syllabary. Finally, the other entries require a city. In favour of *ṣūr* the following points can be made. It has been suggested that the sign value *sù* (which of course has nothing to do with the Assyrian *sù*) represents an affricative pronunciation.[13] Taking account of the difficulties inherent in transliterating one language in a system belonging to another language with a completely different phonetic base, this is not irrelevant. At any rate it is worth noting that the sound was realised as different from the *š* in Aššur. Historically, Tyros would be a natural geographical index for the Phoenician script which in the 8th century B.C. stood shoulder to shoulder with cuneiform as a major medium of trade and commerce.

Assuming that Yariris knew the script of Carchemish and also cuneiform and the Phoenician alphabet, there remains the problem of the identity of the fourth script. The suggestion that Taiman is the Teman in Hanigalbat encounters the serious difficulty that this Teman was not an important place and did not have its own script. Discussion with Hittitologist colleagues whether there could be a different solution, such as *yunan*, Greece, yielded the information that the reading *taimaniti* is assured. Egypt is also excluded since this was known in hieroglyphic Luwian, as elsewhere, as *miṣir*.[14] The suggestion is made here that the quoted passage contains a reference to Taimāʾ and the old south Arabic script. Apart from what has been put forward above, some more general points can be made in favour of this suggestion.

1. As can be seen from other passages in his inscriptions, Yariris was concerned to show his contacts abroad in all directions.[15]
2. While Taimāʾ has been relatively unaccessible in recent times, this was not always so, and the Arab geographer Yāqūt al-Ḥamāwī (c.1179-1229) even considered the town to be on the outer borders of Syria (*fī ʾaṭrāfi ʾl-šām*).[16]
3. Although there is a paucity of archaeological evidence from this period from Arabia the interest in products which could be obtained there is quite clear in contemporary Assyrian inscriptions.

---

[13]H. Craig Melchart, "PIE velars in Luvian*", *Studies in Memory of Warren Cowgill (1929-1985)*, ed. C. Watkins (1987) pp. 182-204. A different view has however been taken by T. Oshiro, "On Hieroglyphic Luwian Sign sú or zú", *Journal of Indo-European Studies* 17 (1989), p. 181.
[14]E.g. J. D. Hawkins in *AS* 25 (1975), p. 152.
[15]J. D. Hawkins, ibid. pp. p.150 (scripts and languages), p.151 ("the king reputed abroad"), p. 152 ("They heard of me in Egypt...").
[16]Yāqūt al-Ḥamāwī, *Muʿjam al-Buldān* s.v. Taimāʾ .

4. Taimāʾ was sufficiently important to be mentioned in the name of a gate of Nineveh in the time of Sennacherib.[17]
5. The existence of a 7th century treaty between Assurbanipal and Qedar shows that Qedar were taken seriously by the Assyrians.[18]
6. The same point could be deduced from the nature of the political affairs and negotiations involving the rulers of Dūmat al-Jandal during the reigns of Esarhaddon and Assurbanipal.[19]
7. The use of the South Arabian script on 5th and 6th century B.C. seals in Mesopotamia argues for some prestige of this script within certain circles; examples have recently been collected and discussed.[20]
8 . In spite of the relatively small quantity of earlier material there is evidence pointing to a greater antiquity of the South Arabic script than was once assumed. J. Naveh places "proto-Arabic" (script) around 1200 B.C. and "south-Arabic" "script" around 800 B.C.[21] More recently, B.Sass assigns the beginnings of the "South Arabian alphabet" to the 10th and 11th centuries B.C.[22]

Finally, one could make the observation that if one only had the quasi-apocryphal information about Nabonidus' stay in Taimāʾ as in the fragmentary Qumran prayer,[23] its historical veracity would certainly be questioned. However, we have not only the inscriptions of Nabonidus and the Babylonian Chronicle but even day to day documents such as those recording the issue of provisions for a journey to Taimāʾ by camel or the transport of the king's own food from Uruk to Taimāʾ.[24] Nabonidus' sojourn in Taimāʾ is an historical fact, although intrinsically much more difficult to explain that a mention of Taimāʾ in an inscription from Carchemish.

Remaining in approximately the same geographical area, the second new piece of evidence for Taimāʾ in the eighth century B.C. can now be brought forward. This is within the context of the correspondence of two governors of Suhu and Mari in the middle Euphrates region, namely Šamaš-rēš-uṣur, long known for his interest in apiculture,[25] and his son Ninurta-kudurri-uṣur. Whereas the significance of Carchemish

---

[17]I. Ephʿal, *The Ancient Arabs* (1982), pp. 124-124 with reference to the sources.
[18]K. Deller and S. Parpola, "Ein Vertrag mit dem arabischen Stamm Qedar", *Orientalia NS* 37 (1968), pp. 464-466; most recently S. Parpola and K. Watanabe, *Neo-Assyrian Treaties and Loyalty Oaths, SAA* 2, (1988).
[19]I. Ephʿal, op.cit., pp. 118-123.
[20]A. Livingstone, "Arabians in Babylonia/Babylonians in Arabia: Some reflections à propos new and old evidence", *L'Arabie préislamique et son environment historique et culturel,* ed. T. Fahd (1989), pp. 97-105.
[21]J. Naveh, *Early History of the Alphabet* (1982), p. 10.
[22]B. Sass, *The Genesis of the Alphabet and its Development in the Second Millennium B.C.* (1988), pp. 166-7.
[23]R. Meyer, "Das Gebet des Nabonid", *Sitzungsberichte der Sächsischen Akademie der Wissenschaften zu Leipzig, Phil.hist. Klasse* , vol 107/3.
[24]See Livingstone, op.cit.
[25]*WVDOG* IV (1903) 10 iv 13-v 6; republished in A. Cavigneaux and B. Kh. Ismail, "Die Statthalter von Suḫu und Mari im 8.Jh. v.Chr.", *BaM* 21 (1990), pp. 321-456; see p. 400.

needs no emphasis, a few words on the historical importance of Suḫu are perhaps not out of place. Stretching from the borders of Babylonia at Rapiqu to around Ḫindanu on the middle Euphrates, the region's principal characteristic was as a buffer zone between Babylonia and Assyria. Periods of more or less actual or nominal vassaldom northwards or southwards alternated with periods when the governors of Suḫu had considerable independent authority. At least through part of the Old Babylonian period Suḫu paid tribute to Babylonia. Tiglathpileser I (1115-1077) conquered Suḫu and the region remained closely associated with Assyria until late Neo-Assyrian times. Depicted on a relief, Šamaš-rēš-uṣur can be seen wearing headgear of Assyrian rather than Babylonian millinery.[26] But under the reign of Nebuchadnezzar II fine wines of Suḫu vintage graced the tables of Marduk and Ṣarpanitu in Babylon.[27] The range of products from Suḫu found in tribute lists attest to rich trade connections. The passage of significance in the newly published text reads as follows:

... ana-ku ^{Id}MAŠ.NÍG.DU.PAP
^{lú}GAR KUR su-ḫi u KUR ma-ri ^{lú}te-ma-ʾa-a-a ^{lú}ša-ba-ʾa-a-a
šá a-šar-šú-nu ru-qu ^{lú}A.KIN-šú-nu a-na muḫ-ḫi-ia ul DU-ku
ù a-na muḫ-ḫi-ia ul it-ti-qu-ú-nu a-na muḫ-ḫi-ia$_{5}$ ma(?) mu
PÚ MAR.TU u PÚ ḫa-la-tu$_{4}$ a-lak-ta-šú-nu TE u it-ti-iq-ma
u a-na ^{uru}ḫi-in-da-a-nu ir-ru-bu-nu ina ^{uru}kar-^{d}A.^{d}IM i-na
AN.BAR$_{7}$ ši-mu-su-nu áš-mi-e-ma ni-ri aṣ-mid ina MI ÍD
e-bir-ma ina šá-ni-i u$_{4}$-me a-di la AN.BAR$_{7}$ a-na ^{uru}az-la-a-a-nu
ak-šu-ud-ma 3 u$_{4}$ -me ina ^{uru}az-la-a-nu ú-šib-ma ina 3-šú u$_{4}$-me
ik-šu-du-nim-ma 1 ME-šú-nu bal-ṭu-su$^{!}$-nu ŠU.II ik-šu-ud 2 ME gam-ma-lu-šú-nu
a$^{!}$-di GÚ.UN-šú-nu SIKI ta-kil-tu$_{4}$ SIKI KASKAL$^{?}$ AN.BAR
na$_{4}$‹BABBAR›.DIL.MEŠ mim-ma mi-reš-ti DU.A.BI
ik-šu-ud ŠU.II-a-a NAM.RI-su-nu ka-bit-ti áš-lu-lam$^{!}$(EL)-ma
ú-še-rib a-na qé-reb KUR su-ḫi MU.7.KÁM
^{Id}MAŠ.NÍG.DU.PAP ^{lú}GAR KUR su-ḫi u KUR ma-ri da-ba-ba
an-na-a da-bi-ib[28]

"I, Ninurta-kudurri-uṣur, governor of the lands of Suḫu and Mari (report as follows): (Concerning) Temanites and Sabaeans, whose country lies far away, from whom no messenger had come to me, and who had not travelled to me, .. , one of their caravans approached the Amurrû well and Ḫallatu well, but passed on and entered the town of

---

[26]J. A. Brinkman, *Political History of Post-Kassite Babylonia, 1158-722, AnOr* 43 (1968), p. 219, n.1376.
[27]S. H. Langdon, *Die neubabylonischen Königsinschriften, Vorderasiatische Bibliothek* IV (1912), p. 90.
[28] See Cavigneaux and Isamil, n. 25 above, pp. 346-7, 351.

Ḫindanu. I heard the news at noon in the town of Kar-Apladad, gave the order to span (the chariots) crossed the river by night and reached Azlajanu before noon on the next day. I stayed in Azlajanu for three days and on the third day they came on. I took hundreds of them alive; I laid my hands on two hundred camels with their loads, blue Tyrian wool, ..wool, iron(?), alabaster(?), all kinds of things one could wish for. I took from them great booty and brought it back to Suḫu. This report was made in the seventh year of Ninurta-kudurri-uṣur, governor of the lands of Suḫu and Mari."

Seen in its own right, this episode is revealing for the trade stability of the times. The comment concerning messengers emphasises the remoteness of Taimā' and Saba': these were lands with which there was no normal diplomatic contact. At the same time there is an element of self-justification. It seems that Ninurta-kudurri-uṣur considered that if he had been approached he might (under whatever terms we do not know) have given right of passage to the caravan. This however not having been the case, he felt that he had a free hand. Seen from the point of view of North Arabia the inscription attests to a certain prosperity of Taimā' as a town involved in long-distance trade in the 8th century B.C.

Thus the philological evidence adduced above supplements the information on Taimā' previously known from Assyrian, Babylonian and other sources, as well as from the inscriptions from Taimā' itself.[29] It remains to briefly consider some historical and archaeological aspects, in the light of the new evidence, including the recently found Aramaic inscriptions from Taimā' . As far as the enigma of Nabonidus' military campaign in Northwest Arabia and this king's extended sojourn and building activities in Taimā' are considered, any evidence which substantiates the importance, prosperity and antiquity of the town and its surrounding region will of course make these events more understandable. In his survey of the present state of knowledge of the archaeology of North-west Arabia referred to above, P. J. Parr pointed out a contrast between two periods which can be distinguished even on the basis of the limited evidence available.[30] He points out that a number of sites in North-west Arabia are characterised by pottery which can safely be dated to the 13th to 11th centuries B.C. At present the best known of these is Qurayya. The present writer can confirm from personal experience the impact made by this site as containing "imposing standing remains of a fortified citadel hill, a small walled settlement, and an extensive area of irrigated fields".[31] In Parr's opinion, these remains, and also some standing kilns are to be associated without doubt with the datable pottery, and are in all probability to be

[29] See K. Beyer and A. Livingstone, "Die neuesten aramäischen Inschriften aus Taima'", *ZDMG* 137/2 (1987), pp. 285-296; "Eine neue reichsaramäische Inschrift aus Taima'", *ZDMG* 140/1 (1990), pp. 1-2.

[30] P. J. Parr, op.cit.

[31] ibid. p. 42.

connected with Egyptian interest in the area (for whatever reasons) which stimulated incipient urbanism. The contrast lies with the lack of evidence for sedentary or urban occupation in North Arabia between approximately the 11th and 6th centuries B.C. Even considering a later period the occupation areas at Taimāʾ and nearby Dedan are limited. The explanation for this may be found in a new role of the Arabian urban center not so much as a center of settlement but rather as a nexus for wider connections, whether trade, religion or as a market center for nomadic peoples. This would at least recall the passage in the mercantile code of Dedan which distinguishes between two groups designated *bkl* and *wbl*, "residents and caravaneers".[32]

In his treatment of Nabonidus' stay in Taimāʾ, W. G. Lambert reviewed previous attempts to explain this sojourn in such a remote place, showing that military strategy can hardly be seriously considered as a reason, and that trade connections in the Hejaz, even if of importance to Babylonia, would not require the personal presence of the Babylonian king for a decade.[33] If a reason can be found, it should probably be sought in connection with other personal idiosyncracies of this king, notably his predilection for the cult of the god Sîn. As has often been pointed out, Taimāʾ had particular religious associations, in which astral and lunar cults are well known to have played a part.[34]

The present contribution will be concluded by reviewing some new items of evidence confirming some of the observations made above. This new evidence consists of inscribed objects excavated or recovered (example C below was found on farmland, completely coated with tar) by the General Department of Antiquities and Museums, Saudi Arabia, to which all credit is due, and published and described in successive numbers of its Journal, *Aṭlāl*. The texts are given here for the convenience of the reader as established in two recent studies, to which the reader is referred for further commentary, and supplied for the present purpose with an English translation.[35]

A. Imperial Aramaic (c. 400 B.C.)

[שנת...בביר]ת תימא	1 [In the year]...in the city of Taimāʾ
[ה]קים פצגו שהרו בר	2 Paḍigū Šahrū, the son of the royal
[מ]לכי לחין העלי בי]ת	3 official of Liḥyān Haʿlay, set up the temple
צ]לם זי רב ומרחבה ו	4 of Ṣalm of Rabb and its extent, and
[ה]קים כרסאא זנה קדם	5 set up this throne before
צלם זי רב למיתב שנגלא	6 Ṣalm of Rabb as a postement for Sengallā

[32]A. F. L. Beeston, "A Minaean Market Code", *BSOAS* XLI (1978), pp. 142-5
[33]W. G. Lambert, above, n. 3.
[34]F. V. Winnett and W. L. Reed, *Ancient Records from North Arabia* (1979), pp. 92-93.
[35]K. Beyer and A. Livingstone, above n. 29 (1990).

ואשימא אלהי תימא	7 and Ašimā, the gods of Taimā',
לחיי נפש פצגו	8 for the life of Paḍigū
שהרו וזרעה מרא]יא	9 Šahrū and for the life of his seed, the lords
ו[ל̊]ח[יי נפשה זי [לה]	10 and for his life.

B. Imperial Aramaic (c. 400 B.C.)

זי קרב תימו בר א̊לה̊ו	1 (This is) that which Taymū, the son of 'Elāhū dedicated
לדרעא לחיי נפשה	2 to the (divinely protecting) arm for his life
ונפשהום זי פרקמננ‹ו›	3 and the life of Parqumannān‹ū›,
בר ועדו (וערו) ‹ו›כרימו ב̊רה זי	4 the son of Wā'edū (Wa'rū) ‹and› of Karīmū, the son of
[פר]קחיו	5 [Par]quḥayyū

C. Nabataean (first century B.C.)

חגרא די קרב אחבול והו פנ̊י חטמ	1 (This is) the sacred object which Aḫbôl, who is under the protection of Ḥaṭmah, has dedicated
ה למנוה א̊להת אלהתא לחיי נפשה ונפ	2 to the deity of deities Mánawah for his life and the lives
ש אחרתה לעלם	3 of his descendants in eternity.

In relation to the outlying contacts of Taimā' this material can be viewed on a general as well as a more specific level. On the more general level the dedication by an individual who was under the protection of an Arab tribe supports the idea that an element of the raison d'être of Taimā' was as a nexus for outside links.[36] Also on a general level all three new pieces of evidence confirm Taimā''s rôle as a suitable place for dedications and as a sanctuary for certain gods, including Sengallā. The uncertainty whether the latter contains the name of the Mesopotamian Sîn has frequently been remarked on.[37] If Sengallā is to be derived from Akkadian, which is uncertain, it would more easily suggest *ušumgallu*, "dragon" which was pronounced in Neo-Assyrian as

---

[36]Ḥaṭmah is known later as a subsection of Judhām, a tribe which settled in pre-Islamic times on the borders of Byzantine Syria and Palestine, holding places such as Madyan, Amman, Ma'ān and Adhruḥ and ranging as far south as Tabūk and the Wādi 'l-Qurā (see 'Umar Kaḥḥālah, *Mu'jam qabā'il al-'arab* (1982), p. 284; *Encycl. of Islam* II, p. 573).

[37]Donner and Röllig and Gibson in their respective commentaries on theTaimā' Louvre stele (see above, note 2), also Beyer and Livingstone, above n. 29 (1987).

šungalle.[38] This could also have astral associations. In any case one notes that the stele on which **A** is written includes in its iconography the winged disc, lunar crescent and Venus star, while example **B** features a primitive bucraneum.

On the more specific level of divine and personal onomastica, Gibson already remarked "Such a cosmopolitan religious situation accords with the position of the oasis at the juncture of trade-routes north-west to Egypt and Syria, east to Mesopotamia, and south to the Yemen; ...".[39] From the new inscriptions the following information can be added. Ašīmā (to be read now also in the Louvre stele, ll.3 and 16) is known from Hamath on the Orontes (II Kings 17:30). This passage parallels Ašīmā of Hamath with Nergal of Cutha, leaving little doubt that Ašīmā was the city god. The passage in Amos 8:14, *han-nišbaᶜīm bᵉʾašmat šōmrōn wᵉʾamrū ḥēj ʾᵃlōhᵃḵā Dān wᵉ-ḥēj dereḵ bᵉʾēr-šabaᶜ* has not escaped in this connection the attention of Biblical criticism, where the alternative suggestions have been made to read ʾᵃšīmaṯ (and refer to the Ašīmā of Hamath) or to emend to ʾᵃšēraṯ, the better known Ashera.[40] It can also be noted that Dān in Samaria was not so far outside the orbit of Hamath, and therefore liable to temptation by its city god. The new evidence at least strengthens the evidence for Ašīmā and suggests that it is more likely that *šᵉwā* has in the course of the tradition been substituted for *ḥîreq* in the Masoretic text in Amos than that the consonantal structure should be interfered with in either passage to yield Ashera.[41] This argument is also supported by the fact that the Septuaginta's translation follows the common meaning of the common Hebrew root which would naturally be associated (correctly or not) with the name Ašīmā.[42] The divine name Bōl, as in Aḫbōl, is particularly common in Palmyrene.[43] The Taimanite *ṣlm* apparently occurs in a Latin inscription from Jawf, where the emphatic ṣ resulted in the a-vowel being heard as o/u: *sanctus sulmus.*[44] The name Haᶜlay is typically Lihyanite. This is not the only example of contact between

---

38*ABL* 951, 12, cited in AHw., o.V.

39Gibson, above n. 2, p. 148.

40H. W. Wolff, *Biblischer Kommentar, Altes Testament, Dodekapropheten 2, Joel und Amos* (Heidelberg 1969).

41See K. Koch et al., *Amos, Untersucht mit den Methoden einer strukturalen Formgeschichte, Teil 1, Programm und Analyse, AOAT* 30 (1976), pp. 224-5. Koch et al. express doubt whether this verse really belongs to Amos, since it agrees better with the thematics of Hosea.

42Septuagint: οἱ ὀμνύοντες κατὰ τοῦ ἱλασμοῦ Σαμαρείας; Vulgate: *qui iurant in delicto Samariae.* Modern translations vary, though the "scholarly" ones favour Ashima: "Ceux qui jurent par Ashima de Samarie, ceux qui disent, "Par la vie de ton Dieu, Dan!" et: "Par la vie de ton Bien-Aimé, Bersabée" ceux-là tomberont pour ne plus se relever.", *La Sainte Bible* (Paris 1956); note that this is marked as a corr(ection) rather than a conj(ecture). The *New English Bible* (OUP/CUP, 1970) translates: "all who take their oath by Ashima, goddess of Samaria". The revised *Zürcher Bibel* (1907-1931) emends: "Die bei der Aschera von Samaria schwören und die sprechen...". A recent German translation of the École Biblique's *Sainte Bible* renders: "alle, die beim Götzenbild von Samaria schwören und sagen: ...", with a note indicating the literal etymological meaning of *ʾašmaṯ*, as in the Sepuaginta, but allowing the alternative possibilities that this is either a goddess ("vgl. 2Kings 17") or a sanctuary in Samaria, referring to Dtn 9:21. The new Deutsche Einheitsbibel also renders "Götzenbild", which is strictly speaking an interpretation. The Lutherbibel opts for "Abgott" while the King James version follows the Septuaginta in translating "They that swear by the sin of Samaria..."

43J. K. Stark, *Personal Names in Palmyrene Inscriptions* (1971) p. 74-5.

44G. W. Bowersock, *Roman Arabia*, p.98f., where no Semitic etymology is given.

Taimā' and Dedan. To restrict oneself to published examples, a Lihyanite king engraved his name three times, in Nabataean script at Khabw al-sharqi, ten miles from Taimā'.[45] A Nabataean inscription from al-ʿUlā from much later (251 of Provincia Arabia, 355/6 A.D.) refers to what may have been a diplomatic marriage.[46] A certain Adnan (prince of Hegra) had married the daughter of his cousin, who was prince of Taimā'.

Addendum

After completion of his work the writer was informed by J. C. Greenfield that he had himself tentatively posed the question with regard to Luwian ta-i-ma-ni-ti-ha whether this could be a reference to Taima and the South Arabic script, in: 'Of Scribes, Scripts and Languages', *Phoinikeia Grammata: Lire et écrire en Méditerranée, Actes du Colloque de Liège,* 14-18 November 1989, eds. Cl. Bauvain, C. Bonnet, V. Krings (Liège-Namur 1991).

[45] JS nab 334, 335, 337.
[46] F. Altheim and R. Stiehl, *Die Araber in der alten Welt*, vol 5, pt. 1, pp. 305-9 with Abb.54.

Cognates Can Be Deceptive : Some Aramaic Distinctives

Alan Millard — University of Liverpool

American visitors to London should take care to walk on the pavement - failure to do so could be fatal! In England the pavement is that part of the street commonly called the "sidewalk" in America.[1] This warning illustrates a common feature of closely related languages, one which has not always been recognised in the past, and is still not understood universally, despite clear evidence.[2] The divergences in the meanings of cognate words between kindred languages is a vast study, and in this essay only a few soundings can be made. Aramaic lends itself well to such investigation because of its links with Hebrew in the west and with Akkadian in the east; its impact on Arabic is well known. The long history of Aramaic would complicate the exercise considerably, so the evidence from Old and Imperial Aramaic, including Biblical Aramaic, will be adduced here, with occasional contributions from other sources.[3] The limited and scattered examples of these earlier stages of the language prevent us from drawing any comprehensive picture.

As a Semitic language, Aramaic shares many words with Hebrew, Akkadian and Arabic in the same meanings: *ʾᵃkal*, *ʾākal*, *akālu*, *ʾakala*, "to eat", *mᵉlēʾ*, *mālēʾ*, *malû*, *malaʾa*, "to be full", *ṣalmāʾ*, *ṣelem*, *ṣalmu*, "statue", *pegrāʾ*, *peger*, *pagru*, "body" are a few. On formal grounds, Aramaic is classed as North or West Semitic, and the lexical stock gives support, numerous words being common to it and to Hebrew and Phoenician, in contrast to Akkadian. "To fall", *nᵉfal*, *nāfal*, Akkadian *maqātu*, is a good example. Another is *mᵉlʾāk*, *malʾāk*, "messenger", Akkadian *mār šipri*.

The feature that deserves more attention first is neither of these, although both could be pursued with profit; rather it is the occurrence of words in Aramaic which have Hebrew or Akkadian cognates, but which have divergent meanings. Often these show Aramaic agreeing with Hebrew against Akkadian, as in *ʾᵃmar*, *ʾāmar*, "to say", Akkadian *amāru*, "to see" (note also Ugaritic *ʾmr*, "to see", but Old South Arabian *ʾmr*, "to proclaim"), or *sᵉfar*, *sēfer*, "writing, book", versus *šipru*, "task, message". This is what would be expected on grounds of comparative grammar, the differences

[1]*Webster's Third New International Dictionary* (Springfield, Mass. 1971) *s.v.* "the artificially covered surface of a public thoroughfare, *chiefly Brit.* sidewalk".
[2]The writings of the late Mitchell Dahood illustrate the point.
[3]In the interests of space few references are given; all the words cited can be traced in the standard dictionaries and lexica.

being matters of historical development which cannot be followed precisely unless many more documents from West Semitic sources of the second and third millennia B.C. come to light. The situation in the second half of the second millennium is obscure, with Ugaritic siding now with one, now with the other (having *spr*, "document etc." as in Canaanite and Hebrew).

Nevertheless, there is a number of words in Aramaic which share the meanings of their Akkadian cognates rather than their Hebrew ones. These are not the loan-words which were gradually absorbed into the language and which Stephen Kaufman treated so thoroughly (some of them obvious, like *niḏbāḵ*, "a course of bricks", some of them revealing valuable information about Akkadian dialects, like *sᵉgan*, "prefect")[4], nor are they words transplanted into Aramaic *faute de mieux*, like *gwgl* ‹*gugallu* and *ʾdqwr* ‹*adakuru*, "overseer of the water works" and "offering vase" respectively, in the Tell Fekheriyeh inscription. These are words like Aramaic *sᵉḥar*, Akkadian *saḫāru*, "to go around". The Sefire stelae exhibit this in the mid-eighth century B.C. in the phrase *malkayyāʾ zî sᵃḥirtî* (*mlkyʾ zy sḥrty* Sefire III 7-8), where the force of the nominal form is the same as the Akkadian *siḫirtu*, "around". Hebrew uses the verb *sāḥar* and its derivatives mainly in the specialised sense of "to go around on business, to trade", a sense found perhaps once with the Akkadian verb, but obvious in its derivatives *sāḫiru*, "peddler" and *saḫirtu*, "small wares", from the early second millennium B.C.[5] In Hebrew the equivalent of Sefire *sḥrty* would be *sᵉḇiḇoṯāy*, but the base SBB had no role in Aramaic, and the Targums use *sᵉḥar* to render Biblical Hebrew *sāḇab* (e.g. Joshua 6:3ff).

In similar ways, the base YQR reveals overlapping shades of meaning and contrasts. Biblical Aramaic has *yᵉqār*, "honour", *yaqqīr*, "honourable" (Ezra 4:10) and *yaqqīr*, "difficult" (Daniel 2:11). Ahiqar adds *yaqqîr*, "heavy" (of debt, 111, 130) and "precious" (93, 95, 108), with the Haphel verb in *hwqr lbb* (98). Akkadian *aqāru*, "to be scarce, precious", lines up with the Aramaic in the third theme, causative, "to give honour (to the gods)", notably in personal names, and in the adjective *aqru*, "precious, rare, dear". Hebrew has *yāqar*, "to be precious", *yaqqîr*, "very precious", *yᵉqār*, "preciousness, price" with the meaning "honour" said to be mainly post-exilic (Est.1:4, 20, etc. but also Ps. 49:13, 21), and *yāqār*, "precious, rare", and in Ecc. 10:1 "weighty". In addition to YQR, Hebrew and Akkadian have *kāḇēḏ*, *kabātu*, "to be heavy, to be honoured", in the causative "to honour, to make difficult", with various derivatives, which Aramaic lacks. (Compare also Ugaritic *kbd* and the gloss *ya-ka-bi-it* on the word-sign dugud in the Canaanite Amarna Letter 245.) Instead, Aramaic subsumes the

---

[4]S.A.Kaufman, *The Akkadian Influences on Aramaic* (Chicago 1974).

[5]On these words see B. Landsberger, "Akkadisch-Hebräische Wortgleichnungen", *Hebräische Wortforschung*, Fs. W. Baumgartner, *Vetus Testamentum Supp.* 16 (1967), pp. 176-90, esp. pp. 179-90.

idea of being heavy in *yᵉqār*. This appears most evidently in the adjective qualifying debt and in the phrase already cited from Ahiqar 98, *hwqr lbb*, which surely parallels Hebrew *hak̲bēd̲ lēb̲āb̲* of Exodus 8:11 etc., "hardening of heart". Where *kāb̲ēd̲* and its related terms stand in Biblical Hebrew, the Targums often have a form of *yᵉqar* (e.g. Gen. 48:10; Ex. 16:7). Both stems appear in Amorite personal names, I. J. Gelb assigning the meanings "to be dear" to YQR and "to be heavy, to be honourable" to KBD, on the basis, presumably, of the Akkadian and Hebrew uses[6]. Plainly, no wholesale transfer of meanings between such cognates can be made without strong support.

Aramaic and Akkadian Cognates

Aramaic shares some members of its lexicon with Akkadian where there is no Hebrew cognate, or where the Hebrew word is likely to be borrowed from Aramaic. Such a noun is *mᵉšak̲*, "skin, hide", the same as Akkadian *mašku*, standing beside *gᵉlad̲*. Ahiqar shows the two clearly in lines 118 and 119 where the leopard asks the goat for *mšky* and the goat replies "Don't take *gldy* from me". Is Aramaic *mᵉšak̲* an Akkadian word borrowed for poetic purposes, or a word of common origin, happening to be rare in our early Aramaic sources, and absent from other West Semitic texts?

Shared verbs include:

Aramaic *bāt̲* "to spend the night" (Dan. 6:19): Akkadian *bâdu, bâtu*;

Aramaic *ṣᵉb̲aʾ*, "to wish, to want": Akkadian *ṣabû*, both with derived nouns (perhaps also Amorite "to desire");[7]

Aramaic *pᵉlaḥ*, "to worship, to serve": Akkadian *palāḫu*, "to fear, to worship, to serve"

The case of *ṣallī*, "to pray", is interesting. Aramaic has a nominal form at Tell Fekheriyeh, *tṣlwth*, and then the verb and a noun in the Imperial period. Akkadian has *sullû*, "to pray" from the third millennium B.C. onwards, but from early in the first millennium also has *ṣullû*. The form with *ṣ* was already current in Ugaritic (I D 39 = CTA 19.39, Aqhat). An ancient bifurcation, with Akkadian succumbing to "Aramaic" influences about 1000 B.C. might be supposed, but one personal name from Ur is apparently written *Sin-ú-ṣe-li* in the eighteenth century B.C.[8] Old South Arabian has a nominal form *ṣlw*, "prayer".

Another verb common to Aramaic and Akkadian is *bᵉʿâ, buʾû*, "to want, to seek". Here the Akkadian is found from Middle Babylonian times, in the latter half of the second millennium B.C., at first in tablets from the peripheral regions in the north

[6] I. J. Gelb, *Computer-Aided Analysis of Amorite* (Chicago 1980) *s.v.*
[7] Ibid.,pp. 34
[8] Cited in *CAD* S 367a from H.H.Figulla, W.J.Martin, *UET* V, *Letters and Documents of the Old Babylonian Period* (London 1953) 493.13.

(Hattusha) and west (Ugarit, Amarna Letters). Again, a western influence on Akkadian might be suspected. This word occurs twice in Biblical Hebrew, Isaiah 21:12, Obadiah 6, where it may well be borrowed from Aramaic.

Aramaic may share a stem with Akkadian or with Hebrew in these ways, but form its own derivative to serve where the other languages have a different term. Thus *m^e^šaḥ*, "to anoint", is well-known to Aramaic, Hebrew, and Ugaritic, yet only Aramaic takes the common noun *m^e^šaḥ*, "oil" from it, where the others have *šemen*, etc., which is also the normal Akkadian, *šamnu.*

Aramaic Alone

Beside these shared words, Aramaic is, of course, distinguished by a body of words which do not occur in Hebrew or Akkadian, although these languages share other cognates for the same concepts.

Aramaic *ʾ^a^zal*, "to go" contrasts with Hebrew *hālak* and Akkadian *alāku* (although *h^e^lak̠* is current in Aramaic also);

Aramaic *ʾ^a^t̠â*, "to come", contrasts with *bāʾ* and *bāʾu* (although *ʾ^a^t̠â* occurs in Hebrew poetry);

Aramaic *n^e^ḥēt̠*, "to go down", contrasts with *yārad̠* and *arādu*;

Aramaic *n^e^faq*, "to go out", contrasts with *yāṣāʾ* and *aṣû;*

Aramaic *s^e^lēq*, "to come up", contrasts with *ʿālâ* and *elû*;

Aramaic *ʿ^a^lal*, "to enter", contrasts with *ʿārab̠* and *erēbu*;

Aramaic *š^e^b̠aq*, "to leave", contrasts with *ʿāzab̠* and *ezēbu.*

Some of these Aramaic verbs do have cognates elsewhere. Ugaritic seems to use *nḥt*, "to go down", in Shahar and Shalim 37ff. Arabic knows *š^e^b̠aq*, and Old South Arabian *nfq*, "to be indebted", is perhaps related to Aramaic *n^e^faq* (note also Arabic *nafaqa*, "to go out").

Finally, there are words for which each language goes its own way. Aramaic *mallel*, "to speak", *millâ*, "word", as opposed to Hebrew *dabbēr*, *dāb̠ār* and Akkadian *qabû*, *qibītu*, *awû*, *awātu*, *dabābu*, with various derivatives, is most obvious. Of particular note is "to write" for which Aramaic uses *k^e^t̠ab̠* with Hebrew, *s^e^far*, "writing" and *sāfar*, "scribe", as in Hebrew, Ugaritic and Canaanite, yet takes over Akkadian *šiṭru*, "document" and *egirtu*, "text". At the same time it has its own verb *r^e^šam*, "to write" (Daniel *passim*) with which it duly renders Hebrew *ḥāqaq* in the Targums (e.g. Is. 10:1).

Our somewhat superficial and unsystematic gleanings from comparative lexicography show that there is a lexical profile which can be drawn for Aramaic. Semitists have been much occupied with investigation of common terms and of basic grammatical features; there is need to notice the peculiarities in each area, too. A proper study will have to await examination of the new Hoftijzer–Jongeling *Dictionary of the*

North-West Semitic Inscriptions and completion of the *Comprehensive Aramaic Lexicon.* Yet some distinctions are clear. Where cognates are concerned, Aramaic is not wholly western, sometimes indeed is decidedly eastern. Where its terms are unique among eastern and western Semitic we may wonder if we reach the true Aramaic. There are words in this class which have Arabic cognates, both Sabaean and later. Again, it is impossible to know if this results from common inheritance or influence in one direction or another. Increasing knowledge about early Arabia may bring enlightenment. Still some words remain peculiar to Aramaic, and among them are terms for ordinary human activities. When thoroughly defined, they may indicate something about the early speakers of Aramaic, their origin and their kin. Their existence points to the development over several centuries before the start of the first millennium B.C. of a distinctive group of people maintaining their identity by speaking "Aramaic".

Neue Materialien zum Christlich-Palästinisch-Aramäischen Lexikon I*

Christa Müller-Kessler — Emskirchen

Die Lexikographie des Christlich-Palästinisch-Aramäischen (CPA) wurde seit der Publikation des *Lexicon Syropalaestinum* von Friedrich Schultheß stark vernachlässigt.[1] Diverse Texteditionen wurden zwar mit Glossaren versehen, doch sind die meisten dieser Wortverzeichnisse unzulänglich und es fehlen vergleichende Hinweise zum Samaritanisch-Aramäischen (SA) und Jüdisch-Palästinisch-Aramäischen (JPA), ganz abgesehen von falschen Lesungen in zahlreichen Textpassagen. Mit der Publikation von Michael Sokoloff's *Dictionary of Jewish Palestinian Aramaic*[2] und einigen verbesserten und verläßlicheren Texteditionen, z.B. Abraham Tals, *The Samaritan Targum of the Pentateuch*[3] oder Zeʿev Ben-Ḥayyim mit seiner Serie LOT[4] und dem *Tibat Marqe*[5] für das Samaritanisch-Aramäische, wurde die Vergleichsbasis für das Westaramäische erheblich verbessert und verbreitert.

Während der Vorbereitungen für die Grammatik des Christlich-Palästinisch-Aramäischen, dessen Wörterbuch und verschiedene Textausgaben begegneten mir zahlreiche Wörter, die in den Erstausgaben oder Reeditionen verlesen worden waren bzw. von den Bearbeitern nicht gelesen werden konnten. Solange die Aramaistik noch auf das *Lexicon Syropalaestinum* von Schultheß angewiesen ist, das teilweise unvollständig ist und viele fehlerhafte Eintragungen aufweist, gilt es, erst einmal den Anfang einer lexikalischen Aufarbeitung zu machen, um so das umfangreiche Material von circa 450 bis 500 fehlenden Lemmata zugänglicher zu machen. Viele Lexeme sind dabei singulär und bedürfen einer eingehenden Untersuchung, bevor sie in ein Wörterbuch aufgenommen werden können. Es fällt gelegentlich schwer, Lesungen neuer Hapax legomena zu akzeptieren, doch bewiesen neue Textfunde gerade für das CPA immer wieder, daß sie öfter als vermutet zutrafen.[6]

---

*Revidierte Fassung des Vortrages. Die Erstellung dieses Beitrages wurde im Rahmen eines Postdoktorandenstipendiums der Deutschen Forschungsgemeinschaft ermöglicht.

[1]F. Schultheß, *Lexicon Syropalaestinum* = LSp (Berlin 1903).

[2]M. Sokoloff, *A Dictionary of Jewish Palestinian Aramaic of the Byzantine Period* = DJPA (Bar-Ilan 1990).

[3]A. Tal, *The Samaritan Targum of the Pentateuch*, vols. I-III (Tel Aviv 1980-83).

[4]Z. Ben-Ḥayyim, *The Literary and Oral Tradition of Hebrew and Aramaic amongst the Samaritans* [hebr.] (Jerusalem 1957–1977).

[5]Idem, תיבת מרקה *A Collection of Samaritan Midrashim etc.* [hebr.] (Jerusalem 1988).

[6]Cf. M. Bar-Asher, *Palestinian Syriac Studies, Source-Texts, Traditions and Grammatical Problems* [hebr.] (Dissertation Jerusalem 1977), 307; Ch. Müller-Kessler, *Grammatik des Christlich-Palästinisch-Aramäischen, Teil I Schriftlehre, Lautlehre, Formenlehre* (Hildesheim 1991), 6.

I) *ʾnkwryṭys*[7]

Schultheß führt in seinem *Lexicon* die annähernd zutreffende Emendation *ʾn[w]kryṭyn* statt *ʾnkwr̈yṭyn*, von griechisch ἀναχωρητής an.[8] Die Eintragung stammt aus der Vita Antonii, Kapitel 41; die Textstelle wurde in der verbesserten Publikation der Taylor-Schechter Fragmente von den Bearbeiterinnen A. Lewis und M. Gibson als *ʾswr*[̈].*ṭ*[.] verlesen.[9] Das Fragment T-S 16.319 bII:2 selber hat *ʾnkwr̈yṭyn* im Gegensatz zur griechischen Version der Vita Antonii, die μοναχοί aufweist. In der *Erzählung aus dem Mönchsleben* ist der Singular emphaticus *ʾnkwryṭʾ* gleich mehrfach und mit der griechischen Nominativendung *ʾnkwryṭys* einmal belegt.[10]

II) **ʾtglgl*

Im Itpalpal tritt die reduplizierte Wurzel *glgl* im folgendem Zusammenhang auf: *nʾṣnyʾ dmtg̈lglyn mn rwḥʾ* "Blüten, die vom Wind umhergewirbelt werden" Jeremia 13,24 T-S 16.322 aII (Le 00:10).[11] Diese Textpassage wurde für Goshen-Gottsteins kritische Textausgabe nicht entziffert.[12] Parallelen zu *glgl*, *ʾtglgl* finden sich im JPA.[13] *glgl* ist darüberhinaus für das CPA die bessere Variante, im Gegensatz zum Eintrag bei Schultheß *glg* I "abstulit, removit".[14] Letzterer basiert auf einer Lesung Lands und gehört zu den Katechesen des Cyrill von Jerusalem, IX, 8.[15] Da die Landschen Lesungen nicht gerade verläßlich sind, muß bezweifelt werden, daß *glg* hier die richtige Wurzel sein kann. Der Eintrag im CPA-Lexikon sollte lauten: *glgl* Palpel "rollen"; Itpalpal "umhergerollt, umhergewirbelt werden".

III) **bʿy npš*

Im CPA wie im Syrischen steht *bʿy npš* für die idiomatische Wendung "jemand nach dem Leben trachten". Dazu findet sich in Jeremiah 45,16 (38,16) Bodl. Heb. e. 73 fol.

---

[7]Sonderzeichen in der Transkription des CPA: ein superlinearer Doppelpunkt kennzeichnet Pluralformen jeglicher Art, der einzelne superlineare Punkt über ʾ *e* oder *i*, π = P-Inversivum, ^...^ superlinearen bzw. sekundären Eintrag in der Handschrift und [...] fehlende Buchstaben.
[8]Schultheß, LSp 13b.
[9]A. S. Lewis, M. D. Gibson, *Apocrypha Syriaca* = Le 02 (Cambridge 1902), 148:2.
[10]H. Duensing, *Christlich-palästinisch-aramäische Texte und Fragmente* (Göttingen 1906), 30:II:22, 28:II:15, 36:II:7; 28:II:3.
[11]Der überwiegende Teil der Taylor-Schechter Fragmente wurde in A. S. Lewis, M. D. Gibson, *Palestinian Syriac Texts from Palimpsest Fragments in the Taylor-Schechter Collection* = Le 00 (London 1900), 46:22 publiziert. Leider ist diese Textausgabe sehr mangelhaft, so daß ich es vorziehe, nach den Bibliotheksnummern zu zitieren. Eine neue Textausgabe ist in Vorbereitung.
[12]M. H. Goshen-Gottstein with the assistance of H. Shirun, *The Bible in the Syropalestinian Version*, Part I (Jerusalem 1973), 86.
[13]Sokoloff, DJPA 129a
[14]Schultheß, LSp 37b.
[15]J. P. N. Land, *Anecdota Syriaca* IV (Leiden 1975), 184:24.

43 recto folgender Beleg: *hlyn db*ʿ*yn npšk* "diejenigen, die dir nach dem Leben trachten".[16] Für einen identischen Sprachgebrauch lassen sich in den anderen aramäischen Dialekten außerhalb des Syrischen keine Belege nachweisen.

IV) **g*ʿ*y*

Die onomatopoetische Wurzel *g*ʿ*y* "muhen" erscheint in dem bisher nicht identifizierten Fragment T-S 12.759 a:3 (Le 00:88) als Nomen *g*ʿʾ*y dtwr̈yn* "das Muhen der Rinder". Die Wurzel *g*ʿ*y* ist gemeinaramäisch und im CPA bereits als Partizip aktiv singular maskulin Peal *g*ʿ̇ʾ in Hiob 6,5 CCR 18: *w*ʾ*n twr*ʾ *g*ʿʾ ^ʿ*l*^ *kwl* ^ʾ*wry*ʾ̇^ *dmzwnh* "und wenn das Rind über seiner Futterkrippe brüllt" belegt.[17]

V) **dwmlyw*

Das eigentümliche und bisher nur im CPA auftretende Adjektiv *dwmly* "tüchtig, genügend" war schon länger bekannt. *dwmly* ist eindeutig die bessere Variante, obwohl Schultheß es in seinem *Lexicon* noch unter *dmwl*ʾ*y* aufführt.[18] Die erste Schreibvariante tritt derart häufig auf, daß das Lemma *dwmly* lauten sollte.

Im 2Korintherbrief 3,5 T-S 20.157 bII (Le 00:46) las Lewis das merkwürdige und keinen Sinn gebende Wort *ḥmsnwtn* "?". Das Fragment hat aber *dwmlywtn* "unsere Tüchtigkeit", das passende Abstraktnomen zu *dwmly*, welches im selben Fragment Vers 5 und 6 im Sinne von "tüchtig" im Status absolutus maskulin plural *dwm̈lyyn* erscheint. *dwmly* setzt sich zusammen aus *d* + *mly* "voll sein" mit regressiver Assimilation.

VI) *ḥyy npš*

Idiomatische Ausdrücke sind in den älteren aramäischen Wörterbüchern nur sehr spärlich verzeichnet. Gerade solche Eintragungen würden bei schwierigen Textpassagen und -rekonstruktionen dem Bearbeiter die Arbeit erleichtern. Eine dieser feststehenden Redewendungen ist *ḥyy npš* "das Leben fristen; am Leben bleiben" Klagelieder 1,11 Bodl. Hebr. b. 13 fol. 12 recto *dyḧwn npš[hwn]* "um am Leben zu bleiben".[19]

---

[16]Siehe Ch. Müller-Kessler, "Christian-Palestinian-Aramaic Fragments in the Bodleian Library" JSS 37 (1992) 207-21, s. u. Fragment III.
[17]A. S. Lewis, M. D. Gibson, *Codex Climaci Rescriptus* = CCR (Cambridge 1909).
[18]Schultheß, LSp 112a.
[19]Siehe Müller-Kessler, Anm. 16, s. u. Fragment V.

VII) *ṭbʿ*

Einträge zu *ṭbʿ* + *b* "einsinken" finden sich bereits im *Lexicon* von Schultheß[20], so das Bibelzitat Hom.Anecd. 191$_{14}$ aus den Kathechesen des Cyrill von Jerusalem. Es wurde von Land verlesen, doch die Handschrift hat richtig *dṭmʿ bšyntʾ* "er versank im Schlaf" wie in der CPA Version der Apostelgeschichte 20,9 CCR 86. So bleibt von den Einträgen bei Schultheß zu *ṭbʿ* nur noch Lukas 9,32 übrig. Ein neuer Beleg ist nun aus dem 2Korintherbrief 3,7 *ʾn dy tšmyšh dmwtʾ dbkẗbyn ṭbyʿ bʾb̈nyn ʾtʿbd btšbḥʾ* "wenn aber der Dienst des Todes, mit Buchstaben in Steine eingehauen (eingeritzt), zur Herrlichkeit gelangt" T-S 20.157 bII (Le 1900:46) zu zitieren.

Sokoloff trennt in seinem Wörterbuch noch die Verben טבע "to stamp" und [2# טבע "to sink"],[21] letzteres bewußt in Klammern, bedingt vermutlich durch den Hinweis bei Schultheß auf *ṭmʿ*. Es scheint sich hier aber eindeutig um dieselbe Verbalwurzel zu handeln, denn ob etwas "einsinkt", "gestempelt" oder "eingehauen" wird, das semantische Umfeld bleibt dasselbe, nur das Material in das etwas "einsinkt" ist verschieden.

Weiter belegt wird die Wurzel im CPA durch das Nomen im Status emphaticus singular *ṭbʿʾ* "Abdruck", welches FMSD 20:18 parallel zu dem Synonym *ḥtmʾ* "Stempel" FMSD 20:19 steht.[22]

VIII) *nhm*

Das bisher nicht identifizierte Fragment T-S 12.759 a:5 (Le 00:88) enthält eine Aufzählung von Bezeichnungen für Laute unterschiedlicher Lebewesen. Das Nomen *nhm* "Brüllen" in *nhm dʾr̈wʾn* "das Brüllen der Löwen" ist eines davon. Als Verb ist die Wurzel bereits in Matthew Black's Glossar zum CPA-Horologion verzeichnet.[23]

IX) *nmr

nmr "Leopard" taucht nur einmal in einer gebrochenen Textstelle auf: *kwšy* [*m*]*škh wnm*˺[*r*] *r̈qwmt*[*h*] "[kann] der Mohr seine [H]aut und der Leopa[rd] seine Flecken [ändern] Jeremia 13,23 T-S 16.322 aII (Le 00:10). Die rechte obere Ecke vom *m* ist abgebrochen, das folgende *r* fehlt, doch ist die Ergänzung aufgrund der Überreste von *nm* und dem Kontext ziemlich sicher. In Jesaja 11,6 Land 166 dagegen gebraucht das CPA anstelle von *nmr* das griechische Fremdwort *πrdwsʾ* πάρδος.

---

[20]Schultheß, LSp 72b.
[21]Sokoloff, DJPA 220b.
[22]A. S. Lewis, M. D. Gibson, *The Forty Martyrs of the Sinai Desert and the Story of Eulogios* (Cambridge 1912).
[23]M. Black, *A Christian Palestinian Syriac Horologion* = CPSH (Cambridge 1954), 62 *nhm* II.

X) *ʿmṣ

In der Vita Antonii, Kapitel 41 T-S 16.319 bI:4 (Le 02:147) läßt sich das Verb *ʿmṣ "schließen" in: *ʿmṣt ʿyn̈y* "ich schloß meine Augen" ausmachen. Dieses Verb für "schließen" wird immer dann gebraucht, wenn vom "Schließen der Augen, der Ohren und des Mundes" die Rede ist. Der gleiche Wortgebrauch findet sich im Syrischen, Mandäischen, JPA und in Maʿlūla.[24]

XI) *pʿy

Eine weitere onomatopoetische Wurzel *pʿy "blöken" neben *gʿy und *nhm* erscheint im nicht identifizierten Fragment T-S 12.759 a:2 (Le 00:88) *pʿʾy dmr̈ʿyʾn* "das Blöken der Schafherden". Die Wurzel *pʿy* ist gemeinaramäisch.

XII) ṣʾy

Bisher war nur das Nomen der Wurzel *ṣʾy* "Exkrement" im Status absolutus *ṣʾy* und Status emphaticus *ṣytʾ* in Black's Publikation des CPA-Horologions belegt.[25] Das Fragment T-S 12.752 a:6 (Le 00:87), welches 1900 von Lewis publiziert wurde, weist aber bereits das Adjektiv für "schmutzig" auf: *[lnp]šʾ yṣpyn dyšlʾ mn ḥšb̈tʾ ṣÿtʾ* "sie sollen sich bemühen, die Seele vor schmutzigen Gedanken zu bewahren". Diese Textpassage gehört ebenfalls zur Vita Antonii, Kapitel 89. Die Wurzel *ṣʾy* scheint gemeinaramäisch zu sein, obwohl sie bisher noch nicht für alle Dialekte nachweisbar ist.

XIII) *ršl

Die Wurzel *ršl* "kraftlos, schwach sein" erscheint im Itpaal an zwei Textstellen. Einmal ist sie als Perfekt in der Vita Antonii, Kapitel 39 *ʾtr̈šlw* "sie wurden entkräftigt" T-S 16.319 bI:13 (Le 02:147) belegt. Ein anderes mal läßt sich eine Partizipialform plural maskulin in den Galaterbriefen 6,9 CCR 154 *wlʾ mtr̈šlyn* "und (wir) sind nicht untätig" nachweisen. Parallelen zum Itpaalstamm lassen sich auch dem JPA entnehmen.[26] Die Wurzel ist gemeinaramäisch.

---

[24]K. Brockelmann, *Lexicon Syriacum* (Halle 1928), 530/1; E.S. Drower, R. Macuch, *A Mandaic Dictionary* (Oxford 1963), 22/3; G. Dalman, *Aramäisch-Neuhebräisches Handwörterbuch zu Targum, Talmud und Midrasch* (Göttingen 1938), 316a; G. Bergsträßer, *Glossar des neuaramäischen Dialekts von Maʿlūla* (Leipzig 1921), 4.
[25]Black, CPSH, 67.
[26]Sokoloff, DJPA 530b.

Aramaic and Syriac Dispute-Poems and Their Connections

Robert Murray, SJ — Heythrop College, University of London

For Sebastian Brock, the Master of this Theme

For the past hundred years, and especially since the publication of M. Steinschneider's *Rangstreit-Literatur* (1908),[1] there has been increasing scholarly interest in the almost world-wide literary genre of debates or rhetorical contests in which two or more figures — mythical or human, animal, vegetable, inanimate or abstract — strive for supremacy. Not only the monuments of the past but also daily evidence of the public taste for watching or reading political or legal debate, or its reflections in fiction, on the stage or on the screen, all make it clear that a good ding-dong verbal battle is one of the human race's favourite forms of entertainment. This view is fundamental to John Huizinga's *Homo Ludens* (1938, ET 1949),[2] which, however flawed and idiosyncratic a masterpiece it may now appear, provides an ideal introduction to our subject in all its aspects. Huizinga illuminates the interrelations between the various kinds of verbal competitive games: human disputes in their social contexts (ch. 3), riddles and riddling contests (ch. 6), heroic disputes recorded in narrative poetry or drama (ch. 7), fables in which animals or trees display human characteristics, and contests between personified abstractions (ch. 8).

This summary already suggests how complicated a task it is to analyse examples of "dispute literature" in almost any culture. A number of genres and styles are distinguishable (and others beside those mentioned are also relevant, for example syncrisis and aretalogy), but few of these are simply subdivisions of dispute; different genres overlap, but also have their own larger fields of play. Sometimes, once we are familiar with the formal characteristics of dispute poems, we can catch echoes of the style occurring in quite other contexts; some examples will come up below. If the following study can claim any value, this is not by its breaking new ground or presenting unpublished texts, but only in so far as it relates Syriac and other Aramaic

---

[1]In the eighty years since Steinschneider, perhaps the most useful general sketches for the purpose of this article were those by Fiore (1966) and Asmussen (1973: for the details see References); now an excellent introduction to the subject, with full bibliography, is provided by G. J. Reinink and H. L. J. Vanstiphout (eds.), *Dispute Poems and Dialogues in the Ancient and Mediaeval Near East* (Leuven 1991) (referred to below as Reinink–Vanstiphout, *DPD*). By the time this article was being revised (see note 3 below) it was possible to see this volume and so reduce overlap with it, though some is inevitable; but in a number of significant respects this article supplements *DPD*.

[2]The English is actually from the German edition of 1944.

examples to each other and to their antecedents and parallels in ancient languages more comprehensively, perhaps, than has yet been done in a single essay.[3]

The Mesopotamian Background

Though the main focus of this article is on Aramaic and Syriac, both the wider terms of reference which are proposed and the fact that Aramaic (including the Syriac dialect) had its cultural cradle in Mesopotamia, make it necessary to give first attention to this earlier matrix. It is not possible here, however (nor is it any longer required), to give more than a sketch to serve as a prelude to the subsequent history of the dispute genre.

Literary debate or dispute is among the human activities for which S. N. Kramer justly claimed that "History begins at Sumer".[4] Indeed many of the related genres likewise made their first known appearances in Sumerian or in (largely dependent) Akkadian literature. Most of the published examples are probably still most easily accessible in J. J. A. van Dijk's *La Sagesse suméro-accadienne* (1953)[5] and W. G. Lambert's *Babylonian Wisdom Literature* (1960).[6] In the same year appeared a valuable survey, with a discussion of classification, by E. I. Gordon (1960);[7] as regards dispute poems this has recently been brought up to date by H. L. J. Vanstiphout in fuller surveys (1990, 1991), taking into account examples of the genre which still await publication.

Owing to Aesop and the other classical collections, it is often the term "fable" which first comes to mind to designate any literary form in which animals or trees speak and witty or didactic points are exchanged. Consequently some scholars treat dispute poems under the heading of "fable",[8] and indeed, some of the exchanges in the course of a dispute may be very similar in style. Yet the dispute form as a whole is quite distinct from the fable; it involves a different kind of activity and of personification, its dialogue frequently concerns the usefulness or moral superiority of the contending subjects, and it has a remarkably constant structural pattern. Gordon argues that the dispute genre should also be kept distinct from the category of "myth"

---

[3]The present article is a thorough revision of one prepared in 1978 for an issue of the *Annual of the Leeds University Oriental Society* which never appeared. At that time Dr S. P. Brock's now numerous series of publications and studies of Syriac dialogues and dispute poems had scarcely begun. Repeatedly in his articles he has done me the embarrassing honour of praising my unpublished article, of which he had a copy. (This explanation is given for the benefit of puzzled bibliographers.) The section on Syriac was not read at the London Aramaic Symposium in 1991. It has now been considerably pruned in view of Dr Brock's extensive studies, so as to keep mainly to earlier texts (especially of Ephrem) which he has treated less fully.

[4]This is the title of the second edition of Kramer's work first published as *From the Tablets of Sumer* (1956). See ch. 18, "Logomachy: the First Literary Debates".

[5]Especially pp. 31-85.

[6]See ch.7, "Fables or Contest Literature". I am grateful to Professor Lambert also for personal discussion of Mesopotamian sources.

[7]Especially pp. 144-147.

[8]See (e.g.) R. J. Williams (1956) and B. E. Perry (1959).

(though mythical elements often occur, especially in the framework of disputes); he also distinguishes "wisdom disputations" proper from the contests or debates occurring in the course of epic narratives such as *Enmerkar and the Lord of Aratta.*[9] However, the Sumerian word for dispute or debate, *a-da-min-dug$_4$-ga*,[10] occurs in both kinds of text (just as we shall see a corresponding overlap of terms in narrative and in formal poetic contexts in Aramaic and Syriac examples). Vanstiphout has emphasised that the Sumerian word just mentioned refers to the debate section of a dispute poem but is not the technical name for the genre, as van Dijk proposed.[11] The latter also speculated about contexts of social activity, being evidently impressed by Huizinga's emphasis on the model of the *potlatch* among the native Americans of the Pacific coastal area.[12]

Before we concentrate on the "wisdom disputation" or dispute poem proper, two other kinds of dialogue should be noted, because when we come to review the forms of dialogue in Aramaic and Syriac literature it may be useful to remember the range and variety of the Mesopotamian antecedents. There are two ethical dialogues in Akkadian.[13] One, the serious discussion commonly called "The Babylonian Theodicy", is an acrostic poem in which a sufferer discusses his plight with a friend.[14] Although acrostics as such cannot be called essential to the dispute genre, they adorn many Aramaic and Syriac disputes and dialogues. The other Akkadian ethical dialogue, between a master and his servant, is satirical.[15] While it differs from the dispute genre in both form and tone, it can offer a point of comparison, since irony, sarcasm and invective have characterised dispute literature throughout its history.

Very different are the Sumerian dialogues or antiphonal songs related to those rituals for which modern scholars have borrowed (from Greek mythology) the term "sacred marriage".[16] Though these have nothing in common with dispute poems except the use of dialogue, it is possible that some echoes of such songs may continue to be occasionally audible in later dialogue literature, even as late as some Syriac *sogyata*.

After these introductory remarks, we may list the known examples of Mesopotamian dispute poems (not all yet published) and summarise the formal

---

[9]Gordon (1960), pp. 144-5; Cf. van Dijk (1953), pp. 33-34; for the Enmerkar text, Kramer (1952). The latter is interpreted by M. Lambert (1955) as almost designed for dramatic performance.

[10]I follow the transliteration used by Vanstiphout rather than earlier forms.

[11]Vantisphout (1990), p. 272, and 1991, pp. 23-24.

[12]*Homo Ludens*, ch. 3, "Play and Contest as Civilising Functions". The *potlatch* is a contest in munificence. It is doubtful whether a particular custom can legitimately be universalised as a model. van Dijk took up Huizinga's analogy (1953, p. 37) and applied it also to *Enmerkar...* in *Orientalia*, N. S. 39 (1970), pp. 302-310.

[13]Discussed, with comparable texts in other literatures, by K. van der Toorn in Reinink–Vanstiphout, *DPD* (1991), pp. 59-75.

[14]W. G. Lambert (1960), pp. 63-91.

[15]Lambert (1960), pp. 139-149.

[16]Imaginatively represented by Kramer (1969). I do not know on what grounds H. Ringgren asserts that banquets celebrating the "sacred marriage" were the occasions when dispute poems were performed for entertainment (*Religions of the Ancient Near East* [1967, ET London 1973], p. 29). However, use of disputes as "floor shows" at banquets seems quite a plausible hypothesis (*cf.* Vogelzang 1991, p. 57, and now Vanstiphout 1992a).

structure which is common to most of them. I follow Gordon (1960, 145-47) and Vanstiphout (1990, 272-78). In Sumerian, Gordon lists Summer and Winter, Cattle and Grain, Bird and Fish, Tree and Reed, Silver and Copper, Pickaxe and Plough, Upper and Lower Millstone. Vanstiphout adds Heron and Turtle, Goose (or Crane?) and Raven, Ewe and Wheat. There is disagreement on the classification of one text, although it is explicitly called an *a-da-min-dug$_4$-ga*: it has a larger narrative element, involving Dumuzi and Inanna, so that Gordon prefers to classify it rather as "myth", while Vanstiphout, following van Dijk, calls it "Herdsman and Farmer", though he recognises its unusual character. In Akkadian there exist disputes of Tamarisk and Palm, Ox and Horse, Wheat and (the grain-goddess) Nisaba, and fragments including one about Willow and Laurel.[17] Details of editions and publications to date are given by Vanstiphout; a complete edition of the known texts by M. Civil has long been awaited.

It was van Dijk who recognised the structural pattern which seems to be basic, despite variations, and this has been further refined by Vanstiphout.[18] It can be summarised thus:

1. Introduction, presenting the parties: brief narrative, sometimes with mythological elements.
2. *Occasio litigandi*, or matter of the dispute.
3. Dispute proper, in which the parties in turn praise themselves and denigrate the other, with vigorous and often comic invective.

[4. Sometimes, narrated actions.]

5. Verdict by a third party; sometimes, reconciliation.

The extant examples seem to show many exceptions to this pattern, but since most of the texts are fragmentary at some points, especially at the beginning or the end, it is not easy to assess the extent of irregularity. The largest part of the extant material comes from the debate sections; this is not surprising since they form the longest part of each poem. Perhaps the most amazing discovery arising from this ancient genre is that made by Pierre Grelot (1958) when he realised that some Syriac dispute poems by St.Ephrem (fourth century CE) reveal virtually the same structure as poems from about two millennia earlier; and this continues to be the case wherever this genre flourishes in Syriac.

The Channels of Influence

Given this remarkable correspondence of genres in literature which arose successively in the same region, it seems reasonable to postulate a continuous tradition rather than mere coincidence. Of course, many other influences were at work in

[17] On the Akkadian disputes see Vogelzang (1991).

[18] van Dijk (1953), pp. 39ff.; Kramer (1960), pp. 287-91; Vanstiphout 1990, notwithstanding his detailed analysis of variations.

Mesopotamia between the decline of Akkadian and the rise of Syriac: Aramaean, Iranian, Hellenistic, Jewish and Christian. So far, however, no evidence seems to tell against the hypothesis. As we shall see, early Aramaic evidence is lacking; the known examples of the genre in other languages seem traceable to Akkadian models, and such innovations as are found in the Jewish-Aramaic and Syriac examples are not so much in form as in subject matter, which largely depends on Biblical themes or Christian developments.

The Hebrew Bible contains no regular example of a dispute poem. D. Daube (1973) found very few instances of fable in the proper sense, though he thought that the story of Balaam's ass (Num 22:21ff) is the reworking of a fable (Daube, pp. 14-16), while more straightforward examples are Jotham's fable of the trees and the bramble (Judg 9:7, Daube pp. 16-19) and Jehoash's brief reference to a story about the thistle and the cedar (2 Kgs 14:8-10, Daube pp. 19-20). Daube considers Ezekiel's allegory of the eagle, the cedar and the vine (Ezek 17:1ff) rather a riddle than a fable (pp. 21-22), while he finds Jesus' parables absolutely distinct from fable.[19] Of the other related genres, we have one example of a riddle-contest in the story of Samson (Judg 14:12-20).

The Hebrew Bible is, of course, rich in dialogue.[20] Are there any passages which betray any hints of relationship to the formal dispute genre? As the books stand, the sober answer is "no". But if the reader will bear with a little imaginative speculation, let us look for a moment at the skeleton structure of the book of Job. It has a narrative introduction strong in mythical elements; an *occasio litigandi* in the determination of Job's "friends" to defend their crude theodicy and to convict him; an extended dispute section, and a concluding divine verdict. Even with this basic similarity of structure, of course, the book of Job is unique and unlike any possible model in Mesopotamian literature, whether the "Babylonian Theodicy" or the (mostly more playful) dispute poems; it contains some of the deepest moral and theological discussion in all ancient literature. Yet imagine, as a hypothesis, a far shorter poem presenting essentially the story as in the actual book with a debate section consisting of alternating speeches by Job and a single opponent. Such a poem would fall within the requirements for a classic dispute as we know the form from Sumerian to Syriac literature and later. I only wish to suggest by this fancy that the author[21] could have been familiar with the dispute form, but rightly realised that his conception was too grand to be confined by its limitations.

---

[19]For suggested reasons for this opinion about Jesus (as previously also the prophets) see Daube (1973), p. 7.

[20]See the summary in Jacobs (1984), pp. 2-5.

[21]I would broadly defend the unity of conception, and consequently of authorship, of the book of Job.

Can we find any more possible but concealed stylistic links? Another book full of dialogue is *The Song of Songs*. S. N. Kramer (1969, Ch.5) suggested that there are some possible similarities to elements in the Sumerian so-called "Sacred Marriage" songs. Such a comparison involves too many uncertainties at both ends to have any solid basis; yet something can be said about one element in the *Song*, namely the praise-sequences. These, like the praises of Sarai in the "Genesis Apocryphon", anticipate the *waṣf* in later Arabic love poetry.[22] But formally such praise-sequences (like aretalogies) are similar whatever person they refer to; in the *Song* it is the beloved, while elsewhere it is often the speaker, as in many ancient royal inscriptions, and also in dispute poems. If I may be allowed another flight of fancy, the personification of Wisdom and Folly, with their speeches, in Prov. 7-9 are not far from what could easily have been expressed as a dramatic confrontation, a dispute of Wisdom and Folly. The author could well have been aware of the genre as an available medium.

There is a variant of the aretalogy style which enumerates not the *aretai* (both virtues and achievements) of one person but the exemplars of a virtue, as in Wis. Sol. 10; or the theme may be inverted as what I have elsewhere called an "anti-aretalogy", listing the devil's evil works and those whom he corrupted.[23] Such enumerations may also be set out by way of comparison, as in the genre of *syncrisis*, which appears in Wis. Sol. 11-19 and in much other Hellenistic literature. These rhetorical forms remain close to forms of argument characteristic of dispute poems; in Syriac they are extensively used by Aphrahat in prose argument, but also Ephrem employs them creatively in his developments of the dispute genre, as we shall see below.

The story in 1 [3] Esdras 3-4, how three young guards or pages at the court of Darius competed for a prize by speeches arguing about what is strongest (respectively wine, the king and women; the third speaker then turns to Truth, which is acclaimed as supreme) is a Hellenistic insertion in material adapted from Ezra and Nehemiah. C. J. Brunner refers to this as a *tenson* (dispute poem),[24] but its structure is quite different from that in the Mesopotamian tradition. Nevertheless it can again be said that the individual speeches are such as could have occurred in a true dispute, if (for example) wine had been disputing with beer or with bread, or woman with man, or even with the king.

These last examples, of course, take us beyond the Hebrew Bible, though they belong to the early "parabiblical" literature. It requires some imaginative reflection to recognise features which are not so distant from elements in the dispute tradition. Yet

---

[22]On the *waṣf* in the Song of Songs see F. Landy (1983), *passim*; on that in 1QGenAp (col. 20) see J. A. Fitzmyer (1971) pp. 119-124.

[23]Cf. R. Murray (1977), p. 120.

[24]Brunner (1980), pp. 195-96. The term (from Latin *tensio*) originated among the troubadours in Provence. Its use in modern discussions of dispute poems seems to be due mainly to S. Fiore (1966). See also J. Asmussen (1973), esp. pp. 46-47 and J. Bottéro (1991).

such reflection may, perhaps, justify us in picturing that tradition flowing underground throughout the period of the Bible's formation, though it never actually surfaces. It remains curious that the Bible, with all the lively dialogue it contains, so rarely reflects the classic patterns of dispute. When we turn to the Aramaic targums, we find places where exegetical problems have been dealt with by inserting a bit of debate: for example, Cain and Abel at Gen 4:8, or Isaac and Ishmael at Gen 22:1.[25] In these instances, though in prose, we instantly hear echoes of the dispute style.

Before we focus on Jewish-Aramaic and Syriac poetry, however, we should examine other clues to the channels of influence. It was Aramaic, of course, which principally succeeded to the place of Akkadian both in Mesopotamia and as a *lingua franca*. A form of Aramaic script was adapted for Parthian, as for other languages further east. Imperial Aramaic is the natural place to look for the link between Akkadian and the later Aramaic literatures; but the link is unhappily all but missing.

The first known non-Akkadian example of the genre is in Egyptian, from the 22nd dynasty (950-730 B.C.E): this is a fragment of a dispute between the Stomach and the Head,[26] pictured as taking place in a law-court before the "supreme judges" and with due rituals. The text says that the Stomach spoke first, but its speech is not given; what we have is part of the Head's speech in which it boasts how essential it is to all the limbs and their activities. G. Maspero, the editor, called the text a variant of a known near eastern fable, and said that it illustrated Egyptian legal procedure. M. Nøjgaard (1964) said that it has exactly the form of Akkadian disputes. J. P. Asmussen went further and said that there must be actual "interdependence";[27] but if the fragment is the only known Egyptian example, and contains real Egyptian features, we should be cautious about how closely it could be related to a Babylonian model.

It is Egypt, again, namely Elephantine, that has left us the first echo of anything relevant in Aramaic: this is a fragment of the Aḥiqar fable material, in which the Bramble and the Pomegranate are briefly heard engaging in mutual recrimination.[28] What remains, however, does not suggest a formal dispute so much as the genre of short fable, although at a point of stylistic overlap. Nevertheless, the Aḥiqar cycle does in a sense bridge our gap, since (whatever its actual place of origin) it pretends to an Assyrian location, is known to have existed at least partly in Aramaic, and is traceable in its subsequent ramifications, including Syriac traditions. One such fragment may be the story of royal riddles preserved in west Syriac manuscripts and published by S. P. Brock (1968). His discussion points to the Aḥiqar cycle, but behind that, he thinks, to

[25]On Gen 4:8 in all Palestinian targum witnesses (including Ps.-Jonathan) see G. Vermes (1975); fragment texts in M. L. Klein (1980) *ad loc.*, (1986), pp. 6-13; Gen 22:1 in Tg. Ps.-Jonathan.
[26]Published by G. Maspero (1886).
[27]Nøjgaard (1964), p. 441, and briefly Asmussen (1973), p. 51.
[28]Published by A. Cowley (1923), pp. 218, 225; text and further bibliography in Asmussen (1973), p. 57.

an Egyptian rather than a Mesopotamian origin for the precise genre of the fragment. Of course the attestation is late (which may render the Egyptian/Mesopotamian distinction less significant), but the genre and style of the fragment seem to point to an earlier stage in cultural history.

All in all, however, we have to regret the almost total loss of a popular literature in Imperial Aramaic, no doubt owing to the decomposition of the material used for writing on. But for this misfortune we might well have many pre-targumic Aramaic examples (whether versions of older texts or new compositions) of the dispute genre, which both had been and was again to be so well loved. As it is, the earliest examples of dispute poems which seem to inherit the Mesopotamian tradition, subsequent to the Egyptian specimen mentioned above, are likewise in languages from farther afield, namely Greek and Middle Persian.

The first of these is a poem by Callimachus (c. 310-c. 235), in the choliambic or *skazōn* metre.[29] It has been recovered from a somewhat fragmentary papyrus, but about 70 lines are virtually complete. He ascribes the story to the "ancient Lydians", which could be a clue to an earlier origin farther east; but we may guess that he discovered his source in Alexandria.[30] The dispute is between the Laurel and the Olive. The latter seems to be winning (some comments on the Laurel could possibly be the words of a referee) when a bramble intervenes to make peace, but is angrily silenced by the Laurel. The conclusion is missing. The editor, C. A. Trypanis, calls the poem a fable which "also employs the technique of the *agōn*", though not strictly.[31] However it is not beyond the range of variation in Mesopotamian dispute poems. As for the *agōn*, the technical name for part of a classical Greek drama, some modern scholars have suggested that precisely this element in the Attic drama could have arisen through oriental influence.[32] Such a hypothesis, for a period well before the Hellenistic age, may be possible but it is hardly provable; drama can develop styles of confrontation and argument with or without foreign influences. (Likewise, the song-contests of shepherds which are given literary form by Theocritus and later imitated by Virgil require no theory of foreign influence, either for their rustic basis or for their sophisticated end-product.)

The Middle Persian example is a complete dispute poem called "The Babylonian Tree" (*Draxt i Asurik*),[33] which has strong echoes of the Akkadian poem "The Tamarisk and the Date", though the opponent of the date-palm is now the goat, which

---

[29]Edited by C. A. Trypanis (1958), pp. 118-127.
[30]*Cf.* Nøjgaard (1964), pp. 440-441.
[31]Trypanis (1958), p. 119.
[32]See W. J. Froleyks (1973), esp. pp. 398-421; from the Sumerian end, H. Sauren (1972) sees *Enmerkar and the Lord of Aratta* and *Lugalbanda and Anzu* as anticipating the *Agōn* (*cf.* also M. Lambert, 1955).
[33]For editions see C. J. Brunner (1980), p. 193.

gains the victory. The first editor of this poem thought that it had an Arabic model and was as late as the ninth century C.E., but C. J. Brunner (1980) emphasises the Parthian elements in the Pahlavi text and proposes a date about the turn of the eras.[34] It seems likely that the geographer Strabo had heard (with more or less accuracy) about this poem or one very like it. He enumerates the virtues of the date-palm in a way that could easily be a summary of points made in the dispute, and then actually says that there is a "Persian song" which names 360 *ōpheleiai* (useful qualities) of the palm.[35] In this case it seems entirely probable that a Mesopotamian dispute poem was so popular as to be adapted into Parthian and known of in the Greek-speaking world; we may also guess that the immediate source of the Parthian text was in Aramaic. But "adapted" must be stressed; there are a number of references to Zoroastrian cult.[36]

Dispute Poems and Fragments in Jewish Aramaic

In post-Biblical Jewish Aramaic we find examples of dispute style in some *piyyuṭim*, some of them also inserted in targums; the latter also contain other echoes of the style, as do the Talmud and early midrash. This gives us at last a fair quantity of Aramaic material to compare with the Mesopotamian antecedents and with the Syriac examples which begin in the fourth century C. E. I am unqualified to attempt to date particular specimens of this Jewish material which developed, both in Palestine and in Babylon, probably from before the common era till after the Muslim conquest;[37] but in view of the longevity and wide extent of the dispute tradition, it is of interest and value to survey and analyse some examples of its Jewish branch.

Among the texts known to me from targum research, two extended examples can be seen as precedence disputes relatable to the established tradition, though both show features not found in the Sumerian models, in that they have multiple contestants and (like many Aramaic dispute poems) are in alphabetical acrostic form. They can be called respectively the Dispute of the Months and that of the Trees. The former occurs, in considerably varying forms, in Palestinian targum fragments at Exod 12:2, or in collections of poetic texts for use in the Palestinian liturgy at the New Moon of Nisan and at Pesach. The targums from Exod 12 to Exod 15 are rich in such poems, many of them acrostic, besides several shorter traces of what might once have been longer disputes. The "Dispute of the Trees" is in the second targum to Esther at 7:10 (in varying forms) and in several related midrashim; curiously, these witnesses divide into two traditions of quite contrary import, as will be analysed below. The poems in Geniza

[34]Brunner (1980), pp. 191-192, 196.
[35]Strabo, *Geography*, VII, ed. H. L. Jones (1930), pp. 214-215; Cf. Asmussen (1973), p. 52.
[36]See translation by Brunner (1980), pp. 291-294, lines 47-52, 100-102.
[37]The collection by M. Sokoloff and Y. Yahalom, *Aramaic Poems from the Byzantine Period*, is eagerly awaited.

fragments relating to the Pentateuch have been edited from many manuscripts by M. L. Klein (1980, 1986);[38] the dispute in the Esther targum II has been studied by P. Grelot (1986).[39]

The Dispute of the Months is particularly interesting because it comes to us in a rich and complex tradition with variants not only in Jewish targums but also in Syriac (where the variants are no less complex), as S. P. Brock has demonstrated (1985). In the targums the dispute is attached to the words "This month shall be for you the beginning of months" (Exod 12:2). In most forms it is told how all the months gathered and each made its claim to pre-eminence; the choice of Nisan to be the head comes as the award of victory. But in some poems the series of months reflects other interests besides providing the contestants for a dispute. The examples gathered by Klein may be analysed as follows:

1. *Fragment Tg, Paris MS.*[40]
Intr.: Before redeeming Israel YHWH examined months.
Matter : to decide (a) in which month Israel should be redeemed,
(b) which should receive the crown.
Dispute : Each month in turn, starting with Iyyar, claims (a) and (b) as a refrain; then gives a reason, either (i) from Biblical history, or (ii) referring to a festival, or (iii) to seasonal fruits etc.
Verdict : Moses decides for Nisan (which has not spoken): in it YHWH did redeem Israel, and will finally.

2. *Genizah fragment, MS T-S NS 186 (acrostic)*[41]
Intr.: (Aleph) All the months gathered.
Matter : In which month shall be deliverance?
Dispute : (Beth-Lamed) Each month, starting with Iyyar, gives reason, either (i) from subsequent Biblical history, or (ii) referring to a festival; each is followed by refrain:

ʾEna hu dᵉnaseb kᵉlila,
dᵉbi yitparᵉqun ʿamma dᵉbet Yisraʾel.

(Nisan does not speak.)
Verdict : God said in prophecy to Moses: I have chosen Nisan.

---

[38]Two examples in the Fragment Targums (1980), text pp. 72-73, 77; translation pp.37-39, 43-44. The volume of Genizah texts (1986) has 29 examples; see index, ibid. p.L.
[39]See now also Grossfeld (1991).
[40]Klein (1980), text pp. 72-73, translation pp. 37-39.
[41]Klein (1986), pp. 186-189.

3. *Fragment of dispute section, Siwan - Marḥešhwan, MS T-S H10.78*[42]

The Bodleian MS Heb. e73 has a series of four poems related to Ex 12:2 under the heading *ʾl pbytyn.*[43] The first, however, never develops either the alphabet or the dispute, but jumps to the victory.

4. *Intr.* : "war" (*pwlwmws*) of the months when the August One (*ʾgwstws*) sent to the land of Egypt.
Matter : Let us cast lots on the zodiac, that we may know in which of us Israel is to be redeemed.
No Dispute.
Victory : Nisan "roared", silencing the others; "It is I who shall deliver".

5. The fourth example in the Oxford MS is not alphabetical; it is a fragment, but apparently of a full dispute:[44]
Intr.: Description of the *Kyrios* (*qyrys*) darkening the eyes of the Egyptians and enlightening the Israelites. The months gathered and said:
Matter : As in (4) without reference to zodiac, and with "which of us will take the crown".
Dispute : Iyyar begins as in nos. 1 and 2 above, but the fragment breaks off here.

Genizah MS T-S H 11.51 has a little collection of poems which introduce new variations on the theme, including more on the zodiac, which was not developed in no. 5 above.

6. The first, alphabetical, is not a dispute but an interpretation of phases and movements of the moon in relation to the months, in terms of predictive prophecy.[45]

---

[42]Ibid., pp. 190-191. See also W. J. van Bekkum in Reinink–Vanstiphout, *DPD* (1991), pp. 80-81.
[43]Klein (1986), pp. 192-195. The mysterious words are a garbled spelling of *ʾlpbytryn (alphabetarion).*
[44]Ibid., pp. 194-195.
[45]Ibid., pp. 196-201; see the study of this text by J. C. Greenfield and M. Sokoloff (1989).

7. The following poem is an acrostic in which the months are assimilated to signs of the zodiac.[46] Now, for the first time among our examples, Nisan disputes with its opponents, but they do not answer back:

Intr.: All the months and zodiacal signs gathered.

Matter : because of Nisan, who is called "the redeemer".

Dispute : Nisan "roared" at each month in turn, starting with Iyyar; most are connected with a sign of the zodiac and often a Biblical reference (e.g. Iyyar/Taurus/the Golden Calf) to prove its unworthiness to be the redeemer.

Victory : claimed by Nisan, who is likened to the *ʾimra* (referring both to zodiacal Ram and paschal lamb).

8. The last poem of this set, also an acrostic, is not a dispute but is apparently all a speech by God: as in the last, the months are related to the signs of the zodiac but also to the twelve patriarchs.[47]

This analysis illustrates how easily different genres can overlap in the area of dispute poems. Despite the many variations in the examples just summarised, the basic form is unmistakable in several of them; but another genre is also drawn on, namely that of epigrams on the members of a set - the months, the zodiac or the twelve tribes. S. P. Brock notes the same fusion of genres in some of the related Syriac variants of the "Dispute of the Months".[48] He uses the Greek term *ekphrasis*, "description"; I prefer to speak more loosely of a series of epigrams, which would cover such sets as the Blessings on the Tribes in Gen 49 and Deut 33. The same kinds of short sayings characterising a season or a month, with its weather, activities, products and festivals, may have been originally at home in pedagogical or mnemonic series, or as literary equivalents of the iconographical series which are found, especially in mosaics, in many parts of the ancient world, including synagogues such as Bet Alpha in Israel and many churches. Alternatively, the kind of points made in such verses could, without too much effort, be turned into riddles; or again, as epigrams, they might express favourable or hostile feelings towards their subjects. In such a form they could easily find a place in dispute poems, either in self-praise or in invective directed against the rival or rivals. Some might become isolated from larger contexts, yet still remain recognisable in type when they occur here or there, just as other fragments of dispute rhetoric can be recognised once one is aware of the genre and its patterns.

---

[46] Klein (1986), pp. 200-204.
[47] Ibid., pp. 204-207.
[48] Brock (1985), pp. 184ff.

With this we may turn to analyse the other example of a longer dispute in the targums, the "Dispute of the Trees" in the second targum to Esther, which is so full of enlargements and additions that it is often judged to be a midrash rather than a targum.[49] The passage has been discussed by P. Grelot on the basis of the printed versions[50] and also as found in an unpublished manuscript in Rome (Biblioteca Angelica), of which Grelot gives a provisional transcription.[51] The insertion occurs between 7:9 and 10. Haman is doomed to be hanged and the question arises, on what. Now begins a dispute which preserves evidence of having been an alphabetic acrostic, although the sequence is somewhat disturbed. Haman apparently appeals to the trees of the garden; these gather to decide which is the highest. Thus we have the Introduction and the statement of the Matter. Now follows the Dispute, in which the trees plead their case in turn. In the printed texts eleven are named, of which one, *ʾdrʾ*, is of debated meaning and one may well be missing.[52] In the Angelica text there are twelve; though Grelot is doubtless right that this is a secondary and tidied-up version, one may guess that the number twelve could be original. We may wonder what the vine and the myrtle are doing disputing height with the palm and the cedar, but the author can hardly have been concerned to achieve verisimilitude. In this first form of the "Dispute of the Trees", they all make excuses, each with reasons of the kind we saw in the dispute of the Months (reasons of dignity arising from Biblical history or from associations with worship); in the Angelica text they all end "it its impossible for me to be defiled by his corpse" as a kind of refrain. Finally the Cedar pronounces the judgement: let Haman be executed on the *ṣliba* [53] he had prepared for himself. But in the Angelica text the Cedar explains that Haman had used a cedar beam, stolen from the ark and hidden in his house; the Cedar now nobly offers itself to serve as the means of expiation.

The second form of the dispute is found in Esther Rabba, and is placed earlier, in chapter 5, at the point in the story when Haman is advised to set up a *ṣliba* to hang

---

[49]It is doubtless considerably later than the poems related to the Exodus: Grossfeld (1991) p. 20, thinks that Targum II is not earlier than 800 C.E. (though this does not date the dispute section).

[50]Grelot (1986). The Aramaic text varies in the MSS. Probably the most accessible form is that in Lagarde, *Hagiographa chaldaice* (1873; reprint, Osnabruck 1967), p. 264. I depend mainly on Grelot, also using the edition in translation by B. Grossfeld (1991), pp. 180-183 and 213-216. But *n.b.* his version of Tg II is based on another MS, Sassoon 282 (1189).

[51]Grelot (1986), pp. 403-406, describes this variant text, Bibl Angelica Or. 72 (A-1-2) and the similar form in MS Paris BN hebr. 110, giving a transliterated text and French version. Unfortunately Grossfeld (in his otherwise valuable edition) refers to the Angelica MS misleadingly as *Roma Anglica* (sic!) Or. 72-73, and his description of it (p. 3) raises doubt as to whether he consulted it for Tg II. However, he gives variants from the Paris MS in his apparatus on pp. 181-182.

[52]Jastrow lists *ʾadara*, "prob. Spanish Juniper" and *ʾidra* (in the present passage) as "fig"; Grossfeld says "wild fig", but see Grelot (1986), p. 401. Also, since the fig-tree follows, one might expect two adjacent trees to be more different.

[53]I leave the word in Aramaic because it is probably "loaded". *Ṣliba* is a stake for impalement or the wood used for crucifixion, and the verb *ṣleb* implies some such execution; but in the Hebrew neither *ʿeṣ* nor the verb *talah* requires or implies such a picture. Given that in Tg II, just before the Dispute of the Trees, there is an obscure phrase about Haman going to something or somewhere (see Grossfeld, p. 180) connected with Bar Pandera (Jesus), and that in Syriac *ṣliba* regularly refers to the cross of Jesus, one may suspect what game is in play. (See also Ginzberg in next note).

Mordecai.[54] This position gives the dispute greater irony, for of course Haman does not yet know what his *ṣliba* is actually going to be used for, but the trees know. This form of the dispute is the converse of the other: each tree in turn pleads its claim to the honour of being the instrument of retribution. In this version fourteen trees speak; finally the decision goes to the thorn-bush, from which Haman had in fact prepared the *ṣliba*. (Again, credibility seems to be no concern.) In comment on this pair of versions on one theme, each the inversion of the other, we may remark that in form they correspond to the "multiple dispute" like that of the months; but in matter they both present distant echoes of Jotham's fable in Judges 9. The "excuse" form is obviously nearer, but in the second form the victory of the thorn-bush reminds us of the bramble's role in the Biblical story. It may be that in tree-disputes this kind of conclusion was especially enjoyed; if the texts of Callimachus's dispute poem and of the Aḥiqar fragment were better preserved, we might perhaps discover that even so small a detail was a common feature of a wide tradition.

Both these dispute traditions, that of the Months and that of the Trees, occur in targums or midrashim to Biblical books, and integrated into narrative contexts (that in Esther 5 with great skill), but both types also look as if they existed in their own right; not surprisingly, since Pesach and Purim provide contexts, both in the liturgy and elsewhere, for such recitations. Another multiple precedence dispute which is loosely attached to a Biblical context, but which suggests a different *Sitz im Leben*, is the "Dispute of the Letters of the Alphabet", the fullest form of which is in the first *Alphabet of Akiba*.[55] The letters came to the Creator, beginning from Tav, each of them pleading its worthiness to be employed to begin the work of creation. Each one appealed to a word of virtue beginning with itself, but each was reminded that it also begins bad words. At last Bet's claim was accepted to serve for *brešit*. Aleph had remained modestly silent up to now, but was rewarded with the privilege of serving for the beginning of the Decalogue.[56] This dispute is thought to reflect a pedagogical and mnemonic origin, probably connected with the Talmudic story of the children in the *Bet ha-midrash* in the time of R. Joshua b. Levi (early third century B.C.E.),[57] but such a *Sitz im Leben* may well be another link with Mesopotamian origins.

Let us now return to shorter examples or echoes of the dispute style in targumic contexts. The brief disputes which are created to dramatise the issues between Cain and

---

[54]ET in *Midrash Rabba* IX, Esther (1939), pp. 111-112; summary in Ginzberg, *Legends* IV, pp. 443-444 and VI, p. 479, n. 184. He notes the two contrary forms of the dispute and the obscure allusion to Jesus; he renders *ṣliba* unequivocally as "cross".

[55]Summarised by Ginzberg, *Legends,* I, pp. 5-8 and V, pp. 5-6, nn. 10-12. Though in Hebrew, this multiple dispute merits mention here as a related variant of the genre. Cf. van Bekkum (1991), pp. 79-80. Brock (1982) has published two Syriac *sogyata* on the Letters of the Alphabet; cf. Brock (1984), p.52.

[56]Cf. *Midrash Rabba* (ET, 1939), *Genesis* I, 10, p. 10.

[57]Cf. *bShab* 104a, ET *Babylonian Talmud* , *Shab.* pp. 500-501.

Abel (Gen 4) and between Isaac and Ishmael (Gen 22) were mentioned above. In the Red Sea episode the Palestinian targums again burst out into acrostics at Exod 14:29-31. The texts published by Klein could mostly be called poetic re-tellings of the biblical story, but one, in the Paris Fragment Targum, with variants in Oxford geniza fragments, includes features of the dispute genre, though more in the "epic" style.[58] From Aleph to He God is instructing Moses to go and command the sea. At Vav he does so; the sea has to respect his staff, but is angry. At Ṭeth begins the actual dialogue. The sea's protest reveals the "matter" of the dispute: which of them has legitimate authority? Moses is junior, the sea having been created before humans. Moses replies "this is no time for dispute" (*dina*); the Creator has sent him. The sea protests once more: no child of a woman shall vanquish it. Moses insists that it is One greater than them both who is to conquer. Finally the sea has to yield and the Israelites pass through. The "epic" context and dramatic style of this short dispute make it distinct from those which could just as well stand on their own as in the Biblical context to which they are attached; nevertheless this is a true variant of the genre, not merely a dramatic dialogue in free style. We shall see comparable examples in Syriac.

At Exod 15:12, in Targums Neofiti, Pseudo-Jonathan and the Paris Fragment Targum,[59] the victory song of Moses is interrupted by a short piece of prose dispute, in the mode not of precedence but of seeking exemption: the land and the sea are heard disputing (*m^edayy^enin*) over the corpses of the Egyptians, which each wants the other to keep. After God promises not to trouble the earth to return them eventually, the latter swallows them.

Passing beyond the Pentateuch, in the Song of Deborah (Judg 5), which is greatly expanded in the targum, there is a fragment of a multiple precedence dispute at v. 5, summarily in some manuscripts but at greater length in Codex Reuchlinianus, and found also in several midrashim.[60] The disputants are the mountains Tabor, Hermon and Carmel. Each claims to be worthy to have the Shekhinah rest on it because of its grandeur and because of the part it played in the history of Israel; but a *Bat Qol* replies that it is the Lord's pleasure for the Shekhinah to rest not on high mountains but on a small, weak one, and he has chosen Mount Sinai.

---

[58]Klein (1980), text p. 77, translation pp. 43-44; Klein (1986) , pp. 236-239 (two versions).

[59]P: ed. Klein (1980), text p. 79, translation pp. 46-47; N: ed. Diez Macho (1970), p. 99; Ps-J: ed. Rieder (1974), p. 104. French translation (with notes) of N and Ps-J by R. le Déaut (1979), pp. 124-125.

[60]In margin of C. Reuchlinianus (f6): text in A. Sperber (1959), p. 54. For examples in midrashim see A. Goldberg (1969), pp. 207-208; W. van Bekkum in Reinink–Vanstiphout, *DPD* (1991), pp. 79-80, including stanzas from the anonymous *piyyuṭ* for Shavu'ot, given in full by T. Carmi (ed. and tr.) *The Penguin Book of Hebrew Verse* (Harmondsworth 1981), pp. 245-246.

Doubtless many other fragments of dispute or related styles can be discovered among the treasures of midrash; for example the debate in heaven as to whether man should be created or not (*Gen. Rabba* 8, 5; ET *Midrash Rabba* I, p.58) or the argument of Abram with Nimrod (*Gen Rabba* 38, 13, ET ibid., p. 311).

It would be wrong to pass over the Talmuds, but I can only mention briefly one or two examples or echoes of the classic dispute style. The talmudic methods of argument have been brilliantly analysed by Louis Jacobs (1984); his first two chapters, including an introduction to the technical vocabulary of debate, contain much that also throws light on other kinds of debate and dialogue, both in Jewish Aramaic and in Syriac. For example, the term for a unit of Talmudic argument, *sugya*, in its Syriac form *sogita* is also a technical term, but one which has links with our present subject; it is the name for the kind of poetic dialogues, sometimes including passages in dispute style, but generally freer in form, providing both entertainment and instruction, which have abounded in Syriac from Ephrem till modern times.

The Babylonian Talmud contains a debate which, though of much richer content, in its basic structure is remarkably comparable to the classic "Dispute of the Months". This occurs in *Rosh-ha-Shanah* 10b-12a.[61] The theme concerns the respective claims of Tishri and Nisan to be the first month of the year. R. Eliezer supports the former, R. Joshua the latter. The debate proceeds with elegant alternation of points adduced in support of each side. The conclusion, though conventional, is especially comparable to that of a dispute poem: *Tanu rabbanan*, "our Rabbis taught", and reason is judiciously acknowledged on both sides. The argument could have appealed to history, since both reckonings have been followed in past and present; but the talmudic method is timeless, as are many of the themes of classic dispute poems. This debate could have been in poetic form; it is in another, no less elegant, genre.

The Talmud can also parody the dispute style, as we find in a short bit of clowning which interrupts a discussion of the libations at Sukkot (*bSukkah* 48b).[62] Apropos of Isaiah 12:3, we are told about two *minim* called *Śaśon* and *Śimḥah*, who disputed which of them was the more important, bandying Biblical texts in which now one, now the other stands in the first place. The passage ends in childish abuse.

I have no doubt that the period of the targums, Talmuds and midrashim could provide many more examples or echoes of the dispute genre in Jewish Aramaic, but these must suffice. It is time to pass on to the evidence in Syriac, which can perhaps show more examples and variations of the genre than any other ancient literature, and continues to produce them.

The Dispute Poem in Syriac

Though our material begins formally with Ephrem, his more conservative contemporary Aphrahat, while leaving us no example of a dispute poem, has a partially related kind of genre which deserves mention here. This is a kind of *syncrisis* in the

[61]Text in L. Goldschmidt (1933), *Roš-Hašanah*, pp. 314-319; ET *Babylonian Talmud, Rosh Hashanah*, pp. 39-43.
[62]Goldschmidt (1933), *Sukkah*, p. 135; ET pp. 227-228.

form of a Biblical comparison-series.[63] In it, Biblical figures are compared with Christ in formal, often rhythmical alternation; the pairs of examples could easily have been points made by parties to a dispute. Thus M. Albert (1976), apropos of Jacob of Serug's Dispute of the Church and the Synagogue, perceptively draws attention to some of Aphrahat's comparison-series,[64] an observation which is supported by the fact that Ephrem uses some of the same type of tradition in his dispute poems.[65]

With Ephrem the Syriac dispute poem appears full-grown. He has two series: the set of dialogues of Death with Satan and with Man in the *Nisibene Hymns (CNis)*[66] and the set of disputes between Virginity and "Holiness" (or better, "Consecration", meaning the practice of sexual abstinence within marriage) in the Hymns preserved in Armenian (*HArm*).[67] It may seem curious for examples of this genre we have been tracing to be classified as "hymns", and this justifies a short discussion on matters of terminology and definition[68].

"Hymn" is the conventional rendering of the Syriac *madraša*, though its basic sense would seem to connote exegesis rather than singing.[69] *Madraše* are preserved with the names of their melodies; they are usually stanzaic, with a refrain, which is not typical for dispute poems. However, if *madraša* has not lost its relationship to *midraš*, it should not surprise us to find that the proper term in Syriac for a dispute poem seems to be *draša*, another formation from the same verb; it is more surprising that Jewish Aramaic seems to have preferred to use *din* and the verb *dayyen*, by a metaphor more forensic than scholastic.[70]

Disputes are also found among the dialogues (*sogyata*), anonymous or ascribed to named authors (though not among those under the name of Ephrem), but the term *sogita* does not precisely denote a dispute poem any more than does *madraša*, of which it is a sub-species. The typical *sogita* contains narrative with dramatic though not necessarily adversative dialogue. Both R. Duval (1907) and A. Baumstark (1922) noted this dramatic quality, as well as the frequency of alphabetical acrostics, which of course is a formal link with the Jewish material just surveyed. Baumstark says of the tendency to dramatisation that it "allows us to recognise the germ of a religious drama which regrettably never developed further".[71] This was a reasonable speculation; but in fact at

---

63 See R. Murray (1975), pp. 42-336; (1977), pp. 110, 114; for a parallel in *Leviticus Rabbah*, see below, pp. 182-83.
64 *PO* 38 (1976), p. 21. (For Jacob's dispute poem referred to, see below, p. 181).
65 Murray (1977), pp. 125ff, and further below.
66 *CNis* 52-68; ed. E. Beck (1961), pp. 73-110 and German tr., pp. 62-98; ET by J.Gwynn in *NPNF* 13, pp. 206-219; Hymn 52, tr. P. Grelot (1958); tr. S. P. Brock (1983).
67 *HArm* 4-9; ed. L. Mariès and C. Mercier (1963), pp. 41-77; Latin tr. ibid.; French tr., F. Graffin (1961).
68 See Brock (1984), pp. 31-34, 57-58.
69 The Armenian equivalent, *kcʿourd*, corresponds rather to "hymn", as something sung all together.
70 Ephrem does use this verb in a dispute context, of the body "going to court" with the soul, in *CNis* 69,5 (Cf. Brock 1984, p. 49; on this theme see below, p. 42).
71 R. Duval (1907), pp. 16-17; Baumstark (1922), pp. 39-40.

least one *sogita*, the dialogue of the "good thief" and the cherubim guarding paradise, is known to be sometimes performed with a dramatic mime in church. S. P. Brock says of this that it "is the only dialogue *soghitha* which ever gave rise to something resembling liturgical drama";[72] yet it seems not improbable that other Syriac dialogue and dispute poems might have been recited dramatically in earlier times.

As remarked above, *draša* seems to be the proper term for a dispute poem; other terms which occur are descriptive rather than technical.[73] Though this use of *draša*, as of the verb *draš*, seems to be a Syriac development, it may well reflect a background in Jewish-Christian controversy, as is suggested by the occurrences of these words and the *nomen agentis*, *daroša*, in Aphrahat.[74] We shall see a specimen of such controversy in a dispute poem by Jacob of Serug.

To turn to Ephrem's texts in more detail, it must suffice to give a formal analysis with brief indications of the subject-matter. Ephrem's "Dialogues of Death" are all to one melody, *O Mawta, la tešta*ᶜ*le* ("O Death, be not puffed up!"): the opening words, in fact, of the last hymn (*CNis* 68). The stanzas are couplets of eleven-syllable lines, the refrain being a couplet of the same length. If the refrains are original, this strengthens the impression, given at many points, that there is an actively interested audience. It is clear both from tradition and from internal evidence that Ephrem used the *madraša* for teaching, encouraging response by the refrain; the extension of this into the dispute genre may well be his innovation, just as we often find him creatively transmuting traditions and adapting or combining genres.[75]

CNis 52, which P. Grelot (1958) analysed in relation to Mesopotamian examples, is "classic":

Intr. and Matter (stanzas 1-2): Death and Satan disputing: which has the greater power?

Dispute (stanzas 3-25): speaking in alternate stanzas, each claims greater power and fearsomeness.

Conclusion (stanzas 26-27): God is confessed as Lord of both: "As we have seen them mock each other here so shall we look on them triumphantly in the resurrection."

---

[72]See Brock (1984), p. 47; he quotes the description by W. A. Wigram, *The Assyrians and their Neighbours* (London 1929), p. 198. The classical Syriac text, with three versions in modern Syriac, are now edited with Italian translation by F.A. Pennacchietti, *Il Ladrone e il cherubino: Dramma liturgico cristiano orientale* (Turin 1993).

[73]See Brock (1984), pp. 39-40 for details and references. Besides *draša* (to which corresponds Arm. *mak*ᶜ*aṙoumn, HArm* 5,1), more descriptive terms are *maṣṣota*, "conflict" (Arm. *paterazm*, "duellum", *HArm* 4,2 and 9,1) and *taktuša*, "contest".

[74]*Draša*: PS I.1, cols. 468.8, 756.3; *daroša*, *ibid.* 512.2, 744.15, 821.2, 825.7. In the Armenian the last three instances are rendered by *mak*ᶜ*aṙoł*, the *nomen agentis* related to *mak*ᶜ*aṙoumn*.

[75]Cf. Murray (1977), pp. 125ff.

(The conclusion suggests a dramatised performance ending in laughter, as Grelot argued.)

CNis 53-57 : the introductions are mostly short and formal. The matter for dispute is mainly drawn from the scriptures. The examples adduced by each disputant form sequences such as are frequent both in Aphrahat and in Jewish sources (*cf.* Murray, 1977); the respective claims frequently reflect "aretalogy" style, while the mutual accusations sometimes form what I have called "anti-aretalogy", a kind of recital which was probably originally connected with exorcism.[76]

CNis 53 has no clear conclusion, but the last speech of Satan apparently continues (st. 24), so that he is made to confess the lordship of Christ in a kind of doxology.

CNis 54 : there is a longer introduction (1-5), addressed to "Free will" (one of Ephrem's favourite themes) though in fact to the audience. In the Dispute section both Death and Satan repeatedly use the "I am he who..." form. Death has the last word and this leads into a formal doxology (st. 22).

CNis 55 : in the dispute the only Biblical examples are Jonah and Job. The speeches grow longer than simple stanzas as Death and Satan complain about the difficulty of their warfare against humanity. They recognise their common interest (10-11), and in face of the challenge of free will they are reconciled (30-32); again the poem ends with a doxology.

CNis 56 continues without an introduction. Bickering breaks out afresh, but from st. 14 Satan and Death are reconciled. There is a formal conclusion with a doxology (22-23).

CNis 57 returns to scripture, in "aretalogy" style or its inversion; the poem is mainly a monologue of Death on Satan's evil acts, though Satan briefly interrupts (sts. 5, 7, 15) to add complacent elaborations. There is no conclusion.

CNis 58-60 play variations on the Dispute: they contain dramatic speeches, but are nearer to dialogue form *(sogita)* than to *draša*. The theme of Hymns 58-60 is Christ's passion and his conquest of death and sin; they do not, however, come so near to the "Descent to Sheol" theme (which regularly involves elements of

[76]Cf. Murray (1977), pp. 120-124.

dialogue between Sheol, Death and Satan)[77] as does *CNis* 36. There are features of dispute style, but rather in the "epic" mode. Death increasingly takes the side of Christ and humanity, which makes Satan furious: Hymn 60 is his monologue of complaint.

CNis 61-68 concern Death and Man: Satan speaks only in 64:3-10. Most of these are monologues by Death. In 67 he attacks the Jewish people in the ugliest of all Ephrem's tirades; in purely rhetorical terms, of course, coarse invective is found in the dispute style from the beginning. The only true dispute poems here are 65 and 68. Hymn 65 is an alphabetical acrostic, like many *sogyata*, though the pattern is incomplete. There is no introduction. The dispute begins in alternate stanzas (1-14): Man expresses faith in resurrection, to Death's discomfiture. In 15-20 Man argues at greater length; in 21-22 Death pleads Adam's guilt and God's just punishment. There is no conclusion. In *CNis* 68 (again without introduction) the dispute continues in alternate stanzas, each bringing scriptural examples: Man, those who escaped death; Death, those who did not. In 16-30 Death sums up in homiletic style, and a doxology (31) concludes the hymn and series.

Ephrem's other set, in *HArm*, also includes dramatic dialogues and monologues beside true dispute poems. This time the disputants are personifications of states of life. The chief character in the set is Virginity,[78] who speaks either alone or in debate with "Consecration" (the state of sexual abstinence in marriage)[79] or with Marriage itself.[80] If we were to restrict our attention to the dispute poems proper (*HArm* 4, 5 and 9), we would not feel the full impact of the subject-matter, which stylistically is similar in the whole set of hymns, being based on sequences of scriptural (mainly Old Testament) figures, adduced as exemplars of the various states of ascetical life. In Hymns 1-3 the sequences exemplify prayer, fasting and virginity, not yet with any personification. In the choice of scriptural examples, the virtues extolled and the thesis that some Biblical personages already exemplified Christian ascetical ideals, Ephrem stands close to Aphrahat, but also (surprising as it may seem) these traditions can be traced back to

---

[77]See the *Gospel of Bartholomew* and the *Descent* section of the *Gospel of Nicodemus* (ET in Hennecke–Schneemelcher–Wilson, *New Testament Apocrypha* I, London 1963), pp. 470ff., 488ff.; summary of theme and further bibliography in Murray (1975), pp. 325-326.
[78]Arm. *kousoutʿiwn* (= Syr. *btuluta*).
[79]Arm. *srboutʿiwn* (= Syr. *qaddišuta*).
[80]Arm. *amousnoutʿiwn* (= Syr. *šawtaputa*).

sectarian Jewish ascetical teaching.[81] Let us now look at the true precedence dispute poems in this set.

HArm 4. *Intr.*: Virginity and "Consecration" are presented.

Matter : Which is superior?

Dispute : in alternating speeches, mostly of 4 cola each, V. speaks seven times, C. six. The matter all concerns conflicting claims to Biblical models. The tone is comparatively courteous, though with the traditional cries of "you are conquered!". V. has last word, advising C. to be more modest in its claims.

Conclusion: God's gifts are not to be boasted about.

HArm. 5. *Intr. and Matter* : similar to Hymn 4.

Dispute : same argument continues, V. speaking eight times, C. seven. First seven speeches are on O.T. saints, then seven on N.T. Virginity has last word.

Conclusion : V. is superior. Hymn ends with a prayer for those who lapse from ascetical commitment (the same preoccupation as moves Aphrahat in his *Dem.* 7.)[82]

HArm 6 is a monologue by Virginity, a sort of aretalogy in which she praises herself for her choice; but soon the poem is revealed as a concealed dispute with Marriage, for there follows a black picture of the trials of that state (a regrettably familiar ascetical *topos*). The superiority of Virginity is then restated in the third person, and this passes into an exhortation to fellow-ascetics.

HArm 9 (not in strict dispute form).

Intr.: Marriage feels overawed by V. and C., but Ephrem will speak up for her.

Dispute: M. claims merit of producing good children (a self-praising aretalogy combined with an exemplary series). V. swiftly deflates M. Marriage replies modestly but then yields the palm to V. with generous praise (61-end). The speeches are of very irregular length.

Ephrem's concealed but real link with Aphrahat has been pointed out. Has he any antecedents in his use of the dispute form for his teaching on states of life?

---

[81]See A. Guillaumont, "À propos du célibat des Esséniens", in *Hommage à A. Dupont-Sommer* (Paris 1971), pp. 395-404; S. Fraade, "Ascetical Aspects of Ancient Judaism", in A. Green (ed.), *Jewish Spirituality from the Bible Through the Middle Ages* (London 1986), pp. 253-288.

[82]See T. Jansma, "Aphraates' Demonstration VII §§ 18 and 20", *Parole de l'Orient* 5, (1974), pp. 21-48.

Formally speaking, none are extant, but there may be two hints in quite different areas. The three voices, respectively of virginity, ascetical marital continence[83] and "ordinary" marriage, are heard in the collection called *Psalmoi Sarakōtōn*, among the "Manichean Psalms" preserved in Coptic.[84] Like many of this collection, the "psalm" is responsorial. The leader evokes in turn "the cry of a virgin", "the cry of an *enkratēs*" and "the cry of a married person". Each is followed by "perhaps she cries to...": the virgin and the *enkratēs* cry in auspicious directions, but the married person always to a symbol of perdition. Though this recitation is quite different from a dispute poem, and though Ephrem in his ascetical teaching is decisively opposed to the encratite condemnation of marriage, it cannot be denied that the Manichaean song makes points similar to those made by Ephrem, but in a harshly encratite sense. If flesh were to be put on its skeleton it could easily become a kind of dispute poem.

Another possible hint of an antecedent tradition of using the dispute form to compare states of life might lie in a remarkable contemporary parallel in Greek, for which we must digress from Ephrem. This is the *Synkrisis Biōn* by Gregory of Nazianzus (329-389), a Cappadocian neighbour of Ephrem, and only a few years younger.[85] The poem is a dispute between two ways of life, the "worldly" (*kosmikos*) and that "of the spirit" (*tou pneumatos*), in the presence of a judge (*kritēs*) who eventually awards the palm, with an air of Attic and academic detachment, to the Spiritual Life. The latter, against rather crudely hedonistic claims by the Worldly Life, describes itself in highly civilised language which nevertheless emphasises virginity and, still more, poverty. Christ is named only once, though there are frequent allusions to him and his teaching. H. M. Werhahn, in his learned introduction and commentary, correctly related Gregory's poem to traditional exercises in the rhetorical schools (pp. 11-15) and in particular to the *diatribē* of Stoic and Cynic popular moral preaching (pp. 15-20). He did not refer to Callimachus' non-ethical example, or to the broader and older tradition of dispute poems; nor did he discuss Gregory's purpose in writing. This, we may guess, was to commend Christian values to non-Christian readers who had stayed with the cultural values which were also familiar to Gregory since his student days in Athens; he starts from where they are, just as Matteo Ricci was to do to attract the Confucian *litterati* in China.[86]

What of the formal and thematic similarities with Ephrem? His reference to "the poison of the Greeks"[87] has been taken too far as a condemnation of everything

---

[83]On these terms and for further bibliography see Murray (1975), pp. 12-16.
[84]See C. R. Allberry (ed.), *A Manichaean Psalm-Book* II (Stuttgart 1938), pp. 179-181; Murray (1975), pp. 27-29 and 13, n. 1.
[85]Ed. H. M. Werhahn (1953).
[86]See E. Malatesta (ed.), Matteo Ricci S. J., *The True Meaning of the Lord of Heaven (T'ien-chu shih-i)* (Taipei-Paris-Hongkong 1985).
[87]*HFid (Hymns on Faith)* 2, 1.

hellenistic, whereas it almost certainly refers to Arian rationalism.[88] Ephrem's controversial treatises show some degree of philosophical sophistication,[89] and rhetorical forms, like other features of hellenistic education, certainly crossed linguistic frontiers, as even Aphrahat demonstrates.[90] But the main impression, surely, if we compare Gregory's cool reasoning with Ephrem's vivid sequences of Biblical vignettes and his far more dramatic, almost comic, debating style, is that the traditions they represent have developed independently; their similarity is at the level of Huizinga's universal picture.

In this article I shall not attempt to investigate whether Gregory had followers in this genre in Greek. We shall glance below at one more Greek poet, the sixth-century Romanos, about whose antecedents - purely Byzantine or partly Syriac - there has been some debate. The case for the latter has been strengthened recently, but the Byzantine origins of the *kontakion* are equally firm. However, discernible links between Gregory's classicising verses and Romanos are not in the area we are considering.[91]

To return to Ephrem, one more text calls for consideration. Though the two sets of poems surveyed above are his only true examples of the dispute poem, he has a subtle variant of it in the hymn-collection which is somewhat arbitrarily titled "On the Church".[92] In Hymn 9, Ephrem lets us into the tension he feels between the theologian-poet's need to use words in speaking of God and the contemplative's conviction that wordless silence is the only adequate approach to the mystery: in technical terms, between the "cataphatic" way (*via affirmationis*) and the "apophatic" way (*via negationis*). This poem sums up the concern, aroused by Arianism, which inspired a large part of Ephrem's *Hymns on Faith*.[93] In *HEccl.* 9 Ephrem describes the debate in his mind; the two points of view are personified, though not to the degree of liveliness that is typical of the genre. To a modern westerner it may seem paradoxical that the "apophatic" voice is that of Intellect or Reason (*maddᶜa*) while the voice justifying bold, even anthropomorphic, expression is that of Love (*ḥubba*).

Introduction (sts. 1-2): Ephrem's perplexity between the urging of Reason and Love.

Dispute (3-19): R. and L. speak in alternate stanzas, first each adducing biblical examples (4-7). After each has spoken three times there is a pause for breath (9), when Ephrem again

88 See S. P. Brock (1982, repr. 1984), pp. 17, 19.

89 Brock, ibid. p. 19.

90 Cf. Murray (1983).

91 See P. Karavites, "Gregory Nazianzinos and Byzantine hymnography", *JHS* 113 (1993), pp. 81-98, esp. pp. 97-98.

92 Ed. E. Beck in *CSCO* 198-199 (1960). For Hymn 9 see tr. and notes by R. Murray (1980).

93 See Murray (1980), pp. 26-31 and Brock (1985), pp. 29-31.

describes his ἀπορία. The debate then continues, Love speaking five times and Reason four (10-16, 18-19), again with some biblical examples.

Conclusion : not formal, but before end, in st. 17; the inevitable solution is found in a due balance of speech and silence under control of both Love and Reason. Love has the last word.

In this striking poem the form is only slightly different from the fully dramatic dispute. (In Jacob of Serug we shall see a similar variant of the genre occurring briefly.) While it is characteristic of Ephrem to adapt and vary literary traditions, we may notice, before leaving him, a few places where he takes up familiar *topoi* but chooses not to treat them as others had done. True to his seriousness as a teacher, he has left us no botanical or zoological precedence disputes, such as have always been popular in the genre; yet in his series of hymns on the *aretai* of the Olive and its oil (*"Hymns on Virginity and on the Symbols of the Lord"*, 4–7)[94] he enumerates points which might well have featured on one side of a dispute with (say) the Vine, while in the *Hymns on the Resurrection* he praises the Paschal month Nisan in terms very reminiscent of the "Dispute of the Months" tradition.[95] But here we must leave Ephrem (for the *sogyata* under his name are neither by him nor do they contain true disputes).

After Ephrem

From this point on, the material originally surveyed in my unpublished article is now covered, and far surpassed in richness, in Dr. Brock's publications. I shall restrict myself to a few analyses and remarks supplementary to his work.

Ephrem's spiritual descendants came to be divided in their understanding of fundamental Christian doctrines, but not in devotion to Ephrem and their common poetic tradition. Let us look at two examples, from either side of the fifth-century division. Among the *sogyata* unreliably ascribed to Narsai and published by F. Feldmann (1896), no. 5, on Nestorius and Cyril of Alexandria,[96] seems to be a true dispute, in that the contestants do not merely converse dramatically, but press their cases and attack each other's positions. This is the first example we have seen of a poem on an acute contemporary issue. It is in the commonest *sogita* form, stanzas of 4x7 syllables.

---

[94]Ed. E. Beck in *CSCO* 223-224 (1962); tr. K. McVey, *Ephrem the Syrian, Hymns* (New York 1989), pp. 275-296.

[95]Ephrem, *Paschahymnen*, ed. E. Beck, *CSCO* 248-249; see *HResurr.* 3, *passim*. In st. 14 Nisan is expressly compared with the other months; cf. Brock (1985), pp.185-186.

[96]See also F. Martin (1899-1900). The dispute is surely later than Narsai. On the collection cf. Brock (1984), pp. 39ff.

Intr. (sts. 1-5): the disputants, the "glorious priests" (Diodorus, Theodore and Nestorius, against "the Egyptian, the ravening wolf", Cyril.

Dispute (sts. 6-47): each side speaks 21 times (except that one verse of Nestorius is missing). The controversy is at an unsophisticated level and uses plenty of invective, but both sides make real points and "Cyril" (or rather, the "Monophysite" voice as the East Syrians understood it) is not entirely caricatured. Nestorius has the last word.[97]

Conclusion (48-49): a doxology, praising God and awarding victory, of course, to Nestorius.

On the opposed, Syrian Orthodox, side stands Jacob of Serug, the greatest Syriac poet after Ephrem. Since he clearly liked dramatic dialogue, we might expect to find many dispute poems, but not many are known. Two are in the genre of anti-Jewish controversy, the contestants being the Church and the Synagogue; I will analyse one of these, no. 6 in the *memre* (metrical homilies) "Against the Jews".[98]

Introduction (lines 1-10) : the contestants are presented and the audience are invited to judge disinterestedly (!) and reach a fair decision (*dina*).

Dispute : each then speaks four times, at some length. S. opens in "aretalogy" style (11-48), recounting favours received from God (15 points in "I" form). C. replies (41-78), acknowledging S.'s claim, and then depicting her own sinful past in idolatry (13 points in "I" form). But at 71 the tone changes to accusation. S. replies that God will not reject her because of the merits of the Fathers, using a classic exemplary series (79-98). C. sharpens accusation, especially that S. mistakenly denies that God can have a son (99-124). S. suggests recourse to a fair audience (125-130). C. and S. each speak once more, bandying texts (131-214). But finally C. has the floor alone for a long speech (215-312), including a short "comparison series".

Conclusion (313-344) : in place of the unbiased judgement asked for by S., C. claims and celebrates victory.

[97]It is interesting to compare this popular style of controversy with the more serious prose debate between an "Orthodox" and a "Nestorian" published by H. Ibrahim and V. Poggi in *OrChrP* 42 (1976), pp. 459-493 (perhaps 7th-9th centuries).
[98]Ed. M. Albert, *PO* 38 (1976).

Evidently Jacob here departs from the traditional form, as also from the fairness he promised.

Apart from his more formal disputes, Jacob also follows Ephrem occasionally in imaginative adaptations of the style. For example, in his *memra* "On the End of the World"[99] he has a passage reminiscent of Ephrem's debate of Reason and Love. The homily is largely on marriage, its joys and sadnesses, and is in a far more sympathetic tone than Ephrem ever adopts. There is a point (73-90) where sadness (*karyuta*) and joy (*pṣiḥuta*) are personified as they debate within the poet's own mind, till the dispute is calmed by knowledge (*ydaʿta*), which brings deeper insight.

Now that this survey has reached the area which Dr. Brock has explored and illuminated so fully, I will conclude my own observations on Syriac dispute poems with a footnote to the theme of "Body and Soul", for which Brock (1984) lists four known examples, one of them ascribed to Jacob,[100] and will close after a few remarks on Romanos.

The first two "Body and Soul" debates have now been presented in English translation, No. I by Dr. Brock himself and No. II by H. J. W. Drijvers (1991), the latter with a valuable commentary.[101] Of these it is the first (perhaps of the sixth century) which seems closer to the dispute form, in that there is real argument and recrimination between Body and Soul, whereas in the second they rather show sympathy and awareness of the need for mutual help, with scarcely any of the rivalry or invective which have characterised dispute poems from their first beginnings. This tone of sympathy, indeed, which seems characteristic of Jacob of Serug, might be added to the considerations advanced by Professor Drijvers in favour of the ascription to him, which have been queried because of its metre and strict alternation which are unusual together in a *memra* by Jacob. Though both Brock and Drijvers classify this as a dispute poem, it seems to fall somewhere between this category and that of purely dialogue *sogita*.

The more typical dispute, No. I, centres on questions of responsibility for sin: does the body drag the soul down by its instincts and desires, or does the soul lead the body on? Questions of responsibility and imputability will always be acute for religious traditions which, like both Judaism and especially Syrian Christianity, strongly emphasise human free will. In fact the essentials of the mutual accusations by soul and body in this poem are expressed, by means of three amusing parables, in *Leviticus Rabbah* IV, 5-6. I do not mean to suggest any literary dependence, but merely to

[99]Ed. P. Bedjan (1910) V, pp. 873-886; this passage, pp. 876-877. There is a (somewhat loose) French translation by J. Babakhan in *ROC* 18 (1913), pp. 358-374.
[100]Brock (1984), pp. 49-50.
[101]In Reinink–Vanstiphout, *DPD*, pp. 121-134.

observe a continuing similarity in religious thinking. The same section of *Lev. Rabbah* also ends (IV, 8) with an elegant Hebrew kind of *syncrisis* which has some formal resemblance to the Syriac "comparison series", mentioned earlier. The Jewish example compares the activities of the soul in the body with those of God in the universe. The comparison also occurs (more briefly and in the reverse order) in the Talmud and in other midrashim,[102] but here the theme is elaborated into "stanzas" of rhythmical prose with a gracefully varying refrain.[103] Among all his many examples of comparison-series, Aphrahat never has one either so complex or so artistic as this; but this form can be added to the many other links, in both form and matter, between Jewish and Christian Syriac literature.

This survey does not aim to go much beyond the sixth century, but a few remarks on Romanos Melodes, his use of dialogue and his relationship to Syriac poetic models will not be out of place. The fact that Romanos was born in Emesa (Homs) has encouraged some to suppose that he was bilingual and thus could easily have known the hymns and homilies of Ephrem and Jacob. Against such a view J. Grosdidier de Matons, the editor of Romanos's *kontakia*, when discussing the origin of this hymnic form, judged that there is no clear evidence for influence of Syriac models, but only for purely Greek roots. The case for some Syriac influence has been renewed by Syriac scholars, cautiously by S. P. Brock (1989), more energetically by W. Petersen (1985); but A. Cameron (1991, p. 94) justly warns against contentiousness in this matter. Similar rhetorical forms, kinds of imagery and particular *topoi* are to be found in writers all round the near east from Palestine to Adiabene, whether they wrote in Greek, as did Cyril of Jerusalem, Severian of Gabala and John Chrysostom, or in Syriac, as did Ephrem and Aphrahat (*cf.* Murray, 1983). Thus on the question of Romanos's cultural background and formative influences it is easier to point to traditions which he evidently knew, by whatever channels, than to prove dependence on particular sources. In the perspective of the present article it is most interesting to note the points where Romanos's dramatic dialogues show him close in themes and spirit to Syriac tradition, whether he knew it in Syriac or not. S. P. Brock (1989) has illustrated this as regards the *ʿAqedah* story (Gen 22). But Romanos comes nearest to something like the dispute style in those *kontakia* which contain dialogues involving Satan, Hades, Death and Adam, especially in the context of Christ's descent to Hades.[104] None of these passages

---

[102]The other examples start each comparison with God. In *bBerakot* 10a there are five points of comparison; in *Deut. Rabba* 2, 37 there are six; in *Pirqe d-Rabbi Eliezer* (tr. G. Friedlander, London 1916), three. Ibn Gabirol re-worked the theme in a *piyyuṭ*; see R. Loewe, *Ibn Gabirol* (London 1989), pp. 87-88 and 176.

[103]Tr. in *Midrash Rabbah, Deuteronomy*, p. 65. As in *bBerakot*, the statements are connected with Ps 103, in which the psalmist five times calls on his soul to bless YHWH, but here there are eight points.

[104]In the edition by J. Grosdidier de Matons, vol. 4 (*SC* 128, Paris 1967), nos. 37, 38 and 42-44. There is also a dialogue of Hades and Death in no. 26, on Lazarus (vol. 3, *SC* 114, 1965).

is in strict dispute form, as are Ephrem's *CNis* 52 and the dispute listed by Brock (1984) as "Death and Satan II".[105] But we should remember that from earliest times the dispute style had a looser variant in "epic" narrative contexts. The dialogues of the infernal powers have such a variant in the *Gospel of Nicodemus*;[106] in this, in the Syriac examples and in Romanos a number of points recur, but we probably cannot argue for more than a common tradition.

To leave the dispute poem in the sixth century is to leave it flourishing, with a history ahead which (in Syriac at least) still shows no signs of ending. But at this point I happily leave it to Dr. Brock and to the authors of the essays on Arabic and other literatures in the Groningen Symposium volume, which provides so rich an introduction to the whole subject, though still leaving many treasures unexplored.

References

Asmussen, J., "A Judeo-Persian Precedence-Dispute Poem and some Thoughts on the History of the Genre", in Asmussen, J., *Studies in Judeo-Persian Literature* (Leiden 1973), pp. 32-59.

Babylonian Talmud, Soncino Press Translation, ed. I. Epstein (London 1935-52).

Baumstark, A., *Geschichte der syrischen Literatur* (Bonn, 1922).

Bottéro, J., "La 'tenson' et la réflexion sur les choses en Mesopotamie", in Reinink-Vanstiphout, *DPD* (see below), pp. 7-22.

Brock, S. P., "A Piece of Wisdom Literature in Syriac", *JSS* 13 (1968), pp. 212-217.

- *Soghyatha Mgabbyatha*, (Glane [Monastery of St. Ephrem] 1982).
- "From Antagonism to Assimilation: Syriac Attitudes to Greek Learning", in *East of Byzantium* (Dumbarton Oaks Symposium 1980, Washington D.C. 1982, pp. 17-34; reprint in Brock, *Syriac Perspectives on Late Antiquity* [London 1984]).
- "Dialogue Hymns of the Syriac Churches", *Sobornost/ECR* 5 (1983), pp. 35-45.
- *The Harp of the Spirit* (ed. 2, London 1983).
- "Syriac Dialogue Poems: Marginalia to a Recent Edition", *Muséon* 97 (1984), pp. 29-58.
- "A Dispute of the Months and Some Related Syriac Texts", *JSS* 30 (1985), pp.181-211.
- "The Dispute Between Soul and Body: An Example of a Long-lived Mesopotamian Literary Genre", *Aram* 1 (1989), pp. 53-64.
- "From Ephrem to Romanos", in E. Livingstone (ed.), *Studia Patristica* XX (Leuven 1989), pp. 139-151.
- "Syriac Dispute Poems: The Various Types", in Reinink–Vanstiphout, *DPD* (see below), pp. 109-119.

Brunner, C. J., "The Fable of the Babylonian Tree", *JNES* 39 (1980), pp. 191-202, 291-302.

[105] Now published with German tr. and study by G. J. Reinink (1991).

[106] Cf. n. 77. Jacob of Serug also has a *memra* "On Death and Satan" (Bedjan V, pp. 641-658); a rubric says it is for the Easter vigil. The dialogue is dramatic, but rather in "epic" than strict dispute style.

Cameron, A., "Disputations, Polemical Literature and the Formation of Opinion in the Early Byzantine Period", in Reinink–Vanstiphout, *DPD* (see below), pp.91-108.

Cowley, A., *Aramaic Papyri of the Fifth Century B.C.* (Oxford 1923).

Daube, D., *Ancient Hebrew Fables* (Oxford 1973).

Denning-Bolle, S. J., "Wisdom and Dialogue in the Ancient Near East", *Numen* 34 (1987), pp. 214-31.

Drijvers, H. J. W., "Body and Soul: A Perennial Problem", in Reinink–Vanstiphout, *DPD* (see below), pp. 119-134.

Duval, R., *La Littérature syriaque* (ed. 3, Paris 1907; reprint Amsterdam 1970).

Ephrem, [*HFid*] *Des hl. Ephraem des Syrers Hymnen de Fide*, ed. E. Beck, *CSCO* 154-155 (1954).

id., - [*HEccl*] *Des hl. E. d. S. Hymnen de Ecclesia*, ed. E. Beck, *CSCO* 198-199 (1960). (For ET of Hymn 9 see Murray).

- [*HArm*] *Hymnes de S. Éphrem conservées en version arménienne*, ed. L. Mariès and C. Mercier, *PO* (=*Patrologia Orientalis*) 30 (1961).
- [*HVirg*] *Des hl. E. d. S. Hymnen de Virginitate*, ed. E. Beck, *CSCO* 223-224 (1962).
- [*CNis*] *Des hl. E. d. S. Carmina Nisibena*, ed E. Beck, Pt. 2, *CSCO* 240-241 (1963).
- [*HResur*] in *Des hl. E. d. S. Paschahymnen*, ed. E. Beck, *CSCO* 248-249 (1964).

Fiore, S., "La tenson en Espagne et en Babylonie: Évolution ou polygénèse?", in F. Jost (ed.), *Proceedings of the IVth Congress of the International Comparative Literature Association (Fribourg 1964)* (The Hague-Paris 1966), pp.982-992.

Fitzmyer, J. A., *The Genesis Apocryphon of Qumran Cave I* (Rome 1971[2]).

Froleyks, W. J., *Der Αγὼν Λόγων in der antiken Literatur* (Inaugural-Dissertation, Bonn 1973), esp. pp. 398-421.

Ginzberg, L., *Legends of the Jews* (Philadelphia 1909-38).

Goldschmidt, L., *Der Babylonische Talmud*, 10 vols. (Haag 1933-1935).

Gordon, E. I., "A New Look at the Wisdom of Sumer and Akkad", *BiOr* 17 (1960), pp. 122-152.

Graffin, F., "Hymnes inédites de S. Éphrem sur la virginité", *OrSyr* 6 (1961), pp.213-242.

Greenfield, J. C. and Sokoloff, M., "Astrological and Related Omen Texts in Jewish Palestinian Aramaic", *JNES* 48 (1989), pp. 201-214.

Grelot, P., "Un poème de Saint Éphrem: Satan et la Mort", *OrSyr* 3 (1958), pp. 443-452.

id., - "La Dispute des arbres dans le Targoum II d'Esther VII, 10", in D. Muñoz Leon (ed.), *Salvación en la palabra* (Madrid 1986), pp. 399-408.

Grosdidier de Matons, J., *Romanos le Mélode, Hymnes* (ed. with French tr.), *SC* 99, 110, 114, 128, 283 (1964-1981).

id., - *Romanos le Mélode et les origines de la poésie religieuse à Byzance* (Paris 1977).

Grossfeld, B., *The Two Targums of Esther, Translated, with Apparatus and Notes* (*The Aramaic Bible*, vol. 18, Edinburgh 1991).

Huizinga, J., *Homo Ludens* (Haarlem 1938; ET London 1949; reprint in paperback, 1970).

Jacob of Serug, *Homiliae selectae Mar-Jacobi Sarugensis*, ed. P. Bedjan (Paris-Leipzig 1905-1910).

- *Homélies contre les Juifs par Jacques de Saroug*, ed. (with French tr.) by M. Albert, *PO* 38 (1976).

Jacobs, L., *The Talmudic Argument* (Cambridge 1984).

Klein, M. L., *The Fragment-Targums of the Pentateuch* (Rome 1980).

- *Genizah Manuscripts of Palestinian Targum to the Pentateuch* (Cincinnati 1986).

Kramer, S. N., *History Begins at Sumer* (Philadelphia 1961[2]).

- *Enmerkar and the Lord of Aratta: A Sumerian Epic Tale of Iraq and Iran* (Philadelphia 1952).
- "Rivalry and Superiority: Two Dominant Features of the Sumerian Culture Pattern", in A. Wallace (ed.) *Men and Cultures* (Philadelphia 1960), pp.287-291.
- *The Sacred Marriage Rite* (Bloomington-London 1969).

Lambert, M., "Le jeu d'Enmerkar", *Syria* 32 (1955), pp. 212-21.

Lambert, W. G., *Babylonian Wisdom Literature* (Oxford 1960).

Landy, F., *Paradoxes of Paradise: Identity and Difference in the Song of Songs* (Sheffield 1983).

Maspero, G., "Fragment d'une version égyptienne de la fable des membres et de l'estomac", in Maspero, *Études Égyptiennes I* (Paris 1886), pp. 260-64.

Midrash Rabbah, Soncino Press Translation, ed. H. Freedman and M. Simon (London 1939).

Murray, R., *Symbols of Church and Kingdom: A Study in Early Syriac Tradition* (Cambridge 1975).

- "Some Rhetorical Patterns in Early Syriac Literature" in R. H. Fischer (ed.), *A Tribute to Arthur Vööbus* (Chicago 1977), pp. 109-131.
- "St. Ephrem's Dialogue of Reason and Love" (*HEccl* 9), *Sobornost/ECQ* 2 (1980), pp. 26-40.
- "Hellenistic-Jewish Rhetoric in Aphrahat" in *III. Symposium Syriacum 1980* (*OrChrA* 221, Roma 1983), pp. 79-85.

Narsai (attrib.), *Syrische Wechsellieder von Narses*, ed. F. Feldmann (with German tr.), (Leipzig 1896).

- *Sogita* no. 5: French tr. by F. Martin, *JA* 9 (1899-1900), pp. 484-492, 515-525.

Nøjgaard, M., *La fable antique, I: la fable grecque avant Phèdre* (Copenhagen 1964).

Perry, B. E., "Fable" in *Studium Generale* 12 (1959), pp. 19-45.

Petersen, W., *The Diatessaron and Ephrem Syrus as Sources of Romanos the Melodist* (*CSCO, Subs.* 74, 1985).

Reinink, G. J. and Vanstiphout, H. L. J. (eds.), *Dispute Poems and Dialogues in the Ancient and Mediaeval Near East* (Orientalia Lovaniensia Analecta 42) (Leuven 1991), cited as *DPD*.

Reinink, G. J., "Ein syrisches Streitgespräch zwischen Tod und Satan" in Reinink–Vanstiphout, *DPD* (see above), pp. 135-152.

Rieder, D., *Pseudo-Jonathan: Targum Jonathan ben Uziel on the Pentateuch* (Jerusalem 1974).

Sauren, H., "Les Epopées sumériennes et la théatre classique", *OLP* 3 (1972), pp. 35-47.

Sokoloff, M. and Yahalom, Y., *Aramaic Poems from the Byzantine Period*, forthcoming.

Sperber, A., *The Bible in Aramaic* (Leiden 1959-1962).

Steinschneider, M., "Rangstreit-Literatur" in *SbKAW* (*Sitzungsberichte der Könichlichen Akademie zu Wien), phil.-hist. Klasse*, 155 (Wien 1908), pp.1-87.

Trypanis, C. (ed. and tr.), *Callimachus: Aetiae, Iambi and Other Fragments* (*LCL*, Cambridge, Mass. - London 1958).

van Bekkum, W. J., "Observations on the Hebrew Debate in Mediaeval Europe" in Reinink–Vanstiphout, *DPD* (see above), pp. 77-90.

van der Toorn, K., "The Ancient Near Eastern Literary Dialogue as a Vehicle of Critical Reflection" in Reinink-Vanstiphout, *DPD* (see above), pp. 59-77.

van Dijk, J. J. A., *La sagesse suméro-accadienne* (Leiden 1953).

Vanstiphout, H. L. J., "The Mesopotamian Debate Poems. A General Presentation", Part I, *Acta Sumerologica* 12 (1990), pp. 271-318; Part II, "The Subject", ibid. 14 (1992).

- "Lore, Learning and Levity in the Sumerian Disputations: A Matter of Form, or Substance?", in Reinink–Vanstiphout, *DPD* (see above), pp. 23-46.
- "The Banquet Scene in the Mesopotamian Debate Poems", *Res Orientales* IV (1992a).

Vermes, G., *Post-Biblical Jewish Studies* (Leiden 1975; 1983^2).

Vogelzang, M. E., "Some Questions about the Akkadian Disputes", in Reinink–Vanstiphout, *DPD* (see above), pp. 47-57.

Werhahn, H.M., *Gregorii Nazianzeni ΣΥΓΚΡΙΣΙΣ ΒΙΩΝ* (Wiesbaden 1953).

Williams, R. J., "The Fable in the Ancient Near East", in E. C. Hobbs (ed.), *A Stubborn Faith* (Dallas 1956), pp. 3-26.

The Dictionary of Jewish Babylonian Aramaic Progress and Prospects*

Michael Sokoloff — Bar Ilan University

At the Aramaic Congress held at the University of Chicago in 1976, I spoke on the topic of the state of research on Galilean Aramaic.[1] At the time I was just organising my ideas for work on a new dictionary of this dialect, and the results finally appeared in 1990 as *A Dictionary of Jewish Palestinian Aramaic*.[2] The present article will deal with the logical continuation of my work on Jewish literary Aramaic, viz. a new dictionary of Jewish Babylonian Aramaic, which will present to the scholarly world the lexical riches of the Aramaic literature of Jewish Sassanian and post-Sassanian Babylonia in an accurate and up-to-date form. The following discussion will present the

---

*The oral nature of the talk has been retained here in the written version, and relevant footnotes have been added. The research for this project is being supported by the National Endowment for the Humanities, Grant No. RT-21038-89. Note the following abbreviations:

Addit.	S. Krauss et al., *Additamenta ad Aruch Completum*, Vienna 1937 (Heb.)
AC	*Aruch Completum*, ed. A. Kohut, Vienna 1928[2]
AIT	J. A. Montgomery, *Aramaic Incantation Texts from Nippur*, Philadelphia 1913
Assaf	S. Assaf, *Gaonic Responsa from Geniza Mss.*, Jerusalem 1929 (Heb.)
BT	Babylonian Talmud
Col	Columbia University, Ms. X893-T141
EA	Eastern Aramaic
Eps, *Studies*	J. N. Epstein, *Studies in Talmudic Literature and Semitic Languages*, 2 vols., Jerusalem 1983-88 (Heb.)
Harkavy	A. Harkavy, *Responsen der Geonim* (Studien und Mitteilungen aus der Kaiserlichen Öffentlichen Bibliothek, VI), St. Petersburg 1887 (Heb.)
HG	E. Hildesheimer (ed.), *Sefer Halakhot Gedolot*, 3 vols., Jerusalem 1971-1987
HP	R. Yehudai Gaon, *Sefer Halachot Pesuqot* (Codex Sasoon 263), ed. S. Sasoon, Jerusalem 1948; Facsimile edition, Maqor Publishers, Jerusalem 1971
IJ	E. S. Rosenthal, "Talmudica Iranica", in S. Shaked (ed.), *Irano-Judaica, Studies Relating to Jewish Contacts with Persian Culture throughout the Ages*, Jerusalem 1982 (Heb.)
J	M. Jastrow, *A Dictionary of the Targumim, the Talmud Babli and Yerushalmi and the Midrashic Literature*, New York 1903
JBA	Jewish Babylonian Aramaic
K	C. J. and B. Kasowski, *Thesaurus Talmudis Concordantiae Verborum quae in Talmude Babylonico Reperiuntur*, 42 vols., Jerusalem 1954-1982
Kutscher, *Studies*:	E. Y. Kutscher, *Hebrew and Aramaic Studies*, Jerusalem 1977
OEL	Outline Etymological Lexicon
OH	*Otzar ha-Geonim*, 13 vols., Haifa-Jerusalem 1928-1943 (Heb.)

[1]See M. Sokoloff, "The Current State of Research on Galilean Aramaic", *JNES* 37 (1978), pp. 161-168. I hope to publish a parallel article on JBA in the near future.

[2]Bar Ilan University (Ramat Gan 1990).

progress that has been accomplished on this project to date, and what I see as the prospects for its successful completion within a reasonable time span.

1. The Texts

The declared objective of the project is to prepare a dictionary of the Aramaic language utilised by the Jews in Babylonia during the Sassanian and post-Sassanian Periods, viz. that contained in the Babylonian Talmud, the Gaonic literature,[3] the incantation bowls from Iraq and Iran and other magical texts,[4] and the remnants of the "Book of Commandments" of Anan,[5] the founder of Karaism. While each of these genres presents its own particular problems, clearly the first two are the most difficult to deal with both in terms of their content and due to their vast scope.

The Babylonian Talmud contains the Amoraic discussions on 33 tractates of the Mishna, and each tractate varies greatly in both its absolute size and in the relative portions of the texts in Aramaic mixed together with Hebrew material. It may come as a surprise to some if we note at the outset that the vast proportion of the BT — which contains about 1.8 million words — is in Hebrew. Leaving aside the repetitive legal terminology, the percentage of Aramaic on average does not exceed 10-15% of the entire text. This percentage, however, varies greatly from tractate to tractate. Thus *Berakhot*, which contains relatively few extensive halakhic discussions, also contains a very small percentage of Aramaic, probably no more than 5%, with most of it concentrated in the later chapters. On the other hand, the Tractate *Neziqin*, i.e., *Baba Qamma*, *Baba Meṣiᶜa*, *Baba Batra*, contains a proportionally larger amount of Aramaic, about 25%, since not only are the aggadic portions in Aramaic, but the halakhic discussions are also to a great extent in this language.[6] While observations such as these have a bearing on the layering of discussions composing the BT and their relative dates, separation of these layers also is both a tedious and difficult task, and so this factor cannot be taken into account at the present stage of research.[7] The reason for this is that, as pilot studies by scholars have shown, such strands may only be

---

[3]See below, p. 194.

[4]E.g. The Sword of Moses (חרבא דמשה), published by M. Gaster, *Studies and Texts in Folklore, ...and Samaritan Archaeology*, I (London 1925-28), pp. 69-104; III, Hebrew section, pp. 69-103.

[5]The texts were published by Harkavy, Schechter, Mann, and Epstein. For details, see J. N. Epstein, *Studies*, 1, pp. 71-84; id., *Tarbiz* 7 (1936), pp. 283-290.

[6]For *Baba Meṣiᶜa*, e.g., the following figures are relevant. Out of a total of 82,482 words in the entire tractate, 24,124 (or 29%) are in the file prepared for analysis (this number includes, however, Hebrew words added to clarify the context).

[7]On the impossibility of deciding what is Amoraic, Saboraic and Gaonic in the Talmudic discussion as we have it before us, see J. Sussmann, ושוב לירושלמי נזיקין in מחקרי תלמוד, (Jerusalem 1990), I, pp. 104-114.

unravelled by painstaking literary analysis, and this has been done for only a small number of sequential texts.[8]

Thus, the goal of the present project cannot include the labelling of such layers and perforce must treat the BT vocabulary as if it were the editorial product of a final redaction, probably some time in the 6th cent. C.E., containing interpolations and additions from the later Saboraic and Gaonic Periods.[9]

The reason for including the other literary types of text which post-date the BT and extend into the Moslem Period is the recognition that on the whole they constitute an organic continuation of the JBA of the Sassanian Period and were written during a period when JBA continued to be the vernacular of the Jewish community of Babylonia.[10] While this is least so in the case of the magic bowls,[11] nevertheless their clear affinity with the other material warrants their inclusion in the corpus.[12]

Finally, a word concerning the Targumic Aramaic texts of the mixed type such as Pseudo-Jonathan and the Targums to the Hagiographa. Indeed, while these texts seem to have an original Palestinian basis, the massive influence of both Onkelos-type Aramaic[13] and JBA upon them is manifest.[14] Hence, it would seem proper that these

---

[8]Work of this type has been done for a long time, and a contemporary practitioner is S. A. Friedman. See e.g. *A Critical Study of Yevamot X with a Methodological Introduction* (New York 1978) (Heb.), where the author brings the rule: כשעברית וארמית משמשות בערבוביה, עיקר ניסוח המימרא הוא העברית, והארמית לשון סתם התלמוד הוא . See now also his *Talmud Arukh, BT Bava Mezi'a VI*, Jerusalem 1990 (Heb.)

[9]It is, of course, clear that the BT contains discernible non-JBA types of texts: supposed inscriptions (e.g. *BB* 58a), statements of Palestinian Amoraim (e.g. the statement of Resh Laqish: דין גרמא דעשיראה ביר *Berachot* 5b), quotations from legal formulae (e.g. a writ of divorce in *Yev* 115b; v. Kutscher, *Studies,* pp. 417-430 (Heb.); S. A. Friedman, *Tarbiz* 43 [1974], pp. 62-64), Targumic quotations of the Onkelos type (see the list in L. Zunz, *Die gottesdienstliche Vorträge der Juden historisch entwickelt* [Hebrew translation] [Jerusalem 1954], p. 252, n. 11), and quotations from earlier documents (e.g. *Megillat Taanit*; v. G. Dalman, *Grammatik des jüdisch-palästinischen Aramäisch* (Leipzig 1905^2), p. 9). It is the author's present position to include in the dictionary words found in the first two categories, and probably in the third, since their style is only quasi-archaic, while the other categories clearly belong to an earlier period.

[10]On the question: Until when did the Jews speak Aramaic in Babylonia?, see J. N. Epstein, *A Grammar of Babylonian Aramaic* (Heb.) (Jerusalem 1960), p. 16ff.

[11]Approximately 120 Jewish magic bowls have been published to date (v. J. Naveh and S. Shaked, *Amulets and Magic Bowls* [Jerusalem 1985], pp. 19-21, for a summary of the publications), and quite a few texts contain many archaic forms, e.g. קדישין מלאכין *AIT* 4:1; מיכלהון *ib.* 6:5; דלא יחטון להון *ib.* 8:10; alongside the regular JBA forms.

[12]There is not yet a complete glossary of the vocabulary of these texts. The publications contain a large number of misreadings and mistranslations. For corrections in the published texts and important lexical discussions, see J. N. Epstein, "Glosses babylo-araméennes", *REJ* 73 (1921), pp. 27-58 [Hebrew version in *Studies*, I, pp. 329-384]). See also Naveh–Shaked, pp. 30-35, with literature.

[13]See e.g., the recent discussion of E. Y. Cook, *Rewriting the Bible: The Text and Language of Pseudo-Jonathan*, UCLA dissertation 1986, pp. 40-43.

[14]This was already pointed out by Zunz (op. cit., n. 10, p. 261, n. 61). To take a few examples out of many: 1. אכוורניקא ‹ Peh **xwarnag* celebration hall in an orchard PsJ Dt 32:50, appears only in BT [see *Addit.* 21]; 2. אמגושא ‹ OP *magus* Mazdean priest ib. 7:15, appears in BT and the other EA dialects [see *Addit.* 30]; 3. In Tg2Jb, the following words known elsewhere in Jewish Aramaic texts only from BT are found גרגישתא, טוש, ככא, מורניתא, שרגא (See R. Weiss, *The*

texts should also be scanned for both new JBA words and corroborative forms not found in the "canonical" texts.

2. Transmission of the Texts

One of the most difficult tasks facing the lexicographer of JBA concerns the transmission of the literary texts[15]. While it is quite clear that the text of the printed editions has been corrupted and should not serve as the basis for a dictionary, it is not clear what in fact constitutes an uncorrupted original text,[16] if indeed such an entity exists. It is a sad reflection on modern academic Talmudic research that to this day no scholarly critical edition of the Talmud has been produced to aid the user.[17] While there exists a consensus concerning some tractates about which manuscript is on the whole the superior one (e.g. the Hamburg Ms. of *Neziqin*)[18] this is not the case with others.[19] Furthermore, it is also quite clear that in some cases different manuscripts of

---

Aramaic Targum of Job [Tel Aviv 1979], p. 102+ (Heb.)). The vocabulary attested *only* in this type of Targum merits a special study.

[15]The epigraphic evidence consists solely of the incantation bowls, some of which also have a history of literary transmission as is evidenced by the variants in parallel bowls. The problems of transmission are both pre-canonical (i.e. before the "redaction" of the Talmudic text) and post-canonical (i.e. the manuscript tradition). Unfortunately, the first is still shrouded in mystery and speculation, while the latter cannot as yet be seriously investigated through lack of critical editions of the Talmudic text.

[16]The current printed text is the Vilna edition of 1880-1888 — an important scholarly achievement at the time — which can be traced back to the first complete edition of the Talmud published in Venice by D. Bomberg between 1520-1523 (on the printing of the Talmud, see R. N. Rabbinovicz, מאמר על הדפסת התלמוד, ed. A. M. Habermann (Jerusalem 1952). On the pre-Bomberg prints, see H.Z. Dimitrowsky, *S'ridei Bavli*, 2 vols. [New York 1979]). While the Vilna text has become today the *de facto* standard, it suffers from cumulative printers' errors, scholarly emendations, and the high hand of the censor. While the rare Bomberg edition is now generally available in reprint (Jerusalem, no date), its value is still limited vis-à-vis the manuscripts.

[17]The only complete critical edition of a tractate is that of H. Malter, *The Tractate Taʿanit* (New York 1930), which gives the variants to the eclectic text that he established. The Complete Israeli Talmud Project of Yad Harav Herzog is working on such a project, but its published volumes of the tractates *Yevamot*, *Ketubbot* and *Soṭa* give the Vilna edition as the basis for variants. Of the critical edition of *Pesaḥim* on which the late E. S. Rosenthal worked for over 30 years nothing has as yet appeared, now ten years after his death. The first two chapters of this tractate were edited critically by B. Na'e, גמרא שלמה, Jerusalem 1960-64. For a survey of critical work on the BT, see S. A. Friedman, in *Researches in Talmudic Literature* (Jerusalem 1983), pp.96-104 (Heb.); D. Goodblatt, *The Babylonian Talmud*, in *Aufstieg und Niedergang der rōmischen Welt*, 19.2, Berlin 1979, pp. 257-336; B. M. Bokser, "Talmudic Studies" in *The State of Jewish Studies*, ed. S. J. D. Cohen and E. L. Greenstein (Detroit 1990), pp. 81-83.

[18]See D. Goldschmidt, *Der Traktat Nezikin ... in photographischer Facsimile-Reproduktion ... und mit textkritische Scholien versehen* (Berlin 1914). For an evaluation of the language of this manuscript, see E. Y. Kutscher, review of J. N. Epstein, *A Grammar of Babylonian Aramaic*, in his *Studies*, p. 227 (Heb), passim.

[19]Thus, while the Spanish manuscript of *Avoda Zara* in the possession of the Jewish Theological Seminary (Rab 0015) was once considered the best witness to this tractate (see *Tractate ʿAbodah Zarah*, ed. Sh. Abramson [New York 1956]), the Paris Ms. (Bib. Nat. 1337) is now considered to be superior (see the remarks of E. S. Rosenthal quoted in D. Rosenthal, *Mishna Aboda Zara: A Critical Edition with Introduction*, Ph.D. Dissertation [Hebrew University 1980], p. 139 [Heb.]).

the same tractate preserve variant traditions containing also variant vocabulary, both *a priori* with a claim to being authentic JBA.[20]

Were the goal of this project the achievement of lexical perfection, we would have to wait until critical editions of the various tractates were prepared and only then could the analysis of their vocabulary begin. This, however, is tantamount to saying that the project should be abandoned for the foreseeable future since to my knowledge very little work is presently being carried out along these lines. Rather, the alternative chosen has been to base the lexical work on one manuscript of each tractate, chosen for its general textual superiority.[21] This text is then completely analyzed and serves as the basis for the lexicon of this tractate. As for the other mss. of each tractate, many are now available in database form from the Saul Lieberman Institute of the Jerusalem branch of the Jewish Theological Seminary and can be quickly scanned for variants.[22] Currently, no one seems to be working on a database of the BT texts from the Geniza[23] or on systematically collecting the important readings in the Gaonic literature[24] and the early medieval commentators, though work of this latter type has been done partially in the past.[25]

---

[20]This is especially true regarding the Yemenite mss. of various tractates, e.g. *Pesaḥim, Yoma, Megilla, Sanhedrin*. See Y. Tobi, על התלמוד בתימן, Tel Aviv 1963; Y. Kara, *Babylonian Aramaic in the Yemenite Manuscripts of the Talmud*, Jerusalem 1983 (Heb.), who deals mainly with the morphology. The importance of the Yemenite Talmudic manuscripts was already especially emphasised by E. S. Rosenthal in his dissertation and in various articles (See Kara, *op. cit.*, for bibliographical details). On his authority, Kutscher chose selections from one of them for his contribution on JBA in F. Rosenthal, *An Aramaic Handbook*, 2/1 (Wiesbaden 1967), pp. 44-45. Some examples of words known to me in JBA only from Yemenite manuscripts are: הרדופא oleander *Pes* 39a (32; Col); זוניתא belt 16a (19; Col); אנוסי perpetrators by force *Ar* 16a (9) [cited in *Midrash ha-Gadol*, Genesis, ed. M. Margoliot (Jerusalem 1947), p. 383:16].

[21]The manuscripts used are the ones employed by the Hebrew Language Academy for their Historical Dictionary of the Hebrew Language which were selected for each tractate following the advice of eminent Talmudists and with regard to their linguistic purity. See E. Weissberg, מצע לעיבוד מסכתות נוספות של התלמוד הבבלי 12, *Proceedings of the Hebrew Language Academy*, 28-30 (1980-81), pp. 332ff. (I would like to thank the Academy and the former director of the Historical Dictionary, Prof. Z. Ben Ḥayyim, for having provided me with the Aramaic portions of these manuscripts in electronic form.)

[22]In its final form the database will contain all of the manuscripts of all of the tractates of the Talmud (currently there is at least one manuscript of each tractate). The database allows quick simple and Boolean searches of strings including wild cards.

[23]The Geniza fragments have now been catalogued by the Mishna Project of the Israel Academy of Sciences under the direction of J. Sussmann (see J. Sussmann, "Talmud Fragments in the Cairo Geniza", *Teʿuda* 1 (1980), pp. 21-32 (Heb)). Some fragments have been published in the past in facsimile (e.g., A. I. Katsch, גנזי תלמוד בבלי, 2 vols. [Jerusalem 1976-79]; S. Morag, *Vocalised Talmudic Manuscripts in the Cambridge Geniza Collections*, vol. I, Taylor-Schechter Old Series [Cambridge 1988]).

[24]On this subject see R. Brody, ספרות הגאונים והטקסט התלמודי, *Meḥqerei Talmud* 1 (1990), pp. 237-303.

[25]Especially in the notes of the important but still incomplete דקדוקי סופרים of N. N. Rabbinowicz, 16 vols., Munich 1867-97.

As to the Gaonic writings, which may be conveniently divided into legal compendia, responsa and commentaries, much important material has been published and systematically collated during this century, especially from the Geniza.[26] Indeed, besides containing vocabulary not found in the BT, the Gaonic writings contain many explanations of difficult Aramaic words.[27] These were already not understood by the people who studied the BT over 1,000 years ago.[28] Unfortunately, for the JBA vocabulary, we do not have a work similar to that of Bar Bahlul or Bar Ali for Syriac, but the collection of these indigenous explanations and their presentation in the lexicon will be of great help in understanding many obscure words.[29] Indeed it has become quite clear that much of the lexical tradition found in the Aruch, R. Ḥananel, and Rashi can be traced back to these Gaonic explanations.[30]

3. The Analysis of the Texts

In order to be able to prepare a proper semantic analysis of JBA a complete as possible database must be prepared, i.e. a Key Word in Context Concordance (KWIC) of the entire corpus as outlined above. From the material gathered to date, I would estimate the JBA corpus to be in the range of 500,000-700,000 words, a figure which would be significantly increased if we were to utilize more than one extant transmission of each tractate. The project's goal is to prepare the computerized database for semantic analysis. While a description of the techniques employed for this purpose lies outside the scope of this paper, a general overview can be given.

---

[26]For a general survey, v. S. Assaf, תקופת הגאונים וספרותה (Jerusalem 1955), pp. 133-222. The important work of B. M. Lewin, *Otzar Ha-Geonim*, 13 vols. (*Berakhot-Baba Meṣiʿa*) whose aim was to collect all of the Gaonic material according to the Talmudic tractates is still incomplete (see also H. Z. Taubes, אוצר הגאונים למסכת סנהדרין [Jerusalem 1966]; A. Kimmelman, "A Guide to Talmudic Commentary in the Gaonic Period", *Annual of the Institute for Research in Jewish Law*, 11-12 (1984-86), pp. 463-542 (Heb); B. M. Lewin, "Index of *Otzar Ha-Geonim* to the Tractates *Bava Batra* and *Hullin*", ibid., pp. 543-588 (Heb); T. Groner, *The Legal Methodology of Hai Gaon* [Chico 1985], pp. 185-187).

[27]The only scholar to study these words systematically was J. N. Epstein, "Notes on Post-Talmudic-Aramaic Lexicography", *JQR*, 12 (1921), pp. 299-390 [= *Studies*, 1, pp. 85-135]. Many additional words are discussed in his other works. The Gaonic literature is replete with replies to lexical queries from the Jews outside of Babylonia. See, e.g. Harkavy, p. 212f; Assaf, p. 155ff.

[28]See J. N. Epstein, *The Gaonic Commentary on the Order Toharot Attributed to Rav Hai Gaon* (Jerusalem 1982), Introduction, pp. xlviii-lxiii (Heb). The following are several examples: כודא haemorrhage after childbirth: לכודא אמרו רוח שאוחזת את האשה על המשכב אחר שתלד נקרא כודא Harkavy 23; מוצא (כלים פ"ט מ"ט) ...ובתלמוד (קיד' נב ע"ב) מוזא והוא פסולת של ירקות, *Gaonic Commentary* 17:12; ... דפקא והצלעות דפקי קורין אותן, ibid. 80:12.

[29]The explanations are composed either in Hebrew, Aramaic or Arabic (for an example of the last, see *Otzar Ha-Geonim, Berachot*, Responsa, pp. 102-114).

[30]See Epstein, *Studies*, 1, pp. 33-34. This can easily be seen in *Otzar Ha-Geonim, passim*, from the material collected by the editor, in the sections of Gaonic explanations.

The computer programs employed were developed for the Comprehensive Aramaic Lexicon (CAL) Project,[31] are written in C, and run under the UNIX operating system. The input is a paginated and line-numbered Aramaic text, and the output is a lem-file, i.e. a file containing on each line a word of text, its lexico-morphological analysis, and its coordinate. The lem-files can then be used to produce KWICs and other lists as desired. The elegance of the system lies in the simplicity of the lem-files, since these are ASCII files which can be updated easily and corrected on the basis of refinements as the project moves along.

4. The Outline Etymological Lexicon

Before embarking on this project I was of the opinion that the untapped lexical material of JBA would be considerably less than that of JPA. After all, the BT has been much more extensively studied than its Palestinian stepsister. In fact, while the opposite conclusion may not be true, it is no exaggeration to say that the number of lexical items not attested in the current dictionaries is easily in the many hundreds.[32] These are of several types:

a. *Words occurring in the (printed) texts but not given in the lexica.* After having prepared a list of the words attested for JBA in the current lexica, many additional JBA words of this type were located by simply canvassing the Talmud concordance of Kasowski.[33] Some of these words are given in the lexica as occurring in other Jewish Aramaic dialects,[34] while others are completely absent from all the dictionaries.[35] The tentative reason for this deficiency lies in the fact that since the time of Nathan b. Yeḥiel, the author of the *Aruch* (11th cent.), each lexicographer has utilised his predecessor's work as the basis of his own, adding more material from his own reading. This project, it seems, is the first attempt to undertake the entire process from scratch.

b. *Words occurring in the mss.* While both Kohut and Jastrow already employed the manuscript variants in *Diqduqe Soferim*[36] in their dictionaries and were

[31]The CAL Project was begun in 1985 and is also supported by the National Endowment for the Humanities. The programs were written under the direction of S. A. Kaufman.

[32]For a survey of the current dictionaries and their defects, see E. Y. Kutscher, "The Present State of Research into Mishnaic Hebrew (especially Lexicography) and its Tasks", *Archive of the New Dictionary of Rabbinic Literature*, 1 (1972), pp. 3-28 [Heb; English summary, pp. iii-x]. The total number of lexical items in JBA — including the Gaonic material — is approximately 7,500.

[33]Some examples: גנז itpe. [K 9:308; quoted in J 258 from Tg]; זרעא [K 12:336; quoted in J 414 from Tg and PT]; חפר [K 14:67; quoted in J 493 from Tg].

[34]Since "Jewish Aramaic" was not differentiated clearly into dialects, the dictionary authors often felt that a reference from one type of text was sufficient.

[35]E.g. גביא collection (*Pes* 113a(21; Col: גבייא).

[36]Rabbinowicz utilised the almost complete Munich Ms. — a late western European manuscript written in 1343 — as his main basis of comparison with the printed text. Variants from other — and generally superior — manuscripts, early prints, and early Rabbinic authorities are quoted in the notes.

able to clarify some words on the basis of these readings, this was not done in any systematic fashion.[37] Indeed, my work to date has shown that each tractate analyzed from manuscripts has contributed new words to the growing inventory of lexical items.[38]

c. *Words occurring in non-canonical sources.* Except for very rare instances, the Talmudic dictionaries do not quote JBA words from non-BT sources.[39] It was the achievement of the eminent Talmudist, J. N. Epstein, the outstanding lexicographer of JBA in modern times, to demonstrate the riches of the post-Sassanian material for the JBA vocabulary, viz. in the Gaonic writings, the incantation bowls, and the writings of Anan.[40] In his articles, hundreds of such words were uncovered and elucidated especially in light of Mandaic and Syriac.[41] Nevertheless, a rereading of these same texts has shown that many more words and meanings are found in them which were not noted by Epstein.[42]

The purpose of the OEL is to organise all of this material in a coherent manner along with the cognates from the related Aramaic dialects and the pertinent lexical discussions in the scholarly literature.[43] The practical aspect of this work is to establish lemmata for use in producing the lem-files, since the vagaries of orthography leave room for both morphological errors and confusion. At any given stage the OEL is used to produce and update the Outline Lexicon which is an essential component of the analytical computer program.

In spite of the large amount of material collected in this pioneering work, it is clear that much was left out, and this achievement, outstanding for its time, cannot be the basis of modern lexical work. Moreover, Rabbinowicz generally omitted orthographic variants.

[37]See e.g. in J: ברזניתא, טפיתא, כריהא.

[38]E.g. 2# ארדא "mast" *BB* 73a(8; Ms. H); בורא "uncultivated land" *BB* 168a(19; Ms. H).

[39]The only dictionary to quote the Gaonic sources to any degree is AC.

[40]See his *Studies*, where all of this scholar's lexicographic articles have now been collected (the non-Hebrew articles are given in a revised Hebrew translation and the original Hebrew articles are reprinted); id., *Gaonic Commentary* [op. cit., n. 28]. Many of the words discussed by him can be located by means of the indices.

[41]Epstein had a thorough knowledge of Mandaic literature, and in his articles he frequently elucidated unclear Mandaic words. Unfortunately, the authors of the *Mandaic Dictionary* seem to have been unaware of Epstein's contributions (e.g. there are no references to his important lexical article "Mandäische Glossen", *Archiv Orientalni* 17/2 (1950), pp. 165-169). I intend to deal elsewhere with Epstein's contributions to Mandaic studies. For Syriac note e.g. 2# אומצא "piece (of bread, meat)", פרהז "to warn", צפא "row".

[42]E.g. אפרא "meadow" HP 68:25, גובייריא "jujube" HG1 97:86, גורא "adultery" OH *Git* 197:25, דרדי "to consume" HG3 387:42, הנזמין "council" HG3 30:14 [Ros, IJ 98[37]], חבן itpe. "to be lazy" HG1 189:59. It should be noted that Epstein's aim was to deal with selected words and not to make a complete inventory of all the Gaonic vocabulary.

[43]For the literature until the 1930s see Krauss, *Addit.*, containing B. Geiger's invaluable notes which both explain the Persian loanwords in the Talmud and act as a corrective to Kohut's Persian excesses (see also the review of the *Aruch Completum* by W. Bacher, *ZDMG*, 47 [1893], pp. 487-514). A new comprehensive study of the Persian loanwords in JBA is being prepared by S. Shaked (see provisionally *Encyclopaedia Iranica*, II, pp. 259-261). Many words have also been treated by E. S. Rosenthal, IJ.

What then are the prospects for the successful completion of the dictionary in a reasonable amount of time? The author has now (August 1992) completed the lem-files for the entire BT, the incantation bowls and Anan's *Book of Commandments*. A great deal of the scattered Gaonic material has been read through and much lexical material excerpted. However, no final decision has been taken as to how to incorporate this large mass of material into the database in the most efficient manner. At some point, it will also be necessary to scan at least several of the other manuscripts of the BT, the Geniza fragments, and pre-Bomberg prints for real lexical items.

In the final analysis the really important work will be the semantic analysis of the database.[44] For a literature such as the BT, studied so intensively for over a millennium and possessing an extensive traditional and modern scholarly exegetical tradition, it will be nigh impossible to gather all of the pertinent secondary material or to assure that credit is always given to the first scholar who proposed a given explanation. Indeed, if what we hope for is not Utopia but a significant improvement over our present-day knowledge, then it is a realistic goal which can be achieved in a reasonable time frame. Utopian scholars may have the ultimate truth on their side, but their reluctance to publish their results only holds back progress and keeps other scholars in the dark.

The work on the dictionary was commenced in 1988, and it is my hope that within the decade a companion volume to my *Dictionary of Jewish Palestinian Aramaic* will be available to the scholarly world.

---

[44]Regarding the commonly occuring lexemes, this is probably one of the most neglected aspects of the current dictionaries which were implicitly written for the traditional Jewish scholar who had an intuitive knowledge of the text and utilised a dictionary for obscure and difficult words only and not for Talmudic neophytes and comparative Semitists. As an example, the reader may compare the following attested meanings for סלק pe. found in JBA with those given in the dictionaries: 1. to go up, ascend; 2. to go, come; 3. to immigrate from Babylonia to Eretz Israel; 4. to result, be reckoned; 5. to occur; 6. to be valid; 7. to agree with something; 8. to be successful; 9. to begin a discussion; 10. to be healed (of flesh); 11. to catch (of a dye).

Papyrus Amherst 63: A New Source for the Language, Literature, Religion, and History of the Aramaeans*

R. C. Steiner — Yeshiva University, N.Y.

When I submitted the title of this lecture to the conference organizers, I had quotation marks around the word "Aramaeans", for I do not believe that everyone who speaks Aramaic deserves to be called an Aramaean. I find now, however, that the quotation marks have been removed, presumably in an attempt to make me feel at home here in England. Somebody wants me to believe that anyone who speaks English, even an American, can call himself an Englishman.

Be that as it may, the document discussed in the present paper, papyrus Amherst 63 (the Aramaic text in demotic script) has an impeccably British pedigree. The papyrus was originally owned by — and still bears the name of — an Englishman: Lord Amherst of Hackney. Even after being sold to J. P. Morgan, it was housed for many years (1913 - 1947) at the British Museum, where it was studied by an eminent British Egyptologist, Sir Herbert Thompson. For these reasons alone, this document would be an appropriate topic for this conference.

It is true that a document discovered in the nineteenth century would not ordinarily belong at a conference devoted to "new sources", but this document is different because it remained largely unknown and undeciphered until the past decade.

And what a source it is! It is filled with new information about a community of Aramaic-speaking exiles in Egypt — its language, literature, history, and religion. I would like to point out a major contribution of the papyrus in each of these areas.

Language

Any literary text as long as this one can be expected to make important contributions to Northwest Semitic lexicography, and this text has already begun to fulfill its promise, shedding considerable light on at least half a dozen rare Biblical and Rabbinic lexical items. In some cases, Amherst 63 attests these lexical items in revealing contexts which resolve a controversy about meaning. Thus, our text corroborates the view that *kāśītā* in Deut 32:15 means "you became fat" rather than

*I would like to thank the Texts Program of the National Endowment for the Humanities (an independent federal agency of the United States Government), the Littauer Foundation, and Yeshiva University for their generous support of my work on this text.

"you kicked/rebelled",[1] the view that *ʿakšûb* in Ps 140:4 means "viper" rather than "spider, tarantula",[2] and the view that *sanwērîm* in Gen 19:11 and II Kings 6:18 means "blinding light" rather than "blindness".[3] In other cases, it confirms a questionable by-form: *ḳiṭran*[4] "pitch" alongside *ʿiṭrān*, *rî* "moisture" alongside *rəwāyāh*, *ṣawʾar* "neck"[5] alongside *ṣawwar*,[6] and possibly *šərošî* "caning, lashes" alongside *sərošî*.

However, the most interesting contribution of the text in the area of language is the light it sheds on the nature of Qumran Aramaic and its relationship to colloquial Aramaic. It is well known[7] that the Genesis Apocryphon contains quite a few colloquial forms which are characteristic of the Palestinian targums — forms like *tmn* "there" and *kmn* "how" (for *tmh* and *kmh*), *ʾḥwy* "his brother" (for *ʾḥwhy*), relative-genitive *d-* (for *dy*), *ʾn* "if" (for *hn*), *ʾaphel* (for *haphel*), and possibly *bʿwn* "they sought", *ʾtwn* "they came" (for *bʿw*, *ʾtw*). There is no serious difference of opinion about the identity of most of these forms, but there is disagreement about their implications. What do these forms reveal about the language of the Genesis Apocryphon? Is it a transitional dialect of Aramaic close to the vernacular, as Fitzmyer[8] believes, or is it Standard Literary Aramaic coloured or contaminated by

---

[1]R. C. Steiner and C. F. Nims, "You Can't Offer Your Sacrifice and Eat It Too: A Polemical Poem from the Aramaic Text in Demotic Script", *JNES* 43 (1984), p. 101.
[2]This is an old controversy, pitting LXX, Peshiṭta, Avot de-Rabbi Nathan, and Ḳimḥi against the targum to Psalms, the Qumran Psalms scroll, Saadia, and Rashi.
[3]E. A. Speiser, *Genesis* (Garden City 1964), pp. 139-40.
[4]E. Y. Kutscher, *Studies in Galilean Aramaic* (Ramat Gan 1976), p. 33.
[5]Cf. S. P. Vleeming and J. W. Wesselius, "Betel the Saviour", *JEOL* 28 (1985), p. 134, where, however, the *e* = ʾ is taken to be a secondary phonetic development. The form צואר has hitherto been unknown in Aramaic outside of BA, and even there it is only a *ketib*. As a result, some scholars have claimed that the BA *ketib* comes from Hebrew; see, for example, F. R. Blake, *A Resurvey of Hebrew Tenses* (Rome 1951), p.94; E. Y. Kutscher, *The Language and Linguistic Background of the Isaiah Scroll* [Hebrew] (Jerusalem 1959), pp. 141-42; M. Sokoloff, *The Targum to Job from Qumran Cave XI* (Ramat Gan 1974), p. 166. This claim is based on the assumption that the Proto-Semitic form is *ṣawwar*, and that the Hebrew א is merely a *mater lectionis*. The evidence of Amherst 63 suggests that the proto-form is *ṣawʾar*, as maintained by other scholars; see Th. Nöldeke, *Mandäische Grammatik* (Halle 1875), pp. 127-28; H. Bauer and P. Leander, *Historische Grammatik der hebräischen Sprache des Alten Testamentes* (Halle 1922), p. 548; J. Blau, "Short Philological Notes on the Inscription of Mešaʿ", *Maarav* 2 (1979-80), p. 148, n. 25; K. Beyer, *Die aramäischen Texte vom Toten Meer* (Göttingen 1984), p. 675.
[6]Not *ṣəwar*, pace Vleeming and Wesselius, "Betel", 134; cf. Nöldeke, *Mandäische*, p. 127-28, n. 2.
[7]Thanks to E..Y. Kutscher, "The Language of the 'Genesis Apocryphon'", *Scripta Hierosolymitana* 4 (1957), pp. 8-9, J. A. Fitzmyer, *The Genesis Apocryphon of Qumran Cave I* (Rome 1966), p. 100, P. Grelot, Review of J.A. Fitzmyer, *The Genesis Apocryphon of Qumran Cave I*, *RB* 74 (1967), p. 102, and A. Diez Macho, *El Targum* (Madrid 1972), p. 69.
[8]*Genesis Apocryphon*, 2nd ed., pp. 23-24. The term "transitional dialect" was borrowed by Fitzmyer from Kutscher ("Language", p. 6), and, as a result, Diez Macho (*El Targum*, p. 47) assumed that the position of these two scholars was identical. However, Kutscher nowhere implies that the language of the Genesis Apocryphon is close to the vernacular. He seems to be thinking rather of gradual change in the literary language due to the increasing influence of the spoken language.

careless intrusions from the vernacular, as Greenfield,[9] Diez Macho,[10] Kaufman[11] and others have argued?

Before bringing Amherst 63 into the matter, we need to examine some of the practical consequences of this controversy — or, to use an Aramaic term, the *nāpəḳā minnah.* The "transition theory" implies that variability in the text is a reasonably accurate reflection of variability in speech. A sociolinguist of the variationist school would be justified, according to this view, in writing variable rules based on the data in the text; a historical linguist would be justified in speaking of a sound change in progress. Take, for example, proclitic *d-*, which occurs only eight times in the Genesis Apocryphon alongside almost 100 examples of *dy*.[12] Based on these frequencies, Svedlund concludes that "the shift from *dy* to the proclitic *d* seems to have been in its early stages at the time of the writing of G[enesis] A[pocryphon]".[13] Somewhat more cautiously, Diez Merino writes that "Qumrán supone un estadio intermedio del paso de /dy/ a /d-/";[14] he explicitly indicates that he is discussing a change in the spoken language by placing *dy* and *d-* between slashes, in phonemic notation.

The "contamination theory", on the other hand, implies that variability in the text is not an accurate reflection of variability in speech. According to this view, the replacement of *dy* by *d-* may well have gone to completion long before the writing of the Genesis Apocryphon.

In the matter of *dy*/*d-*, Amherst 63 settles the matter rather unambiguously in favor of the "contamination theory". The scribe almost always writes the relative-genitive particle without a *y* or a word-divider, and he generally dispenses with demotic *aleph*[15] as well. This evidence is all the more remarkable inasmuch as Amherst 63 seems to be at least two centuries older than the Genesis Apocryphon.

Even when Amherst 63 agrees with the Genesis Apocryphon in exhibiting variability, the relative frequencies may be very different. When we examine the plural perfects of final-weak verbs in the Genesis Apocryphon, we find that there are twelve cases without suffixed *-n* and two possible cases with suffixed *-n*: *bʿwn* and *ʾtwn*.[16] Here again, an advocate of the "transition theory" might speak of an early stage of development, since the suffix occurs only fourteen percent of the time. But in Amherst 63, the suffix occurs fifty percent of the time.[17] By the time of the Genesis

[9]J.C. Greenfield, "Standard Literary Aramaic", *Actes du premier congrès international de linguistique sémitique et chamito-sémitique* (The Hague 1974), p. 286; id., "Aramaic and its Dialects", *Jewish Languages* (Cambridge, Mass. 1978), p. 36.
[10]*El Targum*, pp. 47ff.
[11]S. A. Kaufman, "The Job Targum from Qumran", *JAOS* 93 (1973), p. 326.
[12]Fitzmyer, *Genesis Apocryphon*, 2nd ed., p. 27.
[13]G. Svedlund, *The Aramaic Portions of Pesiqta de Rab Kahana* (Uppsala 1974), p. 14.
[14]L. Diez Merino, "Uso del d/dy en el arameo de Qumrán", *Aula Orientalis* 1 (1983), p. 82.
[15]It is usually assumed that the scribe intended this sign to indicte the presence of a vowel.
[16]A. Tal, "Revadim baʾaramit hayehudit šel ʾereṣ yiśraʾel", *Lešonenu* 43 (1978-79), pp. 171-72.
[17]XVII/9 *hww*, XVII/14 *dlhwwn*, XVIII/1 *dlhwwn*, XIX/10 *ʿnwn*, XX/5 *nsw*, XXI/4 *nsw*, XXI/1 *w(ʾ)twn*, XXII/3 *nsw*.

Apocryphon, the frequency in the vernacular was probably higher, perhaps even 100%.

Another crucial difference between the two theories concerns Palestinian forms which do not appear at all in the Qumran scrolls. Are such forms to be considered later than the ones which do? According to the "transition theory", the answer is yes, but the evidence suggests otherwise. Already in the Persian period, the Hermopolis letters and the Proverbs of Aḥiqar exhibit *pael* and *haphel* infinitives with prefixed *m*-, as Greenfield[18] and Kutscher[19] have pointed out. If these forms are not used at Qumran, it can only be because they were rejected as being too colloquial. Amherst 63 shows that there are other such features which remained totally submerged, without a single slip to betray them: deletion of word-final *n* preceded by diphthong *ay*,[20] omission of *l*- before the infinitive,[21] the *mn* + participle construction,[22] and the *maqṭôlī* pattern for verbal nouns.[23]

Why should Amherst 63 be so much more revealing than the Qumran scrolls? After all, it too is a literary text, and it ought to be written in Standard Literary Aramaic; indeed, Greenfield's classic article on the subject labels it as such.[24] Part of the answer is that it is a transcribed text. Transcriptions and loanwords are extremely effective in piercing the veil which our well-trained scribes have placed over the vernacular. Let me illustrate this with two brief examples.

The first example concerns the Aramaic word *ḳlḳlt*ʾ "rubbish heap" in line 22 of the Tell Fekherye inscription. Greenfield and Shaffer have devoted a delightful study to this word.[25] They note that the word is attested in this fully reduplicated form in the Targum to Prophets and other targumic texts but that "the usual form ... for this word in both the Palestinian and Babylonian dialects of Aramaic, as well as Syriac and Mandaic is *qīqlā* in the absolute form and *qīqiltā* in the determined form".[26] Finally, they point to the attestation of an Akkadian *kiqillutu* with the same meaning: "Of linguistic importance is the fact that the word *kiqillutu* is a loan word in Neo-Assyrian from Aramaic, and this loan word follows the form *qīqlā*, *qīqiltā* known to

[18]J. C. Greenfield, "Dialect Traits in Early Aramaic" [Hebrew], *Lešonenu* 32 (1967-68), pp. 367-368; id., "The Dialects of Early Aramaic", *JNES* 37 (1978), pp. 96-97.
[19]E. Y. Kutscher, "The Hermopolis Papyri", *IOS* 1 (1971), pp. 107-108.
[20]Cf. Kutscher, *Studies*, pp. 43-51.
[21]See W. B. Stevenson, *Grammar of Palestinian Jewish Aramaic* (Oxford 1924), p. 53 (where, however, the statement about BA is not correct); J. M. Lindenberger, *The Aramaic Proverbs of Ahiqar* (Baltimore 1983), p. 111; J. Naveh and S. Shaked, *Amulets and Magic Bowls* (Jerusalem 1985), p. 33); A. Tal, "Hammaqor leṣurotaw berovde ha'aramit hayehudit be'ereṣ yiśra'el", *Hebrew Language Studies Presented to Zeev Ben-Hayyim* (Jerusalem 1983), pp. 207-208.
[22]Cf. Kutscher, *Studies*, pp. 51-58. The construction is used adverbially, i.e., in circumstantial clauses. It may have developed by analogy with the *mn*+*dy*+perfect construction, attested in BA.
[23]M. Sokoloff, "The Noun-Pattern MQṬWLY in Middle Western Aramaic" [Hebrew], *ʿErkhe hammillon heḥadaš lesifrut ḥazal*, vol. 2 (Ramat Gan 1974), pp. 74-84.
[24]Greenfield, "Standard Literary Aramaic", p. 284.
[25]J. C. Greenfield and A. Shaffer, "*Qlqlt*ʾ, *Tubkinnu*, Refuse Tips and Treasure Trove", *Anatolian Studies* 33 (1983), pp. 123-29.
[26]Ibid., p. 123.

us from later Aramaic dialects. Thus both the more literary *qlqlt*ʾ has been found in the Tell Fekherye inscription and the more colloquial *kiqillutu* in Neo-Assyrian texts. This is added evidence for the use of Aramaic as a spoken language in Assyria".

They could have added that it is also evidence for the antiquity and amazing tenacity of the distinction between written and spoken Aramaic. It appears that well-trained scribes succeeded in suppressing a colloquial form for a millennium until the old norms broke down in Late Aramaic. We know this now thanks to a cuneiform scribe whose career did not depend upon mastering the correct, historical spelling of this word. There is a certain amount of poetic justice in this example. Scholars are always turning to the *sēpiru*, the Aramaic scribe, to find out how Akkadian was pronounced; for once we can thank a *ṭupšarru*, an Akkadian scribe, for information about the pronunciation of Aramaic.

The second example is ἐφφαθά "be opened" in Mark 7:34. Here we learn from a Greek scribe that the assimilation of reflexive-passive *t* had already taken place in colloquial Aramaic — assuming, of course, that this is not Hebrew.[27] Here again, no Aramaic scribe would have been caught dead writing such a form in Palestine during that period.[28]

It is thus completely natural that we should find colloquial pronunciations appearing much earlier in Amherst 63 than in normally written Aramaic texts. We should make every effort to use this foreign scribe to outsmart the native scribes who make life so difficult for us.

Literature

Amherst 63 concludes with a story about the Assyrian king Ashurbanipal and his brother, Shamash-shum-ukin — a story which Greenfield has called the "Tale of Two Brothers". This story is, in all likelihood, an ancestor of the Sardanapallus legend known from Greek and Latin sources, whose fiery death scene was the basis for a tragedy by Byron (*Sardanapalus*) and a well-known painting by Delacroix ("The Death of Sardanapalus"). As far as I know, this is the only extant ancient Near Eastern composition, other than the Bible, which has served (at least, indirectly) as the inspiration for modern European literature and art.[29]

---

[27]See S. Morag, "*Ἐφφαθά* (Mark vii. 34): Certainly Hebrew, Not Aramaic?", *JSS* 17 (1972), pp. 198-202 and the literature cited there.

[28]A possible exception is cited by M. McNamara, "The Spoken Aramaic of First Century Palestine", *Proceedings of the Irish Biblical Association* 2 (1977), p. 119; but cf. Beyer, *Die aramäischen Texte*, pp. 464, 466, and 672 s.v. *pšr*. Later Palestinian scribes do record the assimilation; cf. Morag, "*Ἐφφαθά*"; S.E. Fassberg, *A Grammar of the Palestinian Targum Fragments from the Cairo Genizah* (Atlanta 1990), pp. 68-69 and 98, fn. 61; M. Bar-Asher, "Two Grammatical Phenomena in Palestinian Syriac" [Hebrew], *Meḥqarim belašon* (Jerusalem 1987), pp. 114-117; id., "Le syro-palestinien: études grammaticales", *JA* 276 (1988), 50-53.

[29]The tale of Semiramis inspired a tragedy by Voltaire, an opera by Rossini, and a ballet by Gluck, but the original (Aramaic?) version is not extant. Aḥiqar, on the other hand, is extant in its original Aramaic version or something close to it. However, according to J. M. Lindenberger, in *The Old*

This text affords the rare opportunity to study the process by which oriental lore reached the West. Comparison of the Aramaic story with cuneiform sources shows that it is basically a piece of pro-Ashurbanipal political propaganda masquerading as popular history.[30] In Ctesias' Greek version this rather sober narrative has metamorphosed into a legend about a transvestite king. The transformation is so thorough that were it not for the (misapplied) name Saradanapallus and the death scene, there would be no reason to suspect any connection between the two narratives. All of this should provide rich fodder for literary historians and cultural anthropologists with a psychoanalytic bent.

History

In this area, there are some exciting new discoveries to report. I have deciphered a passage reporting a conversation between the king and the young spokesman of a newly-arrived a group of *š.m*^{m} *r̄r̄*[.] ⸢*y*⸣*.n*^{m} "Samaritans". (It is not yet clear whether the king in question is the king of Rash, the original homeland of our community, or the king of Egypt.) The king, whoever he is, inquires about the boy's origin; the boy replies that he is from ⸢*y*⸣*hẇt* (Judea), that his brothers are from *š.mryn.*^{m} (Samaria), and that his sister is now being brought from *y.*⸢*eir*⸣*wš.rm*⸢*.*⸣^{m} (Jerusalem). The king welcomes them and instructs the boy to pick up a *qab* of wheat on his shoulder, predicting that he will achieve great wealth in his new land. What we have here is nothing less than an account of the arrival in exile of men from the Land of Israel — the only such account ever found. That this account was considered very important in antiquity as well is clear from its key position within the papyrus (immediately preceding the sacred marriage ceremony; see below) and from its opening words: "with my own two eyes I watched ...".

The newly arrived group consists only of males and is characterized as a *gayis* "troop" — a word used also in the Tale of Two Brothers. In other words, they are soldiers. Either the Rashans lived among soldiers from Judea and Samaria or (if this is a story about the founding of the Rashan community in Egypt) they were themselves soldiers from Judea and Samaria. Either way, one gets the impression that the Rashan community is somehow connected with the Elephantine community. We are probably dealing, then, with a text produced by the Aramaeans of Syene, the pagan neighbors of the Elephantine Jews, as conjectured by Vleeming and Wesselius.[31]

Testament Pseudepigrapha, J. H. Charlesworth, ed., vol. 2 (Garden City 1985), p. 492, its "influence on Western culture in general has been very slight"; with the exception of a Roman mosaic and Norman French fable, "Ahiqar does not appear to have had any impact on Western literature and art".

[30]For the time being, see R. C. Steiner and C. F. Nims, "Ashurbanipal and Shamash-shum-ukin: A Tale of Two Brothers from the Aramaic Text in Demotic Script", *RB* 92 (1985), pp. 61-65.

[31]"Betel", p. 111.

It is also clear that the Rashans did not go directly from Rash to Syene; they made a stopover on the way. All of the evidence points to Bethel as the place. In one of the dialogues dealing with the history of the community, a man relates that he was forced to abandon his home town — a magnificent "city full of ivory houses (*p̄tȳ š.n*^{m} = *bty šn*)"[32] — when its spring dried up (XI/6-11). The dialogue is immediately followed by the paganized version of Psalm 20 (XI/11-19), which has been linked by Weinfeld[33] and Zevit[34] to Jeroboam's temple at Bethel. Indeed, the occurrence of the name *Bethel* in this prayer is the only one of the nine occurrences in the papyrus which is not written with the Egyptian god determinative. It is not impossible that the priest who dictated the text told the scribe that this occurrence referred to the city of Bethel rather than the god. It appears, therefore, that the drought-stricken city described in the dialogue is Bethel, a city which was indeed renowned for its "ivory houses" - the *bty šn* of Amos 3:14-15. A migration from Bethel to Egypt caused by the drying up of a spring would, if it included native Israelites, conform perfectly to Hosea's prophesy that Ephraim's "fountain shall be parched, his spring dried up" (13:15) and that the resulting famine would lead the Ephraimites to return to Egypt (9:2-3,6). Another possible reference to Bethel comes in a broken context where the words *y.š.k*^{m} and *ʿ.kryk*^{m} occur in close proximity. It is difficult to resist the temptation to interpret the first word as *yšḳ* "will kiss" and the second as *ʿglyk* "your calves", alluding to the practice, derided by Hosea (13:2), of kissing the golden calves at the Bethel sanctuary (V/12). Finally, the text refers to the god Bethel both as Eshe(m)-Bethel (XV/14,15) and as "Resident of Hamath (*t.r̄ ḥ.m.t*^{m})" (VIII/6,10), thereby establishing another link with the city of Bethel, in which colonists from Hamath worshipped a god by the name of Ashima (II Kings 17:28-30).[35]

How did these Aramaeans get to Bethel? There is substantial new evidence indicating that their original homeland, called *rš* and *ʾrš* in the papyrus, is the land between Babylonia and Elam which the Assyrians called Rashu and Arashu.[36] It appears that Ashurbanipal, who captured Rashu in his campaign against Elam, deported its inhabitants to the Assyrian province of Samaria, like the Elamites from Susa mentioned in Ezra 4:9-10. Most or all of them wound up in Bethel, joining the foreign colonists settled there by earlier Assyrian kings.

---

[32]Aramaic *b* is occasionally rendered with demotic *p* in the papyrus, e.g., VIII/5 *i.p.ẖ.n*^{m}=*ṭbẖn* "butchers", XV/6 *t̄t.hp* ⸢*g*⸣ =*ddhb* "of gold".

[33]M. Weinfeld, "The Pagan Version of Psalm 20:2-6: Vicissitudes of a Psalmodic Creation in Israel and its Neighbors" [Hebrew], *EI* 18 (1985), p. 131.

[34]Z. Zevit, "The Common Origin of the Aramaicized Prayer to Horus and of Psalm 20", *JAOS* 110 (1990), p. 224.

[35]This last point calls to mind the Vincent–Albright theory that the Elephantine community came from the vicinity of Bethel; W.F. Albright, *Archaeology and the Religion of Israel*, 5th edition (Baltimore 1968), pp. 171- 173. One of the pillars on which that theory rests is the conjecture that Eshem-Bethel of the Elephantine papyri is to be identified with Ashima.

[36]See now R. C. Steiner, "The Aramaic Text in Demotic Script: The Liturgy of a New Year's Festival Imported from Bethel to Syene by Exiles from Rash," *JAOS* 111 (1991), pp. 362-363.

Religion

It appears from the account in II Kings 17 that the earlier colonists had taken over Jeroboam's temple, where one of the priests, returned from exile at their request, "taught them how to worship the Lord" — presumably a reference to the temple service. If our reconstruction is correct, that temple service included a northern version of Psalm 20, which was later transmitted to the Rashans in paganized form. Even in that altered form, the prayer still retains Israelite divine names, as do the prayers which follow it in column XII.

This Israelite influence is rather superficial. For the most part the religion reflected in the papyrus is not Israelite but pagan, with rituals resembling those of the Babylonian Akitu festival. The papyrus includes the first complete record of a sacred marriage ceremony in a West Semitic language and the first attestation of the actual marriage declaration of this rite in any Semitic language. This is the only extant liturgy of a pagan festival celebrated in the Land of Israel in Biblical times.

The ceremony begins with the celebrant's arrival at the gate leading to the courtyard of the New Year's chapel; he stops there and recites a blessing (III/6-8). A voice from within calls out to him to enter the courtyard (III/8-9). After he enters and washes his hands (III/10-11), the statue of Marah (= Nana, Nanai), the Queen of Rash, is brought into the assembly of the gods (IVA/9-10). The gods rise from their thrones and give the order for her to be seated among them (IVA/11-13). Each of the assembled gods is asked to bless the king (IVA/15-21, VII/1-7). As in the Akitu festival, the king makes a negative confession (VI/3, 9), and is told not to be afraid, that the god will destroy his enemies and bless him (VI/12-17). Sheep are slaughtered and turned into smoke, while sixty singers lift their voices and sixty temple servitors burn myrrh and frankincense (VII/7-13). The chief god is invited to feast on lamb and become inebriated with wine, to the accompaniment of sweet harp and lyre music (XII/1-10). Spoon-stuffed ducks are brought to the table on ivory platters (XV/10-12).

The high point of the festival is the sacred marriage ceremony. The king initiates the rite by declaring: "Nana, thou art my wife" (XVI/7). "In thy bridal chamber, a priest sings" — he continues — "Nanai, bring near to me thy lips" (XVI/8-9). The king and the goddess keep a vigil outside the bridal chamber, a bower erected for the occasion in a cedar grove (XI/1-3, XVII/2-3), with music from a nearby grave preventing them from dozing off (XVI/9-11); one is reminded of the condemnation of grove and grave in Isa 65:3-4. At the appointed hour, the king invites the goddess to enter the bridal chamber: "My beloved, enter the door into our house. With my mouth, consort of our lord, let me kiss thee" (XVI/12). They enter the "perfumed hideaway", where the goddess is lain upon an embroidered bedspread (XVI/13-14). The ceremony culminates in an exchange of blessings between Nanai and Baal of Heaven and a promise by the king to rebuild the ruined capital of Rash (XVI/15-19).

We may recall that, according to II Kings 17:33, the people deported by the Assyrians to Samaria "worshipped the Lord, while worshipping their own gods", including, for example, Ashima of Hamath. However, the reliability of this report has been called into question by Talmon. According to him, "[this] tradition ... is not at all objective historical testimony".[37] It is therefore worth noting that the Biblical record is completely corroborated by Amherst 63. By the time the Rashans migrated to Egypt, they worshipped both Eshem-Bethel, the Resident of Hamath, and, *lehavdil*, the God of Israel.

[37]S. Talmon, "Biblical Tradition on the Early History of the Samaritans" [Hebrew], *Eretz Shomron* (Jerusalem 1973), p. 27.

Some Observations on Word Formation in Samaritan Aramaic: The *qiṭṭūl* Pattern[1]

Abraham Tal - Tel Aviv University

A well established commonplace in Semitic linguistics maintains — in principle with good reason — that nominal patterns are, or at least were, connected with certain categories of meaning. Thus, for example, the Hebrew pattern מִקְטָל designates the location of an event or an action, etc., like מזרח, east, מפרץ, bay, etc.; קַטָּל designates professionals, such as סַפָּן, sailor, טַבָּח cook, and so forth. This principle is very often contradicted by such words as מבטא, expression, מבחן, test, מספק, doubt, etc. Nevertheless, the nominal patterns are usually associated with meaning categories, in the same manner in which the so-called verbal conjugations (a not very apt equivalent for the Hebrew בניין) are held to denote particular kinds of action.

In my work on the Dictionary of SA I was often faced with the problem of classifying nouns. In order to do this properly, I found it necessary to first understand the phonological particularities of SA and how they affect the morphology of the language and, naturally, its morpho-semantics. In the following I shall examine some facets of the nominal system of SA.

The grammatical description of SA suffers from a considerable flaw, stemming from the circumstance of its extinction as a spoken language. From the XIth century on, it was replaced by Arabic in all respects, with the exception of the liturgy, in which, similarly to Hebrew, the use of Aramaic persisted. As a result, any information regarding the phonologic structure of these two languages is necessarily inferred from the pronunciation of prayers and of the Pentateuch in the synagogal service.

The problem is that the extent of Aramaic prayers in the contemporary prayer book is very limited and can hardly provide us with the necessary material for a linguistic description of the Aramaic compositions handed down to our generation. The Aramaic Targum of the Pentateuch used by the Samaritans, as well as their Aramaic Midrash called Tibåt Marqe, were totally abandoned. Contemporary Samaritans have no contact with these two compositions, and, consequently, the main sources of knowledge can be analyzed only in their 'consonantal' representation. Therefore, the only reliable source of evidence regarding the vocalization of SA remains the recitation of the few Aramaic prayers still used at present in the Samaritan liturgy.[2]

[1] Abbreviations: m = Mishnah; MH = Mishnaic Hebrew; SA = Samaritan Aramaic; SH = Samaritan Hebrew; SP = Samaritan Pentateuch; ST = Samaritan Targum; TM = Tibåt Marqe.

[2] Nearly all of them have been reproduced in phonetic transcription by Ben-Ḥayyim in his *Literary and Oral Traditions of the Samaritans* (henceforth LOT), vol. III/b, (Jerusalem 1967).

Attempts have been made by the Samaritans to "improve" the situation. Several Targumic manuscripts (dating from the XIIIth century on) have been partially supplied with various marks intended mainly to distinguish between homographs. However, no systematic means of reproducing the pronunciation, comparable with the Syriac or the Jewish systems, has ever been used in this kind of literature.[3] Recently, the late Samaritan priest Yaʿaqov ben Uzzi made an interesting attempt to provide a manuscript of TM with vocalization marks taken from the Tiberian system! As the manuscript in question is a part of the library of the late Izhak Ben-Zvi, I suspect it was produced at his request. Needless to say, the value of Yaʿaqov ben Uzzi's vocalization is very limited, since he had no clear tradition of pronunciation on which to rely for this particular composition. Of course, I do not accuse him of inventing a purely imaginary reading of this midrash. Actually, I think he reconstructed a vocalization in accordance with what he knew from parallel forms occurring in the liturgy. Nevertheless, not everything deserves rejection and, used with proper care, this evidence should also be considered.

Another important source of evidence is the recitation of the Pentateuch. This has been, and remains, the most stable tradition within the community, carefully cultivated during the course of generations. Two reservations would seem to contest the value of this evidence. First, it is Hebrew evidence, not Aramaic. Second, it is the contemporary pronunciation of the Samaritans, and apparently nothing certifies its value as an indication of the ancient pronunciation. As for the first reservation, Ben-Ḥayyim's investigations have proved that Aramaic and Hebrew shared the same phonological structure in ancient Shekhem.[4] As far as the second reservation is concerned, there are grounds for assuming that very few changes occurred in the pronunciation of the Pentateuch. The great Samaritan grammarian of the twelfth century, Abu-Isḥaq Ibrahim Ibn Maruth, in his *Kitāb at-Tawṭiyya*, describes a linguistic system, prevalent during his time, very similar to what is in use today.[5] This fact suggests that it is not unreasonable to assume that no drastic changes took place from the third or fourth centuries to the twelfth either. Thus, the foregoing reservations ought not to preclude the tentative consideration of the recitation of the Pentateuch as evidence for the vocalic structure of fourth century Aramaic.

Within the limits described above I have investigated the graphic sequence *CCwC* (קטול) in order to discover the nominal patterns it includes and the semantic areas in which it functions. The present paper will treat this sequence insofar as it represents the ancient pattern קְטוּל with its important role in Aramaic grammar.

---

[3]This does not refer to the vocalization system used for the Hebrew Pentateuch of the Samaritans. For a description see LOT V (Jerusalem 1977), pp. 4 ff.

[4]LOT V, p. 256.

[5]Published and translated with commentary by Z. Ben-Ḥayyim in LOT I (Jerusalem 1957), pp.4-127.

The evolution of Samaritan Hebrew and Aramaic phonology caused great changes in the morphology. A remarkable process of de-phonemization of the vowels *o* and *u* put both in complementary distribution: *o* occurs in closed syllables, *u* in open ones.[6] Consequently, a process of fusion evolved, and different patterns merged into one; former צִפּוֹר and שִׁקּוּץ now belong to the same class: *ṣibbor* and *šiqqoṣ* respectively, and so do Hebrew loan-words, frequent in the SA vocabulary, like *gibbor*, *rimmon*, etc. Their plurals have *u* indiscriminately: *ṣibbūrəm*, *šiqqūṣəm*, etc. This systemic process considerably enlarged the domain of the קִטּוּל pattern. The following are cases of non-systemic changes which also contributed greatly to the expansion of קִטּוּל.

1. קִטּוּל and קָטוּל (originally short vowel: qaṭūl)

An evident convert to קִטּוּל was the קָטוּל pattern, which in Hebrew is dominated by the passive participle of Qal, e.g. לָמוּד = taught, accustomed. This form competes with the newly created (probably in post-Biblical times) לִמּוּד = taught, frequent in MH with the same meaning (mTer. 4:3). Similarly, in SA *ålūfəm* (pl. of *ålof)* and *illūfəm* (pl. of *illof)* concur in the sense of 'used, accustomed': *ik dat illof* = 'the way you are used to'.[7] *šibbu* (initially *šibbuʿ*) is the Samaritan pronunciation of שבוע (e.g. Gen 29:27) when it designates *a week* or a group of *seven years* (the vowel *u* is retained in an open syllable which has lost its final guttural). In the same manner שְׁבוּעַיִם is pronounced *šibbuwwå'əm* (Lev 12:5). However, this change did not affect the name of Pentecost שָׁבוּעוֹת (Exod 34:22) which remains *šåbā'ot*, and thus both traditions coexist. The same is true with regard to צפון, *north*, for which the Aramaic form was adopted: *ṣibbūna* (Gen 13:14), although the proper name בעל צפון remained *bāl ṣåfon* (Exod 14:2).[8]

2. קִטּוּל and קְטוֹל

Jewish Aramaic תְּקוֹף, *vigour, force,* represented in SA by the vocalization תקוף in TM (the *qameṣ* represents the *a* vowel that replaced the ancient shewa;[9] see below) also occurs in the form *tiqqof* in the liturgy. So too, the pronunciation of אֵזוֹב (Exod 12:22) and אֵפוֹד (Exod 28:4) is *izzob* and *ibbod* respectively. Since both are Hebrew loanwords, there is little doubt that their pronunciation was similar in SA. And so too, דְּרוֹר (Lev 25:10), *release from servitude,* is pronounced *dirror,* and its equivalent חרור (probably *irror*) in the ST. The same process occurred in שְׁאוֹל,

[6] LOT V, p. 30.

[7] LOT III/b, p. 44.

[8] *Ṣåfon* is the Hebrew-Canaanite form, as attested by the El-Amarna *ṣapuna*. However, MH too gave preference to the Aramaic form (mSanh. 2:6).

[9] The Samaritan phonology does not tolerate shewa: LOT V, pp. 37-40.

vocalized this way in Onqelos (Deut 32:22), which became *šiyyol* in the Samaritan liturgy (in this case the doubled *yy* is to be considered a consonantal glide designed to separate the sequence of vowels that resulted from the drop of the *aleph* in *šēʾol*). The replacement of a simple consonant following a full vowel by a double consonant preceded by a short vowel (i.e. the occasional substitution for an open syllable of a closed syllable, formed by the gemination of the following consonant, which naturally involved a shortening of the vowel: Cv: = CvCC), is an aspect of the general tendency of SA, as well as of SH, to alternate simple and double consonants. This tendency is well reflected in the twofold conjugation of Hebrew *Piʿel: sāfər* (Num 23:10) vs. *tēbaqqəš* (Gen 37:15), in the unconditioned interchange between the passive participle *qəṭīl* (*lēqəṭ*) with the adjective *qaṭṭīl (laqqəṭ),*[10] in the free variation of the Aramaic infinitive *mētor* (infinitive of *twr* = to watch) and *mittor*[11] etc.

On the other hand, the same tendency acted at times in the opposite direction: original קִטּוֹל nouns lost their gemination and left the domain of this pattern. One of the most natural candidates for this transformation was the verbal noun זימון *meeting,* pronounced *zīmon*, undoubtedly connected with the non-doubled variant of *ʾitpaʿʿal: izdāmån.* In both, the originally short vowel was lengthened according to the "compensation rule" mentioned above. Incidentally, this very verb has the same ungeminated form in Jewish Aramaic and in post-Biblical Hebrew. Thus זימון joined other *qīṭol* forms, such as ניצוץ *nīṣoṣ* 'spark'; נימוס 'practice'; מיסון 'middle' (Greek loanword: μέσος), etc.

Loss of gemination produced various affiliations of former קִטּוֹל forms with other noun-patterns. In the now open syllable the original short vowel could no longer be maintained and, unlike the case of *zīmon*, was reduced to *shewa* and a new קְטוֹל form was produced. Since *shewa* was replaced by a full vowel in Samaritan (see above), the form finally became either *qēṭol* or *qāṭol.* In the latter case, the new form merged with the well-known "nomen agentis" frequent in every Aramaic dialect. For example, פִּגּוּל 'abomination', became *fāgol* in Lev 7:18, reflected in the Aramaic of TM, according to ben Ozzi's punctuation: פַּגּוּלִין (277b). However, he also punctuates פֵּגוֹל in 246a.[12]

The קִטּוֹל pattern and its meaning.

Under these circumstances, when, on the one hand, various patterns merged together subsequent to phonologic changes and, on the other, nouns migrated from one category to another, our capacity to associate a given pattern with a particular semantic

---

[10]Occurs in the plural, *laqqīṭən*, LOT III/b, p. 222. The participle singular of the type *qəṭīl* occurs on p. 223, obviously with a geminated second radical: *dalləq*.
[11]LOTS III/b, p. 303.
[12]Cf. the alternation of MH חִפּוּיָן (m.Ed. 2:8) / חֲפּוּיָן (m.Kel. 22:7).

area is very limited. Nevertheless, the fact that in Samaritan morphology קִטּוּל grew beyond its initial limits can be established with certainty. An abundance of nouns occur in SA, the majority of which function as verbal nouns, as exemplified below:

ליתי שבק אהן יתובה... על עודנו 'I do not leave this order as it is' (TM 73b). The pronunciation *yittob* is attested by a poem of Eleazar b. Pinhas (XIVth century) which runs: יתבת כל כלום בטב יתוב = 'you arranged everything in good arrangement' (LOT III/b 315).

חסרן איקר ארעה ובדורה בה = 'lack of the fruits of the land and dispersion in it' — these are Cain's punishments in TM 163a.

ויפרק ית זבון אחיו = 'and he will redeem his sold brother' (lit.: his brother's selling) — Lev 25: 25.

לפצואתך כתורי = 'to your salvation I wait' (lit.: is my waiting) — Gen 49: 18.

טל קדושה = 'the dew of its sanctity'*(qiddūše)* — LOT III/b 96.

ביום מלול יהוה = 'the day God spoke' (lit.: of God's speaking) — Exod 6:28 (Ms A).

סמוי עינים = 'Blindness of eyes' — Deut 28:65 (MSS VB).

The basic aptitude of קִטּוּל to express the general notion of the action enabled practically every verb to generate a noun constructed on this pattern, creating a kind of *nomen verbi*, used with the *verbum finitum*, just as the Masoretic Text uses the absolute infinitive. Thus, קִטּוּל became customary in sequences where a finite verb is preceded by a noun which expresses the tranpositioned content of the action. One should keep in mind that the Masoretic Hebrew absolute infinitive is practically non-existent in the Samaritan Version of the Pentateuch.[13] In its stead, the construct infinitive usually occurs, e.g. Lev 20: 4: העלם יעלימו *(ʿālləm)* = 'they will conceal'. In many instances a noun occurs, e.g. in Deut 7: 26: שקץ תשקצנו *(ašqeṣ)* = 'you shall abhor it'. Many of such combinations are rendered in the ST by a finite verb preceded by a *qiṭṭūl*-type noun bearing the general notion of the action, state, etc. Examples are given in the following:

[13]The same is true for MH. On קִטּוּל in general in MH see Y. Elitzur, "The Stem Qiṭṭūl in the Mishnaic Hebrew according to Cod. Kaufmann" (Hebrew with English summary), *Language Studies* II-III (Jerusalem 1987), pp. 51-65.

נכסף נכספת - סכוי סכית = you longed (Gen 31:30).
נחש ינחש - נסוי ינסי = (my lord) divines (Gen 44:5).
שלם ישלם - שלום ישלם = he will pay (Exod 21:36).
שבר תשבר - תבור תתבר = you will destroy (Exod 23:24).
הפר יפר - בטול יבטל = he may make void (Num 30:13).

The earliest targumic source uses קִטּוֹל in twenty four percent of similar cases. The percentage in the latest source is a little higher: twenty seven.

However, the most intriguing use of קִטּוֹל is its occurrence as a substitute for the construct infinitive,[14] which, unlike the absolute infinitive, maintains its full force in SA as well as in SH. Indeed, this change is by no means a widespread phenomenon. It rather had its beginning in the earlier stages of SA and progressed in the later stages. Thus, in the old MSS of the ST it occurs mostly when the SP has an infinitive in a **nominal status,**[15] so that e.g. in Lev 26:15: להפרכם את בריתי = 'that you break my covenant' (lit. your breaking...) is translated as לבטולכון (MSS JC). Similarly in Lev 5:4: לבטא בשפתים - לפרוש ספון = 'to utter with one's lips' (the ST, according to MS J, opted for a nominal expression under the form of the construct state: "to the utterance of one's lips"). And so does Lev 21:4: לא יטמא בעל בעמיו להחלו - לא יסתב... לחלולה = 'a husband among his people shall not defile himself by his (own) profanation'. Only rarely is an infinitive having a **verbal status** rendered by a *qiṭṭūl* noun in the old MSS of the ST. Such are the two following instances:[16]

לא ימשל למכרה - לא ישלט לזבונה = 'he shall have no right to sell her' (Exod 21:8).

לברך לקחתי - לברוך דברת = 'I was commanded to bless' (Num 23:20).

This restriction was abandoned in the course of time. In the more recent stage of SA קִטּוֹל is used to render the infinitive even in a **verbal status**. This is exemplified by the following passages, taken from later MSS of the ST, mostly A.

---

[14]See M. Florentin, *A Diachronical Study of the Samaritan Aramaic Verb* (Tel Aviv 1982). (Thesis submitted for the M.A. degree at Tel Aviv University [Hebrew]), pp. 40-41.
[15]For our discussion, an infinitive is considered to be in a nominal status when it occurs in a complementary position, usually in the construct state, or with possessive suffixes. In MH, this kind of infinitive no longer exists. An infinitive is in a verbal status when it forms the predicate of a phrase with a finite verb, either alone or with object suffixes. This is the only kind of infinitive existing in MH.
[16]To the best of my knowledge, no other instances exist in this MS. About its age and position see A. Tal, *The Samaritan Targum of the Pentateuch*, vol. III (Tel Aviv 1983), pp. 17-21.

ונהר יצא מעדן להשקות את הגן - ונהר יפק מן גנתה לפלוס ית פרדסה = 'a river flowed out of Eden to water the garden' (var. למשקאה; Gen 2:10).

הקריב לבוא - קרב לעלול = 'he was about to enter' (var. למיעל; Gen 12:10)

ואיש אין בארץ לבוא עלינו - וגבר לית בארעה לעלול עלינן = 'and there is no man on earth to come in to us' (var. למיעל; Gen 19:31).

ויכל יעקב לצוות - וכלל יעקב לפקוד = 'and Jacob finished to charge' (var. למפקדה; Gen 49:33).

Of special significance is the fact that MS A of the ST frequently translates the infinitive לאמר *līmor* as אמור, while the older manuscripts have למימר (e.g. Gen 32:18, 34:20, Exod 7:16, 17:4, etc.). Obviously, this is a novel means of emphasizing the abstract notion of the action.

Other later manuscripts use קטּוּל in this position as well. Thus, one finds in MSS V and B: לחבר את האהל - לדבוק ית משכנה = 'to join the tent together' (var. למדבקה; Ex 36:18). And so has TM: דעתידין לבדור, 'bound to be scattered' (247b); לקבול בלישהתך, 'to receive your prayer' (297a).[17]

This is one aspect of the general tendency towards nominalization, particularly apparent in MH. I refer to the replacement of verbal by nominal forms, e.g. in the frequent interchange of the imperfect form with the participle e.g. of יברך with מברך, which may be considered a process of supplanting of the former by the latter.[18] The temporal use of the participle abounds in TM: כלה בידכון מתחלף = 'every favour reserved for you will change into curse' (144a; lit.: 'everything regarding you will change'). Similarly, in 115b: כהניה לא מקבלין הן הטמאו = 'the Priests will not be accepted, if they will be defiled', etc. To the same tendency belongs the frequent change from infinitive (considered as a part of the verbal system in MH) to participle, in phrases of the type עתידין עוֹשׂין instead of the older עתידין לעשׂוֹת.[19] In SA the type דו הוה עתיד כתב ארהותה = 'for he (Moses) was bound to write the Law' (TM 269b) tended to replace the type דאנה עתיד למוקרך = 'for I am bound to honour you' (279b).

[17] On the later origin of these parts of TM see Z. Ben-Hayyim, *Tibat Mârqe, A Collection of Samaritan Midrashim* (Jerusalem 1988) (Hebrew), pp. 15-24.

[18] Supposedly, this is conditioned by the non-modal content of the verb. This is not confirmed by the excellent study of M.Mishor, *The Tense System in Tannaitic Hebrew* (Jerusalem 1983) (doctoral dissertation, in Hebrew), pp. 117-125; 272-306. See especially p. 305.

[19] See Mishor, ibid., p. 270.

SA קְטוּל has other meanings too, as it has in the cognate dialects and in Hebrew. The most widespread is the expression of the result of an action. Several examples are given below (common nouns having no particular meaning are ignored).

Gen 27:7 (A): והנדי כי ציוד = 'and bring me game'.

Lev 2:6: תגזר יתה גזורים = 'you shall break it in pieces'.

Asatir 6a: זער דזגוג = 'a moon of glass'.

Deut 23:14 (ACE): וסכה תהי לך על זיונך = 'and you shall have a spike with your weapons (lit.: equipment)'.

The abstract character of this pattern is best expressed by words with adverbial force, such as שבוע in Lev 26:18: ואוזף למרדי יתכון שבוע על חוביכון = I shall chastise you sevenfold for your sins.[20] Of a similar nature is the noun כלול: כלול גברי אתרה = 'all the men of the place' (Gen 29:22 - A).[21]

I would like to conclude this paper with an interesting fact. As mentioned above, the קְטוּל form is very prolific in SA. This is well illustrated by nouns, derivatives of foreign roots, which have been restructured according to SA rules of grammar. Such is, e.g. נשוב יתנשב which renders ירה יירה, 'will be shot', in Exod 19:13 (V). This form originates in the Arabic نشب = 'to shoot arrows'.[22] Similarly, תפול יתפל (Num 12:14) renders ירק ירק, '(her father) had spat in her face', from Arabic تفل 'to spit'. נקנצתי קנוץ, from قنص translates גנוב גנבתי, 'I have been kidnapped' in Gen 40:15, etc.

Several nouns, abstract by nature, whose prefix has been taken as a part of the root when one of the radicals no longer appeared, have been treated in the same way. Thus הסוך נסך for הסך נסך = 'pouring out a drink offering' (Num 28:7) is, according to the ST, an abstract noun (Cf. MS B: נסוך), derived from the Afʿel conjugation of the root נסך. Out of the Qal infinitive of נחת a *qiṭṭūl* abstract noun has been derived in MSS MB of the ST: מיות נעתנן (‹ מחות) = 'we came down' (Gen 43:20).

---

[20]According to Ben-Hayyim the word belongs to the root שבח, its meaning being *manifold*. See Hayyim (Jefim) Shirmann Jubilee Volume (ed. S. Abramson et al.) (Jerusalem 1970), p. 42.

[21]Also found in Jewish Aramaic documents from the Geniza: פתורה וכלולה = *the table and all that belongs to it.* See M.A. Friedman, *Jewish Marriage in Palestine* (Tel Aviv 1980), vol II, p. 169.

[22]R. Dozy, *Supplément aux Dictionnaires Arabes* (Leiden 1881), vol II, p. 678b.

Lexical Clues to the Composition of the Old Testament Peshitta*

M. P. Weitzman — University College, London

Introduction

How many translators are responsible for the Peshitta version (P) of the Hebrew Bible? Even in antiquity there was no agreed answer. Theodore of Mopsuestia spoke of an individual (ἕνα τινὰ ἀφανῆ),[1] while the commentary attributed to Ephrem (on Josh 15:28) speaks in the plural of those who translated the Bible into Syriac (*hānon d-paššeq[w] l-suryāyā*). Again, Barhebraeus believed that P originated in a single period (though he preserves three different traditions of when that period fell),[2] while Ishoʿdad of Merv divides the books into two groups, translated in two different periods.[3] The main aim of the present article is to estimate the number of translators, and to delimit, albeit tentatively, the sections which these translators undertook (i.e. the translation units). The degree of cohesion between the translation units is then considered. Only then can we assess the legitimacy of combining evidence from different books of P, e.g. in order to describe translation technique in P as a whole, or to construct any hypothesis about Peshitta origins.

In order to distinguish different translators, we may test the consistency of translation of Hebrew words in P. Differences between books, if sufficiently systematic, would suggest different translators. The Hebrew words whose renderings are to be tested — which may be termed "discriminators" — must be chosen with care. A discriminator must be frequent, since otherwise books cannot be shown to differ systematically in their translation of it. Ideally, the meaning of the Hebrew word should

---

*The help of Piet Dirksen and Konrad Jenner at the Peshiṭta Institute in verifying manuscript readings is gratefully acknowledged, as are the comments of Richard Steiner and other contributors to the discussion at the conference. I am grateful also to Sebastian Brock and Robert Gordon for their comments on an earlier draft. The abbreviation *Symp* indicates P. B. Dirksen and M. J. Mulder (eds.), *The Peshiṭta: Its Early Text and History* (Leiden 1988).

[1]See H. N. Sprenger (ed.), *Theodori Mopsuesteni Commentarius in XII Prophetas. Einleitung und Ausgabe* (Wiesbaden 1977), p. 283 (on Zeph 1:5). In the same way Epiphanius deprecates the minor Greek versions as the work of individuals ("De LXX Interpr" in *PG* 43:374-9), in contrast with the inspired seventy supposedly responsible for LXX.

[2]M. Sprengling and W.C. Graham (eds.), *Barhebraeus' Scholia on the Old Testament* (Chicago 1931), p. 26. The three periods are those of (a) Solomon and Hiram, (b) Asa, the priest supposedly sent by the Assyrians to Samaria, and (c) Addai the apostle and the allegedly contemporary Abgar, king of Edessa.

[3]J.-M. Vosté and C. van den Eynde (eds.), *Commentaire d'Išoʿdad de Merv sur l'Ancien Testament, I. Genèse*, CSCO 126 (text) and 156 (French translation) (Louvain 1950 and 1955), text, p. 3. The periods are those of Solomon and Abgar. As the editors point out, however, Ishoʿdad probably knew all three theories quoted by Barhebraeus, but appreciated that some of the books must have been translated later than the age of Solomon, or even Asa. His two-period theory retains an early date for as many books as possible (see the French translation, p. 4, n. 1).

be uniform throughout the Bible. Failing that, the possibility that the Hebrew word is variously rendered because of variations (real or perceived) of meaning, rather than because of differences of policy among the translators, will have to be controlled.[4]

A number of Hebrew words that can serve as discriminators are studied below. By definition, a discriminator has at least two alternative Syriac renderings. It will always be found that one of these can be characterised as "conservative" — either because it is the oldest Aramaic term, or because it is the Syriac cognate of the Hebrew word. Any alternative rendering may be contrasted as an "innovation". The reason that such an innovation gained currency will lie in some drawback (e.g. ambiguity) in the conservative rendering. The Biblical books vary systematically in the receptivity of their translators to such innovations.

Conservative and Modern Words for "City"

Our first discriminator is עיר "city". P consistently renders by *qrītā* in some books, and by *mdī(n)tā* in others. For example, P in Jeremiah has *qrītā* 127 times and *mdī(n)tā* only twice, while P in Ezekiel has *mdī(n)tā* 59 times and never *qrītā*. This difference cannot be ascribed to different meanings in the underlying Hebrew. In both books the Hebrew usually denotes the same city at the same period — Jerusalem at around the time of Babylonian invasion. In fact P in nearly every Biblical book comes down firmly on one side or the other, as follows:

Renderings of עיר

	Gn	Ex	Lv	Nu	Dt	Jos	Jg	Sam	Kg	Isa	Jer	Ezek	Dodk	Ps
qrītā	45	3	14	49	57	83	53	75	112	34	127	1	2	15
mdī(n)tā	0	0	0	0	0	55	0	1	2	9	2	59	40	5

	Pr	Job	Ct	Ru	Lam	Qoh	Est	Dan	Ezr	Neh	Chr
qrītā	0	2	0	0	4	0	3	2	6	15	99
mdī(n)tā	3	0	3	4	1	5	7	3	1	4	4

[4]For example, the Hebrew word דבר has two Syriac renderings, *meltā* and *petgāmā*. It cannot, however, serve as a discriminator, since the choice between these renderings is largely conditional upon meaning. Most instances are covered by the following rules: (a) *petgāmā* means "thing" or "matter", (b) *meltā* indicates the words of men, except that (c) *petgāmā* is always used with the verbs *y(h)ab* and *afīb*, meaning "answer"; (d) *petgāmā* is always used for a word of God quoted verbatim, e.g. as law or prophecy, but (e) a word of God not so quoted may be either *meltā* or *petgāmā* (e.g. the "word of the Lord" becomes *petgāmā* at Isa 2:3 and *meltā* in the parallel at Mic 4:2). The case is different in P on the New Testament, where *meltā* is usual and *petgāmā* is almost wholly restricted to expressions of answering, with the verbs *y(h)ab, pannī* or *afīb*, the last being already an established idiom in Biblical Aramaic (Dan 3:16). In the Syrohexaplar too, *meltā* is very much preferred.

These statistics exclude the few cases where P renders differently (e.g. by *karkā* at Prov 1:21 or even *ṭalyā* at 2 Sam 20:19)[5] or not at all (e.g. Gen 19:14), and also the cases in Chronicles where the whole verse is translated freely or even omitted.[6] On the other hand, they include cases like the city Ar (Isa 15:1), מעיר at Hos 7:4, and even בעדי עדיים at Ezek 16:7, where the noun עיר is not normally thought present but was perceived by P. The other tables in this paper have been drawn up on a similar basis, so that the total in each column may not agree exactly with the statistics for the Massoretic Text as analysed today.[7]

Some books have a minority of renderings that go against their main policy. These are due, in the main, to sources of interference that will be discussed below. One of the few books *not* to opt overwhelmingly for just one of the two alternatives is Joshua, which nevertheless has a clear policy (see Appendix): a Canaanite city was a *mdī(n)tā* while a city founded by the Israelites was a *qrītā*. By contrast, two books vacillate with no obvious policy between two alternatives: Isaiah and Psalms. We shall later consider why.

Hebrew also possesses the synonym קריה, which is etymologically cognate with *qrītā*. One might have expected that even a translator who avoided *qrītā* for עיר would feel bound to translate קריה by its Syriac cognate. In fact, however, the translators adhere to the same policies as for עיר:

Renderings of קריה

	Dt	Kg	Isa	Jer	Dodk	Ps	Pr	Job	Lam	Ezr
qrītā	2	2	8	1	1	1	0	1	1	3
mdī(n)tā	0	0	2	0	4	0	4	0	0	4

(Num 21:28 and three passages in Proverbs have *karkā*).

Thus *mdī(n)tā* predominates for קריה in P to the Twelve Prophets and to Proverbs, just as for עיר. Evidently these translators felt strongly that *qrītā* did not adequately convey the meaning "city".

---

[5]On this passage see R.P. Gordon, "The Variable Wisdom of Abel: The MT and Versions at 2 Samuel XX 18-19", *VT* 43 (1933), pp. 215-226: 222.

[6]It seems that P's Hebrew *Vorlage* in Chronicles was often illegible, so that the translator often had to guess the sense, or alternatively omit the passage. See S. Fraenkel, "Die syrische Übersetzung zu den Büchern der Chronik", *Jahrbücher für Protestantische Theologie* 5 (1879), pp. 508-536, 720-759: 754-5; M. P. Weitzman, "Is the Peshitta of Chronicles a Targum?", in P.V.M. Flesher (ed.), *Targum Studies*, vol. 2, forthcoming.

[7]Conveniently presented in F. I. Andersen and A. D. Forbes, *The Vocabulary of the Old Testament* (Rome 1989).

The original Aramaic for "city" was, of course, *qrītā* (or rather the absolute: *qryh*). Its rival *mdī(n)tā* originally meant an imperial province, literally a juridical district, from דין. Such is its usage at Elephantine and in biblical Aramaic. The hellenistic period, however, saw the emergence of cities of unprecedented size, which had to be distinguished from the older settlements that had always been indicated by the term *qrītā*. For the new great cities, *mdī(n)tā* seemed an appropriate term, for such a city could dominate a whole province, particularly as a centre from which its justice (דין) was dispensed.[8] Thus, in the almost contemporary account of the flood of 201 C.E., the city of Edessa is called a *mdī(n)tā* while *quryā*, plural of *qrītā*, denotes the surrounding villages.[9] Nevertheless, *mdī(n)tā* was in some measure demoted in going from "province" to "city",[10] and *qrītā* shrank in turn, becoming a mere village. Hence *qrītā* is the traditional rendering, but *mdī(n)tā* the more accurate, and the translators varied in their preference between these rival claims.

This development of the senses of *mdī(n)tā* and *qrītā* was paralleled at Palmyra, where we have the advantage of dated texts. In the bilingual tariff of 18th April 137 C.E., the term for the city of Palmyra is מדיתא; thus 800 denarii are levied for the use of the two wells in the city (ii 58), or for bringing sheep into the city to be shorn (ii 147).[11] This use of מדיתא to denote Palmyra is not surprising, given that the city lay at an oasis in the Syrian desert, dominating the surrounding territory. By contrast, the tariff indicates surrounding villages by the plural קריא (compare Syriac *quryā*); no duty was paid on goods transported between these and the city (ii 112). The tariff uses מדיתא of other cities also (ii 116). In fact, as early as 24 C. E. a Palmyrene inscription from Babylon uses מדיתא of that city; the inscription marks a statue set up by *t[g]ry klhwn dy bmdynt bbl*, which surely means all the merchants in the city, rather than the

---

[8]E.Y. Kutscher, *Words and their History* (Hebrew with English summary) (Jerusalem 1961), p. 20. At the same time *mdī(n)tā* retained its larger meaning "province", and so became ambiguous; but this was evidently accepted as the price of distinguishing the new cities from their modest native predecessors. The shrinkage of *qrītā* may have been accelerated by phonetic resemblance of its plural to χώρια, to which it corresponds in the Greek text of the great bilingual tariff from Palmyra.

[9]C. Brockelmann, *Syrische Grammatik* (Leipzig 1912³), pp. 21*-23*.

[10]One effect of this shrinkage is that in P of Daniel, where *mdī(n)tā* is sometimes used for "city", the translator is reluctant to use that word also for Aram. מדיתא "province", and so prefers *arʿā* at 2:48, 3:1, and *atrā* at 3:30.

[11]*Corpus Inscriptionum Semiticarum, ab Academia Inscriptionum et Litterarum Humaniorum Conditum atque Digestum. Pars Secunda, Inscriptiones Aramaicas Continens. Tomus III: Inscriptiones Palmyreneas* (Paris 1926-1947), vol. 2, no. 3913, ii 58, 147. At Palmyra too, the term מדיתא likewise became ambiguous, in that it retained its older meaning of "province"; *cf.* the phrase רחים מדת(ה) "lover of his land", corresponding to φιλοπάτρις in honorary inscriptions (such as no. 3932 in vol. 2 of the *Corpus*).

whole province, of Babylon (cf. Dan 3:1).[12] This may be the earliest extant occurrence of *mdī(n)tā* as "city".[13]

With the exception of the Targum on Proverbs, which has long been recognised as dependent on P,[14] the Targums normally use *qrītā* (or rather *qartā*) to mean "city", not *mdī(n)tā*.[15] Indeed at Gen 47:21 the Palestinian Targums use *mdī(n)tā* for "countryside": Joseph in Egypt is said to have exchanged the populations of the cities (*quryātā*) and the countryside (*mdīnātā*) lest his brothers be stigmatised as wandering strangers.[16]

To return to P, it is likely that all the translators were aware that *mdī(n)tā* denoted a larger settlement than *qrītā*. They differed, however, as to which should be the normal equivalent of עיר. P in some books (e.g. Jeremiah) prefers the more conservative usage, and in other books (e.g. Ezekiel) the more modern. The reason will be considered after some further variations have been presented.

Towards a Graded Series of Innovations and of Books

Another word differently rendered among the Biblical books is עולה. Here the conservative rendering is *ʿlātā*. However, the rival rendering *yaqdā šalmā*, evidently a calque on Greek ὁλοκαύτωμα, was sometimes preferred. The reason may be that *ʿlātā* possesses an unsuitable second meaning: "hill shrine". The renderings are distributed as follows:

---

[12] J. Cantineau, "Textes Palmyréniens provenant de la Fouille du Temple de Bêl", *Syria* 12 (1939), pp. 116-141: 122.

[13] In the Genesis Apocryphon, the four kings defeated by Abraham are said to have marched via the great valley *l-mdyt(h)wn* (22:4), on their way *l-mdynt drmšq* (22:5). However, it is unlikely that *mdī(n)tā* already here has the meaning of "city". At 20:28, the sense is clearly "province, land" (מדינת מצרים); hence Damascus too may here be viewed as a state rather than a city. See K. Beyer, *Die aramäische Texte vom Toten Meer* (Göttingen 1984), pp. 176, 182.

[14] T. Nöldeke, "Das Targum zu den Sprüchen von der Peschita abhängig", *Archiv für Wissenschaftliche Erforschung des Alten Testaments* II/2 (1872), pp. 246-9.

[15] At Num 24:24, the older printed editions of the Fragment Targum speak of hordes issuing from מדינתא רבתא, which has been taken as Rome or Constantinople. The correct reading, however, is מדינת איטליה; see M. L. Klein, *The Fragment-Targums of the Pentateuch* (Rome 1980), vol. 1, p. 204. At Gen 15:1, in the Palestinian Targums, Abraham fears reprisals that the survivors of the battle of Gen 14 might plan בכרכיהון ובמדינתהון. Even here, however, the sense could be "lands" rather than "(great) cities"; see n. 13 above.

[16] In rabbinic Hebrew, both senses — "city" and "countryside" —are attested in different passages. The former occurs at mTer 2:5, which allows town onions (בצלים מבני המדינה) to be substituted as heave-offering for village onions, but not visa versa, since the former are the food of the wealthier citizens (פוליטיקין). Rabbi Samuel b. Nahman (ca 300 C. E.) likewise explained מדינה in Esth 9:28 as כרך (TJ Meg 1:1 fin). However, מדינה could also indicate the provinces as opposed to Jerusalem, e.g. at mMaaser Sheni 3:4. Some passages (e.g. mShek 1:3) remain ambiguous.

Renderings of עולה

	Gn	Ex	Lv	Nu	Dt	Jos	Jg	Sam	Kg	Isa	Jer	Ezek	Dodk	Ps
ʿlātā	6	13	27	22	0	1	6	14	17	3	4	1	0	0
yaqdā šalmā	0	2	26	30	6	3	0	0	0	0	0	18	3	3
yaqdā	1	2	1	1	0	0	0	0	0	1	2	0	0	3[17]

	Ezr	Neh	Chr
ʿlātā	9	1	31
yaqdā šalmā	0	0	0
yaqdā	0	0	0

(A few other occurrences, including 4 in Chronicles, are rendered by *debḥā*; *qurbānā* also occurs.)

Apparently the innovation *yaqdā šalmā* for "burnt-offering" had gained wider acceptance than the innovation *mdī(n)tā* for "city". Ezekiel and the Dodekapropheton, which showed the modern usage for "city", have the modern rendering for עולה also. However, that modern rendering for עולה also appears in a number of books that had the more conservative usage for "city", notably Leviticus to Deuteronomy. Finally, some historical books (Judges, Samuel, Kings and Chronicles) as well as Jeremiah retain conservative usages for both words. The books thus begin to fall into a graded series, some conservative in rendering both words, some conservative in rendering עיר but modern in rendering עולה, and some modern in rendering both words.

Another discriminator is Heb. כסף, when it denotes silver metal as opposed to money. This distinction is largely anachronistic in terms of the Biblical text itself until after the exile,[18] but was nevertheless perceived by the translators of P. Some retain the native *kespā* even where silver metal is meant. Others reserve *kespā* for the sense "money" and use *sēmā* where silver functions as a material. The innovation is once more a Greek loan word: ἄσημος "unstamped".[19] The statistics are as follows:

---

[17]Including Ps 66:13, where *yaqdā* was corrupted to *ʾiqārā*; see A. Vogel, "Studien zum Pešiṭta-Psalter Besonders im Hinblick auf sein Verhältnis zu Septuaginta", *Biblica* 25 (1951), p. 203.
[18]R. Loewe, "The Earliest Biblical Allusion to Coined Money", *Palestine Exploration Quarterly* 87 (1955), pp. 141-150.
[19]Mishnaic Hebrew אסימון and Persian *sīm* are loans from the same source.

Renderings of כסף in sense "silver metal"

	Gn	Ex	Lv	Nu	Dt	Jos	Jg	Sam	Kg	Isa	Jer	Ezek	Dodk	Ps
kespā	6	28	0	0	0	0	0	2	8	2	2	0	0	1
sēmā	0	2	0	31	1	7	0	0	0	8	2	9	14	7

	Pr	Job	Ct	Ru	Lam	Qoh	Est	Dan	Ezr	Neh	Chr
kespā	0	1	1	0	0	1	2	2	10	0	8
sēmā	11	0	2	0	0	0	0	2	0	0	10

The innovation *sēmā* has made even greater progress than *yaqdā šalmā*. Not only is it preferred in all the books which have *yaqdā šalmā*; it also occurs sporadically in Jeremiah and Chronicles, which had resisted all the innovations so far.

The figures for Genesis and Exodus are based on the text of 5bl, which has *kespā* throughout (except at Exod 11:2, 12:35). The remaining manuscripts have *sēmā*, but the reading of 5bl appears to be original, the other manuscripts having modernised to *sēmā*.[20] This would imply that the renderings within the Pentateuch for the words עולה and כסף are conservative in Genesis and Exodus and modern in Leviticus to Deuteronomy. (The two occurrences of *sēmā* even in 5bl in Exodus will be considered later.) In the same way, the figure for Kings includes one place (2 Kgs 25:15) where *kespā* survives in 9al alone, and that for Ezra likewise includes two places (1:11, 5:14) where it survives in 8h5 alone.[21]

A yet more widely accepted innovation is found among the renderings of the root גלה (including the nouns גולה and גלות) in the sense "go into exile". While the most conservative translators have the cognate Syriac verb *glī* (with noun *gālūtā*), most instead use the passive of the verb *šbā* "capture", with noun *šbītā*. The root *glī* may have been considered ambiguous, given its alternative sense "reveal". Its rival could be due to the influence of LXX, which has the passive αἰχμαλωτεύομαι or αἰχμαλωτίζομαι for Heb. גלה and αἰχμαλωσία for Heb. גלות. The aversion to Syr. *glī* may be gauged from the Aramaic portions of Daniel, where P often does little more than transpose into Syriac characters, but pointedly replaces גלותא by *šbitā* (2:25, 5:13, 6:14). Again at Ezek 12:3 the prophet is commanded to enact a mime: "go into

---

[20]Against this, A. van der Kooij ("On the significance of MS 5b1 for Peshiṭta Genesis", in *Symp*, pp. 183-199) argues that P often translates one Hebrew word by two different Syriac words according to context, so that differentiation between *kespā* and *sēmā* could go back to the translator himself. If *sēmā* is original, however, 5bl must have changed it to *kespā*, and in explanation van der Kooij can only posit vaguely "some alteration" based either on Hebrew or on an Aramaic dialect that used *kespā* for silver (pp. 191n, 198).

[21]C. Moss, "The Peshitta Version of Ezra". *Le Muséon* 46 (1933), pp. 55-110: 78. Dan 11:38 has also been classified under *kespā*, although 7a1 modernises to *sēmā*.

exile (גלה) before their eyes", while in P the instruction takes on the curious sense *eštbī*: "get thee captured". The statistics are:

Renderings of גלה "(go into) exile"

	Jg	Sam	Kg	Isa	Jer	Ezek	Dodk	Lam	Est	Dan	Ezr	Neh	Chr
glī	0	1	17	1	0	0	0	2	4	0	1	2	6[22]
šbā	1	0	0	3	32	17	18	0	0	3	12	0	1

This innovation has proceeded still further than those mentioned above, with P even in Jeremiah coming down firmly on the modern side. P retains the conservative usage in Kings, Esther and Nehemiah regularly, and in Ezra-Chronicles sporadically.

The renderings of חסד show a similar pattern. The Syriac cognate *ḥesdā* has a homonym meaning "disgrace", and *ṭaybūtā* usually occurs instead. The distribution follows:

Renderings of חסד

	Gn	Ex	Nu	Dt	Jos	Jg	Sam	Kg	Isa	Jer	Dodk	Ps	Pr	Job
ḥesdā	1	0	0	0	0	0	1	4	0	0	0	1	0	1
ṭaybūtā	9	4	2	2	2	1	11	1	5	6	12	68	5	2

	Ru	Lam	Est	Dan	Ezr	Neh	Chr
ḥesdā	2	1	2	0	1	0	4
ṭaybūtā	0	0	0	2	1	1	10

In rendering this Hebrew word, most Biblical books including the whole Pentateuch are decidedly in the modern camp. The conservative usage is virtually confined to the historical books, but only in Kings is it dominant (according to 9al and its apographs; the rest have *ṭaybūtā*). Curiously, Ruth is conservative here, despite its "modern" usage of *mdī(n)tā*. A different rendering, viz *raḥmē*, occurs 51 times in Psalms and at 2 Sam 9:1,3, Ruth 1:8, Lam 3:24; similarly in Proverbs we find *raḥmē* (31:26) or *mraḥmānā* (14:22, 20:6).

The conservative tendency of the block Judges-Kings is confirmed in the renderings of חג. Both Judges and Kings show the cognate *ḥaggā*. Books outside Judges-Kings avoid that rendering, apparently because it could also apply to heathen

[22]Including 1 Chr 17:9, where the root בלה was read as גלה.

feasts. Instead these books have *ʿēdā* or the related *ʿadʿēdā*. Mishnaic Hebrew likewise avoids the Biblical term חג, substituting יום טוב. The distribution follows:

Renderings of חג

	Ex	Lv	Nu	Dt	Jg	Kg	Isa	Ezek	Dodk	Ps	Ezr	Neh	Chr
ḥaggā	2	0	0	0	1	5	1	0	0	0	0	0	0
ʿēdā	0	0	0	0	0	0	0	0	2	0	1	2	9
ʿadʿēdā	10	4	2	7	0	0	1	4	8	2	1	0	0

Further evidence of conservatism in the historical books emerges from the renderings of ארון (excluding Gen 50:26, where "coffin" is meant). In Kings, parts of Samuel, and once in Chronicles, we find the calque *ārōnā*. Elsewhere the loan-word *qībōtā* has prevailed:

Renderings of ארון

	Ex	Lv	Nu	Dt	Jos	Jg	Sam	Kg	Jer	Ps	Chr
ārōnā	0	0	0	0	0	0	25	13	0	0	1
qībōtā	26	1	6	8	30	1	24	1	1	1	50

The situation in Samuel is complex:

(1) Up to and including 1 Sam 6:2 we have *qībōtā* (20x).

(2) By 1 Sam 6:13 a shift has occurred to *ārōnā,* which is used up to and including 2 Sam 6:16 (23x).

(3) The remainder of the book displays rapid alternation: *qībōtā* in the next verse (2 Sam 6:17), *ārōnā* at 2 Sam 7:2, *qībōtā* between 2 Sam 11:11 and 2 Sam 15:25 (3x), and finally *ārōnā* at 2 Sam 15:29.

Some More Complex Cases

We may now consider the renderings of the plural of ארץ. Some books simply show the Syriac cognate *arʿātā*. In others, however, the translator recognised that the "lands" of the Bible had become mere provinces in a succession of empires. Such translators therefore render *mdīnātā* "provinces", or less commonly *atrawātā* "places". For all these translators, *arʿā* may have meant primarily "world", and thus lacked a meaningful plural. The distribution is as follows:

Renderings of ארצות

	Gn	Kg	Isa	Jer	Ezek	Ps	Dan	Ezr	Neh	Chr
arʿātā	6[23]	2	3	3	2	3	1	0	0	0
mdīnātā	0	0	0	0	15	0	0	5	2	8
atrawātā	0	0	0	3	0	0	1	0	0	0

Here the "conservative" rendering dominates in Genesis and Kings, two of the most conservative books. It dominates also in Isaiah and Psalms, which have behaved erratically with respect to the other discriminators. Elsewhere, *arʿātā* is avoided, usually in favour of *mdīnātā*. A measure of the aversion to *arʿātā* is the rendering of Ezek 29:12, where God promises to make Egypt "the most desolate of desolate lands, and her cities shall be the most desolate of ruined cities for forty years, and I shall scatter Egypt among the nations and disperse them among all the lands". In this single verse P uses *mdīnātā* four times — twice for the plural of עיר and twice for the plural of ארץ. Even the singular ארץ is sometimes rendered by *mdī(n)tā* (e.g. Qoh 10:16, 1 Chr 19:3) or by *atrā* (Josh 9:6, 10:42, 12:1). Conceivably the substitute *atrawātā* is due to the translator of Jeremiah, who may have assimilated 23:8 ("all the *lands* where I exiled them") to 8:3 ("all the *places* where I exiled them").

The renderings of גר present a more complex picture. First, although the word meant "resident alien" in the Bible itself, it developed in rabbinic Hebrew the sense of "proselyte", which P was often inclined to import into the text, as were LXX and the Jewish Targums.[24] Second, Aphraates' citations offer at two points a different text from the Biblical manuscripts. The first factor leads to a threefold classification of occurrences of גר, which P takes to indicate:

(a) strangers who sojourn in Israel without adopting their faith;
(b) Israelites (or patriarchs or even God) compared to strangers;
(c) strangers who become proselytes.

Examples of (a) occur in 2 Sam 1:13 (an Amalekite) and 1 Chr 22:2, 2 Chr 2:16 (non-Israelites forcibly employed in building the temple). Here P has *gīyōrā*, the native equivalent of גר. As Geiger observed, however, this word carried in Syriac negative overtones, of "alien" and even "adulterer". Hence, when senses (b) and (c) are detected other renderings are usual. For (b) P usually offers *ʿāmōrā* "dweller", based on the verb גור; less often we find *tawtbā*, which properly renders תושב. For (c) we often

---

[23]At Gen 26:3, *arʿātā* survives in 5b1 alone; the others modernise to *malkwātā*.
[24]A. Geiger, *Urschrift und Uebersetzungen der Bibel* (Breslau 1857), pp. 354-5.

find the striking phrase *anyā d-metpnē lwāt(y)* "he that turns to Me". This may be a calque on Greek προσήλυτος, which literally means "one who goes (cf. ἐλεύσομαι, ἦλθον) to (πρός)". The Syriac translator apparently took the unstated object of πρός as God himself; moreover he changed the verb from "go" (which might suggest death or translation) to "turn", with a glance at Isa 45:22: "Turn to me (MT פנו אלי, Targ. אתפנו למימרי) to me and be saved".[25] The distribution is as follows:

Renderings of גר

	Gn	Ex	Lv	Nu	Dt	Jos	Sam	Isa	Jer	Ezek	Dodk
gīyōrā	0	0	0	0	0	0	1	0	0	0	0
ʿāmōrā	2	9	6	0	18	2	0	1	2	0	1
d-metpnē	0	0	15	11	3	0	0	0	0	5	2
tawtbā	0	3	0	0	1	1	0	0	1	0	0

	Ps	Job	Chr
gīyōrā	0	1[26]	3[27]
ʿāmōrā	3[28]	0	1
d-metpnē	0	0	0
tawtbā	0	0	0

The perceived differences in the meaning of גר certainly account for much of the variation in the renderings. Thus in Lev 19:34 the Israelite is commanded to "love the stranger, for ye were strangers in the land of Egypt". P renders the first by *aynā d-metpnē lwāt(y)* and the second by *ʿāmōrā*, sacrificing the correspondence found in the Hebrew. (The same occurs at Deut 10:19.) In Deuteronomy a stylistic factor may have contributed to the variation in P: where the גר is mentioned together with other weaker members of society, the one-word rendering *ʿāmōrā* is preferred, presumably to avoid undue emphasis on any one item in the list (so Deut 16:11 etc., and even 5:14).

Nevertheless, the different books actually differ in translation policy. In Leviticus to Deuteronomy, Ezekiel and the Minor Prophets — books which stand towards the "modern" extreme — the rendering *aynā d-metpnē lwāt(y)* is predominant.[29] Elsewhere it never recurs, apart from a possible echo at Isa 54:15,

[25]There is, however, no echo in P itself at Isa 45:22 (*etqarrab[w]*).
[26]So Job 28:4 (MT *gār*); but at Job 31:32 (MT *gēr*), P has *aksnāyā*.
[27]At 1 Chr 9:2 *gīyōrā* appears once more, to render נתינים.
[28]So Ps 39:13, 94:6, 119:19. At Ps 146:9, P has *meskēnā*, which Geiger thought corrupt for *aksnāyā*; however, the translator may simply have substituted it to fit the parallels ("orphan and widow").
[29]With the exceptions in Deuteronomy noted above. In Mal 3:5 P has a doublet, with *ʿāmōrā* side by side with *aynā d-metpnē lwāt(y)*.

where יגור גור (properly referring to strife or dread) is apparently taken by P (together with LXX) as referring to proselytes: *w-kul d-metpnēn men īday neᶜlūn lek(y).* This distribution is not wholly explained by stylistic factors, nor by differences in the meaning of גר, nor even by the need to confine the phrase "he that turns to Me" to legislation and prophecy. Only differences of translation policy can explain why, in the phrase "if a stranger sojourns with thee", P in Lev 19:33 writes *aynā d-metpnē lwāt(y)*, but P in Exod 12:48 has *tawtbā*. Again, when Zechariah (7:10) appeals to the people not to oppress the גר, P writes *aynā d-metpnē lwāt(y)*, but when Jeremiah (7:6) uses the same phrase, P has *ᶜāmōrā*. We may thus see *aynā d-metpnē lwāt(y)* as a usage which, like *yaqdā šalmā*, characterises the books Leviticus to Deuteronomy, Ezekiel and the Minor Prophets.

Similarly, the confinement of the conservative rendering *gīyōrā* to Samuel and Chronicles, two books with an especially "conservative" record, is not simply due to the fact that גר here in the Hebrew usually has sense (a), viz. strangers who dwell among the Israelites without adopting their faith. That sense is sometimes clear in other books also, as eating forbidden meat (Deut 14:21), or as waxing more prosperous than the Israelites themselves (Lev 25:47,49; Deut 28:43); and in those less "conservative" books, P uses not *gīyōrā* but *ᶜāmōrā* or *tawtbā*. Conversely, the P translator of Chronicles twice uses *gīyōrā* where the interpretation "proselyte" could easily have been admitted, of the sojourners summoned to Asa's sacrifice (2 Chr 15:9 — Heb. *gārīm*) or to Hezekiah's Passover (2 Chr 30:25). This rendering may be due to his "conservatism", rather than any perception of sense (a).

There remains the fact that Aphraates, in an amalgam of Lev 19:10, 23:22 and Deut 24:19-21, never uses *aynā d-metpne lwāt(y)* but instead has (twice) *gīyōrā*. It has been suggested that the Biblical text familiar to Aphraates actually read *gīyōrā*,[30] and moreover that this is a relic from the earlier Jewish Aramaic versions from which P had supposedly developed.[31]

It is unusual to find any major difference between the P manuscripts and Aphraates' citations. Normally the Biblical text cited by Aphraates (when allowance is made for faulty memory or exegetical need) coincides closely with that of the Biblical manuscripts.[32] The explanation for Aphraates' wording here may be primarily theological rather than textual. The sensitivity in P to the negative overtones of *gīyōrā*

---

[30]See most recently R. J. Owens, "Aphrahat as Witness to P-Leviticus", *Symp* , pp. 1-48: 22-25.
[31]A. Baumstark, "Neue orientalistische Probleme biblischer Textgeschichte", *ZDMG* 89 (1935): 89-118: 94. P is not in fact a transposition of an earlier version in Jewish Aramaic; see M.P. Weitzman, "Peshitta, Septuagint and Targum" in *Orientalia Christiana Analecta* 247 (1995), pp. 51-84.
[32]Owens has himself shown this in detail for Genesis to Leviticus. See R. J. Owens, *The Genesis and Exodus Citations of Aphrahat the Persian Sage* (Leiden 1983), together with the article cited in n. 30 above.

may be best explained on the hypothesis that the translators were Jews.[33] Hence the potentially offensive *gīyōrā* was replaced by *ʿāmōrā* and *aynā d-metpnē lwāt(y)*, wherever reference was perceived to the Jews or the proselytes who had joined them.[34] A Christian writer, however, would have no difficulty in applying *gīyōrā* to a convert to Judaism. Hence the reappearance of *gīyōrā* in the P version of the New Testament (Matt 23:15, Acts 2:11, 6:5, 13:43) to denote Jewish proselytes. Aphraates would have known that the long phrase *aynā d-metpnē lwāt(y)* simply meant a proselyte, and he could have substituted the neater and clearer term *gīyōrā* without feeling theological offence. Perhaps, then, Aphraates read the same text as the Biblical manuscripts, but found *gīyōrā* a neater term. The resulting verbal agreement between Aphraates (*gīyōrā*) and MT גר is in that case coincidental.

The Most Conservative Block: Judges, Samuel, Kings

Among the most conservative books, on the evidence considered so far, are Judges, Samuel and Kings; Joshua clearly does not belong here. Two further Hebraic renderings found in individual members of the group deserve mention:

(a) In Judges, אשרה (6:25-30) and עשתרות (2:13, 10:6) are rendered *estrā*, a Syriac form that resembles both Hebrew words and occurs in no other book. For אשרה, other books have a variety of renderings: *glīpā* "graven image" (Mic 5:13), *deḥltā* "object of fear" (frequently in Kings), *ḥešltā* "cast image" (twice in Deuteronomy), *ptakrā* "idol" (twice in Isaiah), *šteltā* "grove" (Deut 16:21). Further renderings appear in Chronicles: *adrianṭā* (from Greek) "statue" (2 Chr 14:2), *ḥugbā* "idol" (2 Chr 33:19), *nemrā* "leopard" (2 Chr 31:1, 33:3)[35] and *ṣalmā* "image" (2 Chr 24:18). At 2 Chr 19:3, where MT has בערת את האשרות, the translator mistook ר for ד, confusing Heb. *ʾăšērāh* with Syr. *ʾešad*, and so rendering *dmā zakyā lā ešadt* "you did not shed innocent blood". As to עשתרות, the occurrences outside Judges fall in Samuel and Kings, where they are rendered *genyātā* "lurking-places" (perhaps by association with סתר).

(b) The overwhelmingly frequent translation of תורה in P is the Greek loanword *nāmōsā*. By contrast the Jewish Targums use אורייתא, reserving נמוס for

[33]See M. P. Weitzman, "From Judaism to Christianity: the Syriac version of the Hebrew Bible", in J. Lieu, J. North and T. Rajak (eds.), *The Jews among Pagans and Christians in the Roman Empire* (London 1992), pp. 147-171, where some non-rabbinic form of Judaism is suggested as the context of P.

[34]Except perhaps in the conservative translation of Chronicles.

[35]Compare the sixth-century reference to the worship of *bar nemrē* at Harran, in J. P. P. Martin, "Discours de Jacques de Saroug sur la chute des idoles", *ZDMG* 29 (1875), pp. 107-147:110 (1.54).

> human decrees, such as those enacted by Joseph in Egypt (Palestinian Targums on Exod 1:8) or by the Israelite king (Tg on 1 Sam 8:9) or by corrupt priests (id. on 1 Sam 2:13) or by foreigners for themselves (Onkelos on Lev 18:3) or for subject Israelites (Tg on Ezek 20:25). The rendering *ōrāytā* is confined to three places in Kings (2 Kgs 22:11, 23:24, 25), plus three in Chronicles (2 Chr 23:18, 34:14, 15).

These examples show that the group of conservatively rendered books Judges-Kings is not homogeneous. Only Judges has *estrā* and only Kings (in this group) has *ōrāytā*. In the case of Samuel, there may even be two hands within this single book, as we shall see.

The Graded Series

The evidence may be summarised in Figure 1. Each biblical book accepts the innovations shown above it, rejects the innovations shown below it, and hesitates in relation to the innovations shown at its own level.

The historical books Judges-Kings clearly belong at the top of the scale. Less conservative than these, but less modern than the remainder, are the books Genesis-Exodus, Esther-Ezra-Nehemiah-Chronicles, Job and Lamentations. These last vary somewhat in lexical policy, but none is more conservative overall than any other. Genesis-Exodus in P are more conservative in rendering עיר, כסף and the plural of ארץ, while the group Ezra-Chronicles (especially Chronicles) has a more conservative record in rendering עולה, גר and תורה. For Job and Lamentations the evidence is scanty, but tends to place these books too in the broadly conservative category; note especially the occurrence of *kespā* for silver metal in Job[36] and the verb *glī* in Lamentations.

[36]Not only for כסף but also for בצר "iron ore" (22:24).

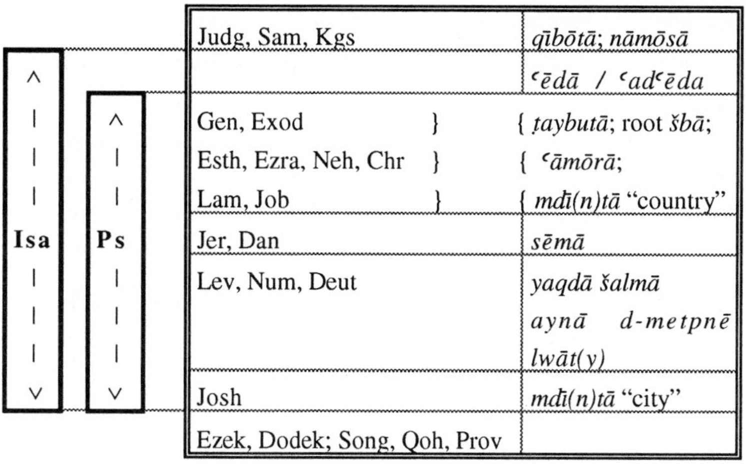

Isa	Ps		
		Judg, Sam, Kgs	*qībōtā*; *nāmōsā*
^			*ʿēdā* / *ʿadʿēda*
|	^	Gen, Exod } Esth, Ezra, Neh, Chr } Lam, Job }	{ *ṭaybutā*; root *šbā*; { *ʿāmōrā*; { *mdī(n)tā* "country"
Isa	**Ps**	Jer, Dan	*sēmā*
|	|	Lev, Num, Deut	*yaqdā šalmā* *aynā d-metpnē lwāt(y)*
v	v	Josh	*mdī(n)tā* "city"
		Ezek, Dodek; Song, Qoh, Prov	

Figure 1

As we move farther down the scale of fig. 1, the grouping becomes finer. The later books of the Torah, Ezekiel and the Twelve Prophets, and the Solomonic books, as well as Joshua, are relatively modern. Jeremiah is somewhat more conservative; Daniel stands at about the same level, despite some inconsistency regarding עיר, כסף and ארצות.

Isaiah and Psalms, however, stand apart as books that treat several of these discriminators with wide inconsistency. For example, they have no clear policy regarding the use of *qrītā* and *mdī(n)tā*. Thus the same phrase וגנותי על העיר הזאת occurs at Isa 37:35 and 38:6; the first passage P has *qrītā* and in the second *mdī(n)tā*. Again, Jerusalem is called "city of God" in Psalms both at 46:5 and at 48:2; the first is rendered *mdī(n)tā*, the second *qrītā*. To posit more than one translator would not account for the pattern, since, for either book, the occurrences of *mdī(n)tā* are scattered over most of the text (amidst more numerous occurrences of *qrītā*, not listed here):

Isaiah: 1:8, 26; 19:2; 32:19; 36:1; 37:26, 35; 38:6
Psalms: 46:5; 59:7, 15; 72:16; 101:8; 122:3

These books are, moreover, peculiar in combining *mdī(n)tā*, the most recent innovation in the list, with such conservative usages as *ḥaggā* (Isa 30:29) or *ḥesdā* (Ps 107:43). Altogether the lack of a coherent policy towards innovations is itself a characteristic of these two books.

Finally, Ruth uses both *ḥesdā* and *mdī(n)tā* and thus cannot be accommodated at all in the scale, according to which the use of *mdī(n)tā* would have implied the use of *ṭaybūtā* in place of *ḥesdā*.

Interpretation of the Series

The above scale has a twofold aspect. First, it is a scale of innovations, running down from the most widely accepted to the least. Second, it is a scale of books, with those most resistant to innovation at the top and the most modern at the bottom.

The most obvious interpretation of the scale is chronological. One could suppose, for example, that the reason the עיר is differently rendered in Jeremiah and Ezekiel is that the translator of Jeremiah worked before the usual term for "city" changed from *qrītā* to *mdī(n)tā*, while the translator of Ezekiel worked afterwards.

A purely chronological interpretation would lead, however, to the odd conclusion that the historical books, which are the most conservative, were translated before the Pentateuch. One cannot lightly abandon the expectation that the books were translated in approximately the same order as in the Jewish canon. This is suggested, first of all, by the analogy of the Septuagint and Jewish Targums; and the absence of Ezra-Chronicles from Nestorian canon and from the Syriac "massoretic" tradition seems to confirm that the last books in the Jewish canon were translated last in P.[37] Furthermore, as shown below, there is some evidence that the P version of the Torah influenced the P version of books that stand later in canonical order, even where the latter are more "conservative" on the scale.

It is not satisfactory, then, to interpret the scale of translators chronologically. Instead, one may view it as a scale of conservatism (or conversely of modernism). At any one time, not all writers are equally open to innovation. For example, both the "conservative" Thucydides and the "modern" Lysias were contemporaries in late fifth-century Athens. Indeed, it is possible for one writer to be more conservative in his language than another who wrote (say) a generation earlier.

Where innovations are entering a language, modern linguistic science tells us that a scale such as fig. 1 is likely to be observed, if we examine the usage of a number of speakers at one point in time.[38] Such a scale is technically termed "implicational", since a speaker's acceptance of one innovation implies his acceptance of all the innovations shown above in the scale. The explanation is that linguistic changes — for example, changes in vocabulary — do not sweep through a whole community overnight. At any one time, some speakers are more modern — i.e. receptive to

[37]R. Beckwith, *The Old Testament Canon of the New Testament Church* (London 1985), p. 309.
[38]J. K. Chambers and P. Trudgill, *Dialectology* (Cambridge 1980), pp. 149-154.

innovation — than others. In principle, the different speakers could be ranked along a scale from the most conservative to the most modern.

That scale may be viewed as a chain of speakers, which comprises the route by which an innovation spreads through the language. (This is of course a model — a simplification from which an analysis can be developed that may yield insight into a more complex reality.) The innovation will first be adopted by speakers at the "modern" extreme of the scale, and then spread along that scale. Ultimately it may be adopted even by the most conservative, but this will take time. Now at any moment, a number of different innovations will be spreading among speakers in this way. Since they will have entered the language (in the sense of being adopted by the most modern speakers) at different times, they will not all have progressed along the scale to the same extent. If we take a snapshot of the process at that particular moment, we shall be able to rank the innovations according to their progress along the scale, and we shall also be able to rank the speakers according to their "modernism" (i.e. the number of innovations adopted). In short we shall observe an implicational scale just like fig. 1.

In the case of P we are dealing not with the free utterance of speakers but with translators, each bound by a source text. However, translators must have had their individual views on the proper balance between tradition (which favoured conservative lexical choice) and intelligibility (which would tend to favour modern usage). Hence different translators will place themselves along an implicational scale, no less than speakers.

In relation to P, the implicational scale is found to be subject to two qualifications. First, absolute consistency cannot be expected. Even a translator with a high degree of consistency in the rendering of a particular Hebrew word may occasionally depart from his normal policy. For example, P in Jeremiah twice translates עיר by *mdī(n)tā*, despite his usual massive preference for *qrītā*. The reasons for this "interference" will be investigated below.

Second, the scale is not quite comprehensive. It does not accommodate all translators, or all innovations. In P of Ruth we find a translator who cannot be fitted into the scale. Here חסד is rendered *ḥesdā*, which according to the scale should imply that עיר is rendered *qrītā*; but in fact עיר becomes *mdī(n)tā*. As to innovations, an example not consistent with the scale is the use of *diatīqī* to the exclusion of the native word *qyāmā* to render ברית. This feature is mainly confined to Joshua and Chronicles — a combination that could not have been suspected from fig. 1. In fig. 1, Chronicles is among the most conservative books; Joshua is more modern, though by no means the most; and the two books stand well apart from each other.[39] More detail is given below.

Clearly it is an over-simplification to assert that all the innovations in the scale spread into the language by exactly the same route. For example, the innovation *mdī(n)tā* (for "city") seems for the most part to have followed in the wake of the innovation *ṭaybutā* (for חסד); but there is one translator (namely in Ruth) who has the innovation *mdī(n)tā* without the innovation *ṭaybūtā*. Again, it seems that the innovation *diatīqī* was first adopted by speakers other than the group of "modern" speakers who introduced the innovations featured in the scale of fig. 1. If we are told that a given speaker has adopted (or rejected) this particular innovation, we shall not be able to draw any inference as to which of the innovations in the scale of fig. 1 he adopts or rejects.

In short, it would be wrong to assert that the renderings in P obey immutable laws. On the other hand, it would be equally wrong to say that they are random. The differences between the translators from book to book are sufficiently systematic to suggest the boundaries between the translation units, albeit tentatively.

The books apparently translated last, namely Ezra to Chronicles, are among the most conservative in lexical usage. Now a "conservative" translator may have worked in the same period as a "modern" one, or even a little later, but (to hazard a guess) hardly more than two generations later. It is a fair conclusion that all the books of the Hebrew Bible were translated within the span of one or two generations, but by translators who were not all equally receptive to innovation. The "modern" usages (e.g. *mdī(n)tā* for "city", *yaqda šalmā* for "burnt offering") naturally became normative for later translations into Syriac, such as the P versions of the Apocrypha and New Testament.[40]

The Influence of the Septuagint

Many of the innovations are Greek loanwords or calques from Greek. In some measure, they seem due to the influence not merely of the Greek language, but of the LXX version.

A striking feature of investigations into the possible influence of LXX upon P is that the results differ between books. Haefeli's survey of research to his own day,[41] published in 1927, shows LXX's influence to be frequent in Ezekiel, the Twelve Prophets and the Solomonic books; sporadic in Genesis, Joshua, Isaiah, Jeremiah,

[39]Some other books (notably Jeremiah) uses *diatīqī* sporadically, while retaining *qyāmā* as the main rendering; but the combination of these with Joshua and Chronicles again does not fit in with the scale of fig. 1.

[40]There are some exceptions. The Old Syriac Gospels retain *gālūtā* "exile" (Matt 1:11, 17) and *kespā* "silver" (Matt 10:9, 26:15, 27:3, 9). Even P in the New Testament has *ōrāytā* as a technical term for the Pentateuch.

[41]L. Haefeli, *Die Peschitta des Alten Testamentes* (Münster 1927).

Psalms and Esther;[42] and insignificant or non-existent in Samuel, Kings, Job, Lamentations and Chronicles. Of course these results were based on studies each restricted to one book,[43] but a correlation between those results and the above scale of lexical usage is clear. Evidently the translators at the top end of fig. 1 were not only conservative in their lexicon but also faithful to the *Hebraica veritas*, and therefore unwilling to consult LXX, even when the Hebrew exemplar was obscure (as in Job) or illegible (as in Chronicles). The translators at the other extreme were prepared to admit not only lexical innovations but also the use of LXX to illuminate the Hebrew. Indeed the two phenomena may converge: thus *yaqdā šalmā* for עולה and *eštbī* for גלה are not only innovations but also imitations of the text of LXX (ὁλοκαύτωμα, αἰχμαλωτεύομαι).

Sources of Interference

The tables above showed that a book which usually favours one rendering may occasionally choose its rival. The main reasons for this may be classified as follows:

Variations of Nuance

Normally, גלה "go into exile" has people as subject. At Judg 18:30, however, the subject is the land. Although P in Judges is normally conservative, the land could not be said to depart into exile. Hence the modern rendering *eštbī* "be captured" (which could apply to the land as well as to people) could not be avoided.

Further examples of attention to nuance appear in the rendering of עיר. Even though most translators had a definite preference between *qrītā* and *mdī(n)tā*, they were aware that *mdī(n)tā* denoted a greater or mightier settlement than *qrītā*. Thus in Lamentations, the mighty Jerusalem of the past is called *mdī(n)tā* (Lam 1:1), but in its ruined state it is called *qrītā* (Lam 2:12, 15; 5:11). Again, P in Esther uses *mdī(n)tā* for Shushan but *qrītā* for the lesser cities. The usage of *qrītā* and *mdī(n)tā* in Joshua is conditioned similarly (Appendix).

Sometimes a contrast in the original forces the translator to use both the conservative and the modern rendering. For example, the Hebrew at 1 Sam 6:18 contrasts עיר מבצר "fortified city" with כפר הפרזי "open village". P needed *qrītā* to indicate the village, and so had to use *mdī(n)tā* of the fortified city. Again, Jer 19:15

---

[42]We may add Daniel, according to M. J. Wyngaarden, *The Syriac Version of the Book of Daniel* (Leipzig 1923), which Haefeli had not had the opportunity to use.

[43]Barnes's brief but nevertheless wide-ranging study anticipated the conclusions reported in Haefeli. The most recent study is by J. Lund, *The Influence of the Septuagint on the Peshitta: a Re-evaluation in Light of Comparative Study of the Versions in Genesis and Psalms*, unpublished diss., Jerusalem 1988. Lund's view is that P has not been influenced by LXX. Unfortunately, Lund restricts himself to Genesis and Psalms, as the existing investigations into possible LXX influence upon these books happen to be the lengthiest. He thus leaves aside those books where LXX influence is clearest.

threatens evil אל העיר הזאת ועל כל עריה. Evidently העיר refers to Jerusalem and עריה to its daughter-cities. To point the contrast, P translates the first word by *mdī(n)tā* and the second by *qrītā*. The case is similar at Neh 11:1 and Zech 7:7; in both passages "cities" contrast with Jerusalem. Parallelism too can force the use of two renderings, i.e. the conservative and the modern; thus at Hab 2:12, the normal rendering for "city" in the book, namely *mdī(n)tā*, appears in the first line (for עיר) and *qrītā* (for קריה) in the second.

Hangover

Although the usual word for "city" in P on Kings is *qrītā*, we find *mdī(n)tā* at 1 Kgs 20:19, 30. This is due to the appearance of מדינות in the Hebrew of 1 Kgs 20:14-19. Likewise in Ezra the occurrence of מדנן in the Aramaic of 4:15 has brought in *mdī(n)tā* for עיר at 4:15,19; by 4:20 the effect has worn off, and *qrītā* is again in use. Conversely, in Ezekiel the usual rendering is *mdī(n)tā*, but *qrītā* appears at Ezek 39:3, as a hangover from 38:13, where the Hebrew had כפיר but the translator read כפר "village" and translated *quryā*.

Initial instability

A translator may revise his initial policy. A striking example occurs at Gen 1:1 and 1 Chr 4:41. In both books the translators first intended to use Syriac *yāt*, corresponding to את, to mark every direct object (apart from named persons, which Syriac always introduces with *l-*). After the first relevant verse, however, they abandoned *yāt*, apparently because they decided that such literalism would impede intelligibility. However, neither translator went back to remove the initial *yāt*.[44]

Initial instability may be detected in the renderings of עולה in Leviticus and Numbers. In each book the translator begins with the "conservative" *ʿlātā*, but seems dissatisfied, tries other renderings and eventually settles on *yaqdā šalmā*. The detailed pattern in these two books follows:

---

[44]On the use of *yāt*, sometimes erroneously claimed as a western Aramaic element, see the article "Peshitta, Septuagint and Targum" (n. 31 above), p. 75.

Lev	*ʿlātā*	1:3, 9, 10, 13, 14, 17; 3:5; 4:7, 8, 10, 24, 25, 29, 30, 33, 34; 5:7, 10; 6:2, 3, 5, 18; 9:7; 14:22, 31; 15:30; 16:5.
	yaqdā	1:6.
	yaqdā da-ʿlātā	7:37; 8:13, 23; 9:2, 3.
	yaqdā la-ʿlātā	8:21.
	yaqdā šalmā	7:2, 8, 8; 9:17, 22; 10:19; 12:6, 8; 15:15; 16:3, 24, 24; 17:8; 22:18; 23:18, 37.
	qurbānā	1:4.
Num	*ʿlātā*	6:14; 7 (13x); 8:12; 15:3, 5, 24; 23:3, 6, 15, 16, 17.
	yaqdā	10:10.
	yaqdā šalmā	6:11, 16; 15:8; 28 (14x); 29 (16x).

A new start is evident at the beginning of Numbers, if not a new translator.

Cohesion within the Pentateuch

Two words are rendered more conservatively in Genesis and Exodus than in the rest of the Pentateuch: כסף is rendered by *kespā* rather than *sēmā*, and עולה by *ʿlātā* rather than *yaqdā šalmā*. It will be recalled that in the 14 renderings of כסף in Exodus where 5bl reads *kespā* and the majority *sēmā*, the rendering of 5bl appears original. Still, there are two passages in Exodus — 11:2 and 12:35 — where even 5bl has the "modern" rendering *sēmā* (as against 28 occurrences of *kespā* elsewhere in 5bl). As to עולה, P at Exod 35:16; 38:1 has *yaqdā*, and at Exod 18:12; 24:5 the full expression *yaqdā šalmā* (as against 13 occurrences of *ʿlātā*). This small minority of "modern" renderings in Exodus can be accounted for in more than one way. One possibility is that in these passages too the original text was *kespā* (or *ʿlātā*) but was ousted from all biblical MSS, including 5bl, by later modernising scribes;[45] it is worth noting that Ephrem's citation of Exod 11:2 actually has *kespā*.[46] On that view the fact that this handful of "modern" renderings occur in Exodus rather than Genesis is not significant. Alternatively, one could suppose that the translators of the adjacent books Exodus and Leviticus conferred, and that the translator of Exodus understood his colleague's misgivings about the intelligibility of *kespā* ("silver") and *ʿlātā* ("burnt-offering"). It may even be that the P version of the whole Pentateuch goes back to the

[45]So M. D. Koster, *The Peshitta of Exodus: The Development of its Text in the Course of Fifteen Centuries* (Assen 1977), pp. 70-72.
[46]R.-M. Tonneau (ed.), *Sancti Ephraemi Syri in Genesim et in Exodum Commentarii* (= *CSCO* 152, *Syr* 71) (Louvain 1955) p. 140.

same translator, who in the course of Exodus began to feel dissatisfied with these two conservative usages, and in the later books came to abandon both.

Agreement Patterns That Cut Across the Implicational Scale

So far we have discussed innovations whose distribution tends to follow the implicational scale of fig. 1, and also the factors that occasionally break the underlying pattern. We now turn to some innovations whose distribution tends to cut systematically across the implicational scale. These help us to break up some of the larger groupings in fig. 1.

We may begin with Hebrew ברית, for which, as already mentioned, the native (though not cognate) rendering *qyāmā* had to compete with the Greek loanword *diatīqī* (διαθήκη), whence the following distribution:

Renderings of ברית

	Gn	Ex	Lv	Nu	Dt	Jos	Jg	Sam	Kg	Isa	Jer	Ezek	Dodk
qyāmā	26	12	10	5	26	0	3	13	25	12	14	15	11
diatīqī	0	0	0	0	0	15	0	0	0	0	7	1	4

	Ps	Pr	Job	Dan	Chr
qyāmā	16	1	1	5	2
diatīqī	0	0	0	2	13[47]

In this case Joshua and Chronicles — which lay towards the modern and towards the conservative end of the spectrum respectively — unite against the other books in preferring the innovation *diatīqī*. The innovation is also not infrequent in Jeremiah, which had a conservative record so far. It is worth noting that Joshua and Chronicles are also linked by their common policy of translating Heb. זקן as *qašīš* rather than *sāʾb*, which is perhaps the earlier usage (see below).

Joshua and Chronicles are divided, however, by the next discriminator, namely ויהי before a phrase or clause of time which introduces another verb. Some books render literally (*wa-hwā*), others omit, and two use the adverb *hāydēn* "then", on the following pattern:

---

[47]P in Chronicles even adds *diatīqī* in some passages where MT does not have ברית (2 Chr 5:10, 7:22, 29:9). Of the rarer renderings of ברית, one may note *mawmtā* (Ezra 10:3, twice in Nehemiah and 5 times in Chronicles).

Renderings of ויהי

	Gn	Ex	Lv	Nu	Dt	Jos	Jg	Sam	Kg	Isa	Jer	Ezek	Dodk
[rendered]	38	16	1	3	1	0	4	28	15	3	5	2	1
[omitted]	21	5	0	5	4	26	20	30	65	0	15	11	2
hāydēn	0	0	0	0	0	0	0	0	0	0	0	0	0

	Job	Ru	Est	Dan	Neh	Chr
[rendered]	2	3	1	0	1	22
[omitted]	0	0	4	2	0	0
hāydēn	0	0	0	0	10	2

The figures for Samuel mask a change occurring somewhere in 2 Sam 6 or 7. Up to 2 Sam 6:13, ויהי is usually rendered (27x) and relatively seldom omitted (10x). From 2 Sam 7:1 onwards, however, ויהי is usually omitted (20x), and only once rendered (2 Sam 8:1). Earlier we noted that a long sequence of renderings of ארון by *ārōnā* ceased at just this point, with *ārōnā* at 2 Sam 6:16 and *qībōtā* in the next verse. To these we may add a third Hebrew word which has two different renderings in Samuel, with a change of policy just here. The divine title צבאות is transliterated in all seven places where it occurs in Samuel up to and including 2 Sam 6:2, but from 2 Sam 6:18 it is rendered *ḥayeltānā* "mighty". The convergence of these three shifts suggests that a fresh translator may have taken over at this point.[48] All three shifts move away from imitation of the Hebrew towards Syriac idiom.

Renderings of צבאות

	Sam	Kg	Isa	Jer	Dodk	Ps	Chr
[transliterated]	7	0	1	12	0	0	0
ḥayeltānā	4	4	58	64	103	15	3

The renderings for ויהי and צבאות both cut across the scale. In the case of ויהי, we observe a difference between Chronicles and the first part of Samuel on the

[48]It is worth noting that in the Septuagint a similar shift occurs in the rendering of צבאות. Lucian's recension usually transliterates σαβαωθ up to 2 Sam 6:18 but always has παντοκράτωρ "almighty" thereafter; see the collations of boc$_2$e$_2$ in A. E. Brooke, N. McLean and H. St-J. Thackeray, *The Old Testament in Greek*, vol. 2 (Cambridge 1935). In the other manuscripts σαβαωθ ceases at 1 Sam 17:45. It may be added that, although חסד is usually rendered *ṭaybutā* throughout Samuel, the cases in the chapters following the breakpoint show some instability, as if a new translator was finding his feet. Thus we have *ḥesdā* at 2 Sam 7:15 and *raḥme* at 2 Sam 9:1, 3, before the regular *ṭaybutā* is resumed at 2 Sam 9:7.

one hand, and the remaining historical books (including Joshua) on the other. The difference is particularly clear in the rendering of 1 Kgs 14:6. Here the translator of Kings omitted ויהי, while the translator of Chronicles — who inserted his own translation of 1 Kgs 12:1-14:9 after 1 Chr 10 instead of the corresponding text of Chronicles — renders *wa-hwā*. As to צבאות, the first part of Samuel allies itself with Jeremiah in transliterating this divine title, against the other historical books, prophets and psalms.

Some Peculiarities of One Book or a Small Number of Books

Ironically, Song of Songs and Qohelet in their Peshitta form, which have a wholly modern attitude to "city" and "silver", are alone in regularly using *yāt* and other Hebraisms (e.g. *twb* for Heb. שוב). Both may well go back to the same translator. Conceivably their literalism is due to the influence of LXX, which in these books follows the literal style of Aquila.

The singular הבל is rendered by its Syriac cognate *heblā* regularly in Qohelet (33x). In Jeremiah the rendering is instead *lā medem* (Jer 2:5; 10:3, 15; 16:19; 51:18). Yet another rendering, namely *lahgā* "vapour", going back to the primary meaning of the Hebrew, is usual in Psalms (6 times).[49] This evidence suggests that the three books of Psalms, Jeremiah and Qohelet all stand apart from each other, as was already apparent from fig. 1.

The P version of Job has a number of innovations peculiar to itself: *šlāmā* for חסד (10:12; 36:14, but *ḥesdā* at 37:13), *aksnāyā* for גר (31:32), and the vague terms *debḥā* (1:5) or *qurbānā* (42:8) for עולה. These must be weighed against the "conservative" performance of Job with respect to the other discriminators.

These renderings, being confined to a small number of books, do not conflict with the implicational scale, but neither do they provide additional evidence for it.

Text-Critical Aspects

Modern usages may be introduced either by the translators or by later copyists, and for the present study the distinction is crucial. Attention must therefore be focused on the oldest readings extant. These are sometimes confined to just one manuscript, or a minority of manuscripts, apparently because in some books a revised edition of P was promulgated at an early stage. The main carriers of the older text are 5bl (Genesis-Exodus), 6bl (Leviticus-Numbers), 7pj2 (Numbers), 8h5 (Ezra-Nehemiah), 10f1

---

[49]The adjective *srīq* (or a derivative) appears in Isaiah (2x), Dodekapropheton (1x), Psalms (2x), Proverbs (1x), Job (2x) and Lamentations (1x). Note also the renderings *abdānā* (Prov 21:6), *ʿawlā* (Prov 13:11) and *ʿelʿālā* (Isa 57:13). The plural of הבל, when it has the different nuance of "idols" (and in P becomes *deḥlātā*), may be left aside.

(Esther) and 9al (Leviticus-Kings, Isaiah-Hosea, Psalms, Lamentations and Chronicles).[50] Thus most manuscripts make Exodus appear a *sēmā* book; only 5bl regularly has *kespā*. In Kings, only 9al preserves *ḥesdā*, while other MSS modernise to *ṭaybutā* (1 Kgs 2:7; 3:6, 6; 8:23). Similarly at Gen 26:3, for MT ארצות, only 5bl has *arʿātā*, while the other MSS have modernised to *malkwātā*.

This suggests that in other cases of lexical variation between the more conservative manuscripts and the rest, the former likewise preserve the usage of the original text. Koster has pointed to passages where the most conservative MSS have Syr. *gmr* for כלה "finish" while the others have *šlm*, namely at Gen 24:45 27:30, Exod 31:18 34:33 (5bl), Num 7:1 (5bl, 6bl, 9al), 1 Kgs 8:54 (9al)[51]. Again, for זקן we find *sāʾbā* in 5bl alone at Exod 17:5, and in 9al alone in Judg 2:7, whilst the other manuscripts have *qašišā*, which presumably is the later reading.

Even where the textual tradition is uniform, lexical equivalences that apply in most passages may justify textual emendation in some of the exceptional passages. Thus at Josh 15:9, where MT speaks of cities (of Mount Ephron), we may reasonably emend *qarnā* to *quryā*. Again, at Judg 20:42 for ואשר בערים the P MSS show *wa-b-qadmītā*, which however seems corrupt for *w-ba-qrītā*. Likewise at 1 Sam 28:3 (MT: בעירו), the existing P reading *b-qabreh* may be corrupt for *ba-qrīteh*. Conversely, the unexpected appearance of a Syriac word normally used in accordance with the equivalences discussed above may be due to corruption: thus at Josh 18:9 for מחנה the P MSS show *mdī(n)tā*, which however could be a corruption of *mašrītā*.

The Translation Units

The work above has indicated differences in linguistic usage in the different books of P. These differences do not of course suffice to indicate the boundaries of the translation units definitively, since one cannot know how much inconsistency to allow in the work of an individual translator. Still, the following units may tentatively be proposed:

Genesis, Exodus
Leviticus, Numbers, Deuteronomy
Joshua
Judges, Samuel, Kings[52]
Isaiah, Psalms[53]

[50] M. P. Weitzman, "The Originality of Unique Readings in 9al" in *Symp*, pp. 225-258.
[51] M. D. Koster, "Peshiṭta Revisited: a Reassessment of its Value as a Version", *JSS* 38 (1993), pp. 235-268: 263.
[52] Apparently different translators (even within Samuel) who nevertheless shared conservative attitudes.
[53] These books share a vague lexical policy, which, however, need not mean a single translator.

Jeremiah, Daniel[54]
Ezekiel, Dodekapropheton, Proverbs[55]
Job
Song of Songs, Qohelet
Ruth
Lamentations
Esther, Ezra, Nehemiah : Chronicles[56]

Links Among the Translation Units

We must now consider any links which might suggest a degree of cohesion between the translation units suggested above. There are certainly a number of common features in the different books of P, such as the regular rendering of the tetragrammaton by *māryā* (compare κύριος in LXX) and the replacement of Aram by Edom.[57] Again, P is generally tolerant of anthropomorphisms applied to God, except for particular expressions which are softened in every book, whatever its lexical usage. One such expression is Heb. *nḥm* "repent" in relation to God, which is always modified, no matter how conservative or how modern the lexical policy of the book concerned. God is instead said to "turn away" (Syr. *ahpek*) evil in the Twelve Prophets (Amos 7:3, Jonah 3:10, 4:2, Zech 8:14), while the conservative translator at 2 Sam 24:16 was equally driven to paraphrase: "and the Lord held back the angel of death who was destroying the people".[58]

We have a second linking feature when a translation in P in a passage in one book appears to have been influenced by P in another book, as in the following examples:

(a) At Gen 49:9, MT represents Judah by three different terms for lion: *gūr ʾaryēh* (lion's whelp), *ʾărī* alone, and *lābīʾ*. P duly renders the first term by *guryā d-aryā* and the second by *aryā* alone. For the third term he has no new Syriac word, and so repeats *guryā d-aryā*. Now the use of *guryā d-aryā* for the rarer Hebrew terms for "lion" is well attested in other books of P, and seems to have spread from this passage. This rendering *guryā d-aryā* re-appears for *lābīʾ* (Num 24:9*, Joel 1:6*), *layiš* (Isa 30:6*, Prov 30:20), *šaḥal* (Job 4:10*), and

---

[54]Note the use of *atrawātā* both in Jeremiah and at Dan 11:42.

[55]Although Ezekiel and the Twelve Prophets seem to go back to the same translator, the same need not hold for Proverbs, where many of the Hebrew discriminators are absent.

[56]These books behave similarly among themselves in relation to the discriminators (in so far as the latter occur), and a little differently from Genesis-Exodus, as noted above. They go together thematically, and share seemingly total freedom from LXX; the use of *hāydēn* for ויהי in Nehemiah and Chronicles is a further link.

[57]N. Walker, "The Peshiṭta puzzle and its implications", *VT* 18 (1968), pp. 268-270.

[58]R. Loewe, "Jerome's Treatment of an Anthropopathism", *VT* 2 (1952), pp. 261-272.

even the mother lioness *lĕbiyyā* at Ezek 19:2. (The asterisk indicates passages where the Hebrew also has another word for "lion", rendered *aryā* in P.)[59]

(b) At Gen 49:14, MT compares Issachar to a bony ass crouching between the *mišpĕtayim*. P renders this last rare word by *šbīlē* "paths". Apparently the translator drew inspiration from the description of Dan three verses later as a serpent (Heb. *šĕpīpōn*) upon the path (Heb. *ʾōraḥ*), which last word P rendered by the plural *šbīlē*. Now the Hebrew word *mišpĕtayim* occurs again at Judg 5:16, and here P again has *šbīlē*. It seems that P on Judges was influenced by P on Genesis.

(c) In Psalms the Heb. verb *ḥwš* "hasten" is unexpectedly rendered by *kattar* "wait", at Ps 22:20, 38:23, 40:14=70:2, 55:9, 70:6, 71:12 and (in 9al alone) 141:1. This curious rendering apparently arose because in all these passages the Hebrew form is *ḥūšāh* or *ʾāḥīšāh*, ending with a cohortative *-h*. These forms were wrongly connected by the translator with the verb *ḥšh*, which could mean "hesitate" (Judg 18:9, 2 Kgs 7:9; elsewhere the verb has its original sense "be silent"). It may be that the LXX rendering of אחישה at Ps 55:9 by προσεδεχόμην (itself perhaps guessed from the context) confirmed the P translator in his interpretation. Now this sense "wait" for Heb. *ḥwš* re-appears at Job 20:2, where MT has *ḥūšī bī* and P renders *kattar(w) lī* "wait for me". Apparently the translator of Job had learnt this rendering from the translator of the Psalms — even though in lexical policy Job is more conservative than Psalms.

(d) At Jer 15:9, the prophet sees the mother of seven breathe away her life; the Hebrew is *nāpĕḥā napšāh*. P renders unexpectedly *nepḥat karsāh* "her belly swelled". This is evidently an echo of the fate of the adulteress at Num 5:27 (*cf.* 21), where MT has *w-ṣābĕtā biṭnāh* and P renders, just as in Jeremiah, *nepḥat karsāh* "her belly swelled". Thus the translator of Jeremiah has associated his Hebrew *Vorlage* at 15:9 with the Syriac text of Num 5:27. This means that P in Jeremiah here depends on, and is therefore later than, P in Numbers.

(e) Neh 13:25 in MT describes Nehemiah's treatment of those who had contracted foreign marriages: *wā-ʾak mēhem ʾănāšīm wā-ʾemrĕṭēm* "I smote some of the men and tore out their hair". In P, however, Nehemiah's behaviour is more

[59]The renderings of כפיר can be left aside, since here the rendering *guryā d-aryā* is natural enough.

violent still: *w-qeṭlet menhōn gabre w-ṭemret enōn* ("and I killed some of the men and hid them"). Apparently the translator of Nehemiah was thinking of Exod 2:12, where Moses smote an Egyptian and hid him in the sand. There P renders *w-qaṭleh l-Meṣrāyā w-ṭamreh b-ḥālā*. The reason that the translator of Nehemiah thought of this passage is that he associated by sound the Hebrew verb *mrṭ* in his *Vorlage* with the Syriac verb *ṭmr* in Exodus.

A difference may be noted between cases (a)-(c) on the one hand, and (d) and (e) on the other. In the former group, a full equation with a Hebrew word on one side and a Syriac word on the other spread between books. Thus, to take example (c), the translator of Job needed to know both sides of the equation Heb. *ḥwš* = Syr. *kattar*, in order to apply it to Heb. *ḥwš* at Job 20:2. This may mean that the later translator consulted his predecessor in person; at the very least it means that he consulted not only his predecessor's Syriac translation, but also the Hebrew original behind it. Cases (d) and (e) are different in that they need only imply that the later translator knew the Syriac version produced by his predecessor; the latest translator's departure from his own Hebrew *Vorlage* suggests, if anything, that in these cases he did *not* seek out the Hebrew original behind his predecessor's Syriac version.

Nevertheless, each of these five cases shows that P in one book could influence P in another. Sometimes the influence goes from the book with the more modern to the book with the more conservative usage (cases b, c). Significantly, however, the book that exerted the influence is in each case the book that stands earlier in the traditional Jewish canon.[60] The evidence is indeed consistent with Beckwith's suggestion that the books were translated in substantially the order traditional among the Jews.[61]

Again, in parallel passages in the Hebrew Bible — such as 2 Sam 22 // Ps 18, or 2 Kgs 18-20 // Isa 36-39 — the P renderings in the two books display a degree of similarity that cannot be put down to coincidence. These cases too suggest consultation among the translators, though here we have to be cautious, given the likelihood of scribal revision to harmonise two obviously parallel passages.

One School of Translators?

It seems that P is the work of a number of different translators. These translators however conferred together, and also had a common approach to the task of translation, both generally (in their striving for plain intelligibility even at the expense of literalness) and in certain characteristic renderings (e.g. the divine title *māryā*). So far as

[60] The influence running from Psalms to Job is noteworthy, given that Job precedes Psalms in Syriac Biblical manuscripts.
[61] See n. 37.

the philological side of translation is concerned, they can fairly be said to belong to a single school.

Within that school, however, we discern opposing trends: conservative and modern. The "modern" translators differed not only in lexical usage, but also in their readiness to draw on LXX. Indeed, they may have differed in matters of doctrine also. Some of the glosses which P places on the Hebrew text indicate attitudes to the Jewish people, and those attitudes seem to vary in different books: sometimes self-identification, sometimes hostility. The former are found to be confined among the more conservatively rendered books, e.g.

Ezra 9:14	we have transgressed thy commandments... leave for us remnants in the world
1 Chr 29:15	thou didst rule over our fathers and commanded them by which way they should go
1 Chr 29:16	save us from all the nations that harm and revile us
2 Chr 15:6-6	we were scattered in every nation for we had forsaken the Lord.

The harsher references occur in more modern books. Here the Israelites are described as despising God's word (Isa 28:13) or delighting in sin (Isa 40:2); they are dropped from passages which in the Hebrew look forward to their joy (Ps 106:5) or resurrection (Ezek 37:12); and we find a call to uproot the palaces of Jerusalem (Ps 48:14). By contrast, the "people" amongst whom the Hebrew Psalmist praised God is changed to "peoples" (Ps 35:18, 107:32). Indeed the term *aynā d-metpnē lwāt(y)* for "proselyte", in some "modern" books, implies that the proselyte's first concern is not with the Jewish people: he turns directly to God. It may be that in the period of the translation the Jews were reeling from the wretched outcome of their uprising under Trajan and the Bar-Cochba revolt. The more conservative continued to identify with the Jewish people, whose plight moved them to guilt and shame. However, there were also innovators, who turned their backs on the Jews as a nation and instead sought salvation for the individual and for their own group, called the "elect" (Ps 30:5, 31:22, 32:6, 50:5)[62] or the "congregation" that God would form at the end-time (Mal 3:17).[63]

Speculative interpretation of the evidence, however, as in the last paragraph, has not been the primary aim of this study. Rather, the aim has been to distinguish the

[62]This divisive term was eschewed by rabbinic Judaism before the Middle Ages; see M.P. Weitzman, "Usage and Avoidance of the Term 'Chosen People'" (Hebrew with English summary), *Language Studies (Jerusalem)* 1990, pp. 101-128.

[63]Both wings are characterised by indifference to ritual, as opposed to faith and prayer (Weitzman, n. 33: pp. 153-156; 159-160). Eventually, it may be that the conservative wing died out in despair of national salvation, while the modern wing was absorbed into the church.

contributions of the different translators, and assess the degree of cohesion among them, in order to narrow the limits which any general description of P, or any hypothesis about the origin of the whole of P, will have to respect.

Appendix : The Rendering of "City" in Joshua

Apart from names (excluded here) the noun קריה is absent from Joshua, so that we are concerned with עיר alone. Here *mdī(n)tā* is used for the cities of the Canaanites — Jericho (14x in ch. 6), Ai (22x in ch. 8), Gibeon (10:2), Kiriath-Jearim (18:14), other southern cities (10:19), Hazor (11:12,14), the giants' cities (11:21; 14:12) and Tyre (19:29). The reason is presumably that many Canaanite cities are stated to have been large and fortified. The only named Israelite settlement called *mdī(n)tā* is at 19:35, but even here the translator was thinking of a Canaanite city: although MT has *haṣ-ṣiddīm ṣēr*, just west of Lake Chinnereth, P translates: "Tyre and Sidon".

By contrast, *qrītā* is constantly used in 19-21 for Israelite settlements. It also indicates the lesser cities of the Canaanites — the obscure Adam (3:16), the cities contrasted at 11:13 with the royal cities called *mdīnātā*, and the dependencies of Hebron and Debir (10:37, 39). The choice of *qrītā* to render "their cities" (sc. of the Gibeonites) at 9:17 seems similar, even though the list includes Gibeon itself and Kiriath-Jearim.

The distinction between *qrītā* and *mdī(n)tā* is emphasised in P's treatment of the summary that conclude each sub-list of cities in these chapters. These summaries give the number of cities in the sub-list, normally using *quryā*; but where the sub-list contained any originally Canaanite city, the summary instead has *mdīnātā* — at 19:38 (owing to the perceived reference to Tyre and Sidon) and at 21:18 (where Gibeon is included). (By hangover, *mdīnātā* also entered the next sub-lists, at 19:48 and 21:26 respectively, where it stands beside *quryā.*) The grand total in 21:42 duly uses (on two occasions) both words: *quryā wa-mdīnātā.*

Very occasionally the influence of a passage in Deuteronomy, in which book *qrītā* is always used, seems to be the reason that *qrītā* is applied to a Canaanite city. The claim at 11:19, that not a single city escaped the Israelites, recalls Deut 3:4, and עיר is rendered *qrītā* in both passages. Similarly, *qrītā* denotes the cities of Sihon and Og in Josh 13, apparently in line with Deut 2-3.

Conversely, an Israelite settlement is exceptionally called *mdī(n)tā* at Josh 20:6, but the reason is to point a contrast with a *qrītā* in the same verse. Here a killer who has served his term at a city of refuge returns to his own city, both being עיר in the Hebrew; P uses *qrītā* for the former and *mdī(n)tā* for the latter.

Only once is עיר rendered other than by these two words: at 10:20, עיר מבצר becomes *karkā*. (On *qarnā* at 15:9, see the text-critical discussion above.)

BIBLIOGRAPHY

Abramson, Sh. (ed.) *Tractate ʿAbodah Zarah* (New York 1956)

Albright, W. F. *Archaeology and the Religion of Israel*, (Baltimore 1968)[5]

Allberry, C. R. (ed.) *A Manichaean Psalm-Book* II (Stuttgart 1938)

Altenmüller, H. "Feste", *LÄ* 2 (1977), col. 171-191

Altheim, F. and R. Stiehl, *Die Araber in der alten Welt* IV (Berlin 1967), V (Berlin 1968)

Andersen, F. I. and A. D. Forbes, *The Vocabulary of the Old Testament* (Rome 1989)

Aruch Completum, A. Kohut (ed.) (Vienna 1928[2])

Asmussen, J. "A Judeo-Persian Precedence-Dispute Poem and some Thoughts on the History of the Genre", in J. Asmussen, *Studies in Judeo-Persian Literature* (Leiden 1973), pp. 32-59

Assaf, S. *Gaonic Responsa from Geniza Mss.* (Jerusalem 1929) [Hebrew]

Assaf, S. תקופת הגאונים וספרותה (Jerusalem 1955)

Astarita, M. L. *Avidio Cassio* (Rome 1983)

Atkinsons, K. "The Legitimacy of Cambyses and Darius as Kings of Egypt", *JAOS* 76 (1956), pp. 167-177

Avigad, N. "Three Ornamented Hebrew Seals", *IEJ* 4 (1954), pp. 236-238

Babakhan, J. "Vulgarisation des homélies métriques de Jacques de Saroug ...", *ROC* 2nd series 18, 8 (1913), pp. 358-374

Bacher, W. Review of the *Aruch Completum*, *ZDMG* 47 (1893), pp. 487-514

Bar-Asher, M. "Le syro-palestinien – études grammaticales", *JA* 276 (1988), pp. 50-53

Bar-Asher, M. *Palestinian Syriac Studies, Source-Texts, Traditions and Grammatical Problems* (Dissertation, Jerusalem 1977)

Bar-Asher, M. "Two Grammatical Phenomena in Palestinian Syriac" in *Meḥqarim belašon* (Jerusalem 1987), pp. 114-117

Bauer, H. and P. Leander *Grammatik des Biblisch-Aramäischen* (Halle 1927)

Bauer, H. and P. Leander *Historische Grammatik der hebräischen Sprache des Alten Testamentes* (Halle 1922)

Baumstark, A. "Neue orientalistische Probleme biblischer Textgeschichte", *ZDMG* 89 (1935), pp. 89-118

Baumstark, A. *Geschichte der syrischen Literatur* (Bonn 1922)

Beck, E. (ed.) *Des hl. Ephraem des Syrers Carmina Nisibena*, pt. 2, CSCO 240-241 (1963)

Beck, E. (ed.) *Des hl. Ephraem des Syrers Hymnen de Ecclesia*, CSCO 198-199 (1960)

Beck, E. (ed.) *Des hl. Ephraem des Syrers Hymnen de Fide*, CSCO 154-155 (1954)

Beck, E. (ed.) *Des hl. Ephraem des Syrers Hymnen de Virginitate*, CSCO 223-224 (1962)

Beck, E. (ed.) *Des hl. Ephraem des Syrers Paschahymnen* (HResur), CSCO 248-249 (1964)

Beckwith, R. *The Old Testament Canon of the New Testament Church* (London 1985)

Beeston, A. F. L. "A Minaean Market Code", *BSOAS* 41 (1978), pp. 142-5

Bekkum, W. J. van "Observations on the Hebrew Debate in Mediaeval Europe" in Reinink and Vanstiphout, *DPD*, pp. 77-90

Ben-Hayyim, Z. "Studies in Palestinian Aramaic and Samaritan Poetry" in S.Abramson and A. Minski (eds.) *Hayyim (Jefim) Shirmann, Jubilee Volume* (Jerusalem 1970), pp. 39-68

Ben-Hayyim, Z. *The Literary and Oral Tradition of Hebrew and Aramaic amongst the Samaritans* (Jerusalem 1957–1977

Ben-Hayyim, Z. תיבת מרקה *Tibat Mârqe, A Collection of Samaritan Midrashim* (Jerusalem 1988)

Benz, F. L. *Personal Names in the Phoenician and Punic Inscriptions* (Rome 1972)

Bergsträßer, G. *Glossar des neuaramäischen Dialekts von Maʿlūla* (Leipzig 1921)

Beyer, K. *Die aramäischen Texte vom Toten Meer* (Göttingen 1984)

Beyer, K. and A. Livingstone "Die neuesten aramäischen Inschriften aus Taimāʾ", *ZDMG* 137 (1987), pp. 285-296

Beyer, K. and A. Livingstone "Eine neue reichsaramäische Inschrift aus Taimāʾ", *ZDMG* 140/1 (1990), pp. 1-2

Black, M. *A Christian Palestinian Syriac Horologion* (Cambridge 1954)

Blake, F. R. *A Resurvey of Hebrew Tenses* (Rome 1951)

Blau, J. "Short Philological Notes on the Inscription of Mešaʿ", *Maarav* 2 (1979-80), pp. 143-157

Blenkinsopp, J. "The Mission of Udjahorresnet and those of Ezra and Nehemiah", *JBL* 106 (1987), pp. 409-421

Bokser, B. M. "Talmudic Studies" in S. J. D. Cohen and E. L. Greenstein (eds.) *The State of Jewish Studies* (Detroit 1990), pp. 81-83

Borisov, A. J. "Epigraficheskie zametki", *Epigrafika Vostoka* 19 (1969), pp. 1-13

Bottéro, J. "La 'tenson' et la réflexion sur les choses en Mesopotamie", in Reinink and Vanstiphout, *DPD*, pp. 7-22.

Bowersock, G.W. *Roman Arabia* (Cambridge-London 1983)

Bowman, R. A. "Aramaeans, Aramaic and the Bible", *JNES* 7 (1948), pp. 65-90

Bresciani, E. "Egypt, Persian Satrapy", in *The Cambridge History of Judaism I: Introduction, The Persian Period* (Cambridge 1984), pp. 358-372

Bresciani, E. *Letteratura e poesia dell'antico Egitto* (Turin 1969)

Bresciani, E. "The Persian Occupation of Egypt", in I. Gershevitch (ed.) *The Cambridge History of Iran II: The Median and Achaemenian Periods* (Cambridge 1985), pp. 502-528

Brinkman, J. A. *Political History of Post-Kassite Babylonia, 1158-722*, AnOr 43 (Rome 1968)

Brock, S. P. "A Dispute of the Months and Some Related Syriac Texts", *JSS* 30 (1985), pp.181-211

Brock, S. P. "A Piece of Wisdom Literature in Syriac", *JSS* 13 (1968), pp. 212-217

Brock, S. P. "Aspects of Translation Technique in Antiquity", *Greek, Roman, and Byzantine Studies* 20 (1979), pp. 69-87

Brock, S.P. "A Syriac collection of prophecies of the pagan philosophers", *Orientalia Lovaniensia Periodica* 14 (1983), pp. 203-246

Brock, S. P. "Dialogue Hymns of the Syriac Churches", *Sobornost/ECR* 5 (1983), pp. 35-45

Brock, S. P. "From Antagonism to Assimilation: Syriac Attitudes to Greek Learning", in *East of Byzantium* (Dumbarton Oaks Symposium 1980, Washington D.C. 1982), pp. 17-34; reprint in Brock, *Syriac Perspectives on Late Antiquity* (London 1984)

Brock, S. P. "From Ephrem to Romanos", in E. Livingstone (ed.), *Studia Patristica* 20 (Leuven 1989), pp. 139-151

Brock, S.P. "Limitations of Syriac in representing Greek", in Bruce M. Metzger, *The Early Versions of the New Testament* (Oxford 1977), pp. 83-98

Brock, S. P. *Soghyatha Mgabbyatha* (Glane [Monastery of St. Ephrem] 1982)

Brock, S. P. "Some New Syriac Documents from the Third Century AD", *Aram* 3 (1991; appeared in 1993), pp. 259-267

Brock, S. P. "Syriac Dialogue Poems: Marginalia to a Recent Edition", *Muséon* 97 (1984), pp. 29-58

Brock, S. P. "Syriac Dispute Poems: The Various Types", in Reinink and Vanstiphout, *DPD*, pp. 109-119

Brock, S. P. "The Dispute Between Soul and Body: An Example of a Long-lived Mesopotamian Literary Genre", *Aram* 1 (1989), pp. 53-64

Brock, S. P. *The Harp of the Spirit* (London 1983[2])

Brock, S. P. "Three Thousand Years of Aramaic Literature", *Aram* 1/1 (1989), pp. 11-23

Brockelmann, C. *Syrische Grammatik* (Leipzig 1912[3])

Brockelmann, K. *Lexicon Syriacum* (Halle 1928[2])

Brody, R. ספרות הגאונים והטקסט התלמודי, *Meḥqerei Talmud* 1 (1990), pp. 237-303

Brooke, A. E., N. McLean and H. St-J. Thackeray *The Old Testament in Greek*, II (Cambridge 1935)
Brunner, C. J. "The Fable of the Babylonian Tree", *JNES* 39 (1980) pp. 191-202; pp. 291-302
Burnstein, S. M. "Psammetik I and the End of Nubian Domination in Egypt", *JSSEA* 14/2 (1984), pp. 31-34
Cagni, L. "Considérations sur les textes babyloniens de Neirab près d'Alep," *Transeuphratène* 2 (1990), pp. 169-85
Cameron, A. "Disputations, Polemical Literature and the Formation of Opinion in the Early Byzantine Period", in Reinink-Vanstiphout, *DPD* pp.91-108
Caminos, R. A. "The Nicrotis Adoption Stela", *JEA* 50 (1964), pp. 71-101
Campbell Thompson, R. *Devils and Evil Spirits of Babylonia* (London 1903)
Cantineau, J. *Grammaire du palmyrénien épigraphique* (Cairo 1935)
Cantineau, J. *Inventaire des inscriptions de Palmyre* III (Beirut 1930)
Cantineau, J. "Tadmorea II", *Syria* 17 (1936), pp. 277-282
Cantineau, J. "Textes Palmyréniens provenant de la Fouille du Temple de Bêl", *Syria* 12 (1939), pp. 116-141
Carmi, T. *The Penguin Book of Hebrew Verse* (Harmondsworth 1981)
Castellino, G. R. "Two Šulgi Hymns (BC)", *Studi Semitici* 42 (Rome 1972)
Cavigneaux, A. and B. Kh. Ismail "Die Statthalter von Suḫu und Mari im 8.Jh. v.Chr.", *BaM* 21 (1990), pp. 321-456
Chambers, J. K. and P. Trudgill *Dialectology* (Cambridge 1980)
Contini, R. "I documenti aramaici dell'Egitto persiano e tolemaico", *Riv. Bibl. It.* 34 (1986), pp. 73-109
Cook, E. M. "The Orthography of Final Unstressed Long Vowels in Old and Imperial Aramaic", in *Sopher Mahir: Northwest Semitic Studies Presented to S.Segert, Maarav* 5-6 (1990) p. 52-67
Cook, E. Y. *Rewriting the Bible: The Text and Language of Pseudo-Jonathan* (UCLA dissertation 1986)
Corpus Inscriptionum Semiticarum, Inscriptiones Aramaicas, III: Inscriptiones Palmyreneas (Paris 1926-1947)
Cowley, A. *Aramaic Papyri of the Fifth Century B.C.* (Oxford 1923; reprint Osnabrück 1967)
Craig Melchart, H. "PIE velars in Luvian*", in C. Watkins (ed.) *Studies in Memory of Warren Cowgill (1929-1985)* (Berlin 1987) pp. 182-204
Dalman, G. *Aramäisch-Neuhebräisches Handwörterbuch zu Targum, Talmud und Midrasch* (Göttingen 1938)
Dalman, G. *Megillat Taanit*: *Grammatik des jüdisch-palästinischen Aramäisch* (Leipzig 1905^2; reprint Darmstadt 1960)
Daube, D. *Ancient Hebrew Fables* (Oxford 1973)
Davis, M. T. and L. T. Stuckenbruck "Notes on Translation Phenomena in the Palmyrene Bilinguals", in *Intertestamental Essays in Honour of J. T. Milik* (Kraków 1992), pp. 265-283
Degen, R. *Altaramäische Grammatik* (Wiesbaden 1969)
Delaporte, L. *Epigraphes Araméens* (Paris 1912)
Deller, K. and S. Parpola "Ein Vertrag mit dem arabischen Stamm Qedar", *Orientalia* 37 (1968), pp. 464-466
Denning-Bolle, S. J. "Wisdom and Dialogue in the Ancient Near East", *Numen* 34 (1987), pp. 214-31
Diez Macho, A. *El Targum* (Madrid 1972)
Diez Merino, L. "Uso del d/dy en el arameo de Qumrán", *Aula Orientalis* 1 (1983), pp. 73-92
Dijk, J. J. A. van *La sagesse suméro-accadienne* (Leiden 1953)
Dijk, J. J. A. van "Note sur le lexique et sur la morphologie d'Enmerkar 147-155", *Orientalia* 39 (1970), pp. 302-310
Dimitrowsky, H. Z. *S'ridei Bavli*, (New York 1979)
Dirksen, P. B. and M. J. Mulder (eds.) *The Peshiṭta: Its Early Text and History* (Leiden 1988)

Dittenberger, W. (ed.) *Orientis Graeci Inscriptiones Selectae* (Leipzig 1903-5)
Dodi, A. *The Grammar of Targum Onqelos According to Geniza Fragments* (Ph.D. thesis Bar Ilan University, Ramat Gan 1981)
Donner, H. and W. Röllig *Kanaanäische und aramäische Inschriften* (Wiesbaden 1962-1976)
Dozy, R. *Supplément aux Dictionnaires Arabes* (Leiden 1881)
Drijvers, H. J. W. "Body and Soul: A Perennial Problem", in Reinink-Vanstiphout, *DPD*, pp. 119-134
Drijvers, H. J. W. "Das Heiligtum der arabischen Göttin Allât im westlichen Stadtteil von Palmyra", *Antike Welt* 7 (1976), pp. 28-38
Drijvers, H. J. W. *Old Syriac (Edessean) Inscriptions* (Leiden 1972)
Drijvers, H. J. W. "Some New Syriac Inscriptions and Archaeological Finds from Edessa and Sumatar Harabesi", *BSOAS* 36 (1973), pp.1-14
Drower, E. S. and R. Macuch *A Mandaic Dictionary* (Oxford 1963)
Duensing, H. *Christlich-palästinisch-aramäische Texte und Fragmente* (Göttingen 1906)
Dunant, C. *Le sanctuaire de Baalshamin à Palmyre, III, Les inscriptions* (Rome 1971)
Dunant, C. "Nouvelle inscription caravanière de Palmyre", *Museum Helveticum* 13 (1956), pp. 216-225
Duval, R. *La Littérature syriaque* (Paris 1907^3; reprint Amsterdam 1970)
Elitzur, Y. "The Stem Qiṭṭūl in the Mishnaic Hebrew according to Cod. Kaufmann", *Language Studies* 2-3 (Jerusalem 1987), pp. 51-65
Encyclopaedia of Islam II (Brill, Leiden 1960)
Ephᶜal, I. *The Ancient Arabs: nomads on the borders of the Fertile Crescent, 9th-5th centuries B.C.* (Magnes Press, Jerusalem 1982)
Epstein, I. (ed.) *Babylonian Talmud*, Soncino Press Translation (London 1935-52)
Epstein, J. N. *A Grammar of Babylonian Aramaic* (Jerusalem 1960)
Epstein, J. N. "Gloses babylo-araméennes", *REJ* 73 (1921), pp. 27-58, 74 (1922), pp.40-72
Epstein, J. N. "Mandäische Glossen", *Archiv Orientální* 17 (1950), pp. 165-169
Epstein, J. N. "Notes on Post-Talmudic-Aramaic Lexicography", *JQR* 12 (1921), pp.299-390
Epstein, J. N. *Studies in Talmudic Literature and Semitic Languages*, 2 vols., (Jerusalem 1983-88)
Epstein, J. N. קטעים חדשים מספר המצוות לענן, *Tarbiz* 7 (1936), pp. 283-290
Epstein, J. N. *The Gaonic Commentary on the Order Toharot Attributed to Rav Hai Gaon* (Jerusalem 1982)
Fales, F. M. *Aramaic Epigraphs on Clay Tablets of the Neo-Assyrian Period* (Rome 1986)
Fales, F. M. "La tradizione assiria ad Elefantina d'Egitto", *Dialoghi di Archeologia* 5 (1987), pp. 63-70
Fales, F. M. "On Aramaic Onomastics in the Neo-Assyrian Period," *Oriens Antiquus* 16 (1977), pp. 41-68
Fassberg, S. E. *A Grammar of the Palestinian Targum Fragments from the Cairo Genizah* (Atlanta 1990)
F. Feldmann (ed) *Syrische Wechsellieder von Narses* (Leipzig 1896)
Feissel, D. and J. Gascou "Documents d'archives romains inédits du Moyen Euphrate", *CRAI* (1989), pp. 535-561
Figulla, H. H. and W. J. Martin *UET* V, *Letters and Documents of the Old Babylonian Period* (London 1953)
Fiore, S. "La tenson en Espagne et en Babylonie: Évolution ou polygénèse?", in F. Jost (ed.), *Proceedings of the IVth Congress of the International Comparative Literature Association (Fribourg 1964)* (The Hague-Paris 1966), pp.982-992
Fitzmyer, J. A. *A Wandering Aramean. Collected Aramaic Essays* (Missoula 1979),
Fitzmyer, J. A. *The Genesis Apocryphon of Qumran Cave I* (Rome 1966; 1971^2)
Florentin, M. *A Diachronical Study of the Samaritan Aramaic Verb* (M.A. thesis, Tel Aviv University, Tel Aviv 1982)

Fraade, S. "Ascetical Aspects of Ancient Judaism", in A. Green (ed.), *Jewish Spirituality from the Bible Through the Middle Ages* (London 1986), pp.253-288

Fraenkel, S. "Die syrische Übersetzung zu den Büchern der Chronik", *Jahrbücher für Protestantische Theologie* 5 (1879), pp. 508-536, 720-759

Franco, F. "Five Aramaic incantation bowls from Tell Baruda (Choche)", *Mesopotamia* 13-14 (1978/9), pp. 233-249

Friedlander, G. *Pirqe de-Rabbi Eliezer* (London ~~1916;~~ reprint New York 1970; London 1989)

Friedman, M. A. *Jewish Marriage in Palestine (*Tel Aviv 1980)

Friedman, S. A. *A Critical Study of Yevamot X with a Methodological Introduction* (New York 1978)

Friedman, S. A. *Researches in Talmudic Literature* (Jerusalem 1983)

Friedman, S. A. שלוש הערות בדקדוק ארמית בבלית *Tarbiz* 43 (1974), pp. 58-69

Friedman, S. A. *Talmud Arukh, BT Bava Meziʿa VI* (Jerusalem 1990)

Froleyks, W. J. *Der Aγὼν Λόγων in der antiken Literatur* (Inaugural Dissertation, Bonn 1973)

Gaon, R. Yehudai *Sefer Halachot Pesuqot* (Codex Sasoon 263) (S. Sasoon (ed.)) (Jerusalem 1948; 1971)

Garelli, P. "Importance et rôle des Araméens dans l'administration de l'empire assyrien", in *Mesopotamien und seine Nachbarn, XXV. R.A.I.* (Berlin 1978), pp. 437-447

Gaster, M. *Studies and texts in folklore, magic, medieval romance, Hebrew Apocrypha and Samaritan Archaeology*, I-III (London 1925-28; reprint New York 1971), pp. 69-104

Gawlikowski, M. "Allat et Baalshamîn", in *Mélanges d'histoire ancienne et d'archéologie offerts à Paul Collart* (Lausanne 1976), pp.197-203

Gawlikowski, M. "Le sanctuaire d'Allat, Palmyre. Aperçu préliminaire", *AAAS* 33 (1983), pp.179-198

Gawlikowski, M. "Palmyre et l'Euphrate", *Syria* 60 (1983), pp.53-68

Gawlikowski, M. "Une coupe magique araméenne", *Semitica* 38 (1990), pp. 137-143

Geiger, A. *Urschrift und Uebersetzungen der Bibel* (Breslau 1857)

Gelb, I. J. *Computer-Aided Analysis of Amorite* (Chicago 1980)

Geller, M. J. "Eight incantation bowls", *Orientalia Lovaniensia Periodica* 17 (1986), pp. 101-117

Geller, M. J. "Two incantation bowls inscribed in Syriac and Aramaic", *Bulletin of the School of Oriental and African Studies* 39, University of London (1976), pp. 422-427

Gibson, J. C. L. *Textbook of Syrian Semitic Inscriptions: Vol. 2, Aramaic Inscriptions including inscriptions in the dialect of Zenjirli* (1975)

Gignoux, Philippe *Incantations magiques syriaques*. Collection de la Revue des Études Juives (Louvain-Paris 1987)

Ginzberg, L. *Legends of the Jews* (Philadelphia 1909-38)

Giron, N. "Note sur une tombe découverte près de Cheikh-Fadl par Monsieur Flinders Petrie et contenant des inscriptions araméennes", *AE* 8 (1923), pp. 38-43

Goldberg, A. *Untersuchungen über de Vorstellung von der Shekinah in der frühen Rabbinischen Literatur*, Studia Judaica 5 (Berlin 1969)

Goldschmidt, D. *Der Traktat Nezikin ... in photographischer Facsimile-Reproduktion ... und mit textkritische Scholien versehen* (Berlin 1914)

Goldschmidt, L. *Der Babylonische Talmud* (The Hague 1933-1935)

Gollancz, H. *The Book of Protection, Being a Collection of Syriac Charms* (London 1912; reprint Amsterdam 1976)

Golomb, D. M. *A Grammar of Targum Neofiti* (California 1985)

Gomaa, F. *Die libyschen Fürstentümer des Deltas vom Tod Osorkons II bis zur Wiedervereinigung Ägyptens durch Psametik I* (Wiesbaden 1974)

Goodblatt, D. "The Babylonian Talmud", in H. Temporini and W. Haase (eds.) *Aufstieg und Niedergang der römischen Welt II*, Principat 19 (Berlin 1979) pp. 257-336
Gordon, C. H. "An Aramaic exorcism", *Archiv Orientální* 6 (1934), pp. 466-74
Gordon, C. H. "An Aramaic incantation bowl", *AASOR* 14 (1934), pp. 141-4
Gordon, C. H. "Aramaic Incantation Bowls", *Orientalia* 10 (1941) pp. 339-360
Gordon, C. H. "Two Aramaic incantations" in Gary A. Tuttle (ed.) *Biblical and Near Eastern Studies: Essays in Honor of William Sanford LaSor* (Grand Rapids 1978), pp. 231-244
Gordon, C. H. "Two magic bowls in Teheran", *Orientalia* 20 (1951), pp. 306-315
Gordon, E. I. "A New Look at the Wisdom of Sumer and Akkad", *BiOr* 17 (1960), pp. 122-152
Gordon, R. P. "The Variable Wisdom of Abel: The MT and Versions at 2 Samuel XX 18-19", *VT* 43 (1933) pp. 215-226
Goshen-Gottstein, M. H. with the assistance of H. Shirun, *The Bible in the Syropalestinian Version*, Pt 1 (Jerusalem 1973)
Graffin, F. "Hymnes inédites de S. Éphrem sur la virginité", *OrSyr* 6 (1961), pp.213-242
Grayson, A. K. "Assyria's Foreign Policy in Relation to Egypt in the Eighth and Seventh Centuries B.C.", *JSSEA* 11 (1980), pp.85-88
Greenfield, J. C. "Aramaic and its Dialects" in H. H. Paper (ed.) *Jewish Languages: Theme and Variations*, Proceedings of Regional Conferences of the Associations for Jewish Studies, held at the University of Michigan and New York University in March-April 1975 (Cambridge, Mass. 1978), pp. 29-43
Greenfield, J. C. "Dialect Traits in Early Aramaic", *Lešonenu* 32 (1967-68), pp. 359-368
Greenfield, J. C. "Notes on some Aramaic and Mandaic magic bowls", *JANES* 5, The Gaster Festschrift (1973), pp. 149-156
Greenfield, J. C. "Of Scribes, Scripts and Languages" in Cl. Bauvain, C. Bonnet, V. Krings (eds.) *Phoinikeia Grammata: Lire et écrire en Méditerranée, Actes du Colloque de Liège, 14-18 novembre 1989* (Liège-Namur 1991), pp. 173-85
Greenfield, J. C. "Standard Literary Aramaic" in A.Caquot, D.Cohen (eds.) *Actes du premier congrès international de linguistique sémitique et chamito-sémitique* (The Hague 1974), pp.280-289
Greenfield, J. C. "The Aramean God Rammān/Rimmōn," *IEJ* 26 (1976), pp. 195-98
Greenfield, J. C. "The Dialects of Early Aramaic", *JNES* 37 (1978), pp. 93-99
Greenfield, J. and J. Naveh "Qamiᶜ mandaᶜi baᶜal arbaᶜ hašbaᶜot", *Eretz-Israel* 18, Nahman Avigad Volume (1985), pp. 97-107
Greenfield, J. C. and B. Porten, *The Bisitun Inscription of Darius the Great, Aramaic Version* (London 1982)
Greenfield, J. C. and A. Shaffer "*Qlqlt*ʾ, *Tubkinnu*, Refuse Tips and Treasure Trove", *AS* 33 (1983), pp. 123-29
Greenfield, J. C. and Sokoloff, M. "Astrological and Related Omen Texts in Jewish Palestinian Aramaic", *JNES* 48 (1989), pp. 201-214
Grelot, P. *Documents araméens d'Egypte*, LAPO 5 (Paris 1972)
Grelot, P. "La Dispute des arbres dans le Targoum II d'Esther VII, 10", in D. Muñoz Leon (ed.), *Salvación en la palabra* (Madrid 1986), pp. 399-408
Grelot, P. Review of J. A. Fitzmyer *The Genesis Apocryphon of Qumran Cave I*, in *RB* 74 (1967), pp. 102-105
Grelot, P. "Un poème de Saint Éphrem: Satan et la Mort", *OrSyr* 3 (1958), pp. 443-452
Gröndahl, F. *Die Personennamen der Texte aus Ugarit* (Rome 1967)
Groner, T. *The Legal Methodology of Hai Gaon* (Chico 1985)
Grosdidier de Matons, J. *Romanos le Mélode et les origines de la poésie religieuse à Byzance* (Paris 1977)
Grosdidier de Matons, J., *Romanos le Mélode, Hymnes*, SC 99ff. (Paris 1964-1981)
Grossfeld, B. *The Two Targums of Esther, Translated, with Apparatus and Notes: The Aramaic Bible*, 18 (Edinburgh 1991)

Guillaumont, A. "À propos du célibat des Esséniens", in *Hommage à A. Dupont-Sommer* (Paris 1971), pp. 395-404
Haefeli, L. *Die Peschitta des Alten Testamentes* (Münster 1927)
Hamilton, V. *Syriac Incantation Bowls* (Dissertation, Brandeis University 1971)
Hamm, J. "Glagoljica", *Enciklopedija Jugoslavije* 4 (Zagreb 1986), pp. 391-398
Harkavy, A. *Responsen der Geonim*, Studien und Mitteilungen aus der Kaiserlichen Öffentlichen Bibliothek 6 (St. Petersburg 1887)
Harviainen, T. "An Aramaic incantation bowl from Borsippa – another specimen of Eastern Aramaic "koiné". Appendix: A cryptographic bowl text or an original fake?", *Studia Orientalia* 51/14 (1981)
Harviainen, T. "A Syriac incantation bowl in the Finnish National Museum, Helsinki. A specimen of Eastern Aramaic 'koiné'", *Studia Orientalia* 51/1 (1978)
Hawkins, J. D. "Assyrians and Hittites", *Iraq* 36 (1974), pp. 67-83
Hawkins, J. D. "The Negatives in Hieroglyphic Luwian", *AnSt* 25 (1975), pp. 119-156
Helck, W. "Petubastis-Erzählung", *LÄ* 4/7 (1982), col. 998-999
Herdner, A. *Corpus des tablettes en cunéiformes alphabétiques découvertes à Ras Shamra-Ugarit de 1929 à 1939* (Paris 1963)
Hildesheimer, E. (ed.) *Sefer Halakhot Gedolot* (Jerusalem 1971-1987)
Hillers, D. R. and E. Cussini "Two Readings in the Caravan Inscription Dunant, Baalshamin, No.45", *BASOR* 286 (1992), pp. 35-37
Hilprecht, H. V. *Exploration in Bible Lands during the 19th Century* (Philadelphia 1903)
Hoftijzer, J. and K. Jongeling *Dictionary of the North-West Semitic Inscriptions* (Brill, Leiden 1995)
Hopkins, S. "Neo-Aramaic Dialects and the Formation of the Preterite," *JSS* 34 (1989), pp. 413-432
Huizinga, J. *Homo Ludens* (Haarlem 1938; English trans. London 1949; reprint 1970)
Hunter, Erica C. D. "Aramaic and Mandaic Incantation Bowls from Nippur", in McGuire Gibson (ed.) *The Sasanian-Islamic Transition at Nippur, Excavations at Area WG* (OIP) [in press]
Hunter, Erica C. D. "Two Mandaic Incantation Bowls from Nippur" *Baghdader Mitteilungen* 25 (1994), pp. 605-618
Ibrahim, H. and V. Poggi "Dialogo fra 'ortodosso' e 'nestoriano' del Vaticano Siriaco 173", *OrChrP* 42 (1976), pp. 459-493
Ingholt, H. "Deux inscriptions bilingues de Palmyre", *Syria* 13 (1932), pp.278-292
Isbell, Charles D. *Corpus of the Aramaic Incantation Bowls*, SBL Dissertation Series 17 (Missoula 1975)
Isbell, Charles D. "Two new Aramaic incantation bowls", *BASOR* 223, 1976, pp. 15-23
Jacob of Serug *Homélies contre les Juifs par Jacques de Saroug*, M. Albert (ed.), PO 38 (Turnhout 1976)
Jacob of Serug *Homiliae selectae Mar-Jacobi Sarugensis*, P. Bedjan (ed.) (Paris-Leipzig 1905-1910)
Jakob-Rost, L. and H. Freydank "Spätbabylonische Rechtsurkunden aus Babylon mit Aramäischen Beischriften," *Forschungen und Berichte* 14 (1972), pp. 7-35
Jacobs, L. *The Talmudic Argument* (Cambridge 1984)
Jansma, T. "Aphraates' Demonstration VII §§ 18 and 20", *Parole de l'Orient* 5 (1974), pp. 21-48
Janssen, J. M. A. "Que sait-on actuellement du pharaon Taharqa?", *Biblica* 34 (1953), pp. 23-43
Jastrow, M. *A Dictionary of the Targumim, the Talmud Babli and Yerushalmi and the Midrashic Literature* (New York-London 1903)
Jean, Charles-F. and Jacob Hoftijzer, *Dictionnaire des inscriptions sémitiques de l'ouest* (Brill, Leiden 1965)
H.L. Jones (ed.) Strabo, *Geography* VII, (London 1930)
Kaḥḥālah, ʿUmar *Muʿjam qabāʾil al-ʿarab* (Beirut 1982/1402)
Kahle, P. *Masoreten des Westens* II (Stuttgart 1930)
Kàkosy, L. "Atum", *LÄ* 1, 3 (1973), col. 550-552

Kàkosy, L. "Heliopolis", *LÄ* 2, 7 (1977), col. 1111-1113
Kara, Y. "Babylonian Aramaic in the Yemenite Manuscripts of the Talmud: Orthography, Phonology and Morphology of the Verb", *Eda weLashon* 10 (1983), pp. 175-178
Karavites, P. "Gregory Nazianzinos and Byzantine hymnography", *JHS* 113 (1993), pp. 81-98
Kasowski, C. J. and B. Kasowski *Thesaurus Talmudis Concordantiae Verborum quae in Talmude Babylonico Reperiuntur*, 42 vols. (Jerusalem 1954-1982)
Katsch, A. I. גנזי תלמוד בבלי, 2 vols. (Jerusalem 1976-79)
Kaufman, S. A. *The Akkadian Influences on Aramaic* (Chicago 1974)
Kaufman, S. A. "The Job Targum from Qumran", *JAOS* 93 (1973), pp. 317-327
Kimmelman, A. "A Guide to Talmudic Commentary in the Gaonic Period", *Annual of the Institute for Research in Jewish Law* 11-12 (1984-86), pp. 463-542
Kitchen, K. A. *The Third Intermediate Period in Egypt (1100-650 B.C.)* (Warminster 1986[2])
Klein, M. L. *Genizah Manuscripts of Palestinian Targum to the Pentateuch* (Cincinnati 1986)
Klein, M. L. *The Fragment-Targums of the Pentateuch* I (Rome 1980)
Koch, K. et al. *Amos, Untersucht mit den Methoden einer strukturalen formgeschichte 1: Programm und Analyse*, AOAT 30 (Kevelaer 1976), pp. 224-5
Koldewey, R. *Die Königsburgen von Babylon. 1: Die Südburg*, WVDOG 54 (Leipzig 1931)
Kooij, A. van der "On the significance of MS 5b1 for Peshiṭta Genesis", in P. B. Dirksen and M. J. Mulder (eds.) *The Peshiṭta: Its Early Text and History*, (Leiden 1988), pp. 183-199
Koopmans, J. J. *Aramäische Chrestomathie* (Leiden 1962)
Kornfeld, W. *Onomastica aramaica aus Ägypten* (Vienna 1978)
Kornfeld, W. "Onomastica aramaica und das Alte Testament", *ZAW* 88 (1976), pp.105-112
Koster, M. D. "Peshiṭta Revisited: a Reassessment of its Value as a Version", *JSS* 38 (1993), pp. 235-268
Koster, M. D. *The Peshiṭta of Exodus: The Development of its Text in the Course of Fifteen Centuries* (Assen 1977)
Kraeling, E. G. *The Brooklyn Museum Aramaic Papyri* (New Haven 1953)
Kramer, S. N. *Enmerkar and the Lord of Aratta: A Sumerian Epic Tale of Iraq and Iran* (Philadelphia 1952)
Kramer, S. N. *History Begins at Sumer* (Philadelphia 1961[2])
Kramer, S. N. "Rivalry and Superiority: Two Dominant Features of the Sumerian Culture Pattern", in A. Wallace (ed.) *Men and Cultures* (Philadelphia 1960), pp.287-291
Kramer, S. N. *The Sacred Marriage Rite* (Bloomington-London 1969)
Kutscher, E. Y. "Babylonian Talmudic" in F. Rosenthal, *An Aramaic Handbook* 2/1 (Wiesbaden 1967), pp. 43-45
Kutscher, E. Y. *Hebrew and Aramaic Studies* (Jerusalem 1977)
Kutscher, E. Y. "New Aramaic Texts", *JAOS* 74 (1954), pp. 233-248
Kutscher, E. Y. *Studies in Galilean Aramaic* (Ramat Gan 1976)
Kutscher, E. Y. "The Hermopolis Papyri", *IOS* 1 (1971), pp. 107-108
Kutscher, E. Y. *The Language and Linguistic Background of the Isaiah Scroll* (Jerusalem 1959), pp. 141-42
Kutscher, E. Y. "The Language of the 'Genesis Apocryphon'", *Scripta Hierosolymitana* 4 (1957), pp. 8-9
Kutscher, E. Y. "The Present State of Research into Mishnaic Hebrew (especially Lexicography) and its Tasks", *Archive of the New Dictionary of Rabbinic Literature* 1 (1972), pp. 3-28
Kutscher, E. Y. "Two 'Passive' Constructions in Aramaic in the Light of Persian", in *Proceedings of the International Conference on Semitic Studies held in Jerusalem, 19-23 July 1965* (Jerusalem 1969), pp. 137-138

Kutscher, E. Y. *Words and their History* (Jerusalem 1961)
Lagarde, P. de *Hagiographa chaldaice* (Leipzig 1873; reprint: *Phophetae Chaldaice*, Otto Zeller, Osnabruck 1967)
Lambert, M. "Le jeu d'Enmerkar", *Syria* 32 (1955), pp. 212-21
Lambert, W. G. *Babylonian Wisdom Literature* (Oxford 1960)
Lambert, W. G. "Nabonidus in Arabia", *Proceedings of the Fifth Seminar for Arabian Studies* (1972), pp. 53-64
Land, J. P. N. *Anecdota Syriaca* IV (Leiden 1875; reprint Jerusalem 1971)
Landsberger, B."Akkadisch-Hebräische Wortgleichnungen", *Hebräische Wortforschung*, Fs. W. Baumgartner, VT Supp. 16 (1967), pp.176-90
Landy, F. *Paradoxes of Paradise: Identity and Difference in the Song of Songs* (Sheffield 1983)
Langdon, S. H. *Die neubabylonischen Königsinschriften*, Vorderasiatische Bibliothek 4 (Leipzig 1912)
Layard, A. H. *Discoveries in the Ruins of Nineveh and Babylon* (London 1853)
Leclant, J. "Kuschitenherrschaft", *LÄ* 3/6 (1979), col. 893-901
Leclant, J. "Taharqa", *LÄ* 6/3 (1985), col. 156-184
Leclant, J. "Tanutamun", *LÄ* 6/2 (1985), col. 211-215
le Déaut, R., *Targum du Pentateuch* (Paris 1979)
Leichty, E. and A. K. Grayson *Catalogue of the Babylonian Tablets in the British Museum. VII: Tablets from Sippar 2* (London 1987)
Leichty, E., J. J. Finkelstein, C. B. F. Walker *Catalogue of the Babylonian Tablets in the British Museum. VIII: Tablets from Sippar 3* (London 1988)
Lemaire, A. "Manuscrit, mur et rocher en épigraphie nord-ouest sémitique", in R. Laufer (ed.), *Le texte et son inscription* (Paris 1989), pp. 35-42
Lemaire, A. and J. M. Durand *Les inscriptions araméennes de Sfiré et l'Assyrie de Shamshi-ilu*, HEO 20 (Geneva-Paris, 1984)
Levias, C. *A Grammar of Galilean Aramaic* (New York 1986)
Levine, B. "The Language of the Magic Bowls", in J. Neusner *A History of the Jews of Babylonia* V (Leiden 1970), pp. 348-9
Levy, B. *The Language of Neophyti 1: A Description and Comparative Grammar of the Palestinian Targum* (Ph.D. thesis New York University 1974)
Lewin, B. M. "Index of *Otzar Ha-Geonim* to the Tractates *Bava Batra* and *Hullin*", *Annual of the Institute for Research in Jewish Law* 11-12 (1984-86), pp. 543-588
Lewin, B. M. *Otzar Ha-Geonim* (Haifa-Jerusalem 1928-1943)
Lewis, A. S. and M. D. Gibson *Apocrypha Syriaca* (Cambridge 1902)
Lewis, A. S. and M. D. Gibson *Codex Climaci Rescriptus* (Cambridge 1909)
Lewis, A. S. and M. D. Gibson *Palestinian Syriac Texts from Palimpsest Fragments in the Taylor-Schechter Collection* (London 1900)
Lewis, A. S. and M. D. Gibson *The Forty Martyrs of the Sinai Desert and the Story of Eulogios* (Cambridge 1912)
Lichtheim, M. *Ancient Egyptian Literature III* (Berkeley 1980)
Liddell, H. G. and R. Scott, *A Greek-English Lexicon* ((Oxford 1864^5, 1888^7; new edition H. S. Jones and R. McKenzie 1940)
Lidzbarski, M. *Ephemeris für semitische Epigraphik III* (Giessen 1909-15)
Lidzbarski, M. *Das Johannesbuch der Mandäer* (Giessen 1905)
Lidzbarski, M. *Handbuch der nordsemitischen Epigraphik* (Weimar 1898)
Lidzbarski, M. "Uthra und Malakha" in C. Bezold (ed.) *Orientalische Studien Theodor Nöldeke zum Siebzigsten Geburtstag* (Giessen 1906), vol. I, pp. 537-545
Lindenberger, J. M. "Ahiqar (7th-6th Century BC)" in J. H. Charlesworth (ed.) *The Old Testament Pseudepigrapha* 2 (Garden City 1985), pp. 479-507
Lindenberger, J. M. *The Aramaic Proverbs of Ahiqar* (Baltimore-London 1983)
Lipińksi, E. "De fenicische inscripties uit Karatepe", in K. R. Veenhof (ed.) *Schrijvend Verleden* (Leiden-Zutphen 1983), pp. 46-54
Lipińksi, E. "Phoenicians in Anatolia and Assyria", *OLP* 16 (1985), pp. 81-90

Livingstone, A. "Arabians in Babylonia/Babylonians in Arabia: Some reflections à propos new and old evidence", in T. Fahd (ed.) *L'Arabie préislamique et son environment historique et culturel* (Strasbourg 1989), pp. 97-105
Lloyd, A. B. "The Inscription of Udjaḥorresnet", *JEA* 68 (1982), pp. 166-180
Loewe, R. *Ibn Gabirol* (London 1989)
Loewe, R. "Jerome's Treatment of an Anthropopathism", *VT* 2 (1952), pp. 261-272
Loewe, R. "The Earliest Biblical Allusion to Coined Money", *Palestine Exploration Quarterly* 87 (1955), pp.141-150
Lund, J. A. "On the Interpretation of the Palestinian Targumic Reading WQHT in Gen 32:25," *JBL* 105 (1986), pp. 99-103
Lund, J. A. "The First Person Singular Past Tense of the Verb הוה in Jewish Palestinian Aramaic", *Maarav* 4/2 (1987), pp. 191-199
Lund, J. *The Influence of the Septuagint on the Peshitta: a Re-evaluation in Light of Comparative Study of the Versions in Genesis and Psalms* (unpublished dissertation Jerusalem 1988)
McCullough, W.S. *Jewish and Mandaean Incantation Bowls in the Royal Ontario Museum* (Toronto 1967)
McNamara, M. "The Spoken Aramaic of First Century Palestine", *Proceedings of the Irish Biblical Association* 2 (1977), pp. 95-138
Macuch, R. "Altmandäische Bleirollen", in Fr. Altheim, R.Stiehl, *Die Araber in der Alten Welt,* IV (Berlin 1967), pp. 91-203; and V/ 1 (Berlin 1968), pp. 34-72
Macuch, R. *Grammatik des samaritanischen Aramäisch* (Berlin-New York 1982)
McVey, K. *Ephrem the Syrian, Hymns* (New York 1989)
McWilson, R. *New Testament Apocrypha* I (London 1963)
Malatesta E., S. J. Matteo Ricci (eds.) *The True Meaning of the Lord of Heaven (T'ien-chu shih-i)* (Taipei-Paris-Hong Kong 1985)
Malter, H. *The Tractate Taʿanit* (New York 1930)
Mariès, L. and C. Mercier (eds.), *Hymnes de S. Éphrem conservées en version arménienne*, PO 30, fasc. 1 (Paris 1961)
Martin, F. "Homélie de Narsès sur les trois docteurs nestoriens", *JA* 9/14 (1899), pp. 446-492; French translation, *JA* 9/15 (1900), pp. 469-525
Martin, J. P. P. "Discours de Jacques de Saroug sur la chute des idoles", *ZDMG* 29 (1875), pp. 107-147
Maspero, G. "Fragment d'une version égyptienne de la fable des membres et de l'estomac", in Maspero, *Études Égyptiennes I* (Paris 1886), pp. 260-64
Melchart, H. Craig "PIE velars in Luvian*", in C. Watkins (ed.) *Studies in Memory of Warren Cowgill (1929-1985)*, Papers from the 4th East Coast Indo-European Conference, Cornell University, June 6-9, 1985 (Berlin-New York 1987), pp. 182-204
Meriggi, P. *Manule di Eteo Geroglifico* Pt. 2 (Rome 1967)
Meulenaere, H. de "Une statuette égyptienne à Naples", *BIFAO* 60 (1960), pp.117-129
Meulenaere, H. de *Herodotos over de 26ste Dynastie (II, 147 - III, 15)*, Bibliothèque du Muséon 27 (Leuven 1951)
Meyer, R. "Das Gebet des Nabonid", *Sitzungsberichte der Sächsischen Akademie der Wissenschaften zu Leipzig, Phil.hist. Klasse* 107, 3 (1962), pp. 1-112
Midrash ha-Gadol, Genesis, M. Margoliot (ed.) (Jerusalem 1947)
Midrash Rabbah, Soncino Press Translation, H. Freedman and M. Simon (eds.) (London 1939)
Milik, J. T. *Dédicaces faites par des dieux* (Paris 1972)
Millar, F. "The Problem of Hellenistic Syria", in A. Kuhrt, S. Sherwin-White (eds.) *Hellenism in the East* (Berkeley-Los Angeles 1987), pp. 110-133
Millar, F. *The Roman Near East 31 BC - AD 337* (Cambridge-London 1993)
Millard, A. R. "*ʾbgd ...* — Magic spell or educational exercise?", *Eretz-Israel* 18 (Nahman Avigad Volume, 1985), pp. 39*-42*
Mishor, M. *The Tense System in Tannaitic Hebrew*, (doctoral dissertation Jerusalem 1983)
Moller, Garth I. "Towards a new typology of the Syriac manuscript alphabet", *Journal of Northwest Semitic Languages* 14 (1988), pp. 153-197

Montgomery, J. A. *Aramaic Incantation Texts from Nippur* (Philadelphia 1913)

Montgomery, J. A. "A Syriac incantation with Christian formula", *American Journal of Semitic Languages and Literatures* 34 (1917-18), pp. 137-139

Mopurgo-Davies, A. and J. D. Hawkins, "Il sistema del luvio geroglifico", *Annali della Scuola Normale Superiore di Pisa* 8/3 (1978) pp. 755-6

Morag, S. "*Ἐφφαθά* (Mark vii. 34): Certainly Hebrew, Not Aramaic?", *JSS* 17 (1972), pp. 198-202

Morag, S. *The Yemenite Tradition: Historical Aspects and Transmission, Phonology, The Verbal System* (Jerusalem 1988)

Morag, S. *Vocalised Talmudic Manuscripts in the Cambridge Geniza Collections* I, Taylor-Schechter Old Series, (Cambridge 1988)

Moran, W. L. *Les lettres d'El Amarna*, LAPO 13 (Paris 1987)

Moss, C. "The Peshitta Version of Ezra", *Le Muséon* 46 (1933), pp. 55-110

Müller-Kessler, Ch. "Christian-Palestinian-Aramaic Fragments in the Bodleian Library", *JSS* 37 (1992), pp. 207-21

Müller-Kessler, Ch. "Eine aramäische Zauberschale im Museum zu Berlin", *Orientalia* 63/1 (1994), pp. 5-9

Müller-Kessler, Ch. *Grammatik des Christlich-Palästinisch-Aramäischen I: Schriftlehre, Lautlehre, Formenlehre* (Hildesheim 1991)

Muraoka, T. "A Study in Palestinian Jewish Aramaic," *Sef* 45 (1985), pp. 7-9

Murray, R. "Hellenistic-Jewish Rhetoric in Aphrahat" in *III. Symposium Syriacum 1980*, OrChrA 221 (Rome 1983), pp. 79-85

Murray, R. "St. Ephrem's Dialogue of Reason and Love" (HEccl 9), *Sobornost/ECR* 2 (1980), pp. 26-40

Murray, R. "Some Rhetorical Patterns in Early Syriac Literature" in R. H. Fischer (ed.), *A Tribute to Arthur Vööbus* (Chicago 1977), pp. 109-131

Murray, R. *Symbols of Church and Kingdom: A Study in Early Syriac Tradition* (Cambridge 1975)

Myśliwiec, K. *Studien zum Gott Atum II: Name, Epitheta, Iconographie* (Hildesheim 1979)

Na'e, B. גמרא שלמה (Jerusalem 1960-64)

Narsai, *Sogita* No.5 (French tr. by F. Martin) *JA* 9 (1899-1900), pp. 484-492, 515-525

Naveh, J. *Early History of the Alphabet* (Jerusalem -Leiden 1982)

Naveh, J. *The Development of the Aramaic Script*, Proceedings of the Israel Academy of Sciences and Humanities 5 (Jerusalem 1970)

Naveh, J. "The Scripts of Two Ostraca from Elath", *BASOR* 183 (1966), pp. 27-30

Naveh, Joseph and Shaul Shaked, *Amulets and Magic Bowls: Aramaic Incantations of Late Antiquity* (Jerusalem - Leiden 1985)

Nøjgaard, M. *La fable antique I: la fable grecque avant Phèdre* (Copenhagen 1964)

Nöldeke, Th. "Das Targum zu den Sprüchen von der Peschita abhängig", *Archiv für Wissenschaftliche Erforschung des Alten Testaments* 2/2 (1872), pp. 246-9

Nöldeke, Th. *Mandäische Grammatik* (Halle 1875)

Ockinga, B. "Inschrift Darius I. aus Susa", *TUAT* 2/4 (1988), pp. 552-554

Odeberg, H. *The Aramaic Portions of Bereshit Rabba with Grammar of Galilaean Aramaic*, (Lund-Leipzig 1939)

Oelsner, J. Review of J. Naveh and S. Shaked *Amulets and Magic Bowls: Aramaic Incantations of Late Antiquity*, in *Orientalistische Literaturzeitung* 84/1 (1989), cols. 38-40

Oelsner, J. "Weitere Bemerkungen zu den Neirab-Urkunden," *AoF* 16 (1989), pp. 68-77

Oshiro, T. "On Hieroglyphic Luwian Sign sú or zú", *Journal of Indo-European Studies*, 17 (1989), p. 181

Owens, R. J. "Aphrahat as Witness to P-Leviticus", in P. B. Dirksen and M. J. Mulder (eds.), *The Peshiṭta: Its Early Text and History*, (Leiden 1988), pp. 1-48

Owens, R. J. *The Genesis and Exodus Citations of Aphrahat the Persian Sage* (Leiden 1983)

Parpola, S. and K. Watanabe, *Neo-Assyrian Treaties and Loyalty Oaths*, SAA 2 (Helsinki 1988)

Parr, P. J. "Archaeology of North-west Arabia", in T. Fahd (ed.) *L'Arabie préislamique et son environment historique et culturel* (Strasbourg 1989), pp. 39-66
Payne Smith, J. (ed.) *A Compendious Syriac Dictionary*, (Oxford, 1896-1903)
Payne Smith, R. *Thesaurus Syriacus* (Oxford 1890-1901)
Peiser, F. E. *Babylonische Verträge des Berliner Museums* (Berlin 1890)
Pennacchietti, F. A. *Il Ladrone e il cherubino: Dramma liturgico cristiano orientale* (Turin 1993)
Perry, B. E. "Fable" in *Studium Generale* 12 (1959), pp. 19-45
Péter, R. "*Pr* et *šr*, note de lexicographie hébraïque", *VT* 25 (1975), pp. 486-496
Peters, J. P. *Nippur*, (New York 1897)
Petersen, W. *The Diatessaron and Ephrem Syrus as Sources of Romanos the Melodist*, CSCO, Subsidia 74 (Louvain 1985)
Petrie, W. M. F. *Tombs of the Courtiers and Oxyrhyncos*, BSAE 37 (London 1925)
Pognon, H. *Inscriptions Mandaïtes des Coupes de Khouabir* (Paris 1898)
Porten, B. *Archives from Elephantine* (Berkeley 1986)
Porten, B. *Select Aramaic Papyri from Ancient Egypt* (Jerusalem 1986)
Porten, B. "The Identity of King Adon", *BA* 44 (1981), pp. 36-52
Porten, B. and A. Yardeni, *A Textbook of Aramaic Documents from Ancient Egypt I-III* (Jerusalem 1986-93)
Postgate, J. N. *Fifty Neo-Assyrian Legal Documents* (Warminster 1976)
Prignaud, J. "Notes d'épigraphie hébraïque I. Un grand vengeur", *RB* 77 (1970), pp. 50-59
Rabbinowicz, N. N. דקדוקי סופרים, (Munich 1867-97)
Rabbinovicz, R. N. על הדפסת התלמוד מאמר ed. A. M. Habermann (Jerusalem 1952)
Redford, D. B. "Necho I", *LÄ* 4/3 (1980), col. 368-369
Reinink, G. J., "Ein syrisches Streitgespräch zwischen Tod und Satan" in Reinink and Vanstiphout, *DPD*, pp. 135-152
Reinink, G. J. and H. L. J. Vanstiphout (eds.) *Dispute Poems and Dialogues in the Ancient and Mediaeval Near East*, Orientalia Lovaniensia Analecta 42 (Leuven 1991)
Rey-Coquais, J.-P. "La Syrie romaine", *JRS* 68 (1978), pp. 44-73
Rieder, D. *Pseudo-Jonathan: Targum Jonathan ben Uziel on the Pentateuch* (Jerusalem 1974)
Ringgren, H. *Religions of the Ancient Near East* (London 1973)
Robert, J. and L. Robert (eds.) *Bulletin Epigraphique* (Vienna 1977)
Rosenthal, D. *Mishna Aboda Zara: A Critical Edition with Introduction*, (Ph.D. Dissertation, Hebrew University 1980)
Rosenthal, F. *An Aramaic Handbook* (Wiesbaden 1967)
Rosenthal, R. E. S. " Talmudica Iranica ", in S. Shaked (ed.) *Irano-Judaica, Studies Relating to Jewish Contacts with Persian Culture throughout the Ages* (Jerusalem 1982)
Sartre, M. *L'Orient romain: Provinces et sociétés provinciales en Méditerranée orientale d'Auguste aux Sévères* (Paris 1991)
Sass, B. *The Genesis of the Alphabet and its Development in the Second Millennium B.C.*, Ägypten und Altes Testament 13 (Wiesbaden 1988)
Sauneron, S. and J. Yoyotte, "Sur la politique palestinienne des rois saïtes", *VT* 2 (1952), pp. 131-136
Sauren, H. "Les Epopées sumériennes et la théatre classique", *OLP* 3 (1972), pp. 35-47
Schmitt, R. "Die Ostgrenze von Armenien über Mesopotamien, Syrien bis Arabien", *Die Sprachen in römischen Reich der Kaiserzeit*, Beiheft der *Bonner Jahrbücher* 40 (1980), pp.198-205; 205-209
Schott, S. *Altägyptische Festdaten* (Wiesbaden 1950)
Schulthess, F. *Grammatik des christlich-palästinischen Aramäisch* (Tübingen 1924)
Schulthess, F. *Lexicon Syropalaestinum* (Berlin 1903)
Segal, J. B. *Edessa and Harran* (London 1963)

Segert, S. *Altaramäische Grammatik mit Bibliographie, Chrestomathie und Glossar* (Leipzig, 1973, 1983^2)
Seyrig, H. "Inscriptions grecques de l'agora de Palmyre", *Syria* 22 (1941), pp. 167-214 (= *Antiquités Syriens* 3 (Paris 1946), pp. 223-270)
Shaked, S. "Bagdana, king of the demons, and other Iranian terms in Babylonian Aramaic magic", *Acta Iranica* 25 (1985), pp. 511-525
Smelik, K. A. D. "An Aramaic incantation bowl in the Allard Pierson Museum", *Bibliotheca Orientalis* 35, (1978), c. 174-177
Soden, W. von *Akkadisches Handwörterbuch* (Wiesbaden 1976)
Sokoloff, M. *A Dictionary of Jewish Palestinian Aramaic of the Byzantine Period* (Bar Ilan 1990)
Sokoloff, M. "The Current State of Research on Galilean Aramaic", *JNES* 37 (1978), pp. 161-168
Sokoloff, M. "The Noun-Pattern MQṬWLY in Middle Western Aramaic", in *ʿErkhe hammillon heḥadaš lesifrut ḥazal* 2 (Ramat Gan 1974), pp. 74-84
Sokoloff, M. *The Targum to Job from Qumran Cave XI* (Ramat Gan 1974)
Sokoloff, M. and J. Yahalom *Aramaic Poems from Eretz Israel of the Byzantine Period* (forthcoming)
Spalinger, A. "Assurbanipal and Egypt: A Source Study", *JAOS* 94 (1974), pp. 316-328
Spalinger, A. "Esarhaddon and Egypt: An Analysis of the First Invasion of Egypt", *Orientalia* 43 (1974), pp. 295-326
Spalinger, A. "Notes on the Military in Egypt during the XXVth Dynasty", *JSSEA* 11 (1981), pp. 37-58
Spalinger, A. "Psammetichus, King of Egypt", *JARCE* 13 (1976), pp. 133-147; 15 (1978), pp. 49-57
Spalinger, A. "The Foreign Policy of Egypt Preceding the Assyrian Conquest", *CdE* 53 (1978), pp. 22-47
Speiser, E. A. *Genesis* (Garden City 1964)
Sperber, A. *The Bible in Aramaic* (Leiden 1959-1962)
Spiegelberg, W. *Demotische Texte auf Krügen*, Demotische Studien 5 (Leipzig 1912)
Spiegelberg, W. *Der Sagenkreis des Königs Petubastis* (Leipzig 1910)
Spitaler, A. *Grammatik des neuaramäischen Dialekts von Maʿlula (Antilibanon)*, Leipzig 1938)
Sprenger, H. N. (ed.), *Theodori Mopsuesteni Commentarius in XII Prophetas. Einleitung und Ausgabe* (Wiesbaden 1977)
Sprengling, M. and W. C. Graham (eds.) *Barhebraeus' Scholia on the Old Testament* (Chicago 1931)
Starcky, J. *Inventaire des inscriptions de Palmyre* X (Damascus 1949)
Starcky, J. and M. Gawlikowski, *Palmyre* (Paris 1985)
Stark, J. K. *Personal Names in Palmyrene Inscriptions* (Oxford 1971)
Starke, F. *Untersuchungen zur Stammbildung des keilschriftluwischen Nomens*, Studien zu den Bogazköy-Texten 31 (Wiesbaden 1990)
Steiner, R. C. "The Aramaic Text in Demotic Script: The Liturgy of a New Year's Festival Imported from Bethel to Syene by Exiles from Rash," *JAOS* 111 (1991), pp. 362-363
Steiner, R. C. and C. F. Nims "Ashurbanipal and Shamash-shum-ukin: A Tale of Two Brothers from the Aramaic Text in Demotic Script", *RB* 92 (1985), pp. 60-81
Steiner, R. C. and C. F. Nims "You Can't Offer Your Sacrifice and Eat It Too: A Polemical Poem from the Aramaic Text in Demotic Script", *JNES* 43 (1984), pp. 89-114
Steinschneider, M. "Rangstreit-Literatur", *SbKAW* (*Sitzungsberichte der Könichlichen Akademie zu Wien), phil.-hist. Klasse* 155 (Vienna 1908), pp.1-87
Stevenson, H. J. *Assyrian and Babylonian Contracts. With Aramaic Reference Notes* (New York 1902)
Stevenson, W. B. *Grammar of Palestinian Jewish Aramaic* (Oxford 1924, 1962^2)

Stolper, M. W. "Belšunu the Satrap," in F. Rochberg-Halton (ed.) *Language, Literature, and History: Philological and Historical Studies Presented to Erica Reiner,* American Oriental Series 67 (New Haven 1987), pp. 389-402

Stolper, M. W. "Empire and Province: Abstract of Remarks on Two Late Achaemenid Babylonian Archives," *Paléorient* 11 (1985), pp. 63-66

Stolper, M. W. *Entrepreneurs and Empire* (Leiden 1985)

Stolper, M. W. "The Kasr Archive," *AJA* 92 (1988), pp. 587-88

Stolper, M. W. "The Kasr Archive," in H. Sancisi-Weerdenburg, A. Kuhrt ed. *Centre and Periphery. Proceedings of the Sixth Achaemenid History Workshop, Groningen 1986, Nederlands Instituut voor het Nabije Oosten* (Groningen 1990), pp. 195-205

Streck, M. *Assurbanipal und die letzten assyrischen Könige bis zum Untergange Niniveh's* II: Texte, Vorderasiatisches Bibliothek (Leipzig 1916)

Sussmann, J. "Talmud Fragments in the Cairo Geniza", *Te'uda* 1 (1980), pp. 21-32

Sussmann, J. ושוב לירושלמי נזיקין in מחקרי תלמוד I, (Jerusalem 1990), pp.104-114

Svedlund, G. *The Aramaic Portions of Pesiqta de Rab Kahana* (Uppsala 1974)

Szubin, H. Z. and B. Porten, "Royal Grants in Egypt: A New Interpretation of Driver 2", *JNES* 46 (1987), pp. 39-48

Tadmor, H. "The Aramaicization of Assyria: Aspects of Western Impacts", in *Mesopotamien und seine Nachbarn XXV. R.A.I.* (Berlin 1978), pp. 449-470

Tal, A. "Hammaqor leṣurotaw berovde ha'aramit hayehudit be'ereṣ yiśra'el", in *Hebrew Language Studies Presented to Zeev Ben-Hayyim* (Jerusalem 1983), pp. 207-208

Tal, A. "Layers in the Jewish Aramaic of Palestine: The Appended Nun as a Criterion," *Lesh* 43 (1979), pp. 165-184

Tal, A. "Ms. Neophyti 1: The Palestinian Targum to the Pentateuch. Observations on the Artistry of a Scribe", *IOS* 4 (1974), pp. 31-43

Tal, A. "Revadim ba'aramit hayehudit šel 'ereṣ yiśra'el", *Lešonenu* 43 (1978-79), pp.171-72

Tal, A. *The Samaritan Targum of the Pentateuch*, vols. I-III (Tel Aviv 1980–83)

Tallqvist, K. L. *Assyrian Personal Names* (Helsingfors 1914, reprint Hildesheim 1966)

Tallqvist, K. "Neubabylonisches Namenbuch zu den Geschäftsurkunden aus der Zeit des Samassumukin bis Xerxes", *Acta Societatis Scientiarum Fennicae* 32/2 (Helsingfors 1902), pp. 1-338

Talmon, S. "Biblical Tradition on the Early History of the Samaritans", in J. Aviram (ed.) *Eretz Shomron* (Jerusalem 1973), pp. 19-33

Taubes, H. Z. אוצר הגאונים למסכת סנהדרין (Jerusalem 1966)

Teixidor, J. *Bulletin d'épigraphie sémitique (1964-1980)* (Paris 1986)

Teixidor, J. "Deux documents syriaques du IIIe siècle après J.-C., provenant du Moyen Euphrate" *CRAI* (1990), pp. 144-166

Teixidor, J. "L'hellénisme et les 'barbares': l'exemple syrien", *Le temps de la réflexion* 2 (1981), pp.258-274

Teixidor, Javier and Joseph Naveh "The Syriac incantation bowls in the Iraq Museum", *Sumer* 18 (1962), pp. 51-62; Naveh, p. 151

Temerev, A. "Social Organisations in the Egyptian Military Settlements of the Sixth-Fourth Centuries B.C.E. *dgl* and *m't*", in C. L. Meyers, M. O'Connor (eds.) *The Word of the Lord Shall Go Forth, Essays in Honour of D. N. Freedman* (Winona Lake 1983), pp. 523-525

Thompson, R. Campbell *Devils and Evil Spirits of Babylonia*, (London 1903)

Tobi, Y. על התלמוד בתימן (Tel Aviv 1963)

Tonneau, R.-M. (ed.) *Sancti Ephraemi Syri in Genesim et in Exodum Commentarii* (= CSCO 152, Syr 71) (Louvain 1955)

Toorn, K. van der "The Ancient Near Eastern Literary Dialogue as a Vehicle of Critical Reflection" in Reinink andVanstiphout, *DPD*, pp. 59-77

Trypanis, C. (ed. and tr.) *Callimachus: Aetiae, Iambi and Other Fragments* Loeb Classical Library (LCL) (Cambridge Mass.-London 1958)

Tuplin, C. "Xenophon and the Garrisons of the Achaemenid Empire", *Archaeologische Mitteilungen aus Iran* 20 (1987), pp. 167-245
Vanstiphout, H. L. J. "Lore, Learning and Levity in the Sumerian Disputations: A Matter of Form, or Substance?", in Reinink andVanstiphout *DPD*, pp. 23-46
Vanstiphout, H. L. J. "The Banquet Scene in the Mesopotamian Debate Poems", *Res Orientales* 4 (1992), pp. 9-22
Vanstiphout, H. L. J. "The Mesopotamian Debate Poems. A General Presentation", *Acta Sumerologica* 12 (1990), pp. 271-318; 14 (1992), pp. 339-367
Vattioni, F. "Epigrafia Aramaica," *Augustinianum* 10 (1970), pp. 493-531
Vattioni, F. Review of E. Lipiński, *Studies in Aramaic Inscriptions and Onomastica* I, (Leuven 1975), in *Orientalia* 48 (1979), pp. 136-45
Vermes, G. *Post-Biblical Jewish Studies* (Leiden 1975; 1983^{2})
Vleeming, S. P. and J. W. Wesselius "Betel the Saviour" *JEOL* 28 (1985), pp. 110-140
Vogel, A. "Studien zum Pešiṭta-Psalter Besonders im Hinblick auf sein Verhältnis zu Septuaginta", *Biblica* 32 (1951), pp. 198-231
Vogelzang, M. E. "Some Questions about the Akkadian Disputes", in Reinink and Vanstiphout *DPD* , pp. 47-57
Vosté, J.-M. and C. van den Eynde (eds.) *Commentaire d'Išoʿdad de Merv sur l'Ancien Testament: I. Genèse*, CSCO 126 (text) and 156 (French translation) (Louvain 1950 and 1955)
Walker, N. "The Peshiṭta puzzle and its implications", *VT* 18 (1968), pp. 268-270
Watterson, B. *The Gods of Ancient Egypt* (London 1984)
Weinfeld, M. "The Pagan Version of Psalm 20:2-6: Vicissitudes of a Psalmodic Creation in Israel and its Neighbors" *EI* 18 (1985), pp. 130-140
Weiss, R. *The Aramaic Targum of Job* (Tel Aviv 1979)
Weissberg, E. מצע לעיבוד מסכתות נוספות של התלמוד הבבלי 12, *Proceedings of the Hebrew Language Academy*, 28-30 (1980-81), pp. 332ff.
Weitzman, M. P. "From Judaism to Christianity: the Syriac version of the Hebrew Bible", in J. Lieu, J. North and T. Rajak (eds.) *The Jews among Pagans and Christians in the Roman Empire* (London 1992), pp. 147-171
Weitzman, M. P. "Is the Peshitta of Chronicles a Targum?", in P. V. M. Flesher (ed.) *Targum Studies*, vol. 2, forthcoming
Weitzman, M. P. "Peshitta, Septuagint and Targum", in *Orientalia Christiana Analecta* 247 (1995), pp. 51-84
Weitzman, M. P. "The Originality of Unique Readings in 9a1", in P. B. Dirksen and M.J. Mulder (eds.) *The Peshiṭta: Its Early Text and History* (Leiden 1988), pp. 225-258
Weitzman, M. P. "Usage and Avoidance of the Term 'Chosen People'", *Language Studies* (*Jerusalem*) (1990), pp. 101-128
Welles, C. B. *Royal Correspondence in the Hellenistic Period: A Study in Greek Epigraphy* (London 1934)
Werhahn, H. M. *Gregorii Nazianzeni ΣΥΓΚΡΙΣΙΣ ΒΙΩΝ* (Wiesbaden 1953)
Wessetzky, W. "Die Familiengeschichte des Peteêse als historische Quelle für die Innenpolitik Psammetiks I", *ZÄS* 88 (1962), pp. 69-73
Wigram, W. A. *The Assyrians and their Neighbours* (London 1929)
Williams, R. J. "The Fable in the Ancient Near East", in E. C. Hobbs (ed.) *A Stubborn Faith* (Dallas 1956), pp. 3-26
Winnett, F. V. and W. L. Reed *Ancient Records from North Arabia* (1979)
Wolff, H. W. *Biblischer Kommentar, Altes Testament, Dodekapropheten 2, Joel und Amos* (Heidelberg 1969)
Wyngaarden, M. J. *The Syriac Version of the Book of Daniel* (Leipzig 1923)
Yamauchi, Edwin *Mandaic Incantation Texts*, American Oriental Series 49 (New Haven 1967)
Yehudai Gaon, R. *Sefer Halachot Pesuqot* (Codex Sasoon 263), ed. S. Sasoon, (Jerusalem 1948; facsimile edition, Jerusalem 1971)
Yoyotte, J. "Le martelage des noms royaux éthiopiens (591 av. J.-C.)", *RdE* 8 (1951), pp. 215-239

Yoyotte, J. "Les inscriptions hiéroglyphiques: Darius et l'Egypte", *JA* 260 (1972), pp. 253-266

Yoyotte, J. "Néchao ou Néko", *Dictionnaire de la Bible, Supplément* 6 (1960), col. 363-393

Yoyotte, J. "Prêtres et sanctuaires du nome Héliopolite à la basse époque", *BIFAO* 54 (1954), pp. 83-115

Zadok, R. *Geographical Names According to New- and Late-Babylonian Texts*, Répertoire Géographique des Textes Cunéiformes 8 (Wiesbaden 1985)

Zadok, R. *On West Semites in Babylonia During the Chaldean and Achaemenian Periods* (Jerusalem 1977)

Zauzich, K. Th. "Demotische Fragmente zum Aḥikar-Roman", in H. Franke, W.Heissig and W. Treue (eds.) *Folia rara W. Voigt LXV* (Wiesbaden 1976), pp. 180-185

Zauzich, K. Th. "Neue literarische Texte in demotischer Schrift", *Enchoria* 8 (1978), pp. 33-36

Zevit, Z. "The Common Origin of the Aramaicized Prayer to Horus and of Psalm 20", *JAOS* 110 (1990), pp. 213-228

Zunz, L. *Die gottesdienstliche Vorträge der Juden historisch entwickelt* (Hebrew translation) (Jerusalem 1954)